DOWN AND OUT IN
SPECIAL EDUCATION

Meditation and Wisdom on the
Road Less Travelled

Robert Bartlett

A True Story (Memoir)
This is a true story. All the people, events, places, organizations, and conversations are real. Names of private people have been fictionalized to provide a small measure of privacy. In addition, names of organizations have been replaced with descriptors except for public institutions whose formal identity was essential to the authenticity of the story. As a memoir, the story relies heavily on the author's memories of past events: any deviation from an actual event is unintentional and will probably not diminish the gist of the situation.

Publisher:
Published by Robert Bartlett on June 10, 2020, in Oakland, California
rwb3publisher@earthlink.net

Dedicated to the approximately 795,000 children who receive special education services in the public schools of California each year.

Warriorship refers to realizing the power, dignity, and wakefulness that are inherent in all of us as human beings. It is awakening our basic human confidence, which allows us to cheer up, develop a sense of vision, and succeed at what we are doing. Because warriorship is innate in human beings, the way to become a warrior—or the warrior's path—is to see who and what we are as human beings and cultivate that. If we look at ourselves directly, without hesitation or embarrassment, we find that we have a lot of strength and a lot of resources available constantly.

CHOGYAM TRUNGPA FROM OCEAN OF DHARMA—THE EVERY-
DAY WISDOM OF CHOGYAM TRUNGPA

CONTENTS

CHAPTER ONE

First Steps

Escape from Unemployment

I wasn't just looking for a day job. I was looking for right livelihood. I wanted to get back to my core values. I wanted to set an example. I wanted my occupation to express my beliefs about democracy and the value and dignity of every individual.

I had just turned forty. It was the summer of 2002. The summer before, I had watched the Twin Towers of the World Trade Center come crashing down live on special coverage. Although living in Danville, an eastern suburb of San Francisco, I saw the terrorist attack live because that spring I had been laid off from my product-marketing position. Unemployment left plenty of time for the luxury of morning television. I wrote "laid off" on job applications, but "driven out" and "fired" might have been more accurate. Or maybe "bored," "indifferent," and "totally disgusted."

Employers were not responding to my applications. For over a year, I had been searching vigorously, using all the latest technology and the most-polished pitches. The last time I searched for work, back in the late nineties, I was frequently juggling two interviews a day. Now, in 2001-2002, I was literally getting no interest for the same skills. The media called the situation a "credit crunch."

I was laid off as a result of a credit crunch—my employer, a relatively major software company, had paid for the prosperity of the late nineties with a huge loan that came due at the turn of the century. As a product-marketing manager for key products, I was at ground zero of the company's efforts to stimulate some sort of brand miracle that would save them. In my first year, I actually pulled off a small miracle by incorporating an acquired product line into the brand—at a profit. But looking for a bigger miracle, my employer got itself acquired in a stunt designed to repay the huge loan.

In this stunt, my role was to rework the brand again, at top speed, for the second time in two years, even though the ink had barely dried from the last revision. At first, I showed some enthusiasm for the big miracle. I reworked large parts of the brand in just a few months—I'm talking truckloads of printed materials. But then came a maniacal stream of minor projects at top speed. I got completely bored. I stopped meeting deadlines. They threatened me, apparently forgetting my recent miracles. I ignored the threats. They fired me. The stunt, as represented by their out-of-town HR rep, had no room for shirkers like me, even though I had received a merit raise a few months prior. One might speculate that a highly-paid copywriter like me was a hindrance to repaying the huge loan. I started to worry that investment bankers might pose an insurmountable obstacle to my business enlightenment. I started to doubt whether business, given my meager role in it, was the path to right livelihood for me.

So, after a year of vigorous searching with no responses, while contemplating doubts of my business enlightenment, I decided to make a change. I had been formulating a career change for a while. For about seven years, I had been considering the possibility of revisiting occupations involving psychology, which was my major in college. I was thinking about psychotherapy or organizational psychology. I was serious, but I could never get my marketing career stabilized enough to embark on this change.

An unexpected perk of unemployment, I had more time to visit my sister, who was in graduate school studying to be a psychotherapist. A few times over the course of that year, she had mentioned that several of her classmates were working as special-ed teachers and aides. In my Buddhist community, that would be called an auspicious coincidence. She suggested that teaching in the public schools might be a gateway to psychotherapy or some other application of my psychology degree.

I had worked in a couple of special-ed settings during my undergraduate career, in the years before I drifted into the computer business, which was my field at graduation time. I knew what special education was like. It was a lot less glamorous than my career-change fantasies, which consisted of visions of me giving penetrating advice to the burnt out of business in my swank therapy office in a Beat neighborhood. But I did a little research, despite the prospect of downward mobility at the fantasy level.

My alma mater listed special education as a career path for applied psychology. I could teach for a while and then maybe become a school psychologist, or maybe use teaching as a gateway to a psychotherapy degree. There was definitely a shortage of properly-trained teachers, and No Child Left Behind (NCLB) was increasing scrutiny of teacher qualifications. Schools and credential programs were hungry for teaching candidates—at least that was the story portrayed in the media. Expectations were on the rise. No longer would schools be allowed to employ under-qualified teachers. The occupational outlook looked promising—to the naïve like me, anyways.

So, in the summer of 2002, I decided to turn my attention toward finding a teaching position and away from product marketing.

Networking My Way to Change

First I had to gain admission to a credential program. Changing fields from marketing to education was going take some selling, so I drew on my copywriter skills to position the product to maximum effect. Interestingly, I embraced people skills to a greater degree than I had in my business years. My entire career, which started in the mid-eighties after graduation, had been in the computer industry, anchored by my knowledge of the nascent personal computer. Over the years, I changed my occupation from sales tech to telemarketer to full-blown corporate sales to finally writer for marketing-advertising. I acquired some impressive career-changer skills in that journey. My major influences were the books *What Color is Your Parachute* and *Never Eat Alone*.

Networking would be the key. I asked nearly everyone in my life if they knew of a teacher who would be willing to offer an informational interview. In addition, I interrogated qualified relatives and friends at various gatherings. It worked: weddings, Thanksgiving, a spouse of my mother's co-worker, an uncle's neighbor, classmates in my sister's graduate program, and even friends of my sister's classmates. These interviews yielded valuable guidance, some of which I still follow today.

At the culmination of the interviews, which were accumulated over about six months, I chose to heed powerful advice from an older cousin who was teaching history in California and studying to become an administrator. She warned me to start my teaching career with the proper California state credential. The state's drive to implement No Child Left Behind, she advised, meant the end of starting one's career as an "emergency" teacher, meaning without training and under a temporary contract. Reform guidelines mandated that teachers earn their credential before entering the classroom. Theoretically, there would be no more emergency teachers.

Journalistic and academic sources that I researched to familiarize myself with the credentialing process verified her advice. In theory, the emergency path was outlawed. Rhetoric circulating on the topic was quite convincing, and I didn't spend any time looking into an emergency position. I decided to go with the flow. Actually, I was pleased to find that the credential training would be a route to a permanent position. My plan was starting to look feasible. I just needed to locate the appropriate university and gain admission. As an experienced pitchman, I figured that I had a pretty good shot at closing a deal with some local college.

Through online research, I checked out special-ed credential programs at the three Bay Area campuses of California State University. In one last round of networking, I invited myself to informational interviews with two education professors at my alma mater, California State University, Hayward (Cal State). Those conversations solidified my plan to use the credential program as a gateway to a secure teaching position—it seemed workable. I also attended Cal State's application workshop for credential candidates. My research culminated in an application to Cal State's teacher education program.

They turned me down. But they gave me a path to future acceptance. The rejection letter included a list of prerequisites that I would need to complete before entering the program. I had met all requirements except one: recent volunteer or paid experience in a special-ed setting. I confirmed with the department that I would be admitted once I had completed the prerequisites. The university hadn't bought into my pitch that volunteer and paid special-ed experiences in my college years satisfied the requirement. They needed to see recent experience in a relevant setting.

My pitchman instincts drove me to appeal—don't fold the deal after just one rejection. I sent a written objection to the chair of Cal State's teacher education department. I tried to reiterate and intensify my belief that my college experiences were sufficient. Unfortunately, I argued more like an ad man than an aspiring teacher, including allusions to my rejection being a matter of female chauvinism preventing the professors from seeing a strong Anglo male like me as a person of compassion. This would be the first of what would become many occasions where I experienced gender anxiety while working among the women of education, in a workforce at seventy-two percent female in California.

The department graciously considered my objection, despite its not-entirely-professional tone. And then rejected it. They stuck with their original demand. So, in the summer of 2002, I resigned myself to spending a year acquiring the required experience.

Then something auspicious happened. Or maybe serendipitous. That same summer and fall, a few local organizations operating under California's district internship laws introduced credential programs for special education. Launched in 1987, district internships stem from state law authorizing, encouraging, and funding non-university organizations formed to accelerate the hiring and credentialing (i.e. training) of teachers. Non-university internship organizations work in partnership with school districts to train teachers on the job. The aim of the district internship laws was to expand the state's capacity to respond to teacher shortages caused mainly by rapid population growth and class-size reduction legislation. These organizations were now turning their attention to fulfilling the promise of NCLB to train all teachers before they enter the classroom, even in special education, where shortages were severe.

District internship organizations are sanctioned and monitored by the same state agency that authorizes universities to train teachers, and the non-university semester credits are given the same weight by school districts and often graduate schools. In other words, as a credential holder, one has the same status as a teacher trained by a university. I learned about the district internship legislation when I noticed an ad in the local newspaper's employment section from Project Pipeline, one of the leading organizations operating under the legislation. They were holding an informational meeting in the nearby town of Concord, in partnership with Mt. Diablo Unified School District. Project Pipeline had formed a partnership with the district to help fill their special-ed openings. I did some background research online, made a reservation, and attended the meeting. Project Pipeline, a non-profit institution headquartered in state capital Sacramento, had been training teachers in the Bay Area and other parts of Northern California for over ten years, with one of the state's highest rates of retention for teachers surviving past their first five years. They were new to special education, but they had been a force in fulfilling California's class-size reduction act for primary- and elementary-age students. Credential classes would be held in Mt. Diablo's facilities, which were a convenient twenty-minute commute from my home in Danville. The organization seemed credible, even substantial. Project Pipeline's administrator for the Mt. Diablo program reminded me of friends from special-ed experiences in college. One goal of the district internship laws was to support the recruiting of mid-life career changers like me. It all seemed of a piece. I decided to apply.

When I encountered the Project Pipeline recruitment ad, I was looking in the employment classifieds for some type of sustenance job to sustain me while I attended Cal State's credential program for two years as a full-time student. Those two years, which would include unpaid student teaching, would be followed by five years in the field as a Level I teacher, which would be followed by one and a half more years as a full-time student, including additional unpaid student teaching, which would yield a master's degree and Level II status. An odyssey. It might help to note that in California, teacher credentialing must occur on a post-graduate basis (i.e. after undergraduate degree).

Project Pipeline, on the other hand, involved half-time study for three years straight, with classes held on weeknights and weekends to accommodate working teachers. After receiving provisional admission from Project Pipeline, the candidate must secure a teaching contract with intern status at one of the school districts that partner with the program. The intern applies directly to the district. An intern contract pays the same or slightly less (typically within five percent) as the salary for a new credentialed teacher at the same number of semester units, and includes full benefits, even retirement contributions. Pay rises as semester units are accumulated. Interns have the same duties as all other full-time contract teachers, plus the responsibility of making good progress in credential studies. The district deducts tuition payments from the intern's salary on behalf of Project Pipeline at each pay period. The total cost for the three years was $10,000, spread out over thirty months (program was also subsidized by the partnering districts and state budget). At the end of the three-year program, the intern receives Level II perman- ent status, and with 48 semester units, a salary close to those afforded a master's degree.

So, if I could get admitted to the credential program and then land a contract with a district, I would have the susten- ance job that I was looking for. One or two more pitches, and I could get this thing moving forward. Savvy readers might pause to wonder if I had contemplated the implications of jumping straight into a full-time teaching position in the spe- cial-ed department of a large public school. I hadn't. I was still a pitchman: my mind was on the short-term close. I could fig- ure out the details later.

Selling Me as a Teacher

Applying to a credential program requires an essay and interview: two requirements where my pitchman skills could provide a bridge. And with Project Pipeline, the Mt. Diablo school district would have similar requirements in its hir- ing process. I crafted a unique selling proposition that I felt would win at both organizations and implemented it into an essay and application letter. When asked interview questions, I could reiterate the selling proposition.

This was not a cynical process. I meditated on my motiv- ation. I knew that my qualifications were a bit thin, since they mostly consisted of experiences in college twenty years earlier. Truth be told, success would have to come from motivation. I was barely qualified, but highly motivated. My heart, I felt, was in the right place. My essay and letter lightly covered my psychology degree and special-ed field experiences, and I lightly mentioned transference of communication, time management, and writing skills from my business years. The greatest weight was given to motivation.

I was kind of an Anglo male bombshell at that point in my life (with some Irish thrown in). A helpful comparison might be a young Ryan O'Neal, Ted Kennedy, Bill Clinton or even George W. Bush. Maybe a little more athletic than those individuals—like if G.W. Bush had played fullback or cornerback at Yale instead of baseball. I was cruising at 5'11", 190, with 35" waist and 44" chest. Collar-length, thick, full, wavy brunette. Clean shaven. Green eyes. Fair-but-tanned-and-ruddy complexion. Mildly-broad brow, cheeks, and chin with aquiline nose. Going by appearances, I looked more like a senatorial candidate than a teaching credential candidate. I had to say something that would show that my inner life was a good fit for the task. That might distract them from the outer anomaly long enough for me to prove myself on the job.

To come up with my angle, I recalled my own experiences as a special-needs student—maybe "difficult" student would be more appropriate. I was a gifted behavior problem, as teacher-ed literature might refer to the situation. Gifted seems a little too flattering, but in the spectrum of students with behavior problems, I would be on the gifted side versus the learning-disabled side. My problems were clearly rooted in upbringing and attitude—I was rich (relatively) and spoiled.

Interventions into this problem were sometimes dramatic and quite explicit. For some reason, my parents frequently tell friends and relatives about the time that I declined to accelerate to the next grade in middle school. In seventh grade, teachers held a meeting with my parents to discuss my proclivity for finishing my work ahead of peers and then having time left over to disrupt them. Teachers felt that I might need greater challenges. They asked me if I wanted to move up to eighth grade; they really felt that I should, all things considered. I declined. My parents interpreted that response as indication of an innately free spirit or maybe a bit of shyness. But in my mind, when asked that question, I envisioned eighth-grade jocks beating me up and picking on me—they already showed disdain toward me for being kind of smart and pretty for a boy: "No thank you. I promise to do better in my classes. I just want to stay with my friends in seventh grade." My parents use this story to convey their feeling that I'm a free spirit and no one has ever been able to manage me.

My strongest memories of this problem come from meetings held by the high school principal in which he tried to convince my mother to place me in the honors program. I started high school in a suburban Catholic boys' school, which was more like a prep school than like the old Chicago parish schools my parents went to. But then I transferred to my neighborhood public high school (which was actually a richer crowd than the private school). I didn't like the six-mile daily commute each way to the private school, and I felt that most of my classmates were aggressive snobs.

I had attended elementary and middle grades in my suburban neighborhood public schools within easy walking distance, so I was just rejoining my class. Not that I was popular or anything like that. It just seemed like the public school snobs and jocks were a little less aggressive than the private ones. Due to geographic factors of my parent's house-owner ambitions, I wound up the only child to attend public school in a long tradition of Catholic education, which included even my siblings. My choice to attend public school, even in the face of my parent's desire to bring me in line with the family tradition, added further evidence to their growing claim that I was a hopelessly free spirit.

Adlai E. Stevenson High School was a volatile mix of expanding suburban affluence and family farms in decline. The towns it served were defined by enclaves of modern luxury homes with spacious groomed and treed lots interspersed with mildly dilapidated farms, some with active livestock and crops and some with abandoned structures and fallow fields. The affluent enclaves were conspicuously yet tastefully carved out of these farms in a way that preserved the rural ambience of this Republican area of Lake County, Illinois. In other words, it was the middle of nowhere, and these rich settlers wanted to keep it that way. It was Republican Phil Crane's district, and it was staunchly and consistently conservative. The demographics were at 98% White and 2% minority, with crime at zero. It didn't take a doctorate in economics to figure out that affluent White commuters were becoming the crop of choice. When it came to the faculty, the hicks of yore were still regrettably in the majority. Their teaching technique could best be characterized as blah, blah, blah, memorize, test, reward or punish, repeat to infinity. In my senior year, after our promising varsity football team experienced a mediocre season, the coach told the local newspaper, "I just can't get these affluent creampuffs to play with any kind of intensity." I was on that team, and possibly the main offending cream puff. The coach was dismissed the next year. I would describe myself as more of a bored brat than a cream puff.

At thirty-three miles northwest of downtown Chicago, which was the destination of my father's commute, the bucolic region was the eastern edge of rural corn country and the western edge of urban life emanating from nearby Cook County. A small minority of the 1,100-strong student body was actually from the agricultural culture, but almost the entire student population had a father in an upper echelon corporate occupation, in small business ownership, or in a profession. The wealthiest enclaves were distinguished by stately names such as County Club Estates, Hoffman Estates, Kildeer, and Lincolnshire, and included close proximity to a couple of the richest country clubs in the Chicago metro area.

Basically planted in the middle of a few farms, the grounds of the modern high school, which featured a long, rectangular, red brick multistory building with hints of Frank Lloyd Wright in its overhangs and stylish use of long parallel lines, were surrounded by open spaces with no housing in sight for a quarter mile or so. The prevalence of Camaros, Trans Ams, Corvettes, Mercedes, and Jeeps in the parking lot for students created a stark contrast to the blowing grasses and dense groves.

The wealthiest enclaves were the ones closest to the school, meaning within two miles. I rode the school bus four miles each way though the active farm fields of Prairie View in my commute from Buffalo Grove (Lake County side), a planned community creatively carved into the gentle rolling hills, pastures, and fields of a former family farm. A large farm house and barn were actually preserved on a hill at the end of my block; I was friends with the tenants for a while. The farm house was replaced with a museum commemorating the area's rural and agricultural roots.

Many areas of the rolling farmland were still open space when I moved there as a nine-year-old from our rented duplex second-story flat in the Beverly neighborhood of Chicago's Irish Catholic South Side, which was the motherland for my big Irish family. Our development was kind of nestled into the open spaces. In my family's first years there, you really could imagine buffalo grazing in the open hillsides, which featured green grassy meadows, creeks and ponds, and groves of oak. I actually spent many hours of my childhood exploring among these expansive fields far and wide, with hardly a care in the world. I even had a couple of friends whose families worked the farms where they were tenants, and I occasionally visited and explored their farms. Small herds of deer occasionally transgressed into the enclaves, and mobs of wild rabbits ravaged my garden each summer. For most of our years there, we had to travel three miles south across a hilly farm road to get groceries or any other kind of service in merchants located in the Cook County side of town.   Nearly everyone's father had an upper middle class occupation, but the school culture still featured a social stratification based on make and model of car, designer label clothes, depth of tan from Vail or Florida after spring break, the number of lift tags dangling off your ski parka, size of parent's home and lot, father's income, attendance at wild house parties, healthy skin, straight teeth, trim physiology, sports prowess, and last and least your grades and college plans. The prevailing culture might be best characterized as nouveau riche.

My neighborhood featured a predominance of spacious two-story American colonials of three types in deliberately winding and rolling streets, with a minority of large ranch houses and an occasional one-story American colonial mingled in. We lived in one of the nine-room colonials with four bedrooms, two and a half bathrooms, full basement (finished into a rec room), and two-car garage, which was a much bigger house than my parents could own affordably in the city. But our lots were a quarter acre whereas the lots in upper echelon enclaves were two to five acres. Our landscaping featured lush lawns, shrubs, evergreens, and young planted trees, whereas many wealthier enclaves had sprawling lawns and old growth or second growth trees. We were the middle class aspect of upper class. My dad was a publisher's rep (i.e. magazine advertising sales person) for one of the nation's leading media and publishing companies, and he experienced his first move to management a few years after we arrived. As the young side of nouveau riche, many of my neighborhood friends' youngish fathers were in similar corporate roles headed for middle management.

After my friends and I got our unrestricted driver's license at sixteen, we typically borrowed our mother's domestic station wagon or compact car at the end of its useful life whereas the upper echelon drove late-model American sports cars and European luxury cars. We weren't allowed to borrow our fathers' late-model cars yet, which in my case was typically a Chevrolet Impala, Oldsmobile Cutlass, or Buick Electra. We went skiing in Wisconsin or Michigan clad in our Levi's and parkas from Sears, but the richer students went to Colorado or Utah at least once a year dressed in the latest sleek fashions from Head. I dressed pretty expensively (although indifferently), I looked kind of preppy with my long, shaggy hair and Anglo physiognomy, I worked out with weights a lot, and I skied a lot, so I got along fairly well with the upper echelon. But I always felt a bit awed by their snobbery and not really part of them.

The friends in my social circle shared this visceral trepidation about our more glamorous and popular peers, but we had enough social savvy to never express it out loud. Whereas the upper echelon might be holding a rip roaring house party, one of us would secure our mother's car, pick up the all-male group for the evening's outing, drive to our favorite country main street for submarine sandwiches and Cokes, and catch the latest action flick at the theater down the street. We were typically home by eleven, at which time we might indulge in the outrageous act of watching Saturday Night Live with our parents—our maybe the Three Stooges on our own (my favorite). I had to be ready for mid-morning mass on Sunday at the Catholic church and elementary school founded by the town's leading farming family in 1852, which was best accessed by means of an unevenly paved tractor path that ran a about a country mile between our neighborhood and the parish campus, which explains why my city-raised, not-driving-well-yet Irish mother delayed the enrolling of her children in that school (the tractor path was eventually repaved into a smooth road).

At the start of my first year in public high school, which was my sophomore year, the principal, a tall dapper fifty-something White gentleman of Scottish descent, met with my mother and me to schedule my classes. After reviewing the cumulative file of my entire school career, which included scores from annual standardized tests and my high-school entrance exam, he felt it was essential that I attempt the school's honor classes for college-bound students—basically I should study with the college bound. My mother replied by saying that my father had never been much of a student and he had done quite well for himself in advertising; she wasn't sure if I really needed that kind of challenge. Stunned by her answer, and looking a bit nonplussed for a minute, the principal merely looked down at his papers, filled in some sort of schedule, and ended by saying that he would see me on the first day of school. I had no idea what he had written on that schedule. I just showed up and kind of did my best now and then.

These meetings became a kind of ritual with the principal goading me into keeping up with the college bound. Mainly, it was the principal asking my mother to enroll me in summer school so that I could catch up and thus continue with the college bound next school year. The first time, at the end of my sophomore year, mother indulged him and took me to summer school. The second time, at the end of my junior year, she told the principal that I just wasn't worth that kind of effort: he had wanted me to get some extra time in on pre-calculus so that I could attempt calculus in my senior year. Senior year, I dropped out of the college-bound cohort and repeated pre-calc with non-honors students. There was definitely a marked difference in atmosphere—and it wasn't positive. Ultimately, I just dropped math since I had already met my graduation requirements. Throughout high school, there were frequent meetings with subject teachers complaining that they just didn't get me and couldn't I just get my act together.

My mother's predictions were quite accurate. I graduated high school with a sub-2.00 grade point average. I was never a great student, and then I basically dropped out of senior year. I probably completed my graduation requirements, but I have a sneaking suspicion that the school administration just didn't want any trouble from my corporate dad. When I went to college the next year, I had no work habits and no feeling for scholarship, behaved deplorably, and dropped out after one year. Alarmingly, the quaint private university had admitted me on the basis of being a gifted behavior problem: my ACT score exceeded their standards even though my grades were deficient.

I wasn't a disgruntled genius. I have a few tricks up my sleeve, but I'm no genius. As I stated earlier, on the spectrum of students with behavior problems, I'm on the gifted side. By the way, I'm not hyperactive—the problem is definitely in my attitude. I wasn't engaging in delinquent behavior during those problem years, but I found lots of fairly benign ways to be off task: building model rockets, model railroads, cultivating a collection of fish species, working out with weights like in *Pumping Iron*, interscholastic football, Boy Scouts, band, snow skiing, skateboarding, going to the movies, playing pool or ping pong with friends in the rec room, watching television, restoring a vintage Alfa Romeo, among others.

I was a slacker, but my life was completely free of delinquency. Yet those years exposed me to what it was like to be out of alignment: to be a problem child that wasn't meeting anyone's expectations, to be considered a loser. My pitch to the credential program centered on this feeling of kinship with special-ed students.

Eventually, in my free-spirited way, I developed work habits and skills in scholarship—at least somewhat—and the ability to accomplish difficult projects basically on deadline. These work habits and skills transferred to the workplace—most of the time. And, most gratifying of all, I have enjoyed so many enriching experiences through being a life-long learner. So, I basically kind of grew up, at least compared to the problem years of my youth. I'm not a loser anymore, at least not most of the time.

My essay and letter developed the theme that my feeling of kinship with students, who are struggling under the burden of labels, school failure, and learning disabilities—in other words, feeling like a loser—will give me the motivation needed to maintain compassion and hope while helping them move forward in their education. Moreover, my own experience of changing, of growing out of problem years to eventually develop powerful skills in communication and management, makes me hopeful and curious about ways to help students experience similar changes (properly scaled to their ability level). Finally, I added that these noble motives would be enhanced by skills in communication, time management, and writing acquired during my business career.

The pitch achieved the intended effect. In spring of 2003, Project Pipeline Teacher Credential Program granted me provisional admission, with full admission upon securing a contract at a partnering school district. Shortly after that, in the summer, Mt. Diablo Unified School district offered me an intern contract to teach at a middle school for academic year 2003-2004. I was set to start the first training course, called Pre-Service, in July. I had a job to survive on while training and a convenient three-year route to a full credential, which should lead to a secure, permanent teaching contract. Pitch successful. Deal closed. Now for the details. I was hired for a position called Resource Specialist. I had not one iota of experience or knowledge for this position. Luckily, I had read enough online to fake my way through the interviews at the district. I was counting on the first credential course to fill me in.

CHAPTER TWO

Inspiration

Born with a Question

I now realize that there was a kind of metaphysical itch that I kept impulsively scratching throughout my college years, which steered my course selections in directions that were antagonistic to inheriting my father's ad man ways. My decision to try teaching was the culmination of a lifetime of simmering rebellion. I wasn't just becoming a special-ed teacher. I was becoming *not* an ad man and *not* any other type of businessman. The negative quality of the decision added force and energy to my intention to help my country in an area of great need.

Dad sent me to a small Presbyterian university in agricultural central Illinois with a solid reputation for placing its business students in corporate jobs after graduation: an excellent choice for a Chicago ad man and his son. The sweeping lawns, ancient oaks, and prominent grand gothic architecture conveyed its loyalty to the highest principals of the industrial revolution, which is when it was founded in 1901 by the rancher-turned-industrialist-banker James Millikin. So I studied pre-med (biology) and flopped socially and academically within one year. One should really be a good student before studying biology at a fine four-year university. I chose biology because it was *not dad*, instead of because I had an affinity for the subject or the study habits and inspiration of a doctor. At least I learned something about making choices. I also learned a few things about drinking parties, carousing, flirting, brawling, road trips, rock music, and junk food. Keen observers may detect a latent talent for the ad game (a chip off the old block!).

Next year, dad's work brought the entire family to New York State: specifically, Ft. Salonga, a verdant, bucolic hamlet on the North Shore. Our spacious two-story American colonial on a two-acre treed lot was just a quarter-mile walk from beaches on Long Island Sound. Dad's daily commute was forty minutes (i.e. thirty miles) westward to Garden City, which was basically in the middle of Long Island. He worked at a branch office of a major national publishing and media empire, in which he was the publisher of a major trade magazine in office automation (i.e. middle manager). Occasionally he drove fifty miles to the firm's world headquarters in New York City (NYC) for corporate meetings. He quickly found an ancient Catholic parish a mile eastward down the shore, and enrolled my sister in an elementary school and my brother in a high school, both Catholic in shore towns within easy driving distance. The hamlet's demographics and economics were almost identical to Buffalo Grove and the other towns in my high school district in Illinois. And we were again the middle-class aspect of a substantially upper class area that might best be characterized as nouveau riche.

Demonstrating his typical dogged persistence, dad drove me eastward down the shore to State University of New York (SUNY) at Stony Brook a few weeks after we moved in. It took about twenty minutes by a lovely scenic route. He drove up to the administration building, prompted me to walk in and investigate, to do a little prospecting. I approached an admin sitting at her desk monitoring the entrance. I humbly told her of my desire to shed last year's courses and explore a fresh start at Stony Brook. She gave me the paper work. I filled it out. After a preparatory year as an open-university student, I became a matriculating member of that very fine university. Basically, I earned my way in.

Covering two square miles, with a total student population of approximately 16,000, SUNY Stony Brook was tastefully integrated geographically with the forested, rolling hills and small towns of the eastern end (i.e. the rural end) of Long Island's North Shore. The campus was ensconced in wooded open spaces such that if you didn't know where the entrances were, you might not even know that the campus existed. The campus was just a short walk down a country lane from the historic colonial-era village of Stony Brook.

Although founded in 1957, the university's modern grounds were developed in the 1960s and beyond. In contrast to the colonial architecture of the nearby shore's small towns, the modern campus featured large governmental multi-story buildings characterized by parallel lines, rectangles and squares, concrete and brick, and glass and steel. Although modern and functional, the buildings were modestly elegant in exterior and interior, and conveyed the grandeur associated with a great university. The landscape featured a central plaza with major buildings for administration, library, fine arts, student union, and a few of the bigger academic departments, with the remaining buildings connected to the plaza by park-like walkways in spoke-and-hub fashion. Student dormitories were located on the outskirts of the grounds away from the academic buildings, and they were connected to the campus by a looping roadway with a shuttle bus. The commuter parking lot, where I started, was a half-block-long rectangle on the farthest outskirts of the grounds with a shuttle bus to transport students into the meandering, park-like campus. The main campus was almost totally free of auto traffic.

Stony Brook Station of the Long Island Railroad was located on the northern shore side of the campus, and served the university and nearby small towns. This stop was considered outside of normal commuting range for Penn Station in Manhattan, which was sixty miles away, but it was a comfortable distance for the occasional day or weekend trip into the city for residential students, and some students actually commuted from NYC. The southern inland side of the grounds abutted a flat region called middle island, which provided a connection to the Long Island Expressway, and thus a convenient route for students in other parts of New York State, especially the NYC metro area, to drive in daily or for each semester. The commuter parking lot was connected to the middle island area. Commuter students in the shore towns like me could walk in, ride a bike, or drive their used car at the end of its useful life a short way along country roads. The rural campus's proximity to major transportation routes leading to the NYC metro area provided an explosive mix of rural, suburban, and urban influences in this haven of modernity among the coastal villages of the American Revolution. The tuition at this leading (i.e. emerging) research university was about $1,200 per year, so basically free to students and an act of generosity by the state's taxpayers.

As Stony Brook and Ft. Salonga had been seats of the colonial rebellion, my own dissenting also made some serious headway. I felt pretty guilty about losing a year's worth of courses. I reflected carefully on my motivation. If I follow my heart, I thought, my study habits and concentration might rise to the occasion: in other words, I might finally acquire those essential traits. In the preparatory year, I selected courses strictly on the basis of curiosity, as if each course was a book that I might have bought to read in my spare time. I paid no heed to graduation requirements—I needed some kind of spark to get started.

I selected cultural anthropology, concepts of the person, comparative politics, contemporary morality, American government, and sociology. All courses were at the freshman level. Seeds for the ground of rebellion. Obviously, I wasn't aiming for a business degree.

Senior year of high school, I read *The Final Days* by Bob Woodward and Carl Bernstein for a history class. The assignment had simply been to report on a demanding book of your choosing. Dad was a genuine ad savage, a sales maniac, but interestingly, he was a life-long learner with an impressive

27

collection of books in his home office. I just grabbed it from there, with no idea of the implications of its contents. Richard Nixon's conduct struck a chord in me: egomaniacal, domineering, impulsive, sneaky, ruthless, pig-headed, and pushy. Dad!! It was a story about dad. It was a story about maleness in America. It wasn't just about the presidency. It was about manhood. So many of the fathers in my town and their sons were following the same model of maleness that led Nixon to his rise and demise. Were all of us Americans in a rise on that basis that would end in our demise? A question, which seemed like I had been born with it, had been brewing in my mind throughout high school, and *Final Days* solidified it. Do we Americans, especially men, have to be so snobbish, competitive, paranoid, and maniacal? Can we do better? Is there something better? Or should I just get on the dad path with my high school classmates?

Stony Brook, which had a reputation for rebellious students and professors, was a totally unexpected turn in my life, but just what the doctor ordered (i.e. the best medicine for anomy and apathy). It was a very egalitarian place. The teachers were astoundingly generous, and taught with their full hearts to what amounted to a student population of typically humble origins. In fact, the high quality of the teaching was a kind of populist rebellion in itself. The NYC-rooted social climate was multi-cultural, inter-class, diverse-ethnic, and mad with upward-mobile dreams of every stripe. Chinese, Vietnamese, Korean, Iranian, Indian, and Russian students were present in force from both local immigrant communities and international programs, interacting transparently with the White majority. In addition, many of the White students were from a variety of relatively recent European immigrant roots. That atmosphere was mind-blowing ether to a discontented brat from the affluent, White, stilted, paranoid suburbs of Republican Illinois. My heart and mind literally soared.

The reduced preparatory schedule and curiosity-based courses proved to be fertile ground for developing study habits—at least nascent ones. I earned the required g.p.a. (3.78 actually) and matriculating status. Under the guise of a political science major, I continued to indulge my curiosity. The poli-sci department offered a unique opportunity to study law from a scholarly perspective as opposed to a lawyerly view in a minor called Law and Society—a rare opportunity for an undergraduate. I studied law from several angles: business, tort, civil liberties and civil rights (thoroughly), philosophy of law, and legislative process. Democracy dharma!! These courses featured matter-of-fact discussions about controversial issues that would completely unnerve an ad guy but energized me. Paranoia-free education!! Not-Dad education!! I also completed the core curriculum of the poli-sci department, in courses such as american defense policy, world politics, and organizational-decision theory, and I actually even slipped in a few of the university graduation requirements (I completed the college algebra and English composition requirements in my first full-time year to make sure that I really belonged there).

I mentioned nascent study habits. Stony Brook's close proximity to NYC provided lots of extracurricular activities on school nights and weekends, especially in Manhattan: my favorites being congenial drinking expeditions of all sorts (with fairly dignified levels of social interaction), cavorting and exploring the landscape, development of truly precious friendships, the youth scene of Greenwich Village (which was going yuppie in the 1980s), and interesting forays into hipster outlets such as Studio 54 and Mud Club. Keen observers might once again detect a latent talent for the ad game.

Dad was holding out on me monetarily. He was goading me into working my way through school. Noticing my intermittent study skills and passion for extra-curricular life, he probably figured I should drop out after two years like he did and go to work in sales somehow. Stony Brook professors routinely proclaimed their opposition to working students. The professors wanted to maintain high standards, and out of respect their students should not waste time working in menial jobs when they should be studying. But I held a job for most of each semester. For a couple of years, I worked in a popular high-end ski shop on Long Island, in nearby Huntington. It was fun, but a big distraction, especially during Christmas and the rest of ski season. I withdrew one semester to take a high-paying landscaping job (tree work) in Huntington. Between working in Huntington and partying in NYC, I barely had time to study.

Even worse, I kept taking courses out of curiosity. In the hindsight of middle-aged maturity, I can see that I should have streamlined my schedule down to the barest minimum needed to achieve the political science major with the law and society minor. Trying for a minor was really stretching my limited skills, but I loved studying democracy. I branched out into the classics and extra courses in philosophy, and these meanderings were complicated by taking an extra course each semester to accelerate my progress (i.e. catch up). Frequently in over my head, I flunked a few courses. My transcript started to look like Swiss cheese. So time management was a "future skill" as we say in special education.

I earned good grades in my poli-sci courses and a few others. Those achievements offset the failures and drops enough to keep me in good standing, but my g.p.a. was sinking a little each semester. One very cold fall semester, while living in a decrepit farm house (on farmland) near Stony Brook with almost no heat or hot water, I decided to take my rebellion blue collar. I had tried to live without a job that semester, but I got fed up with the austerity. I started reading on Zen and other Buddhist topics, inspired by a close friend's suggestions: she was trying to channel my rebellious impulses (and maybe tame them). Those teachings made me want to pull myself together. I figured that a together blue collar worker was better than a disorganized, downhearted, and frequently drunk college student.

Even though I had earned almost all the upper division credits needed for a political science major and minor, and many of the university graduation requirements, I packed up and left for Northern California at the end of fall semester 1984. If I had stayed through that semester, I could have graduated in two or three more semesters, but I had worn myself down in three and a half years of cavorting, partying, road trips, jobs, and juggling too many difficult courses. I felt a little stupid and reckless for leaving, but I was looking forward to the noble life of a blue collar worker with a penchant for lifelong learning: as a blue collar man, I would still be studying how to be *not dad*.

My parents had moved to the San Francisco Bay Area to accommodate dad's career. It was almost as beautiful geographically as Long Island. I was going to stay with them at their new place in Round Hill Country Club in Alamo while I looked for work—blue collar. All things considered, I had accomplished much on Long Island: I gained great knowledge and insight about our country's heritage while studying democracy dharma; I absorbed the enlightened atmosphere of the not-paranoid culture at Stony Brook; I enjoyed penetrating friendships and beautiful scenery with my friends in various meanderings and adventures in NYC and all around the Mid-Atlantic and New England regions; and I had held several semi-respectable jobs blue collar and white. Not too bad for a gifted behavior problem in his early twenties. My question about whether there was a better way to live than the dad path was more on my mind than ever.

Seminal Moments

The question arises as to why I would want to be a teacher, given my obvious lack of affinity for the scholarly life: the blue collar plan sounds about right. In fact, one wonders how and why I earned a degree at all. Summer jobs in my first two years at SUNY Stony Brook turned out to be unexpected seminal moments in my quest to be *not dad*. They were my first experiences working with children, and they left a psychic echo that

I acted on when I decided to try a mid-life change to the teaching profession.

In the summer of 1982, after my first year at Stony Brook, I found a position as a residential counselor at Camp Alvernia in Centerport, just a few very scenic miles west of my parent's house in Ft. Salonga on the North Shore. The camp was located down a quiet country lane, on a gentle hillside grove that led down to Centerport Harbor. The waterfront access and rural setting were valuable assets so close to NYC. There was swimming in the harbor and in a pool, boating, sports, outdoor games, and typical camp fun such as water balloon fights and movie nights. My role was to supervise a group of fifteen fifth-grade boys in all phases of their camp experience during their two-week residential stay. The summer job consisted of two 2-week sessions.

I can't recall the exact basis of my qualifications. I had attended Boy Scout camp as a camper and as a mentor-supervisor. And the previous summer I worked as staff on a roller coaster at Marriot's Great America in my last months in Illinois. So I had some experience supervising young people in sensitive situations. Maybe that was my pitch. I recall going to the main office for an interview with the camp director, a Franciscan brother (Friar). I was responding to a flyer mailed to my parents targeting them as a family with a child in St. Anthony's, a Franciscan high school where my brother was a junior. The flyer was recruiting staff for Franciscan summer programs. Franciscans are a powerful presence in the NYC metro area, operating high schools, faith-based charitable organizations, and even universities—their mission is direct service to the people. This flyer could be called an auspicious coincidence, since I only sought the position out of lack of interest in other forms of employment such as working in a restaurant or store. I had no special interest in helping children or friars, but the job seemed better than sitting around.

The summer turned out to be a lot of fun, definitely better than being cooped up in a business. I guided the children from activity to activity with relative ease. I kept them safe and free of injury or illness, maintained a fair and non-aggressive atmosphere with no bullying, and even started to appreciate each child as an individual. I did okay with the campers: slightly on the tyrant side, but not over the top. The prime mover for me, however, was the extracurricular activities. I really enjoyed my time with the staff, who mostly hailed from NYC with some coming from Sweden, Switzerland, and Holland as part of an exchange program for teachers. We had lots of time off to enjoy the nightlife of the North Shore, beautiful South Shore beaches, and even a couple of trips to Manhattan. It was a real change of scene from my corporate upbringing. Almost all of the staff were teachers or interested in becoming educators in some way. There is an ease and warmth to people outside of the more avaricious occupations. I really enjoyed their companionship.

I was pretty satisfied with my performance at Camp Alvernia, until the following summer (1983), when I worked at Rosemont Camp, a residential camp run by special-education administrators from New York. I learned about the position from a classified ad in Newsday, and I interviewed for it at a camp administrator's house near Stony Brook. The camp was situated on a high meadow in the rolling hills of the Appalachian Range in Pennsylvania (one might call it a mountaintop): the nearest town was Honesdale. The lush, green meadows that hosted the camp were surrounded by dense woods, which led to wilderness areas and game preserves. The only signs of human life nearby were small dairy farms along the county highway, which was accessed through a mile-long dirt driveway.

The camp directors started the year with a training program that really made an impression on me. The staff contained various levels of specialization and expertise. Specialists focused on a specific area such as swimming or academic learning. General counselors accompanied their campers throughout the day, supporting the specialists and attending to the campers' basic needs. Specialists as a rule had extensive experience working with special-needs children, most were already employed in education. I was a general counselor, which for my position meant a surrogate parent for eight fifth-graders—we even shared a cabin like a family. Nearly all of the general counselors were upper-division special-ed majors from universities in New York, some were even on formal internships. I was definitely the least qualified person on the staff. My political science studies weren't much help, but, in light of recent reform initiatives, maybe there was some kind of providence or prescience there.

All camp activities were organized under a master schedule, with periods and transitions similar to a school day. Each period was taught by a specialist, who ran the activity like a school teacher. As far as time management, the atmosphere was more like a boarding school than a camp. As I learned, the formal structure is an aide to special-needs students, who typically experience difficulty with transitions and staying focused: consistency is favored over spontaneity. Keen observers might anticipate trouble ahead for me, a chronic school discipline problem.

The training program was basically a crash course in classroom management, meaning the craft of creating environmental controls that help the student stay focused on the assigned task: for instance, how the staff should respond when a student can't or won't start an activity or task. Now, as I write this book thirty-two years later, with intense training on this topic in the last twelve of those years, it's hard to cull out the memories that started at Rosemont. The crux of the camp training was professionalism. When a child goes off task or fails to act on a directive, we the staff don't respond intuitively by emulating our mother or father, or even our own experience as students, instead we have a view and a method that control our response.

The view has a couple of aspects to it. First, one learns to perceive behavior as a kind of neutral communication more than a wrong or right, a mistake or success. Second, behavior is often the result of psychological or physiological antecedents or causes more than the student's attitude about the activity. So, failure to follow a direction is often a problem of learning or disability rather than a result of conscious opposition.

Method refers primarily to the way one responds to the child's apparent misbehavior. For example, the child won't jump off the peer for his swimming test. As a professional, the first step will be to refrain from any kind of threat or suggestion of punishment; in addition, we will refrain from taunting or teasing the child into action. The best move would be to gain an understanding of the child's motives at that point. My style would be to ask a nonchalant question: "How come you don't want to jump in?" I might offer help: "How about if I go in with you? I'll swim next you." Jumping in is a problem we can solve together.

Method dictates that the response should be rooted in the antecedents. The counselor can always do a quick assessment of the environmental conditions. Maybe the child is skinny and today the air and water are just too cold: better wait until a warmer day. Physiological and neurological factors should be checked: with hearing aid removed, a perceptually-impaired child might panic—he will need some extra demonstrations and a few visual cues before he will be ready to jump. The underlying philosophy says that the child probably wants to comply with the direction, but the antecedents are stacked against it, so when the counselor helps the student cope with them, the child completes the task. At Rosemont, tolerance and accommodation were the prime movers of method, but in other organizations, a motivation plan might also be applied (i.e. carrot on a stick).

The goal of professionalism is to engage the child in growth-oriented tasks without inducing levels of anxiety that might intimidate the child or lead him into oppositional behaviors. A growth-oriented task might be improving the camper's swimming level from beginner to intermediate. We offered real swimming instruction, not just unstructured play. Counselors needed to maintain a positive, supportive tone with the children or they would just freeze up and refuse to participate, even if threatened with punishment.

My campers were classified as Low Incidence under special-ed law. Low Incidence children typically have a perceptual disability affecting either auditory functioning or visual functioning or sometimes both simultaneously. Perceptual refers to the accurate or inaccurate processing of sensory input as it is received and then transformed into some kind of expression such as movement or speech. Life with a perceptual disability is like walking on ice while wearing smooth, hard-soled shoes—a kind of precarious, wobbly relationship with reality. In the case of my campers, they all had some vision, some hearing, some speech, and basic motor skills for their age, but all of these abilities were a little wobbly, and thus led to problems with confidence and social relationships. Potential for academic learning was limited, and some had signs of intellectual disability (i.e. low IQ). The term Low Incidence refers to the small percentage of the general population that has these disabilities—less than one percent.

The few days of training were crucial. I wouldn't have been able to handle the job without them. I had no knowledge of or experience with special-needs children. My campers in particular, as I figured out in the first few days of camp, would need a lot of prompting and encouragement before engaging in any activity. Their perceptual disabilities gave them a kind of natural inclination toward inaction. Method training, which I mentioned earlier, also taught counselors how to give physical support to campers when they first try an activity and then to gradually withdraw it to foster independence. For instance, a counselor might start the summer swimming with beginning swimmers, even allowing them to hold on to him in moments of panic, but finish the summer watching them from the pier. It might seem natural to offer a helping hand—the professional knows how to withhold it, and the training emphasized both aspects.

Besides view and method, the training also covered the basic ethic of high expectations in special education: why we don't just have unstructured or informal play, why we work hard to engage the students in growth-oriented challenges, why we follow a fixed schedule, and why we don't just let the camper sit back and refuse to participate. In other words, why Rosemont was pushier than most camp environments. But the most compelling aspect for me was the view and method of tolerance and accommodation as opposed to pressure and intimidation. More seeds of rebellion.

I have hinted at my Buddhist inclinations. It might be helpful to note here that I had not yet learned about Buddhism while I was at Rosemont. In fact, it was a friend from Rosemont that nudged me in that direction a year later. So, I experienced tolerance and accommodation in a raw, hands-on way. It was like a shock to my system—a kind of encounter with a burning bush.

The Way of Tolerance and Accommodation

The training program at Rosemont turned out to be good preparation for my role. I took it to heart and it gave me the skills needed to give the campers a growth-oriented yet relaxed and fun experience. My campers did well. I particularly recall enjoying my time with them at the waterfront. Midwesterners love their fresh-water lakes, and my youth reflected it: lakefront cottages, lake swimming and life-guard training, fishing, backcountry canoeing and rafting, and water skiing. I probably had a subconscious affinity. Waterfront activities were conducted in a natural spring-fed lake, like a large pond, on the grounds. The water was cool, clear, with a tint of emerald green giving it that magical texture of a natural mountain lake. It was alive with plant life and who knows what else—especially frogs and birds. The camp installed piers in a square structure to create a swimming enclosure and to support boating.

My campers worked hard at their swimming lessons, and a few even increased their level. In addition to swimming, we enjoyed paddling in light plastic canoes that the campers could paddle themselves or ride in with an adult. My warmest memories are of canoeing. Sometimes the waterfront specialists, who were PE teachers, pushed us to practice our paddling maneuvers, but often my gang just fell into leisurely floating in the sunny, fresh breeze. Swimming was a bit more goal-oriented, more like work, but my campers put their shoulder to the wheel and truly showed some guts.

My campers also did well with the classroom teacher. Every week day, the campers completed about an hour's worth of academic work. Campers' teachers from back home sent curriculum for the summer, which was administered by Rosemont's academic specialist, who was a credentialed special-ed teacher (low incidence) from NYC. I acted as a tutor in the classroom, supporting individual students as they attempted their day's assignment. Most of the work was meant to reinforce the previous academic year's accomplishments, as opposed to new information, and predictably the students enjoyed going over tasks that they understood. The teacher interspersed some of her own art lessons in with the workbooks from home for variety.

The teacher was kind to me, and she started giving me a short break while she taught my students. I was never sure whether she was trying to help me or avoid another incident. One day, gripped by gifted-behavior-problem karma, I painted a smiley face on the t-shirt of one of my campers during an art lesson. He returned the inspiration by painting one on mine. Then I painted another on him, and he painted another on me. Then a classmate, moved by our shenanigans, painted a smiley face on a nearby camper. And around it went until every camper's clothes were covered in water-soluble tempera paints. Even the teacher joined in. She thought the paint fight had been great harmless fun, and no harm done. But privately, I was a little shaken up by the karmic aspect of it, and made sure to stay on the straight and narrow after that.

Overall, the campers and I did pretty well in the sole four-week session. We made it to meals on time. My campers ate with satisfactory decorum, in sufficient quantities, and with acceptable variety. They slept well and kept up with the fairly rigorous master schedule. No one had to leave because of behavior problems or illness. Our weakness was the field activities, which were typical phys-ed curriculum. Often, they boiled down to me holding the camper under the arm pits and scooting him through like a puppeteer—P.E. would be a future skill for my campers.

I adapted well to the way of tolerance and accommodation. My campers and I engaged in many activities that summer with delight and minimal conflict or acting out. But the summer was not a complete success. In my weekly supervision meetings, conducted by qualified educators, the feedback was that I was a little permissive for the educational environment. For instance, I had not attended to the goal of improving campers' self-care in skills such as tying one's shoes, folding and storing clothing, and making beds. When it was time for those things, the supervisors noticed, I would just dash around doing everything for the campers. I mildly defended my methods, citing my successes in the prime movers of waterfront and academics. They agreed, but insisted that high expectations meant that we don't settle for that alone but instead strive to reach the whole child. I listened and didn't get mad, because I knew they were just trying to be professional.

Overall, the directors were pleased with my performance and complimented me on a good summer. They invited me back the next summer, but I had moved into a construction-manual labor phase in search of higher wages by then, so I declined. I wasn't sure if I really deserved their praise. They might have occasionally seen the campers and I reclining in the meadow near the swings, lying supine in the tall grasses and flora, taking in soft breezes and gentle Appalachian sunshine like philosophers contemplating the gods, and thought, "They're getting along so well. How lovely." But if they checked the master schedule, they would have noticed that we had abandoned the transition from classroom to waterfront and were shamelessly playing hooky. My killer app was to give up on the schedule for a period or two when I sensed the campers were about to break. Maybe I was too permissive. I had to think about it.

A Moment of Insight

Ensconced in a large staff of educated young adults, I was bound to find my way into extracurricular activities. As with the previous summer, I found them to be one of the main attractions. Teachers are more adventurous than one might guess. One of my favorite activities was convivial drinking outings to local (i.e. townie) bars located on the highway to Honesdale. Teachers really know how to wash their troubles away. I managed to take a couple of road trips to the Scranton area. My favorite outings involved just hanging out in beautiful natural settings. I didn't have a car at camp, but somehow I found lots of rides.

I fell in with a clique of five counselors who had travelled from SUNY campuses in upstate New York: two men and three women. They were all upper-division special-ed majors. They came from disperse locales around upstate New York, but they all knew each other from SUNY. As I recall, none had fathers who were ad men or any other kind of big corporation man. I guess anthropologically we were the young end, or tail end, of the baby boom, and we looked like it. This was an attractive group, socially and physiologically, as fabulous as the up and coming yuppies of NYC: there was not a hint of inferiority in their choice to be teachers. Maybe I was following their passion for extracurricular activities or maybe they were contaminated by mine.

We did many things together that summer and fall. Visiting them after camp, I travelled to Finger Lakes, Lake Ontario, Buffalo, Lake Erie, Plattsburg, and Lake Champlain. Late summer and fall are simply stunning in upstate New York and Vermont. Once, they came down to NYC. At camp, my two favorite activities with them were late-night singing of (or listening to) folk songs in high meadows at the edge of the camp area and swimming in and around the granite falls of a back country river. A few other counselors with upstate SUNY affiliations joined the core clique intermittently on these adventures, enriching them with their vitality and fresh perspectives.

I would have to write a poem to capture my impressions of those remote mountain meadows. Gentle. Cool. Moist but not humid. Still. Vast. Dark, dark starry nights. Some pages ago, I mentioned an echo. The falls are part of that echo. There were about two cascades at twenty feet of height each. The land formation consisted of huge grey granite slabs that jutted out where the water careened down them. The river was considerable. Upstream it was about one hundred feet wide and could get as deep as ten or more feet. It slowed down and formed pools as it approached and exited the falls. It flowed fast and hard through the falls. The granite walls formed a one hundred and eighty degree amphitheater around the river, and we could camp out on the massive upper layers and enjoy the cool breezes and soothing sounds of the translucent water rushing by below. The river bank hosted typical Appalachian groves of oak, maple, ash, birch, hickory, and beech.

We had to veer off the main highway onto a barely marked country road, which we followed through uninhabited farm land and open space for about five miles. We spent about four separate days at the falls. We would stock up on provisions in town and then settle into the falls for a long, lazy day. I remember lots of cheap beer, but I don't remember any food. Somehow we maintained minimal nutrition—maybe we stopped for breakfast on the highway.

We talked about our experiences with the campers, our futures, and our personal lives. Basically, we shared. We also just swam around, napped, and soaked up the sun. The other members of the clique were more settled than I was. They were education majors headed for teaching jobs in upstate New York, whereas I was indulging my curiosity about politics, with a vague, uninformed notion of going to law school. Unbeknownst to them, I was tuning into their settledness, connecting to it. As I mentioned earlier, many teachers have a kind of gentility not found in the more aggressive occupations. On those falls, in their company, in that summer, I was out from under Manhattan's spell, and Chicago's too. A human being, me, might be more than just a social-climbing, money-obsessed, status-seeking, paranoid workaholic. I was getting a glimpse of that possibility, induced by shimmering groves, gentle sunlight, cool breezes, and rushing water.

On those falls, I felt warmth. For most of my young adulthood, I felt the heat of the summer, especially as I got older. But that summer, I noticed the warmth. The sublime energy that comes from stepping out of the master race for a moment and just thinking for yourself—and appreciating a beautiful landscape and celebrating the humanity of good society. After a summer of living a life of tolerance and accommodation, a kind of space opened up in my thoughts, a kind of spaciousness. First, the space was a feeling of ease and calm in the mind, face, shoulders, chest, and the rest of the torso—relaxation and repose. Maybe it was a glimpse of inner peace.

Then a before-and-after quality arose in my thinking, most starkly demonstrated in feelings of regret about the way I had treated the children the previous summer at Camp Alvernia. At Rosemont, I followed a view and method and experienced a healthy self-awareness when I was with the campers: I felt that I had been kind, considerate, and fair. Upon reflection, I realized that I had been the opposite at Camp Alvernia. I had acted almost solely on impulse and an intuitive sense of order: reactive, with no sense of direction or self-awareness.

I was basically kind and patient at Camp Alvernia, and always proper. But occasionally I would become a tyrant when the children were ignoring my directions. My dinner rules were a particular source of regret. Almost nightly, my campers would fall into rivalries. They would steal things off each other's plates, hurl put downs, and push, pull, and swat. Dinner was a somewhat formal occasion, with the friars at a head table with formal setting, so my campers' mischief was making me look bad in front of the authorities. That made me mad, so I developed a secret weapon: dessert. If even one camper got out of line, the whole group had to skip dessert and instead sit silently arms-length apart in the soccer field up the hill. If the campers appeased me by calming down, I would let them move on to the evening activity. If they didn't appease me, they went to our cabin and waited on their bunks for bedtime. This punishment was inflicted on the gentle lads about three times in each two-week session.

The soccer field was lit, within the main grounds, and the Long Island weather was balmy and still on summer nights. The silent sitting was not meant to scare them. It was just a time out. None of the children broke into tears or showed any other sign distress. The punishment worked. Misbehavior at dinner decreased. With no view and no method, my mind found its way to the cruelest punishment that would produce the fastest result: efficiency first. But it wasn't fair. It punished the whole group for the activities of actually one chronic bully and a couple of his victims.

Most of the campers were quite pleasant at dinner. Like the amateur that I was, I seated the best-behaved campers close to me at one end of the table so that I could enjoy dinner, mistakenly leaving the bully at the other end of the long rectangular table to have his fun. In hindsight, I should have seated the bully next to me and maybe even his usual victims, and let the children with more self-control preside in peace at the other end of the table. Misbehavior would have stopped and everyone would have received their dessert. And if the bully still persisted (unlikely), I should find assistance and only re-move him during dessert. That would be the way of tolerance and accommodation. In special-ed parlance, this would be called "preferred seating." An ounce of prevention is worth a pound of cure.

Punishing innocent children for the sake of controlling a group of their peers is bad form. How did I arrive at such cruelty? I considered myself a broad-minded liberal person, someone with the vast vision of social democracy. How did I, on impulse, become such a tyrant? A utilitarian? Even worse, toward children. Where do these unsettling impulses come from? Back then, as I moved on after Rosemont, I called it my "Inner Dad": a kind of karmic jarhead perfectionism prone to ends-means thinking. My dinner rules were something that would appeal to dad, who was an actual jarhead in his youth and now a corporate jarhead. I became concerned that my "Inner Dad" was more severe than my actual dad.

At Camp Alvernia, we received no formal training. I re-call that the counselors reported for dinner the night before campers arrived and then received them the next morning. To their credit, the Franciscans had a friary on site. There were lots of clergy around all the time and many of the staff were from Franciscan or other Catholic educational organizations. But, still, not much supervision. I was mildly shocked by the difference between my actions with view and method, and my actions without view and method. I felt good about my summer of tolerance and accommodation: it brought me the experience of peace. So, the other part of the echo, in addition to the warmth of my Appalachian Rosemont summer, was the insight to develop some kind of view and method to live on my own two feet and to avoid being tugged this way and that by my "Inner Dad."

Discovering Modesty

After my Appalachian summer in 1983, I spent one and

a half more years on Long Island before heading off to San Francisco. On the return trip from Pennsylvania that summer, I spent a couple of weeks travelling around upstate New York with my SUNY friends: Finger Lakes, Lake Ontario, Lake Erie, and Buffalo. A couple of other counselors joined us for the adventure. Basically, the upstate group used a variety of family-owned accommodations to house the travelers. In late summer and fall, after returning home, I made a few road trips up to Plattsburg to visit them at school.

In one late summer trip, I had an automotive mishap that caused me to miss the first week of classes at Stony Brook. Unfortunately, I had planned to register that week. Missing that week made registration nearly impossible because of scheduling problems, so I decided to take the semester off with the intention of making some money. I quickly found a job as a manual laborer in a small tree-maintenance business. The Newsday classified ad said, "Looking for ex-football player in need of fast money." Good fit. So I found a job within the first few minutes of looking and began my blue-collar phase. The money was pretty good, much higher than retail, and we were paid in cash (if you know what I mean).

The job lasted into late November. The North Shore of Long Island is one of the most beautiful geographies in America. It's a forest really—of oak, maple, cedar, elm, sycamore, hickory, birch, and pine—and home owners have been ingenious in integrating into the woodlands more than clearing them, so huge trees are interspersed among most neighborhoods. In addition, fertile conditions mean planted trees grow tall and wide. Primarily, we trimmed healthy trees that were threatening structures or growing disruptively tall, and occasionally we cleared a tree that was diseased or otherwise in the way. An interesting twist on recycling, we turned the trunks and limbs into firewood to haul back to our storage yard for sale or to leave with the homeowner as part of the service. We also turned trimmings into wood chips for sale.

The owner and his assistant were the skilled workers,

climbing up into the trees and working with bigger chain saws. I was the main ground worker. I processed all the discarded trunks and limbs by either feeding them into a large chipper or turning them into firewood. We had axes, mauls, and a hydraulic splitter for firewood. I also worked with the skilled men as a team for tackling larger trees, although with me still on the ground. Occasionally, a temporary ground worker would join us. I enjoyed the work. An extreme workout every day in the mind-expanding ether of fall on the North Shore. We worked hard five days a week from eight in the morning until dusk, squeezing every dime out of every day. The owner closed down for the winter and headed for Florida.

I didn't apply at the ski shop that fall or look for another job. I saved enough money to matriculate in second semester without holding a job. I took a brief break and returned to my studies at Stony Brook in January. In the brief break, having money with no classes or homework left plenty of resources for extracurricular activities. I took the opportunity to visit Plattsburgh a couple of times and the gang came down to Long Island once. Lots of convivial drinking and cavorting about, but we also had a nice way of sharing our experiences and plans in conversations. Through our various excursions during these visits, I developed a very nourishing friendship with Kathleen, the academic specialist at Rosemont, who was a credentialed deaf-education teacher in NYC public schools for her regular job.

We were both rich (relatively), spoiled Catholic young adults from the North Shore, although she was from a richer clan in Cold Spring Harbor—the Gold Coast. Her family lived in a grand three-story Dutch colonial. We were both Irish half breeds: she was half Italian, and I was half Anglo (Puritan New England). Both our fathers were corporate-climber sales types. Athletic and curvy, at medium height, with full cheeks, opaque complexion, soft chin, smiling eyes, button nose, and collar-length black curly hair, Kathleen was more matronly than the toned female archetypes of the mini-skirted eighties. She favored cable-knit cardigans, turtle necks, plaid wool skirts, dark tights, and loafers or oxfords. In the summer, she often turned to khaki walking shorts and polo shirt, with hiking boots, walking shoes, or sandals. She was clean cut, perky, energetic, and industrious, and she could hold her own in an argument.

My only close friend outside the SUNY system, Kathleen earned her undergraduate degree at a small Catholic women's college in Boston, and she was working on her master's in deaf education at Hunter College of the City University of New York. Three years older than me, she had found a separate identity from her family without rejecting them.

I admired her independence. She had an apartment in her grandmother's brownstone in the Brooklyn Heights-Park Slope area, which became a favorite destination for extra-curricular activities. She was outgoing with lots of interesting friends outside the corporate-climber set. She was a helpful sounding board for me, and I really appreciated her time. She was very generous to put up with me. So the extra money and time allowed me to connect with her at a time when I was starting to think of my own independence, or disturbingly, drink about it more than think about it.

Second semester went okay. I developed the ill-fated plan of taking an extra course each semester to accelerate my progress, so I was in six courses instead of five, which kind of nullified the benefit of staying out of part-time work. That was a frustrating experience. Time management involves more than just pushing yourself past the limits of reason, it also involves self-awareness and recognition of your limitations and style. Despite working harder than ever, my grades dropped slightly. But I was still inspired by political science and the not-paranoid atmosphere.

After second semester, I chose the blue-collar approach for my summer job of 1984, looking for higher wages than camp employment. I joined a pool construction and renovation company operating out of Huntington: a prosperous small business. The owner was a Stony Brook graduate in applied math who had inherited the business from his father. I found the job through a classified ad in Newsday. We started each morning in the shop yard where we were assigned a work order for the day. Then your crew of two or three workers loaded their truck with the necessary supplies and equipment and snuck off to the deli down the hill for breakfast, using a trip to the building supply store as an excuse. We were authorized to work as many as hours as required to complete the work order, so we were in no rush: "Don't come back until the work is done!!" However, we often kept at the job until dusk, completely sore and spent, in atonement for our deli shenanigans. I recall that there were five or six crews in the field on any given day.

I was subtly nudged into being a crew boss, managing one or two laborers: the term managing being stretched to the limit (because I would do all the work myself when they got tired). My work orders typically involved digging plumbing trenches by hand among tricky landscaping, laying the plumbing in (luckily real blue-collar men were available to rescue me), cleaning up after various stages of construction, and supporting the gunite contractor as they poured ("shot") the pool. We squeezed every dime out of every day.

I enjoyed gunite days the most, because I positioned myself as free labor for the gunite contractor's crew. I could work with a shovel all day, and they had to do all the skill work. I threw sand and dry gunite mix into the hopper, and then threw wet gunite up twenty to thirty feet to form steps, ramps, landings, and other formations during the troweling. The work order said "supervise" the contractor, but gut instinct told me that helping Hells Angels was probably the best way to supervise them. Bare-chested, it was fun in the sun for me. The customers were almost all on the North Shore, some even in mansions on the Gold Coast. We went up into a few estates in the Queens area too. I always enjoyed the outdoors on the verdant North Shore, even in the heat of summer.

Interestingly, my coworkers in the pool company were mostly White, with a few of the seasonal laborers coming from elite private universities. I remember that a few Mexicans filtered in toward the end of the summer—they spoke English well, and didn't seem like immigrants. It might be interesting to note that the owner of the tree-maintenance business and his assistant both had undergraduate degrees from upper echelon universities, both were White. I have particularly strong memories of working-man's delis on Long Island. Fresh, flavorful meats, eggs, cheeses, rolls, and vegetable fixings served up fast in manly portions by macho countermen (and occasionally a macho counter gal). A quart of fresh-brewed iced tea—yumm!! Reminiscing about my blue collar days, I'm wondering about the political shibboleth that says, "Immigrants are here doing jobs that Americans just don't want to do anymore." Maybe a better view would be that Americans and immigrants should work together to makes things happen for everyone.

The summer went well. I held the pool job right up to the start of fall semester. All that hard work limited my extra-curricular activities, so I wound up with savings, which allowed me to study without a part-time job. My contact with Rosemont Camp friends gradually phased out, except for Kathleen, the deaf-education teacher who lived in Prospect Park. Over the course of the year since camp, I had started to visit her on a fairly regular basis, about once every three weeks on average. She had a full life in the city. Three years older than me, she was starting to live a grown up life. She was confident in her classroom skills. That seemed to bring confidence to everything else. She had an occupation as a public-school teacher, and she had already started her master's degree.

The things Kathleen and I did together had an atmosphere of civility. For the most part, my friends from Stony Brook gravitated towards more of a party atmosphere or extreme conduct of other sorts: like partners in crime. We did more drinking about things than thinking about things, in incredible glamorous locales around Manhattan and the North Shore. I'm talking about my close friends. I had casual friendships with wholesome people: for instance, I dabbled in bicycle road racing and got to know the university team. But my close friends were definitely a little twisted.

With Kathleen, I could sit down and have a drink with her at the Gaslight, a corner pub where she knew everyone. It was very much like the ideal of the Irish pub as far as everyone knowing each other and not everyone being so very rich. It was a crowd of grown-ups—no undergraduates. I mixed right in with patrons after a while. We moved around to other pubs in Brooklyn Heights, which were cozy, but I liked the Gaslight, because it was a low key hang out. Sometimes I met Kathleen along with friends from her Manhattan school for Friday happy hour at their favorite bar and grill in Manhattan's Lower West Side: teachers mixing in with the yuppies for some high energy banter on the way home.

We went to Greenwich Village now and then to do a club crawl. Kathleen had a knack for going off the beaten path, and so did I. We had lots of gentle fun. With my Stony Brook friends, we often stuck our nose in where it didn't belong, like First Avenue, the preppy equivalent of a singles club. Denise went where we did belong, like the smaller music-dance clubs on Eighth Avenue. We explored affordable eateries, usually of an ethnic bent, and we always found what we needed. Sometimes her friends joined us.

As I reminisce about Greenwich Village, memories of many nights come flooding back, involving several different cliques that I moved into and through: really pleasant memories of good sociable companionship. But usually, it was we kids, in a little over our heads, living like our parents. Denise, on the other hand, had a modest yet adventurous, full life. Her friends also seemed to have a knack for subtly resisting the status seeking that dominated the Manhattanshpere (which apparently now includes most of the world), even though some were actually elites. The modesty had the greatest impact on me: it raised the possibility of life outside of corporate elitism. There might be a way to live, I started to think, outside of the status seeking that my parents were trying so hard to convince me was the only way that a decent person could ever live.

Grappling with Tradition

To my parents, Brooklyn was a ruin: the remnant of a bygone immigrant era. As with the South Side of Chicago, a place they had ascended out of. The Catholics were now in Huntington. The Jews had cleared out for Dix Hills decades ago. That left Brooklyn with mostly Blacks, Hispanics, and Puerto Ricans, refugee groups better avoided per my parent's South Side sensibilities. The Hasidim defy categorization and are admired for their obstinacy. As for other Whites, they must be socialists or ne'er do wells. Surely they won't amount to anything. I think only a medical emergency of a close relative could get my parents to go to Brooklyn. Of course, their trepidations weren't so severe that they couldn't give Kathleen the benefit of the doubt, especially given her grandmother's ancient Catholic ties to the neighborhood.

Actually, the Brooklyn Heights-Park Slope area was becoming a quiet, uplifted bohemia. The two neighborhoods formed the core of uptown Brooklyn, which was primarily a residential area that encircled the NYC borough's corporate and governmental buildings. The area's aesthetic was characterized by two square miles of row houses, many of them stately and sturdy brownstones, arrayed in tightly-woven rectangular, treed city blocks. Interspersed among the numerous blocks of housing were niches of independent merchants and restauranteurs, providing an ample diversity of restaurants, delis, pubs, cafes, bookstores, and other vital services for the active, young residents. The NYC subway system provided numerous stations and routes into nearby Manhattan, which was only a five-mile commute to most destinations. The East River was to the immediate west and Prospect Park, an urban oasis of winding lanes, wooded groves of tall trees, lakes, and green meadows was to the immediate east, giving the atmosphere a uniquely breezy, verdant quality. A variety of smaller picturesque parks were interspersed throughout the area. The Statue of Liberty could be seen from parks along the East River. Brooklyn Bridge loomed large in the western horizon, reminding everyone of the borough's ancient past. The spirit of the area's Victorian roots could still be faintly felt.

In the wake of White flight and the near-bankruptcy of NYC in the seventies, these diamond-in-the-rough Brooklyn neighborhoods were a bargain hunter's paradise. For the most part, the area's residents were White, younger workers in government services, entry-level corporate positions, and the service industry. In my limited time there, it seemed like an oasis of middle-class bonhomie amid the growing rancor of the Manhattanshpere, where, encouraged by Reaganomics, the investment community propagated all-out warfare on the gentle, indulgent ways of the American workforce. Expanding the vision of the Great Society past just the War on Poverty, now *everyone* would be under scrutiny in the cause of the global investor master race (euphemistically called global competitiveness).

Anxiety about my place in the master race was putting me under attack, and Kathleen apparently noticed it. I wasn't ready to join. Moreover, I had political views that were starting to separate me from more-compliant friends and acquaintances. I started to notice the basically hateful rhetoric flowing through the media, mostly in feature articles, identifying unionized workers as the source of all that was evil in humankind: inflation, drops in GDP, loss of efficiency, crime, divorce, addiction—all their fault. The persecution started with the unions, but pretty much spread to all American workers. Americans were a problem, and investors were going to smote them out in their quest to become the global master race. Americans were a problem that the global investors would be better off without. We Americans better get competitive, measure up, or get lost—investors seemed to be saying. After my three years of studying democracy dharma, I felt pretty darn good about Americans. I felt they were becoming a great people. The incessant criticism and ridicule from investors was an affront to this evolving tradition of civil liberties and social justice. Aren't we going to stand up to the elitists on Wall Street? Who made them God? Are we going to just sit here and take it—in the land of the people, by the people, for the people!

One time when I delivered this soliloquy in a class discussion, a classmate asked me if I hadn't heard the astounding good news of the democratization of investing. With incredible advances in electronic trading, he said, all will be controlled by individual Americans exercising their investment and consumer dollars. No longer will we live on the shaky ground of the U.S. Constitution. Finally, investors will rule over our entire existence in a grand era of manifest destiny. Investors seemed to have appropriated manifest destiny into their quest to be the global master race. With investors in total control, prosperity was sure to follow! It felt like Wall Street wanted to colonize Americans, as if they wanted to finish up where King George (III) had left off.

Investment bankers may feel that their interests make up America's interests—but isn't that just the crux of the problem. Wall Street was an elitist minority putting their interests ahead of all others, I thought. I really wanted to represent the people. I'll confess to being of protectionist, isolationist bent. Americans should not hesitate to use the law to shape our economy in ways that empower our people to work together to meet each person's needs. Of course, friends routinely reminded me that investment bankers controlled or influenced most of the lucrative employment in NYC and metro area. My friends planned to suck up long enough to accumulate some wealth and then speak up. I reminded them that they were selling out pure and simple.

Most people accepted that my defiance was rooted in genuine metaphysical angst stemming from my studies at Stony Brook and the slightly socialist atmosphere there. But in hindsight, I see that it was also about skill and motivation. I hadn't developed any skill or knowledge that would empower me to jump in and hold my own with the hyper-competitive elitists. Corporate life looked like hostile territory and mildly intimidating. I didn't see a place for me in it.

Dad had a different theory, though. Sergeant Advertising reporting for duty!! Every day, dad took up his position on the front line, penetrated enemy territory, asserted his message, made alliances, and captured the deals with the intensity of a soldier charging a bunker on D-Day. A true Marine—on the front, in the line of fire, without hesitation or doubt. Dad would stress that all I needed was to emulate his dogged persistence and utter lack of hesitation and I too could join the ranks of the corporate elite. I didn't need good grades. I didn't even need a degree. I just needed to start selling something for one of America's top corporations and everything would fall into place for me.

Dad's theory was not without precedent. At that point in his career, he had worked almost exclusively for America's leading publishers in advertising sales (he started in an ad agency but jumped to publishing). He was well established at the territory-rep level and was climbing in middle management. At the beginning of his career, he had accomplished two years of introductory business courses at Chicago's DePaul University, and the merit of rising to the rank of sergeant in the U.S. Marines. Dad had been working his way through night school after leaving the Marines when he decided to move forward on the working and drop the school.

David Ogilvy, father of the modern advertising agency, left the world of higher education at England's Oxford without a degree to learn on the job. His career started with a stint as a successful door-to-door salesman. Based on his success in that role, he was recruited to join a London advertising agency. Eventually, Ogilvy worked with connections from there to start his own agency in Manhattan. By working hard to do notable work for his early clients, his agency eventually went on to become a major force in American advertising. Scottish-born Andrew Carnegie, one of the founders of U.S. Steel, had little formal education and no college education, and basic-ally educated himself through reading and attending night school. He started his career with business skills from a trade school (thus Carnegie's philanthropic interest in life-long learning and libraries). And probably the greatest example of all, Benjamin Franklin, author, publisher, printer, inventor, statesman, coauthor of the Declaration of Independence, and delegate to the Constitutional Convention had no formal edu-cation whatsoever.

Dad's theory wasn't off the wall. It just had one fatal flaw. I wasn't him. I was me. Dad has always had a hard time under-standing why I'm not him, although it makes perfect sense to me. I wasn't going to make friends with the corporate elite by joining one of their sales forces, even though mom and dad were strenuous champions of that approach. But I hadn't thought of an alternative. I didn't have a plan for engaging with the workforce. Part of my problem was that my parents had raised me in a kind of corporate sphere, where all activ-ities outside of the corporate set were considered suspect and even preposterous: for instance, government service was con-sidered a greater demerit on one's reputation than a felony. Our family's clothing, vacations, home décor, restaurants, neighborhood, and schools were all carefully chosen for their cachet with the corporate crowd. I was like a child reared in a remote wilderness who couldn't think of any other way to live.

The corporate approach might seem odd for my Irish Catholic parents from Chicago's South Side, who were born, raised, and married in the parishes. Many of my maternal relatives actually worked within the Daley machine. Maternal grandfather was a detective in the Chicago PD, and great-grandfather was a beat cop (from Ireland). Grandpa Bartlett, on the other hand, was a small-business banker in the Catholic neighborhoods: an Anglo Protestant from a rural Minnesota mining family (operators—great grandfather was a mining engineer) who found himself a Catholic wife from free Ireland and converted to Catholicism. Between the two influences, government and business, mom and dad had given their blind faith to business. To them it was a magic conveyance out of the murky waters of ethno-religious politics into the rarified, privileged ether of the corporate comfort zone. Mana! Valhalla! They were quite proud of themselves for climbing out of the South Side (of the racially divided 1960s).

As with many other Irish social climbers of the 1960s, the allegiance to business was accompanied by a move to the suburbs. My parents moved to Buffalo Grove in 1971, in the Lake County side, which is to say the rural part of town actually abutting active family farms. The town was thirty-three miles northwest of downtown Chicago, the location of my dad's office. The Cook County side was basically the western edge of the Chicago metro area, whereas our side of town was the eastern edge of northern Illinois corn country. We could have reasonably identified with Iowa instead of Chicago. Wisconsin's hilly wilderness was only forty minutes north, and I had many wonderful travel, adventure, and recreational experiences in that pristine state. We were connected to Cook County by only a stretch of barely-paved farm road about five miles in length, surround by fields of corn and other vegetables. Our planned community had been skillfully carved into the rolling green hills of former dairy and cattle country. In my family's first years there, you really could imagine buffalo grazing in the open hillsides, which featured green grassy meadows, creeks and ponds, and groves of oak. I actually spent many hours of my childhood exploring among these expansive fields. This is the bucolic haven of the corporate middle-class that I described in the account of my years as a gifted behavior problem at Adlai E. Stevenson High School, which lied in the staunchly conservative 12th District of Republican Congressman Phil Crane.

I too was born in a South Side parish, and went to Catholic school there until age nine, when my parents moved to the suburb Buffalo Grove and enrolled me in public school, which they thought would be temporary. Through a twist of fate, I wound up staying in public school through high school, as I mentioned earlier, but my parents found a way to return my siblings, both younger, to catholic education. It might be interesting to mention that I was church raised: I received religious education through our Buffalo Grove parish (where my siblings attended school), received all the sacraments, and was churchgoing into my early twenties. This is the already described Catholic parish founded in 1852 by the town's leading farming family, which was a mile or two away down an unevenly-paved farm road. Basically, the move to the suburbs didn't interrupt my parents' devoted Catholicism—it enriched it.

As one might guess, my parents were pretty agitated by my growing interest in politics and law while at Stony Brook. To them, church, corporate life, and the halcyon culture of Buffalo Grove were one faith: the Holy Church of the Catholic-Corporate-Suburban Climber. Regarding Jewish and Protestant neighbors, they were regarded as the Holy Church of the Corporate-Suburban Climber. I'm not engaging in hyperbole. At least one half, and maybe even three quarters, of the children in my neighborhood had a father involved in some way with an upper-echelon corporation (Lake County side of the town), usually at the sales, specialist, or middle-management level. The remaining fathers were typically small businessman with a smattering of professionals, mostly young doctors. There were probably less than five lawyers in the entire village of 18,000 residents. There were two officers and one patrol car in the police department, and one firehouse. Essentially, there was no city government, although the park district was a powerhouse. There were almost no career women, especially if you exclude nurses and teachers: my mother was a homemaker. Color and race were not an issue—all corporate climbers were welcome. The demographics were 98% White middle-class; the crime rate was zero.

Toward the end of my time on Long Island, I was starting to contemplate law school. That was heresy to my parents, and they told me so. They held corporate sales in much higher esteem. They equated lawyers with the slippery dealings of the South Side. For them, to have a son in that field would be backsliding. Occasionally, I would consider journalism, as a reporter. That, to them, was the lowest a person could fall (even though dad sold advertising for magazines): publisher, advertising sales manager—anything but reporter.

Bicycling friends at Stony Brook had started to suggest that I might like to teach history and civics on Long Island after graduation. They planned to teach during the school year and then race and tour over the summers. My parents denounced this option vigorously: "We're not like those people," "How will you ever afford the lifestyle you've had with us?" and "How will you get married, or buy a house, or raise a child?" To list a few of the more potent objections.

If I was an anthropologist, I might proffer a theory that Irish Catholics, in response to the euphoria of escaping the murky social and political conditions of the city, transferred their faith in church and country (often intensified by military service) to the corporation with an intensity not justified by a more-objective appraisal of corporate life. Possibly, a more balanced approach may be indicated by reality. In other words, they became paranoid, snobbish, and materialistic.

So, at the end of my Stony Brook years, hanging out in the modesty of Brooklyn Heights middle-class bohemia, I felt at a loss, without a guide. I didn't want to step into the trap set by my parents. On the other hand, I had no escape plan—no real ground for rebellion. At the gut level, my school experience up to that point didn't add up to law school: it was possible, but it would be a push. I started to deal with this percolating insecurity through impulsive acts of random stupidity.

I started to invite myself to Kathleen's place on school nights and times like mid-terms and finals when I used to keep to myself. Drinking outings near school and in the city became less convivial and more about my boorish venting. One night in the fall, with Simone, my closest Stony Brook friend, we went out to a quiet country pub for a gentle outing with two women students, friends of his. I was quite tame during the evening, but when it was time to leave around eleven, I declared that I wanted to stay until closing. But Simone was the group's driver. He and I had a tacit pact of encouraging spontaneity in each other, so he just said, "No problem. See you later." The two ladies wanted to check: "Are you okay? Are sure you don't want to come home? How will you get home?" The pub was about five miles from my decrepit rented farm house. I gave a characteristic answer for those days. "I'm making a practice lately of doing exactly what I feel, whenever I feel it. I feel like staying. Don't worry. I'll find my way home." With that, Simone said "cool," and out the door they went without me.

I stayed until closing at one o'clock, spending most of my time flirting with an inebriated town girl, and then walked the five miles home, in the dead of night, in the cold air of approaching winter. Country roads, in the stillest part of the night, with a numbing chill, are very dramatic. I let my appreciation of the environment energize my legs. I crashed in the all-night study lounge on the way, went to class, and then walked the rest of the distance home. Simone and I were reading Carlos Castaneda: we were exploring spontaneity as a route to deeper levels of consciousness. In other words, we were both growing increasingly depressed and crazed over our similar career problems. By the way, Simone was an Italian Catholic brat from the North Shore (with a Czech streak) —a poetry major. He lived with his family in their spacious two-story American colonial on a two-acre wooded lot in the heavily-wooded, secluded hamlet of Head of Harbor, which was located on the shore immediately across from the Stony Brook campus. Simone's sister went to the same Catholic girls' prep school as mine.

Kathleen did something really interesting that fall, towards winter. It was one of the few times in my life that someone connected to my consciousness almost by extra-sensory perception and did just the thing I needed, even though I never would have done that thing myself, as if a guardian angel had appeared.

A Path to Independence

I remember that it was a visit to Kathleen's apartment in Brooklyn when I probably should have been studying at home in Stony Brook. She handed me a fresh copy of the book *Illusions: Adventures of a Reluctant Messiah* by Richard Bach. I had never heard of the book or its author. It was the first time she had given me a book. Bach is most famous for *Jonathon Livingston Seagull*, a book I later came to love. Doing research for the present book, I came across the fact that Bach and I were both born in Chicago's outer neighborhoods—he in Oak Park (West Side), me in Evergreen Park (South Side). We both graduated from California State University, which is interesting too.

Basically, *Illusions* is a story about intelligence, will power, and potential. A reluctant messiah, the main character, emerges from the life of an ordinary auto mechanic when the community notices he can perform mechanical miracles on a relatively minor scale. His miracles attract attention from the public, and strangers start seeking him out, to ask for guidance on all manner of hang ups. To avoid the supplicants, the messiah goes on the road selling biplane rides. While on the road, he accepts an apprentice pilot, who tells readers the messiah's story. In the course of their time together, the apprentice becomes a student messiah, receiving teachings on the art of making miracles. Thus the reader becomes an apprentice too.

The subtle message in Illusions is that through relaxation and an open mind, we might find latent intelligence that can help us overcome what might seem like insurmountable limitations in the moment. Things that seem like limitations or obstacles might just be *illusions*. A mind of nonjudgmental openness and playful curiosity is the best ground for reaching one's full potential. When you're ready to let almost anything happen, then something finally will happen.

When attempting a miracle, exertion is a higher value than outcome. That's the opposite of America's short-term gratification ethic, which puts a premium on predictability and quick pay offs. Most people experience a lot of pressure to perform NOW, and so fearing the ridicule that might come from creative trial and error, give up before they even start.

Kathleen was definitely cognizant of the rivalry with my parents. She must have sensed that I was up against my limitations. I didn't want to follow in their footsteps. But I didn't have a feel for doing anything else. My intermittent study habits, limited academic skills, shaky financial condition, and passion for extracurricular activities made law school seem like hyperbole. Besides, law school was an outcome. I had not yet figured out that my purpose lied in living by certain core values that existed above whatever particular occupation I might try. I didn't have a sense of commitment or direction. *Illusions* started me on the path of seeing beyond any particular outcome. It lightened my mood. It ignited the mind of nonjudgmental openness and playful curiosity that might become the energy for living on my own two feet. I didn't have a plan. But I started to have hope that there would be a place in the world for me.

During that same time, in my last months on Long Island, another book on limitations and obstacles fell serendipitously into my hands. Shortly after reading *Illusions*, I came to possess a copy of *Shambhala: Sacred Path of the Warrior* by Chogyam Trungpa. When I first began telling Trungpa's students the story of how I encountered his teachings, I related that Kathleen had given me the book at an auspicious moment. But then I started to doubt my memory. Either Kathleen gave it to me directly, or *Illusions* and my conversations with her inspired me to start browsing the New Age section of city bookstores as we strolled our favorite streets. I recall buying it on a leisurely weekend morning in NYC.

Chogyam Trungpa, or more formally, Venerable Chogyam Trungpa Rinpoche, was a highly-trained Tibetan Buddhist monk who in 1959 fled the Communist invasion of Tibet. After studying religion at Oxford as a refugee, Trungpa determined in 1970 that the purpose of his life was to bring Buddhist wisdom to the West. He felt that Buddhism could be a great source of relief in what he saw as a dark age: nuclear proliferation, break-up of the family, racism, domestic violence, urban blight, generational conflict, materialism, moral ambiguity, class conflict, Vietnam, etc. His first major milestone in the West was to ensconce himself as the guru in a Buddhist center in remote Vermont called Tail of the Tiger. A group of lay practitioners had established the center as an outpost of the Kagyu lineage, a Tibetan Buddhist monastic tradition in which Trungpa was a lama. There were no clergy, until Trungpa arrived.

For six years, Trungpa taught Western lay practitioners what came to be his own special brand of Kagyu wisdom. He taught lay practitioners directly, in the way previously only monks had been taught, including the secrets of Buddhist meditation. Trungpa was an innovator in this respect, especially in giving detailed instructions on meditation. A few other Buddhist monks were starting to operate in a similar way in the West, but they weren't as open and democratic as Trungpa. Literally any one with the time (more) and money (less), assuming minimal social skills, could join in. And Trungpa was willing to teach relatively large groups.

After the six years of teaching Western lay practitioners, Trungpa began to notice a self- destructive streak in his mostly young students. Studying the dharma seemed to be an excuse for sloth and torpor, a means for avoiding the challenge of full adult living. Students were becoming expert critics of the West, without accomplishing much to stand for in their own lives. Trungpa decided to change his relationship to his students, and thus emerged Vidyadhara Chogyam Trungpa Rinpoche, which stands for "Warrior of Warriors" in the mythical spiritual kingdom of Shambhala.

The myth, which some with a literal bent may want to call a legend, begins with a Tibetan king, Dawa Sangpo, seeking out the Buddha and requesting teachings on how to practice the path of enlightenment while ruling a typical secular kingdom. Dawa Sangpo did not want to leave his family or his kingdom, which was the typical way for Buddha's devoted disciples, who almost all became mendicant monks. The Buddha granted the request. Thus emerged the Shambhala teachings and tradition, since Dawa Sangpo's kingdom was known as Shambhala. I'm referring to the origin of Shambhala teachings as mythical, but the teachings and tradition have been influencing Tibetan society for many centuries: they are quite literal. Up until Trungpa, monasteries and monks were the progenitors of Shambhala teachings. Trungpa brought them to the mainstream by founding the Shambhala community, which started by converting Tail of the Tiger in Vermont, and then blossomed into an international network of Shambhala teaching-and-meditation centers. They currently have about 200 centers and 10,000 members worldwide.

In addressing the West, Trungpa didn't limit himself to a narrow transmission of the traditional Shambhala teachings. He incorporated his knowledge of Tibetan Buddhist monastic lineages, Tibetan culture, Zen, Anglo culture, and other influences from his days as a religious scholar at Oxford. He integrated all those influences into one Shambhala dharma, which he taught as the foundational teachings of the nascent Shambhala community. He felt that he had developed a path of enlightened living for Western secular practitioners in ordinary life. Trungpa felt that this new Shambhala path would bring relief to Westerners in this dark age, which was still his ambition, and would address the spiritual hindrances he had seen arise in his Kagyu lay students.

The practice of spiritual warriorship forms the core of Shambhala. Warriors, for the most part, are mothers and fathers, or more generally, people of family. Everyone is from a clan, thus our spiritual life grows from good relationships with parents, siblings, spouses, children, and so on. In addition, warriors acknowledge the need for good society, thus Shambhala teachings guide the warrior in harmonious, effective relationships with coworkers, especially, and all those one depends on and serves generally. For monks, the Buddha's first commandment is to withdraw from society and meditate. Shambhala warriors, on the other hand, celebrate their place in social life and aspire to lead the world to enlightened society.

Shambhala teachings essentially instruct warriors on how to order one's own life and how to relate to others. Enemies are snobbery, sloth, and materialism because of their tendency to elicit aggression, inaction, and anxiety. Victory is hard-working, harmonious families and work places. It's not enough to merely point out the perils of snobbery and materialism. The teachings provide a pathway to the alternative— the warrior transforms into an uplifted, confident leader who celebrates life and brings relief from suffering to friends, family, and firm.

I'm sounding a bit analytical and militaristic. Actually, Shambhala training is a personal journey that unfolds amid the warm, supportive companionship of community members. And the ground of the path is the practice of noticing the potential for basic goodness in every situation: as one learns to appreciate the goodness of their ordinary life, one can experience relief from the destructive emotions and wasted motion that come from always striving for bigger and better.

At the time of this writing, I am considered an advanced

student of the Shambhala dharma. I've done many retreats and training programs, and much Buddhist meditation with the community. I studied what has come to be known as Shambhala Buddhism. In the forty years since Trungpa's launching of Shambhala, the community came to embrace a fluid interaction of Buddhist (Kagyu-Nyingma) and Shambhala teachings, yet always with the focus on warriors in ordinary Western secular life. The most intense point in my studies coincided with the zenith of this interaction between Buddhism and Shambhala: I surged forward when the two were explicitly combined in a hierarchical course of study. I even took the bodhisattva vow, administered in a ceremony conducted by one of the community's preceptors (i.e. lay master).

I'm one of a minority of Shambhala students who studied the two influences in a linear, curricular fashion. In the thirty years since Trungpa sparked my interest in Buddhism and warriorship, my faith in the Buddha and Buddha dharma has matured to the point where I should possibly be known as a Buddhist warrior, except that such a thing does not exist. Despite the growing precision of my Buddhist knowledge, I'm not going to abandon my warrior's ways for the monk's robes. Even in Buddhism, I seem to be a gifted behavior problem.

On my own two feet, I will continue to deepen my Buddhist meditation and knowledge, but my focus will remain on the possibility of spiritual warriorship in ordinary American life, which subtly indicates the possibility of enlightenment outside of the monastery. As a warrior, my primary aspiration is to guide my fellow Americans in developing hard-working, harmonious families and workplaces, but I'm also exploring the possibility of enlightenment. I'm not solely a devotee of Chogyam Trungpa and Shambhala. Trungpa's teachings on spiritual warriorship and Buddhism have penetrated and improved every aspect of my life, but I have also received great benefits from teachings of other Buddhist masters, including the Fourteenth Dalai Lama, Lama Surya Das, Shunryu Suzuki

Roshi, and Master Thich Nhat Hahn. I'm also familiar with ancient classic texts such as Shantideva's *Way of the Bodhisattva*, the *Dhammapada*, and the Pali Cannon. In a two-year hiatus from my studies with the Shambhala community, I studied Soto Zen in depth, including formal intensive training in meditation, forms, and traditional meditation retreats.

But, back in early winter of 1984, freezing in my decrepit farmhouse rented room near Stony Brook, I discovered a kindred spirit when I read *Shambhala: Sacred Path of the Warrior*. Trungpa was so independent in his frank discussion about anxiety that arises in materialistic environments, about longing for renunciation, and about feeling stuck when one should be moving forward. He talked about findings one's spot in the world, starting where one is at now, letting go, and moving forward. But in Trungpa's vision of rebellion, one didn't move forward into Marxist revolt, or underground hipsterism, or even artistic reverie, rather one opened up to the goodness of society largely as it is. In a parallel with *Illusions*, Trungpa pointed the way to an open, relaxed mind that could move forward creatively into the organic, good aspects of society while still rejecting the temptations of materialism and aggression. The warrior's weapons against temptation were generosity, patience, exertion, meditation, loving-kindness, modesty, and an organic sense of priorities.

Trungpa openly rejected the harmful materialism and snobbery that I felt were blossoming on Wall Street and intimidating me generally. Yet he did it without harsh words, without requiring me to withdraw from family or country, without the idea of vengeance or retribution, and in a way that led me to appreciate normal society. It didn't happen all at once, but a switch had been thrown: self-destructive rebellion off, nourishing, self-actualization on. I sensed a solution, and not the final solution Wall Street had in mind. I was definitely stuck and longing to renounce snobbery and ready to renounce my own harmful habit of drinking about things when I should be thinking about them. I could be a together blue-collar worker now, I thought, without waiting for some magical pot of gold like a degree. I could work with what I had in the present moment: pretty good mechanical aptitude and a strong, flexible body. I could move forward into a healthy, work-oriented life, with an open mind, and let life teach me whatever lessons I needed to learn. No more living like an impecunious student bum. So, after a couple of visits to my parent's two-story basically mansion (i.e. Monterey Colonial) on a country club in the ranch lands of California's Mt. Diablo foothills, I decided to move out there immediately and start my life as a noble blue-collar man with a passion for life-long learning.

Point of Departure

In December 1984, a few weeks after returning to Stony Brook after a Thanksgiving visit to my parent's new place in the San Francisco Bay Area, I began plotting my departure. No more impecunious student bum. Go west young man! It was a rainy year in the Bay Area, meaning the hills, mountains, and redwoods were lush green as early as November. Typically, the landscape is a dusty, parched brown at that point, but I had to learn that the hard way. That year, the hills and ridges of Mt. Diablo were verdant and vibrant, and I was impressed by the contrast with Long Island, which was in an early winter cold snap—dark, bare tree branches, grimy winter mud accumulating, and cold, driving rain. Between gentle morning showers, Mt. Diablo was a breezy fifty to sixty degrees with a bright California sun. Of course, Long Island's North Shore would blossom in spring with incredible grandeur, but I had to regret that the hard way.

The vibrant environment enhanced the family's celebration of prosperity. Dad had moved across the country to pursue a transfer upward to regional vice president of sales for the national publishing and media empire where he worked on Long Island. He would support the sales force for a small group of trade magazines addressing the office automation field, which were experiencing interesting interactions with the high tech side of infotech. Thus a branch office was maintained in Santa Clara, which was evolving into the capital of high tech.

His daily one-way commute was forty-five miles south and west over lightly-trafficked highways. The longer commute was no big deal since Santa Clara and Mt. Diablo were both in the middle of nowhere in 1984. Commuters in the Mt. Diablo area were typically oriented toward San Francisco, which was thirty miles due west, but dad was in the vanguard of the new southward view elicited by the tech boom. He bought a nearly-new Cadillac Fleetwood to handle the commuting and secured a new Chevrolet mid-size station wagon for mom's domestic transportation needs. Dad's affinity for General Motors stemmed from his involvement with Delco Electronics Corporation and other aspects of the Midwestern automotive industry back when they were the capital of innovation in electronics and he was an advertising sales rep for a magazine on electronics. This might be an interesting spot to interject that Robert Noyce, lead inventor and "father" of the type of electronic circuit that led to the popularity of the PC (i.e. personal computer), was born and raised in Grinnell, Iowa, and earned his B.A. in physics and mathematics at Grinnell College there. He was one of the founders of Intel Corporation (i.e. the heart of the PC revolution), which was a prime mover in Santa Clara's growing fame.

I had gradually stopped going to class after Thanksgiving, until I just roamed the NYC metro area when I should have taken finals. I basically pulled up lame a few weeks early, like a sprinter with a pulled hamstring. I was reading Bach's *Illusions* and Trungpa's *Sacred Path*. I gave myself over to reading *Sacred Path* for a few days, skipping all my classes. After three years of juggling jobs and school, getting in over my head academically, partying hard, travelling widely, and growing increasingly apprehensive about finding a place in the global investor master race, it felt ecstatically good to just let go, to fall apart. A few days of falling apart and I was hooked. There was no turning back.

When Christmas came, my parents sent me a ticket to spend winter break at their place. I packed a couple of oversized army-surplus duffels with clothing, making secret plans to leave Long Island for good. I left all my other belongings behind. After a week or so at my parent's place pretending I was still a student, I started soft selling my plan to become a noble blue collar worker. The whole family was there: my sister was still in a local Catholic girls' high school and my brother was in from St. Bonaventure University (of upstate New York). Nobody panicked or got upset by the news. But a plan was hatched for me to return to Stony Brook after break to salvage as many courses as possible. Should I change my mind someday, it would be nice have those credits to fall back on.

Christmas break was nice in the mansion. The pool area was especially entertaining. We felt like we were on a tropical vacation, even though the Bay Area was technically in winter. I used my pool construction skills to clean and heat the large oval gunite pool. It was in mild disrepair, but somehow I got it up and running. I renovated it over the next few years. Most memorable, we discovered our family in-ground Jacuzzi at the back of the lot. It abutted the length of the pool, but actually had its own filtration and heating, so we could heat it separately. It was roughly equivalent to a luxury hotel Jacuzzi: ten feet long, five feet wide, four and half feet deep, with a wide bench all around. It was simple but spacious and deep, and it could hold everyone, like a Japanese bath.

Behind the Jacuzzi, along the fence line, was a stream and creek bed rich with oaks, and behind that a horse ranch. Sometimes the horses would intrude on our reverie, or maybe join it. From there it was all ranch land up to the Mt. Diablo State Park. The view from the back yard was open space as far as the eye could see. Our half-acre lot was toward the crest of a mild hill, so we had a panoramic vista. There was a hedge and high redwood fence around the yard's perimeter for seclusion. Most nights in the Diablo area are cold, crisp, and clear. It was truly relaxing to sit under the stars and gaze out over the rolling peaks and oak-lined ridges in the dark, starry night—with no white noise in the rural area. We started a family ritual that Christmas. At least once a month, we would heat the Jacuzzi and finish up a Sunday dinner or holiday celebration with a long, family soak. The warmth of the water brought out the warmth of the people, aided by a modest snifter of Grand Marnier or Bailys Irish Cream. Over the six years that my parents lived there, we had many delightful conversations in our Japanese bath. It may sound bourgeois, but our soaking ritual made us better people.

After a nice few weeks with the family, I packed some clothes and headed back to Long Island. We hadn't done anything too exotic. We mostly stuck to hanging out in the house and going out around the Mt. Diablo area. After growing up in or near Chicago and Manhattan, San Francisco seemed a little dingy, like some kind of failed experiment, like an artifact of the gold rush or shipbuilding era. Mountains and ranches seemed more archetypal at that point.

When I returned to Stony Brook, I rushed around contacting my professors, begging for mercy. They all found a way to accommodate me with some kind of extension. But that didn't really solve much, since I then had to pass five final exams and write a couple of papers. I stayed for about a month and salvaged half of my six courses, which means that I flunked the other half. I earned high grades in the courses that I passed, so I was still in good standing. I could go back someday if the inspiration ever came. The flunked courses were all classics topics that I didn't need, that I took out of curiosity: time management was definitely an "area of need" as we say in special ed. I took comfort in my good standing, but mostly I was determined to drop out.

On this departure, I vacated my decrepit rented farm house. I sold most of my belongings and shipped the rest to my parent's place in California. Now I was really done. Student bum out. Hard-working, thrifty blue-collar man in. Except my parents had apparently hatched a different plan while I was away. They hired a consultant who helped families locate the right college for their child. She was like a professional guidance counselor. She even had software that printed a report of recommendations. She recommended California State University, Hayward—Cal State for short. Cal State had a welcoming attitude toward returning students, which means students who dropped out in their youth but wanted to return some number of years later. The average student age was twenty-seven. I had only dropped out a month earlier, but I was already twenty-two-and-a-half-years old, and thus clearly out of alignment with the corporate set's expectations for youthful ambition. Students were typically mature and careerist, and many even worked at occupations. I could live at home and commute, at least at first, since Cal State was twenty miles west by means of a winding road through ranches. It overlooked San Francisco Bay from a high ridge. I guess the consultant felt that it would be a good place for a late bloomer like me to give the situation another try.

But I was pressing on with my blue-collar ambitions. I started by looking in the employment classifieds of the Contra Costa Times and San Francisco Chronicle. A position as a garbage truck attendant caught my eye. I recall that the company was Waste Management. In Chicago, garbage collection was part of the city works and thus a relatively high-status occupation: they were a real presence in my childhood neighborhood. I figured a position as a garbage truck attendant was a pretty dramatic affront to materialism and snobbery. I interviewed over the phone, and they invited me in to give it a try.

But I didn't follow through. At that point, my parents offered to pay the out-of-state tuition for me to start at Cal State immediately. They pleaded. I guess they panicked when they realized I really meant to follow the blue collar path. I submitted my transfer application in February and enrolled as a full-time student for Spring Quarter, 1985, which started in March. My parents were getting pretty diabolical at that point in their attempt to redirect me toward the corporate sphere. My first step en route to blue-collar glory was going to be a solid, Japanese compact car. They seemed to be the model of thrift. I was thinking about Honda, Datsun, or Toyota—especially Honda. No more amateur efforts at vintage car restoration. I wanted serious thrift and stability. Dad offered to co-sign, so we went out shopping on a sunny winter morning. We headed for a Honda dealership over near Cal State. On the way to the dealership, driving on a country road in Alamo, Dad eyed a vintage 1972 MGB roadster in pretty good shape. It was in a front yard with a "for sale" sign on it. He stopped for a look. I tensed up. He said, "Come on. Let's just take a look. You don't see chariots like this anymore." I begrudgingly cooperated: "Okay. Nice. Let's get to the Honda dealership." "Let's give it a test drive," Dad said, testing me. "What can it hurt?" he said, "They don't make'em like this anymore." So, we talked to the owner a bit, and he let us take it on a test drive. You just don't jump in a well-tuned roadster, top down on a sunny Diablo winter morning, crank it up leaving the on-ramp, and emerge unscathed. That is like giving an alcoholic a drink to celebrate his sobriety. And this junky fell for it hook, line, and sinker.

I was trying to reform from my days of struggling with the renovation of a 1968 Alfa Romeo Spider in high school and on Long Island. I had relied on my Alfa Romeo, a hand-me-down AMC Hornet Wagon (from mom), and a recently-acquired 1971 BMW 2002 for transportation on Long Island—all precariously approaching the end of their useful life—and I wanted to upgrade to a reliable, up-to-date car.

Dad signed me up for a loan at the neighborhood branch office of his bank and we delivered the check to the MGB owner a few days later. I knew dad was thinking of his friend Arthur from the publishing field. With me within earshot, Dad routinely mentioned his nice friend Arthur in the ad game who lived in downtown Manhattan and possessed a really cool Morgan roadster. Arthur was nice to dad: he even let us stay in his West Hampton beach house a couple of times. But still, I'm not him. I made good use of my MGB in the five years that I owned it, but not in the ways my father had hoped.

In that chariot of youthful joy and splendor, I practically travelled over every inch of Northern California (two times over): Pacific Coast Highway up through Oregon and down to Newport Beach, Sierra Range, Yosemite Valley, Cascade Range, Santa Cruz, Monterey, Diablo Range, Gold Country, Central Valley, Folsom Lake, Lake Tahoe, San Joaquin Valley, and the list could go on much too long. By the way, I also commuted to Cal State. And I developed problem-solving skills in many repair and renovation projects, since I couldn't afford to hire a mechanic for more than a tune up. My brother picked up a vintage 1969 Alpha Romeo Spider at the same time. More than a few times, we turned my father's garage into an auto repair shop with both cars on jack stands. We probably should have put a shingle out and started to take ourselves seriously. We might have been wealthy small businessman instead of corporate wage slaves.

Founded in 1957, Cal State, with 12,000 students and covering 342 acres, was very similar to SUNY Stony Brook in its modern architecture and park-like grounds, except that it was on a less grand scale. It sat on a modest rectangle of land etched into the high ridgeline of an affluent suburb (i.e. Fairview) overlooking San Francisco Bay. At that point in its history, the main architectural elements were squares, rectangles, concrete, brick, glass, and parallel lines in multi-story buildings of five floors or less.

The campus's eighteen buildings were distributed evenly through the block-long grounds, with well-tended lawns, planters, gardens, and trees tastefully located along walkways and outdoor seating. The interiors were clean and orderly. Nearly all students were commuters, and two large parking lots abutted the campus, one in the rear and one on the side, at an easy walking distance from all buildings. A few modest dorms were situated at one edge of the grounds, just across the street from the campus. The environment was calm and calming, and, for me, sometimes maddeningly sedate and settled. The tuition was roughly the same as SUNY at $1,200 a year. The ethnicity demographics were diverse for the Bay Area in the eighties at approximately 60% White, 10% Asian, 10% Hispanic, 5% Black, 5% Indian, 5% Filipino, and 5% Other Asian.

I had my Italian road racing bike shipped to California. I was moderately competent as a bicycle mechanic too. The Diablo area offered many lightly-trafficked and wide-open spaces for riding. Later, I would commute by bike when my MGB broke down (I got into pretty good shape). With a sound car, and a couple of month's rest and bike riding, I headed off to Cal State for my first day as a commuter student there. I was going to study business administration with a specialty in accounting.

CHAPTER THREE

Learning to Listen

Embracing the Enemy

So far, I've been engaging in some pretty vigorous complaining about the corporate set and the global investor master race that emerged with Reaganomics. One might wonder why someone with views like mine would study business administration, the very thing that I said was intimidating me. I was pretty determined to drop out when I left Stony Brook. I felt that I had a good plan. I was making a spiritual decision. But my family had eroded my confidence, and even I was a little unsettled by the outrageous prospect of working on a garbage truck. I reflected on my motivation. My core intention in dropping out was to become a work-oriented, together person: someone with a home, solid car, pocket money, healthcare, maybe even a fiancée or wife. Of course, my corporate parents couldn't see blue-collar work leading to those things, at least not with the global investor master race out to destroy the American working class.

I honed in on the work-oriented aspect of my spiritual decision. Cal State actually had a real reputation for turning out employable business students. My parents had picked that up through the grapevine. Maybe I could meet them in the middle. Instead of going straight into business as a blue collar man, I could first get trained in management at the Cal State business school. That meant that the home, pocket money, and fiancée would have to wait, and I was really looking forward to those, but the best things in life often involve a little waiting. I figured studying business was almost as work-oriented and together as working in one. Impecunious, semi-Marxist, semi-academic student ne'er do well cavorting and venting around NYC out! Hard-working, serious student business worker in!

By studying business, I wasn't going into foreign territory. My business education had an interesting foundation. On Long Island, Dad had a routine of bringing the *Wall Street Journal*, *New York Times*, *Fortune*, and *Forbes* home from the office in timely intervals. These publications were almost always arrayed on the coffee table of the family room. I actually read them quite often. It was like peering into a secret world. Despite my reservations about the master race, business still had a positive quality to it. At their core, businesses delivered products and services that people needed, whereas academia seemed to stand back and point out people's flaws, a process which sometimes left one feeling ineffectual and alienated. I was intrigued by the positive quality of meeting people's needs. Maybe I could connect to it.

Trungpa's vision of spiritual warriorship was also on my mind. He advised the warrior to be wary of the habitual tendency to like or dislike when neutrality may be the more appropriate view. The warrior can learn what needs to be learned, can listen when it's time to listen, by refraining from the intense emotions of rejecting and accepting. This tendency to like or dislike what in fact is a neutral situation often impedes our ability to meet our needs and keeps one mired in unnecessary conflict. Businesses meet people's needs: that is essentially a neutral situation, even one with obvious goodness. I would test my nascent warriorship by learning what needed to be learned, and by listening to what needed to be heard, without accepting or rejecting.

One of Trungpa's most famous axioms was his warning to avoid the traps of hope and fear. Westerners' habitual preoccupation with quick, successful outcomes, meaning intense feelings of hope, leads to a fear of failure so intense that one tends to give up before even trying. Moreover, anxiety over a quick outcome often cuts off creative thinking needed for eventual success. Regarding my business studies, I was experiencing a bit of math anxiety (i.e. fear). Maybe skipping calculus in high school would come back to haunt me. My choice of poli-sci at Stony Brook was partially motivated by a desire to avoid heavy math. But Trungpa and Bach had opened my mind to an adventurous spirit. If I encountered an obstacle, I could dig deeper, including catching up on my own. The first step will teach you the next, which shows you the next, and so on, even if you eventually decide to change direction. It rarely hurts to take the first step, and sometimes something wonderful happens.

The warrior develops an organic sense of priorities. Trungpa introduced the Tibetan tradition of lu, nyen, and lha to explain this process. Basically, every aspect of life has a quality of foundation or ground (lu), middle or path (nyen), and summit or fruition (lha). These qualities arise whether one is making a sandwich or designing a space shuttle. Learning how to notice these qualities helps the warrior put first things first. For instance, it's better to do one's homework on the day assigned rather than cram all of it a few days before the final exam. Doing homework every day has a foundational lu quality to it, so it should not be delayed for the sake of a party. Hold the party after the final exam, as a form of fruitional lha. Taking the tests throughout the semester is the nyen. Inspired by lu, nyen, and lha, I have actually learned to solve problems in a step-by-step, hierarchical fashion, and my life has definitely benefitted greatly.

I've also come to use lu, nyen, and lha as a system of diagnosis. I was basically a working student. My shifts often severely interfered with daily homework, thus lu was not properly accomplished. Without daily study, test performance suffered, interfering with nyen. Gaps in test performance made final exams difficult, sometimes even to the extent of failure, interfering with fruition, so sometimes there wasn't much to celebrate at the end of the semester. Even worse, when gaps in nyen (test performance) arose, I would get mad and just party every weekend, consequences be damned. The lesson here is that we Americans have a tendency to cram too many activities into our lu, in our habitual workaholic way, and consequently experience a lot of failure. The warrior must learn how to resist competing priorities, to slow down and focus on one thing at a time—put first things first—to experience true accomplishment.

Armed with new wisdom from Trungpa and Bach, I was looking forward to a new and improved experience at Cal State. I chose accounting for my specialty. First, it was the polar opposite of advertising sales and thus had the quality of being *not dad*: counting beans had a concrete solidity to it—almost as good as being a blue collar man. Second, a matrilineal uncle had risen from big accounting firm auditor to assistant CFO in a major manufacturing corporation, so I knew at least one accountant. Finally, accounting offered a detailed view of the results that I had read so much about in the business press. I'll confess to the *not dad* aspect being the most compelling factor.

Keen observers might notice a change in direction from my days of harassing conformist friends in NYC about their intention to sell out. In fact, I had changed direction. A warrior does not so easily caste dispersions on the plans of their basically hard working, decent friends. One avoids alienating allies with casual judgments of accepting and rejecting in situations that are basically neutral, and instead focuses on basic goodness. Of course, some judgments must be held: for instance, I still had reservations about the demonic intentions of the global investor master race.

At that point, I envisioned myself as a future business rebel. I really had no idea what I was doing, but somehow I would be a businessman who wasn't a snob, who wasn't materialistic, who wasn't a workaholic, and who balanced the needs of customers, workers, and country—and I guess investors had to fit in their somehow too. Such was my state of mind as I began my first quarter at Cal State as a business major in March 1985.

Transference

Accountants may be thinking I was headed for trouble at Cal State. Someone should have told him, they might think, that bookkeeping (i.e. bean counting) is only a fraction of what the corporate accountant does. Deposits must be made, checking accounts must be reconciled, bills must be paid, and payroll must be run, but that is merely the nitty gritty of the bookkeeper. Cal State's mission was to train corporate auditors: the accountants who certify that companies traded on NYSE or NASDAQ follow the rules of winning and losing. Accountants can work as bookkeepers, but the prestige and riches are for those who produce and audit financial statements for major corporations like the Fortune 500. Cal State was successful in training accountants for those environments in significant numbers. Accounting professors warned that only aspiring corporate auditors should study at Cal State: generalists looking for a broad business background would be driven out by the demanding curriculum.

I heard the professor's warning, but I didn't flinch. It turns out that my minimal math background and years of legal studies at Stony Brook were good preparation for accounting. An accountant relies on math skills learned in the ninth grade and maybe basic college algebra. The real demands are in memorizing and applying the extensive rules of success and failure: in other words, applying laws, regulations, and industry guidelines. Investors, lenders, and tax authorities need a consistent, regulated means of understanding a company's progress and comparing it to competitors. Progress is reported in the income statement, and net worth is reported in the balance sheet. Accountants ensure that those reports follow the applicable guidelines for a company's industry.

Accounting can get quite biblical. It's all about resisting

temptation. Occasionally, strong emotions in the moment override the more sanguine judgement of long-term stability. "We need to report that forty million dollar contract with the power utility this quarter," says the CEO of a software development firm to his CFO. "The customer signed the lease agreement yesterday, but the quarter ends today," say the CFO, in a nonchalant tone. "You mean to tell me that you're gonna make me wait sixty days for that lease check to land in our bank," roars the CEO. "Yep." "You know I'm gonna fall short of my projections to Wall Street without that contract," roars the CEO even louder. "Yep," even more nonchalant. "Do you even care about me or this company?"says the CEO reaching a crescendo. "Yep." "Then why in God's name won't you let me report that sale now, when you know it's a done deal?" "Because it ain't done until that lease is fully processed and the cash is transferred to our bank," says the CFO reminding the CEO of industry guidelines and company policy. "Moreover, you and I both know that the sales person promised a few things that aren't exactly deliverable at this particular moment in time." The utility company's executives, upon discovering this futureware, might renege on the contract over the next thirty days, causing the CFO to amend the quarterly income statement to reflect the over-reporting of forty million in sales, triggering Wall Street to cry foul, and possibly eliciting criminal prosecution for securities fraud. Thus the intersection of law and accounting. The wise man, said the Buddha, sees the security of restraint where others see the gain that might come from deceit. Wait until that deal is good and done before showing it on the income statement.

Every question is loaded in accounting. What is a sale? What is an expense? What is an asset? What is a liability? One could spend a lifetime on each of those questions. The modern philosophers are in the accounting department. Stony Brook prepared me well. I earned high grades at Cal State in accounting—As and Bs. I advanced through the professional-level courses for the income statement and balance sheet. I veered off of accounting when it was time to study auditing and special topics such as pensions—the last few professional courses of the specialty. Accounting brought business to life for me. Accounting might seem like it's full of cold numbers. But it's actually full of drama: decisions, theories, relationships, hierarchy, theft, deceit, fraud, ambition, temptation, restraint, success, honesty, and integrity. When one studies accounting, one studies life.

Accounting relied on basic math operations. But other parts of the business major activated my math anxiety. Cal State's business school was following the quantitative approach to decision-making: they offered only a bachelor of science. "Quantitative" basically means looking at problems through the lens of rigorous statistical and mathematical analysis, including some calculus. Amazingly, I completed the business math curriculum, which included serious amounts of linear algebra and trigonometry, and a modest amount of calculus. These areas of math were also integrated into advanced courses that I took, such as marketing management and micro economics. The core math courses looked at a variety of applications, including quality assurance, materials planning, sales projections, profit, finance, public works, and direct marketing.

Although the quantitative approach kept me on edge, it brought me valuable critical thinking skills, which I treasure and now use almost instinctively. Basically, the quantitative approach involves looking at every process as a result of its component factors, with a very rigorous examination of those factors. Typically, at least in the academic setting, these factors can be expressed in a mathematical function or some other kind of equation or theorem: often the function or equation produces some kind of line or curve on a graph.

My favorite functions involve diminishing returns. Sometimes increasing a company's sales can create the need for greater investment which can lead to losses unless sales go even higher: so the function for diminishing returns creates a graph that shows the point at which increasing sales will trigger losses. Empowered with this information, executives can plan for increased investment at the point of diminishing returns to keep growth flowing smoothly. Bigger and better is not as always as easy as it sounds in the land of unlimited opportunity.

Now thirty years later, my memories of actual equations and functions are pretty dim, but I translated the discipline of quantitative reasoning into some fairly powerful skills in using tables and basic graphing for planning—I'm pretty sharp with a spreadsheet. Whereas a professor of economics might produce a single elegant curve on a graph, I might use the relationship of two lines on a graph, backed up by two spreadsheets, one for each line. For instance, a city proposes to fund the renovation of a city block. It wants to justify the expense by the increased revenue that will come from revitalized merchant tenants. One spreadsheet could plot the costs of renovation over time. The other spreadsheet could plot the projected tax revenue over time. The final graph will have two lines showing the progress of costs and revenues over a set time period, providing visual support for calculating the exact date at which revenues will have exceeded costs and the renovation will become a net gain to the taxpayers: a red vertical line could be drawn at the break-even point where net gain begins. For the graph to be helpful, assumptions about the factors involved in costs and revenues must be thoroughly examined. They must be honest. The graph could also be used as a management device to compare actual to projected costs and revenues. Break-even points in a variety of contexts were a major area of study.

So, in addition to the accounting curriculum, I developed a theme of quantitative reasoning in my course selections, most evident in marketing management and micro economics. Those courses emphasized careful budgeting and planning, and truly digging into the factors of whatever projection one was making, whether in the effect a sales discount or advertising campaign would have on the bottom line or estimating the true costs of a public works project. I didn't become an advanced mathematician, but I did develop a kind of intuitive calculus that quickly comprehends the factors of a decision. I'm sufficiently cautious around red flags such as "Savings will pay for the investment," "Increased revenue will pay for the investment," "Increased volume will pay for the discount," "The good will is worth the cost," and other shibboleths of self-deception and imminent bankruptcy.

I matured during my business major years. Time-management skills advanced from "future skill" to "emerging skill." I integrated to-do entries into my lecture notes for every course. Every day, I carefully listed the preparation needed for the next class period, and made running ticklers for writing projects and tests. I carefully reviewed each course's syllabus to anticipate peak loads. I developed the daily homework habit and studied for tests incrementally, without cramming. I followed the hierarchy of major and degree requirements precisely. In six full-time quarters of studying business, from spring 1985 through fall 1986, I completed twenty-one courses with a g.p.a. of 3.15, including significant upper-division progress. Disturbingly, I still hadn't fully embraced streamlining: I dropped a couple of math courses taken merely for depth, pulling my grades down sharply. But I was markedly more focused than at Stony Brook, where my final g.p.a. dropped to 2.27. And I held a part-time job as a store clerk in a retail catalog outlet store for general merchandise.

In Buddhism, the paramount virtue is honesty, expressed as the directive to avoid all forms of deception. The quantitative approach showed me a path for making decisions in a thorough and honest light. Forevermore, I would be sure to consider carefully all factors before making a projection or embarking on a project. Quantitative analysis can be a powerful tool in avoiding self-deception and detecting corruption. The business curriculum's tone of careful and thorough planning echoes into my teaching practice today. California's professional standards for evaluating teachers include the requirement of "planning and organizing subject matter content for a variety of learners." I have received high marks on this criterion in every evaluation, across a variety of evaluators and educational settings.

Even accounting has some transference value. In compliance with the guidelines of No Child Left Behind, every California school publishes an annual *school accountability report,* with vital statistics on student achievement. The report's contents are shaped by laws and guidelines. Most important details are disclosed, but some are withheld, such as how many special-ed students opted out of a diploma. Every spring, school accountability tests are administered to students to determine the quality of the school's teachers—there are some interesting assumptions behind that method of auditing. These tests are based on state subject-matter standards and each teacher is audited on the basis of state professional standards. The Western Association of Schools and Colleges and the California Department of Education conduct periodic audits of the school plan and educational setting of each school. So, like business, education is a workplace controlled by laws, industry standards, governing agencies, and audits.

A drastic reduction in opportunities for extracurricular activities was the prime mover in my improved academic performance. New to the Bay Area, with all my friends still in the NYC area, my studies were the best entertainment available. Cal State's commuter culture, combined with the mature returning-student population, provided a slightly stoic experience, which was just what I needed to finally develop some study habits. Kathleen came out to California for a visit after my first quarter. We put some serious summer miles on the MGB, covering San Francisco, Berkeley, Tahoe, northern Sierra Nevada range, and parts of Yosemite. We were on the road for about five days, plus we spent a few days at my parent's place. We were both on summer break, and the trip was a healthy vacation. My part-time retail job didn't pay much, but I kept it firmly in the background, which meant it only occasionally impeded my study schedule. As I started to make friends, I found the will to put them on hold until studying was done.

My year and a half in business courses was a solid experience. After such a favorable outcome, you might wonder how I arrived at the psychology degree mentioned at the beginning of this story—what twist or turn must be coming up. Remember my question from high school, that itch I seemed born to scratch: my curiosity about the paranoid, aggressive manhood that Nixon seemed an archetype of. Could there be an alternative? In a completely unexpected and almost inexplicable turn of events, my question interacted with Cal State's vision of a well-rounded business person to send me suddenly off in a new direction.

Recidivist Curiosity

Cal State's business major included the incredibly romantic concept of the business person as a renaissance man. In that vein, I fulfilled my communications requirement with speech writing. The small class size, about twenty-five students, meant each student could give four speeches over the quarter. The course text and lectures instructed students on appreciating and writing speeches. Tests were actual speeches given to the class. I really enjoyed the course. My final speech was on the probability of the Soviet Union collapsing, with its deteriorating industrial infrastructure as the prime mover. Speech writing went well. Then I moved on to mandatory psychology 101, and thus began the unraveling of my newfound dispassionate work ethic.

The psychology department at Cal State was part of the college of science. Like the business school, it emphasized a quantitative approach. In psychology, which is principally the study of human behavior problems, a quantitative approach indicates the relatively strict adherence to the scientific method, including precise experimental controls and statistical rigor. Double-blind drug trials are a popular example of these experimental controls. Essentially, scientific psychologists use statistical methods to identify the true cause of whatever is being observed. For example, one might hypothesize that promotions are based on gender at one's workplace: typically one might claim that men unfairly receive more promotions per capita than women. But closer analysis might reveal that hours of overtime are the strongest correlation to promotions, regardless of gender, thus availability for unpaid overtime is the real culprit. In another example, the global investor master race might claim that teachers are the greatest factor in student achievement. More on that later.

At that point, as a budding business major, psychology 101 had only given me the barest glimpse of using scientific methods to identify the true causes of problematic human conduct. But almost reflexively my questions about paranoia and aggression and their role in American manhood were triggered. What caused these powerful tendencies? Could they be eliminated through training? Should they be eliminated? Maybe they should be exalted? The prospect of a rigorous method for exploring these questions was intoxicating. I was hooked almost instantly. Within one quarter of taking psychology 101, I changed my major to psychology and collected my business courses into an official minor in business administration, which in my case was just a few courses short of a double major.

Now, I thought, I might discover a method for being *not dad*, though dad was actually a pretty nice person, at least as far as his family knew him. He was a generous father. I would need two pages to list all the opportunities for mental and physical growth—there would be fifty items at least. And all was given with no strings attached. If he had the pocket money, I was given funds for a lift ticket. He never stopped to check my grades first: children need exercise and fresh air to grow up industrious and energetic. It was the same with hobbies, Cubs tickets, camps, scouting, band, pool table, water skiing, etc.— all seeds for an industrious and energetic life.

There was no corporal discipline in our family. There were no rules, actually, yet the tone was puritan somehow. The children pretty much followed orders on the few occasions they were issued. I never made so much trouble in school that dad would bother to take notice of it. As a descendent of rural Methodist America, dad, I believe, had instinctual reservations about placing too much faith in school authorities. Dad shared with me that he felt his father had been a little heavy-handed. Dad wanted to raise his children in a more liberal, accommodating way.

Despite dad's generous, accommodating ways, I still felt he had a fatal flaw. His mind was absolutely shut to any idea that wouldn't pass muster with corporate elites, who tended to lean toward arch conservative. The only thing that ever made dad actually angry was my occasional attempts to introduce ideas of social democracy into a family gathering. Then he would get a little aggressive, although only mildly. I might complain that investors alone would not be able to counteract the streamlining effects of automation or the exodus of manufacturing work: society might be massively destabilized if we don't augment investing with at least limited central planning. "What the hell do you know about manufacturing?" he would grumble, exploding into a soliloquy. "I've been selling advertising to manufacturing executives since you were born. Do you know even one person in manufacturing?" leaning in, like a drill sergeant scolding an uppity recruit. "Is it you publishing a magazine about office automation? Do you know even one person in automation?" he said with a steely stare meant to finish me off. The scholarly response would have been to object to dad's ad hominin approach, but I just shrugged my shoulders, drank more of his champagne, ate his prime rib, and maybe enjoyed a good soak in his Jacuzzi.

Dad was pretty passive compared to most conservatives.

He always tolerated my interest in Buddhism, for instance. I'm not a prude, but I have gravitated toward the puritanical as I've grown older. Dad never had to contend with me suggesting free love, legalization of marijuana, or Communism. It was an egalitarian household—so no need to fight over racism or sexism. So, dad and I could co-exist fairly easily, as long as I played dumb around topics of political economy. As I embarked on my psychology studies, my motivation was to uncover the root cause of a closed mind. Paranoia and aggression, the typical conservative reactions to any new idea about government or society, had possibly been identified as parts of a syndrome. Maybe there was a cure, which would help conservatives see the need for the economy to meet every one's needs, not just the needs of the corporate set. In hindsight, one can easily see that my expectations were bit unrealistic, but back then, still in the grip of youthful curiosity, I just had to avail myself of the opportunity to study the mind.

Since I've said so much about my rivalry with dad, a few words about mom might be in order. She was a homemaker. She stopped working upon the birth of her first child, me, in 1962. She had been married two years, and she was in her early twenties. She had two more children: my brother, who is two and a half years younger, and my sister, who is eight years younger. She had been working as an administrative assistant downtown at Chicago's premier national bank up to that point, starting after graduation from Catholic high school in the South Side. She returned to the workforce as my sister finished college and even rose to be a manager of sorts.

Mom was an organized and efficient manager of the household. She kept everyone and everything on schedule. She kept abreast of all the various opportunities for exercise, outdoor recreation, and culture: in the South Side and then in Buffalo Grove. She kept all the children busy in healthful activities: camps, libraries, band, sports, hobbies, toys...whatever they needed. A tasty, balanced diet at all times, maybe a little on the rich side, cooked and served by her with style and decorum. The house's décor could pass muster with any Puritan on Beacon Hill—a modest combination of French provincial and Early American. Despite the touch of high style, she wasn't above housecleaning or pressing the children into chores.

Mom wasn't neurotic. She didn't have episodes of depression or bouts with alcoholism. She cultivated friendships and was active in the community, although no busy body. She liked to exercise but only in the most amateurish way —tennis with friends as an adult beginner. She had wide-ranging friendships and made sure to have some fun in life. She dressed like the feminists of her day, but with a tilt toward the preppy. Petite and nimble, she had a trim but matronly figure, and she favored formal fashions in dresses and pant suits. She was more like Jacqueline Kennedy Onassis than Pat Nixon, but she could hold her own with both of them. She could have been a style consultant to the first ladies. On rare occasions, she would don walking shorts or jeans, but always with a high waist, full cut, and accompanied by an oxford blouse or polo shirt, sometimes with a sweater or jacket appropriate to the weather. T-shirts were always out of the question, although tasteful warm-up suits were embraced for mundane activities. She steered the children's wardrobes in preppy directions too, with occasional trendy flourishes in response to the times.

She could be an Irish moralizer, so we children tried to keep our distance as much as possible. She was definitely the daughter of a Chicago PD detective. Her view of boy rearing was the best place for a child was anywhere but underfoot, and she daily prodded my brother and me into the finished-basement recroom, out into the neighborhood in search of playmates, or into an organized activity.

Mom was a neutral presence. As a good manager, she knew how to stay out of power struggles. Dad was a bit of a maniacal workaholic, a style which he applied to everything from his occupation to do-it-yourself carpentry. Mom, on the other hand, gave us the example of a consistent, steady presence. She wasn't much of a scholar, but we were a business family, after all, and therefore too much interest in scholarship might be unseemly. Looking back, as I write, I realize that my life has been shaped by the interaction of my *inner dad* and my *inner mom*, a struggle which will hopefully lead to some sort of healthy balance. In studying psychology, I was pursuing my rivalry with dad, looking to explain his paranoia and aggression. Mom was almost totally silent on issues of politics or any other controversial issue. I never stopped to wonder if she was playing dumb around dad too.

Dad's fashion statement was similarly presidential and preppy. At 5'8" with a round cheerful face, full head of close-cropped dark hair, intelligent blue eyes, rimless glasses, clean shave, broad brow and chin, aquiline nose, and medium athletic build, Dad emanated the burly confidence of Teddy Roosevelt. He habitually wore three-piece tailored suits exclusively of classic style in gray flannel or blue worsted wool, with white broadcloth or pinpoint oxford dress shirt and mini-print or stripped tie. An occasional pinstriped variation would be added for flair. Florsheim wing-tipped leather oxfords in black or burgundy for footwear, with tasseled loafers appearing as a show of confidence in middle age. London Fog trench coat for outerwear, matched with mother's. Dress casual had gradually penetrated dad's rare leisure moments (only); he started to accumulate a small selection of sport coats and dress slacks, and even experimented with chinos and sport shirts. For chores outdoors and other infrequent casual occasions, he put his guard down and wore jeans, flannel shirts, and sweaters, with old sweatshirts and canvas top-siders for do-it-yourself home remodeling. In short, he was a consummate Chicago Irish Catholic social climber.

More Transference

Inspired by my dream of uncovering the root cause of paranoia and aggression, I energetically embarked on a psychology major. Some of my psych courses actually did touch on inquiries into the possible causes of aggression and paranoia, with abnormal psychology and individual differences as the most significant. Scientific psychologists try to go deeper than the conventional theory that behavior problems are rooted in the home environment, so mostly I studied the framework for making deeper inquiries, as opposed to learning about existing theories. We learned about brain structure and how it interacts with depression and schizophrenia. We learned how to observe and measure changes in neurological processing. We learned about personality inventories, which attempt to understand and predict problematic behavior by means of personality traits. We looked at measures and theories of intelligence. We looked at developmental factors, including early childhood. We even looked into attempts to relate television viewing and other situational factors as triggers for disturbed behavior. Both nature and nurture were scrutinized as possible causal factors for whatever problematic behavior was under consideration.

Despite the thorough training in methods and case studies, I didn't encounter a cure for the closed minds of the corporate set. The garden-variety paranoia and aggression of conservatives were not considered problems serious enough for scientific inquiry. Interestingly, though, I had inadvertently started my special-ed career. Special education is the most-focused and best-informed area of cognitive psychology.

An eight-year-old boy deliberately drops his textbook on his teacher's well-shoed toes during math period. The teacher sends the boy to the principal's office: he is suspended from school for three days. Parents ask the child why he did it. He says, "I don't know," and shrugs his shoulders. Upon returning to school, the child once again drops his textbook on the teacher's toes in math period. He is sent to the principal, who suspends the student for three more days. Parents and teacher are shocked: Johnny has been a cooperative student. But afterwards, the principal calls in one of his special-ed teachers. He asks him to chat with the math teacher. The special-ed teacher makes a hypothesis: the boy's violent behavior might stem from problems with auditory processing—a learning disability with neurological origins.

On the day Johnny first assaulted his teacher, the math book introduced addition with regrouping. After his suspension, the teacher tried to return to that topic. Possibly Johnny was having problems processing the more-complicated auditory instructions involved in learning math for bigger numbers. He may not be retaining the teacher's demonstrations at the board. He assaulted the teacher when she offered to help after she saw him skip the practice problems. His violence was a childish attempt to avoid something stressful and the person triggering the stress. The principal, parents, and math teacher agree to have the school psychologist conduct some assessments. Her assessments, which are based on the principles of cognitive psychology (i.e. focused on neurological development and processes), detect a handicap in auditory processing. Principal, parents, math teacher, school psychologist, and special-ed teacher agree as a team (mandatory) to make Johnny eligible for special-ed services under the category of specific learning disability. The special-ed teacher draws up a plan for accommodating Johnny's auditory handicap, which becomes the Individualized Education Plan (IEP). If Johnny's teachers follow the plan, violence toward teachers will end and progress in math will resume.

In special-ed theory, violence, meaning abnormal behavior, is often the result of stress caused by learning differences. Once the impact of the learning difference is lessened through accommodations—such as tutoring from an instructional aide in a quiet area—the abnormal behavior will subside. This is a psychologically-savvy, up-to-date view of problematic behavior. By the way, the assessment process includes the ruling out of causal factors rooted in family background or other attitudinal factors.

In addition to the subjects already mentioned, I eventually took a course each in cognitive psychology, physiological psychology, psychological testing, psycholinguistics, social psychology, psychotherapy, experimental methods, and learning theory—most of them upper division.

Experimental methods provided an introduction to the kind of reasoning skills used in behavior intervention, one of the main services of special education. Cal State's psychology department included direct instruction in experimental methods and also weaved the theme throughout all its other courses. In addition, I chose a degree path in scientific research. In a nutshell, when applied to topics of psychology, scientific research aims to clarify causes and effects, so that one can be clear on the true causes of problematic behavior and thus intervene in or prevent them with greater effectiveness.

My senior seminar in experimental methods featured an experiment in social psychology that provides a good example of my nascent science skills. The professor chose a format whereby he led students in conducting an actual experiment. We set out with the plan of following the scientific method to arrive at a final paper, which would approximate a journal article published for peer review. We started by brainstorming on a research question. We arrived at some questions on the topic of conformity, which is an area of social psychology. We identified Solomon Asch's famous conformity experiments at Swarthmore College in the 1950s as our starting point. Specifically, we were taking issue with the results of an experiment that pitted a minority of one versus a unified majority. In Asch's experiment that created that situation, he found that roughly seventy-five percent of the 123 male college students tested (i.e. subjects) significantly betrayed their senses by following the majority's inaccurate matching of lines based on length: the subject would imitate the majority's spoken mismatches even though the subject could state the correct matches when asked in private later. With the ex-

93

perimenter acting as examiner, the matching exercises were conducted in a small group classroom setting, with all seven participants sitting around a table. Asch concluded that this lapse in judgement had been caused by the presence of six peers who preceded the subject in making the same misjudgment aloud. The six peers were confederates. Asch concluded that peer pressure had caused the subject's misjudgment over other possible factors such as vision problems or personality traits. So, Asch theorized that peer pressure exerts such a powerful force that it can even cause one to betray one's senses.

Our professor felt that the level of overt pressure in Asch's experiment might amount to a kind of practical joke more than a real reflection of human nature. We formed a question: Would the rate of conformity increase or decrease if subjects were only exposed to subtle, covert peer pressure? In response to the professor's prejudice, which we of course all shared, we formed a hypothesis: The rate of conformity would decrease when the subject was exposed only to subtle, covert peer pressure. We focused in on *Minority of One* because it involved the judgement of an obvious visual stimulus. We designed an experiment whereby a subject would give their evaluation aloud of ten 8"x10" pictures previously identified by researchers as neutral. Pictures depicted social scenes. The subjects would make their evaluation by giving each picture three grades, each one on a scale of one to ten, each scale following a positive(1-3)-neutral(4-6)-negative(7-10) progression. Each of the three grades was based on the subject's emotional impression of the picture: in control/no control, love/no love, safe/not safe. The neutral imagery and multi-dimensional evaluation of each picture were meant to avoid presenting the subject with a situation that would contradict his senses or force a snap judgment: in other words, an open, low-pressure task. Conformity pressure was applied in the form of two confederates whose evaluations aloud preceded the subject's evaluation, also made aloud. The confederates' responses were rigged to create a bias condition for each grade: in other words, they always both answered either positive, neutral, or negative. So, as an example of bias, the first grade for the first picture might go confederate one says "1"(meaning positive), confederate two says "2" (meaning positive), and then the subject says "???" (1-10, whatever it might be). Two people express the same opinion of the picture (i.e. confederates), and then the subject expresses his or her judgement. This was considered by the team to be subtle, covert peer pressure. Confederates' biased responses were scattered randomly to avoid projecting any kind of obvious pattern.

We gained permission from the university's committee on research involving human subjects and recruited twenty-five subjects from among psychology 101 students, balanced by gender (50/50). Subjects were satisfying a psych 101 course requirement. We created a schedule of trials, trained our confederates and experimenter (who showed the pictures), divided up the workload, and ran our twenty-five trials. In addition to their spoken response, subjects were given a printed survey to record their grades for each picture. These surveys were used to calculate the statistics that would support our conclusion. Confederates had the same printed survey but with their biases surreptitiously marked in. After our trails, a statistics professor came to our rescue by using the university's statistics software to calculate our results. She provided us with the mean response for each confederate bias condition (positive/neutral/negative). Her statistics indicated that subjects' grades for each picture, on average, had conformed to the confederates' biased responses. For example, when the confederates' scores were set to positive—grade of 1-3—the average score for subjects was 2. So, subjects were definitely influenced by the confederates, despite experiencing only subtle, covert peer pressure. My classmates stopped there and finished their paper.

But in a true moment of gifted-behavior-problem karma, I

asked the professor for permission to dig deeper. I felt that we hadn't answered the hypothesis. We needed a proper hypothesis test, as it is called in statistics. We needed some sort of rate to compare to Asch, to show an increase or decrease in conformity. I ran another group of twenty-five trails to create a control condition. The subjects were shown the same pictures and asked to give the same exact type of grades for each picture, but in silence with no confederates present. I removed the peer pressure, but kept everything else the same. In the control group, I found that each subject had responded with a grade of 5 on every emotion for every picture.

Basically, the average score, with a narrow distribution indicating almost no variation, was neutral, expressed as "5". That showed that subjects, when free of the biasing presence of peers, will uniformly respond with neutrality. This new baseline of neutrality indicated that subjects had been markedly influenced by the confederates. Emboldened by this baseline, I analyzed the average variance between subjects' responses and confederates' biased responses for each bias condition (positive/neutral/negative). Were subjects' responses scattered about or did they cling closely to the confederates? I found that there was almost no variance between the bias conditions and subjects' grades. The subjects had clung tightly to the confederates.

I monkey-wrenched my data into a hypothesis test for each bias condition. After my hypothesis tests, I found that confederate bias controlled the subjects' responses with one-hundred percent certainty. I had a rate—100% conformity, literally meaning no independence among the subjects. Asch's *Minority of One* indicated a conformity rate of seventy-five percent and an independence rate of twenty-five percent. To answer the hypothesis: When exposed to only subtle, covert peer pressure, subjects showed higher rates of conformity than in Asch's *Minority of One*. I proved the null, meaning I contradicted our hypothesis. Our hypothesis at the start of the experiment predicted lower rates of conformity and higher rates of independence, but we found the opposite. I finished the experiment with a conclusion: subtle peer pressure might be even more powerful than overt peer pressure. Moreover, I identified peer pressure as the cause of subject responses over any other factor such as the emotion being graded, the imagery of the pictures, sex, or even personality traits. Subtle peer pressure was clearly the cause of subject behavior.

From an education perspective, this study of peer pressure has some interesting implications for school culture. A school culture without discipline, where students are not compelled by school authorities to maintain positive speech toward teachers and classmates, can become a breeding ground for the worst sorts of peer pressure, especially in distressed urban neighborhoods. Students need strong role models, especially in their parents and teachers, to counteract some of the toxic elements of pop culture (which has become God Almighty). Thus a lesson in how a scientific conclusion can spawn all sorts of social philosophy.

Scientific methods relate to behavior intervention in the identification of the true cause of the problematic student behavior. An intervention is really just a kind of experiment. A Behavior Intervention Plan, as it's called in special-ed terminology, starts with a teacher's complaint about a student's problematic behavior. Then the special-ed specialist does an investigation. They precisely define the problematic behavior and then collect data regarding the circumstances surrounding the behavior: time of day, family conditions, subject matter, teacher, classroom, student seating, diet, and other relevant conditions. The specialist tries to isolate the condition most responsible for triggering the problem behavior. For instance, the behavior only occurs during language arts period, and it occurs every day.

The specialist might run a few experiments to rule out aspects of language arts period other than the subject matter. She might change the student's seat for a while. She might change the language arts period to make it after lunch. But if after testing other factors, the specialist determines that the subject matter itself is the prime mover, a plan is made to alter the teaching of language arts. A motivation plan might be added to language arts to help the student overcome mild anxiety about the subject. Possibly the student will receive language arts in a small-group setting with a specialist. To replace acting out, the student will be taught to ask for help or a break when he feels frustrated with his reading work. Basically, the intervention plan will prescribe modifications to instruction and the teaching of replacement behaviors to decrease the frequency of the problem behavior. A hypothesis will be formed predicting that modifying language arts instruction will eliminate the problem behavior. Data will be collected to determine the effectiveness of the plan. The effectiveness of the plan will rest on the accuracy of the specialist's "scientific" investigation. In California, school psychologists and special-ed teachers are both taught the principles of behavior intervention.

Learning theory, another one of my senior courses, turned out to be not just transference but an actual preview of my teaching credential. In the course, we studied the two major stage theories of development: Erikson and Piaget. Essentially, stage theories posit that the path of maturity from childhood to adulthood includes critical experiences that if missed will lead to problematic behavior in the individual. Of course, these theories are supported by research. Both Erikson and Piaget were featured in credential training. Interestingly, the stage approach is also applied to certain academic skills such as defining critical periods for phonics instruction.

The other major theorist studied was B.F. Skinner. His theory of motivation underlies many of the interventions applied to problems of school achievement. In fact, Skinner's investigations into motivation were initially motivated by his desire to help school children who were experiencing difficulties in the classroom. Studying the history of these theorists was good preparation for education. But the reasoning process probably yielded the greatest transference. The professor stressed radical doubt when studying these theories. Had the theorists in fact isolated the true causes of the problematic behaviors in question? Or were there other explanations? The rigorous consideration of all possible causal factors of a conclusion and the detailed examination of methods brought me detective skills that have helped me in my attempts to develop effective solutions for students experiencing achievement problems.

Competing Priorities

As a psychology student, I became an expert detective regarding the causes of other people's problematic behaviors, but some of my own were still vexing me. Time management was still an "emerging" skill. During my last year of full-time study, Fall 1987 through Spring 1988, I found myself juggling a girlfriend who became my live-in fiancée, a counseling internship at a school for emotionally-disturbed students, my remaining ten quarter-length courses, and a sales-tech position at an innovative computer store that evolved into a management position.

I met my fiancée, Wynda, in spring of 1987, in the experimental methods course described in the previous section. We were teammates on the conformity experiment, a situation I exploited maximally as an opportunity for flirting. She was an Irish-Scottish lass, from an Episcopalian family, a year younger than me, of medium height and build, so there was that ancient Celtic factor. We started dating that summer, and moved into an apartment on the ridgeline just below campus in spring 1988. She graduated from Cal State with a psychology major right after we met. After graduation, she continued to work part-time at the leading national retailer (department store) where she had worked part-time since high school. She was still working part-time when we set up house. I worked part-time at the innovative computer store and tried to finish my degree.

At work, Wynda favored tight knee-length skirts, snug short-sleeve silky blouses, matching jacket, dark nylon stockings, and high heels, and she didn't need a push-up bra or shoulder pads to turn a few heads. At school and on dates, she often wore tight high-waist knit black leggings or skinny jeans, low-healed black leather boots, black leather jacket to waist length, and black silk blouse. Her well-trimmed reddish brown hair was cut short in a bob or even crew cut, which complimented her opaque skin, oval facial features, button nose, full lips, and almond-shaped brown eyes. She was more rocker than preppy, as in opposites attract. She was slightly formal and edgy for Cal State, which probably came from working her way through college as the child of a humble single mother, but she had a flower-child side too, which showed when she wore her full denim overalls with tank top and Birkenstock sandals. After we got to know each other better, I noticed a marked increase in the frequency of her appearing in high-waisted cotton full-cut walking shorts, button-down oxford blouse or polo shirt, one of my cable-knit sweaters, and topsiders or designer sandals. Apparently, my preppy background was rubbing off on her.

To raise money just before we moved in, I dropped out for a quarter to work full-time, which set a trajectory I never reversed. At first, when were both part-time workers, we had loads of fun, especially driving my MGB all over Northern California—Pacific Coast, Sierra Range, Central Valley, Gold Country, etc. We developed a passion for road trips of all sorts. When the MGB faltered, we put Wynda's old Toyota Tercel to the test. Eventually, we bought a new GEO Tracker jeep 4WD convertible to replace the MGB we had worn out, which of course meant payments. I pushed on with my courses, but Wynda got really bored and lonely when I practically disappeared for weeks a time to keep everything moving forward. Attending to a relationship becomes part of time management too.

My study habits were still pretty good. They were still much improved over Stony Brook, but I was juggling extra-curricular activities again and my grades dropped slightly. As I was finishing up my extension of the conformity experiment, which was dragging on, the professor offered to help me apply for graduate school in experimental psychology. My life was such a madcap juggling act that I couldn't envision myself as an authority figure. I didn't follow up on his offer, and even worse, I basically dropped out without properly finishing the course (although I did pass).

After about six months of living together, Wynda became a store-level manager in accounting for the retailer. I became a salaried full-time sales tech at the computer store, which quickly led to working as an assistant to one of the principals of the small business, which had grown to four mall locations. In fall of 1988, I essentially walked away from Cal State without a degree and started my working life. I had squeezed out eight of my remaining ten courses in the time I had courted and moved in with Wynda, but work, bills, and relationship pulled me away from attempting the last two courses. I went without a degree the first few years of my career. Keen observers might note a disturbing similarity to dad, who dropped out of his second year as a part-time student into a full-time advertising career and fatherhood. Wynda was twenty-five-years old at this point, and I was twenty-six, just three years older than my parents had been when they started their married life.

The six-month internship began while we dated and ran through our first three months living together. La Chaim School was a non-profit organization providing school services for students with serious emotional disturbance. Local school districts placed students in La Chaim's schools and paid the entire tuition. I worked at a small elementary school in Albany, an urbanized suburb across the bay from San Francisco and just north of Berkeley and Oakland. Up until the 1980s, Albany had been a blue collar town centered in steel fabrication, auto manufacturing, ship building, military bases, and even oil refining. In winter of 1988, the town was on the verge of making the transition to office workers and the information economy. Oakland, home for many of the school's students, and Alameda County in general, were making the same transition.

Housing prices were depressed during this transition time, creating an opening for poor families to take up residence. Many of the school's students were from poor families, and all were from humble origins. Under special-ed law, the diagnosis of emotional disturbance rules out family and economic factors, meaning the disturbance must arise from a persistent, neurologically-rooted condition, but historically this diagnosis arises more among disadvantaged families. La Chaim had an avowed spiritual mission of serving poor and disadvantaged families.

As a volunteer counseling intern, who worked two half-days a week, I was assigned to work with two Black fifth-grade boys from disadvantaged families. I did one pull-out session a week with each student. Both lived in crime-ridden areas of Oakland with a single mother below the poverty line. In addition to the pull-out sessions, I was invited to weekly staff meetings, including professional-development activities. I could also observe my two students during class time.

Both boys were similar in appearance. They were short for their age, tending toward stunted at 3'5" feet tall. But they were lean, wiry, and strong. They were well-groomed and clean cut, with a daily uniform of nice button down shirt or polo, jeans, and clean athletic shoes or occasionally some nice hard-soled leather shoes. Bright-eyed and well-smiled, they were quick-witted with a strong spoken vocabulary and good social skills. They were both allergic to academic learning.

The content of the pull-out sessions was left to me, but they were conducted on school grounds under the watchful eye of teachers and school administrators. Basically I took a big-brother approach. Special-ed environments often put students under a lot of pressure. The boys' classroom was following a level-points motivation system, which meant maximum structure and pressure. I decided to provide an hour or two of non-contingent time, as it's called in behavior-mod lingo: a time just to be a kid, without too much expected of you. Special-ed guidance recommends including non-contingent time somewhere in each student's day—it helps the student develop trust in the school.

My approach was rooted in the Rogerian concept of unconditional listening. Trungpa's spiritual warriorship also emphasized the healing power of nonjudgmental listening—for listener and speaker. My plan was to support each student's self-esteem by allowing them to engage in nonjudgmental dialogues with me, a supposedly healthy role model. I helped each student choose a format for our sessions. Roland selected PE activities such as free throws, around the world, one-on-one, and batting practice. Alex chose to build a soap-box derby type of cart to use on the school's incline.

These sessions taught me some valuable lessons about special-ed students. Alex and Roland were pretty reverent during the sessions. We would typically spend some time on the structured activity, PE or cart, and then just lay back in the sunny school yard and chat about topics of their choosing. I didn't have to chide them about being appropriate or in some other way redirect their speech. They were pretty friendly. Their occasional bouts of anger were mild enough so that I could downplay them and let them regain their composure. But these two students were notorious for disruptive outbursts in the classroom, especially during academic lessons. Most of all, I learned about the difference between students under stress in the classroom and students in an activity of their choosing. I also learned a lot about Roland and Alex, their lives and goals. I was frustrated by the odds they were facing. At least we had some fun on the school's dime, said the gifted behavior problem. I should have gotten some snacks involved. My Robin Hood skills have improved since then.

At the end of the internship, La Chaim offered me an assistant teacher position at that school. But Wynda and I were already starting to think like corporate workers. We were already cleaning our financial houses, thinking ahead to a big church wedding, our GEO jeep, furniture, medical care, etc. I declined the offer, explaining that I had some bills to resolve before I could consider something like that, which was true. That summer, I was promoted to manager at the computer store and with the increased salary got myself on solid ground financially. Wynda did the same thing. She increased her hours and made other moves that eventually landed her in the retailer's management training program. We were headed for life in the corporate comfort zone, or so we dreamed in our computer-industry entrepreneurial fantasies.

At that point, it was summer of 1988, roughly three years after I arrived in California with a plan to become a together blue collar man. My goals from that plan had been somewhat achieved. My job at the computer store was half tech and half sales. The tech half involved installing and testing components for IBM-compatible computers. Back then, nearly every function required an add-in: video, hard drive, sound, printer, modem, etc. The retail sales part just involved helping customers when they came into the store. We had a few brands of computer, but I gravitated toward the IBM-compatible. Being a computer tech in those days was a lot like auto repair. So, I was a blue collar worker of sorts in the nascent PC industry. I found the fiancée and we had a modest home, our apartment in Hayward on a high ridge overlooking the Bay. And we eventually bought a new car—a Japanese compact (i.e. GEO Jeep)!!

Business Warriorship

I had accomplished some of my ambitions for warriorship. But I had definitely taken a few unexpected turns. Instead of going straight to work as a landscaper without a degree, a strictly blue collar route and my original plan, I almost earned a degree and was in a hybrid white collar situation where I was only half blue collar. And I was a fledgling supervisor. I reevaluated my spiritual aims. I reflected on my philosophy at the start of my business major years: I wanted to be a business rebel. I would be a businessman who wasn't a snob, who wasn't materialistic, who wasn't a workaholic, and who balanced the needs of customers, workers, and country—and I guess investors had to fit in their somehow too. I was going to transcend the authoritarian ways of Wall Street.

Three years at Cal State had only emboldened my naivety. I looked forward to implementing my philosophy somehow in the wide open field of PC technology. I was okay with drifting into a white collar role. My business spirituality resonated with a principle of warriorship called Ashe. The 1980s were marked by a turn toward social philosophies that viewed aggression as a helpful, primordial trait, with leadership reserved for those with the highest levels of aggression. The theories didn't honor outright aggression but subdued forms of aggression such as dominance, competitiveness, and upward mobility. The rugged individual, fighting off and transcending all contenders, was the archetypal hero.

In contrast, Ashe views good society as the aim of the hero. Ashe refers to a primordial drive to thrive through interdependent action. It views the individual as wired to communicate and cooperate more than compete. The Ashe leader, through a lifetime of study and spiritual practice, guides others in living by virtues that promote cooperation and interdependence, and that lead away from habitual tendencies and cultural fads that hinder good society. The Ashe leader is more of a wisdom keeper than a dominator, and his authority stems from naturally arising feelings of gratitude in those he serves. It's a servant view of leadership more than a dominance philosophy. Upon taking my first full-time white collar job, I was curious about Ashe and how it might work into my occupation—I was still young enough to have hope.

So with my warrior's idealism still intact, in summer of 1988, I started my career as an entry-level manager at an innovative computer store in one of the company's four mall locations. We were right next to a main indoor entrance to a leading national department store. Bayfair Mall, about five miles from Cal State, was located in San Leandro, a middle-class commuter town with a healthy mix of condominiums, apartments, and single-family houses. Just south of Oakland on the Bay, it had somehow emerged from the deindustrialization of Alameda County as an oasis of affluence. My role was to supervise the swing shift each day, which usually had one to three other staff, and to help the principal running the store with bookkeeping.

The innovative aspect of the company was in the targeting of the home market for PCs with personal service: a kind of high-end boutique approach to selling computers for home use. In contrast, most full-service computer dealers aimed at business users. I already mentioned the mechanical dimensions of the position: assembling and testing customized IBM-compatible computers. We also carried off-the-shelf PCs from Commodore and Atari, which only required minimal assembly at home. We sold a wide variety of software applications: office, art, desktop publishing, music, video editing, games, educational, and others. Although I could tinker with everything, I evolved toward word processing, desktop publishing, and other productivity applications. With desktop publishing and word processing especially, I was energized by the democratic spirit of empowering homes with powerful communication tools.

I was adequate at sales. The sales hounds on the staff typically beat my numbers, since I was kind of passive in that area —I just enjoyed helping people. My specialty was in keeping my shift honest. I caught the owners' attention when I developed a couple of tables for reconciling the daily physical inventory with the computerized point-of-sale system. My rigor in bookkeeping sent up red flags that helped the owners detect a pattern of serious internal theft and prompted them to renovate their accounting system. Basically, I was pretty firm about following all the company's guidelines. I was also pretty knowledgeable, gradually becoming a student of the business and the PC industry.

Keen observers might wonder what preparation I had for the position. A friend I made at my part-time job in a general merchandise catalogue outlet asked me if I wanted to join a store he had opened for the computer retailer. With no PC industry experience and minimal knowledge, I accepted the offer and then figured everything out from there. Free training! I enjoyed getting to know the key principals at the computer retailer. I was part of a regime led by two of the original founders. Prior to launching the computer retailer, they had been career middle-managers for a leading national department store. Bill, who was running the Bay Fair store, wrote the company's point-of-sale software in Ashton Tate's dBase, which was state-of-the-art back then. That accomplishment was notable because Bill had a political science degree and had worked in the finance department of the leading department store. He was the quintessential PC industry entrepreneur: an amateur living his dream of creativity and independence.

Despite the utopian conditions for we amateur technologists, all was not well. Mail order marketers were slashing prices by selling PCs and software direct to the user, with no service outlet needed. As buyers became more knowledgeable, this kind of sales operation grew more popular. In addition, computer superstores appeared for the small-business and home-office market. We were obsolete. The principals sold the company to raise money, but they still stalled at four stores and closed about six months after I moved on. My affinity for IBM-compatible computers and office applications became the ground for my next job. It seems that I had caught on to something big. A manager who I had worked with when I was just a part-time sales tech at the computer retailer invited me to join him as an assistant at a computer dealer specializing in software and computers for law offices. When I left the retailer, in spring of 1989, I had worked there two years. I had learned a lot, about computers, business, and life.

My friend, Fred, who hired me at the legal tech firm, introduced me to Peter, the founder and principal of the tiny business. Peter had a master's degree in computer science from Santa Clara University, an upper-echelon Jesuit college on the border of Silicon Valley. His undergraduate degree in computer science was from California State University, Chico. Perhaps most interesting, Peter was a Taiwanese-American from a Chinese Catholic family that had fled the Communist takeover of the mainland. They had been Catholic in China. Our small business consisted of Peter, Fred, Peter's wife (also a programmer from CSU Chico), and me. Fred was a high-school graduate of a technical bent, with a strong aptitude in salesmanship.

Fred and I had the mission of helping Peter find new customers for his PC-based legal billing software. Peter had started his career writing a legal billing application for a major office-automation manufacturer. Disenchanted with corporate culture, he decided to apply his skills on his own. He had already built up a modest customer base and now he wanted to expand some more. Just after I arrived, Peter placed a full-page display ad in *California Lawyer* magazine to generate leads for the billing software. While waiting for the leads to come in, I was assigned the task of studying sales manuals from Wang and other office-automation manufacturers. These manuals taught me the niche-marketing approach to selling office-automation products to law offices. From that start, I became a student of niche marketing.

The leads never really materialized. Apparently, Peter didn't have the required skills when it came to communications. Some leads did come in, and we were in a few directories, so there was a trickle of incoming calls. Fred started hustling each lead for a PC sale, kind of like a car dealer might, trying to grab quick cash by discounting and underselling. I confess to sitting back and watching Fred my first month or so. I only wanted to be a sales tech, answering incoming calls at the most. A month or so of observing Fred and Peter's futile efforts inspired me to grab for power. One weekend, I went home and wrote a marketing plan on my home PC. On Monday, I told Peter that I was leaving if he didn't follow the plan. Fred got angry at the plan and resigned. Peter, his wife, and I moved ahead according to my plan.

I proposed to create a full-service computer dealer for law offices, using the latest PC-based automation. That meant office-level PC networks with shared printers, shared files, and shared applications, even e-mail. In addition, the PCs would be Microsoft compatible, a new trend, so that in addition to network capabilities, each user could avail themselves of the incredible variety of productivity tools arising based on Microsoft. Peter already had appropriate sources for all the software and hardware we would resell.

By handling so much of a law office's automation needs, we would develop a deep relationship with the customer, which would lead to long-term revenue. Moreover, they would eventually adopt our billing software. I wrote a full-page display ad for California Lawyer and I sent out direct mail using their list. I also wrote sales literature to send to incoming leads. Stacks of leads came in, from new customers and Peter's existing customers. We converted the leads into sales at a fairly rapid pace—maybe too rapid. We were running hard, especially since we had to perform much of the installation and service work ourselves. We worked 24x7, at prospecting, proposals, deals, and installations. Peter found some help on the mechanical-tech side, or we wouldn't have had a chance. The size of each office deal grew, and in our last deal, we came close to twenty-five users on the network. That was at the end of our first year, and that was the last deal before I left.

We had hit the point of diminishing returns. My marketing plan had quickly exceeded our ability to deliver. We were making promises that were getting progressively harder to keep. Yet Peter really wanted me to go from sales tech to sales manager, spending all my time on marketing, sales, and closing deals. In addition, I was occasionally pushing Peter into following my vision of integrity: he wanted to improvise a little, while I was oppressively fair to the customer. Peter and I had some kind of acrimonious conversation. I knew he really wanted me to be his sales guy and just follow directions, so I quit. He was never that successful again, but he hung onto his expanded tiny business—so my year with him was a success of sorts.

Vulture Capitalism

In the first few minutes of my job search after leaving Peter's law-office automation business, I found a lead in the SF Chronicle classifieds for a computer dealer in downtown San Francisco specializing in law offices. It was a fairly well-established small business, founded and run by former computer-industry sales managers. It was a sales-tech position, but weighted toward sales. The door was padlocked in my first weeks as part of a bankruptcy proceeding. It was the summer of 1990. The economic downturn from the Crash of 1987 (i.e. Junk Bond Crunch) and the Savings and Loan Crisis was taking hold, as well as price slashing by mail-order dealers in the PC industry.

A couple of weeks after the padlocks, I found a lead in the SF Chronicle classifieds for a networking-equipment sales specialist at a major PC manufacturer. I was hired because of my relative technical expertise in arranging PCs into office networks. The expectations for sales output were high. I really didn't want to be in sales, but I was attracted to the potential stability of a manufacturing concern that had recently held its IPO on NASDAQ. The bills were starting to grow at home, so I took the job on the flimsy basis of a learning experience. My role was primarily to promote a new line of networking products to the company's established dealer base in the Mid-Atlantic (U.S.) region. I would be working with the dealers by phone. Selling to existing customers seemed like a manageable situation, even for someone with my wobbly motives. And I would be selling to computer dealers like the one Peter and I had run for a while.

There was a catch, though. After its IPO, the company's growth had trailed off and even reversed slightly. Economic downturns in the late 1980s and price slashing by mail-order PC operations were threatening the manufacturer's strategy of selling to dealers who resold the products to business users. A few PC manufacturers had started to sell their products by mail-order directly to business users, eliminating the need for dealers to act as middle man, consultant, and service outlet. With these mail-order manufacturers, quality was improving and prices were dropping.

Selling network products was an attempt by my manufacturer to appeal to dealers whose business customers required higher levels of service than the mail-order operators could support. Networking was still complicated and expensive. We would penetrate the high end as a way of staving off losses on the cheap end of the market, where mail-order was surely going to rule. We were going high end.

The plan didn't work. About six months into my employment, venture capital transformed into vulture capital. The executive suite and their Stanford MBA analysts didn't think so, and they were scrambling madly to redirect the company's gradual descent. We on the sales floor, however, knew we were feeding off carrion. We of the Mid-Atlantic region made a handsome feast of the carcass before moving on, while hardly even trying. We worked about three weeks of the three years I was there. A company struggling to keep up appearances has to tolerate a lot from its workers, since the company knows it can't find replacements. In desperation, the company tolerated the sales force waiting for business to come to it, instead of sales reaching out to stimulate business. The desperation

111

compensation plan made this passive approach even more viable.

As a specialist to an established sales force, I sat back and waited for the sales reps to direct orders right into my hands. At a modest pace, I sent networking sales literature to current and past dealers, and then called them to introduce myself, but it didn't help much. The management demanded forty customer calls a day, which I felt was onerous from the moment I heard it. I made about eighty a month, mostly in response to incoming leads, which I felt was exceedingly fair. As the company's descent progressed, the entire sales force developed a knack for sitting back, but the desperation compensation plan still yielded the highest pay of their career. The easy working conditions supported a convivial atmosphere among the sales staff. We got to know each other, went out for long lunches, and socialized outside of working hours. Dominators of business take head: you might dominate your workforce for short-term gain, but if you develop a weakness, they will exploit it for revenge and destroy you.

We of the Mid-Atlantic region, and the company's sales force generally, were a cozy cohort of dressed-for-success twenty-somethings in the prime of our youth and beauty. I wore a classic two-piece single-breasted wool suit every day, typically in blue or gray, with white pinpoint button-down oxford dress shirt, mini-print or striped tie, and wing-tipped black or burgundy oxford leather shoes. Of course, it goes without saying that the leather dress belt always matched my shoes. My suits were from designer labels, since I got a great deal on them through Wynda's department store, where the tailor made sure they fit just right. But I wore them plainly, kind of like corporate fatigues, although occasionally I added a daring touch like tasseled oxford leather loafers. I tossed in a London Fog trench coat with removable liner for outerwear.

Some men of a more dapper inclination expanded out from the two-piece classic suit to don separates in stylish combinations of jackets and dress pants with the latest fashions in ties and footwear. Women favored two-piece wool suits in blue, brown, olive, or grey, with a nice blouse, stockings, and leather pumps. Well-trimmed short hair styles were in force for men and women, although a few of the women showed some novelty and let their hair grow longish. We were conforming to the dress code for the company and the times. Almost no one was overweight or plain, and many were fit and toned. The demographics were 90% White and 10% minority (mostly Asian). Sex was at 50/50, which was a radical experience even as late as 1990. (Regarding the local plant's manufacturing force, the demographics were 90% Asian and 10% White.)

In college and all my indoor jobs up to that point, I had dressed casually, relying habitually on Levi's straight leg corduroys and jeans, cotton button-down oxford dress shirts in a variety of colors and patterns, polo shirts, cotton or wool cable-knit sweaters, and Bass weejun loafers or moccasin-style rugged leather outdoor shoes. A rain shell or ski parka was sufficient for outerwear. If pressed to dress up, I could resurrect khakis cotton or grey flannel dress slacks combined with a fresh button-down oxford dress shirt and designer sweater, yet still with the Bass weejun loafers; I had pretty much lost track of my blazers and ties, which I occasionally donned back in New York. It was my fashion unstatement: or maybe the survival mode of a working student. In the weeks leading up to the legal-tech job in San Francisco, I had decided to upgrade my wardrobe as way of invigorating my business warriorship. That didn't work out due to the legal-tech firm's bankruptcy, but the new suits turned out to be a perfect segue to the formal business climate at the PC manufacturer. My fashion sense met the company's expectations, and so did my technical knowledge, so I guess they made an exception for my lack of a college diploma at hiring time in 1990 (i.e. I was still two course short).

My success as a vulture wasn't totally rooted in pessimism. About a year and a half into my three years with the company, I was transferred to a new role. In response to my consistently helpful and friendly presence in the face of the firm's flagging fortunes, I was made the sole sales rep for the entire state of New York, including New York City. We were still a fairly popular brand in the city. I was empowered to sell the full range of products manufactured by the company: complete computer systems, computer components, office laser printers, networking supplies, modems, and other add-in components. I earned commission based on revenue with only minimal pressure on the profit side (i.e. the desperation compensation plan). I quickly became one of the top sales reps in terms of revenue for the entire enterprise, and my profit margin wasn't too bad either, but much lower than required to trigger a return to profitability. At this point, the goal of the sales staff was to keep the cash flowing and payroll rolling: profit would be a "future skill." Once I had New York underway, a few other territories were added to my empire. Wynda and I were approaching a joint annual income of $100,000 in my last year and a half with the company.

I couldn't take much pride in my leadership status, since I didn't really believe that the company would return to profitability. I was grateful for the increased income, but the experience felt a bit mercenary. There was one accomplishment that I did enjoy. My approach to sales was anything but aggressive. My style was helpful, patient, and tolerant, with cheerfulness for the killer app. I really loved being the top sales rep on that basis. I was a business warrior!

In my last few months with the manufacturer, key teammates in my New York sales empire had left the company and business was slowing down. Growing tired of mediating the conflict in time zones between the Pacific and Atlantic coasts, I transferred to become the sales rep for Northern California, which of course was our home turf and capital of the PC revolution. This territory was pretty lucrative too, and it gave me an opportunity to visit customers occasionally and grow in the direction of major-account development. But the growth experience felt a bit insincere, since almost all of my close friends had left the company and the probability of a return to profitability was low. While working the Northern California territory, I made plans to move on, following in the footsteps of nearly every one of my colleagues from the Mid-Atlantic region.

A sales rep in the Mid-Atlantic region, who I had befriended during our excessive free time on the job, offered to recommend me for a corporate sales position at one of the world's dominant software companies. Her husband had worked there during the growth surge before and after the software company's IPO, and now the couple was moving to the Sierra Range to live the good life with their capital gains and stock holdings. They would still need to work, but in laid-back, mountain style. I could replace her husband if I passed muster with management. It's interesting to note that her husband had a business degree from Cal State Hayward. In my last six months as a vulture, the PC company filed for Chapter 11 bankruptcy and its stock was delisted. The company continued to gradually contract until it disappeared about two years later. By the time I left in the fall of 1993, I had spent many working hours reading up on networking products and the industry, which left me well-prepared for my next career move.

The vulture approach had an element of warriorship to it, although a controversial one. The warrior knows when to retreat and merely survive. Overachievement, perfectionism, and the quest for dominance are not always the answer. Both the vulture and hawk have a place in nature, and sometimes the vulture is better adapted to hard times. The American Bald Eagle, for instance, is both scavenger and hunter, and occasionally even steals prey from other species of eagle. This balance is known as inscrutability, since the warrior refrains from committing to one camp or the other. This balance has Buddhist roots in the principle of equanimity.

Despite the presence of a junk-bond fueled recession, I celebrated a few key milestones of adult life in the late '80s and early '90s. At the end of my time with Peter, computer consultant to law offices, Wynda and I married in an Episcopalian church wedding with lots of family and friends. The wedding placated Wynda's mother, who was a bona fide church lady. As a church-raised Catholic, it was an accommodation I was willing to make. Wynda had continued with her store-level management position at the leading retailer at markedly lower wages than mine but with more stability. Wynda and I paid for the wedding.

In accord with gifted-behavior-problem karma, Wynda and I learned about the impending arrival of our first (and only) child as we packed for our honeymoon road trip to Alaska. Wynda had seemed a little emotional during the wedding—a home pregnancy test the next day revealed the cause. At that point, we had been married de facto for two years, including full co-mingling of funds. We had agreed at the start of our relationship to accept whatever pregnancy might arise, so we knew how to proceed. Personally, my warrior's faith in the basic goodness of society outweighed any worries about career or financial considerations. May Ashe provide!!

We modified our Alaska road trip to northward up the Pacific Coast to Seattle, where we headed due east and then south at the Washington border, camped in Oregon's Blue Mountain wilderness, and then meandered down the eastern borders of Oregon and Northern California. We had an awesome few days of camping in a remote of area of California's Mt. Lassen volcanic preserve. It was late August 1990. The cool, wet coastal climate was refreshing and then the moonscape-like desolation of the arid inland geography was stunning. The trip took about a month. We replaced tent camping with motels for a few destinations and applied other inventive strategies to help Wynda cope with her pregnancy. It was a nice trip. The controversy over old-growth logging was a big topic on the radio. We saw a lot of logging activity. The lumber companies were panicking. Use it or lose it, and acquired lumber companies had junk bonds to pay off. Apparently, growth was a controversial process in the land of unlimited opportunity. The wise man, the Buddha might have said, will realize the bounty of restraint where the fool will experience the paucity of panic.

After our daughter Aileen was born, Wynda took a year of partially-paid leave from the retailer. As a long-time employee, she was entitled to up to one year of leave with some basic job protection. Between Wynda's leave pay and my vulture compensation plan, we pulled it off, but it was close rations. We two psychology majors just couldn't bring ourselves to put our daughter in day care before her first birthday. At the end of her leave, Wynda's retailer received her back into the job that she had left. We did find professional infant and toddler day care providers that we trusted, and Aileen eventually became a precocious preschooler.

In the six months after the wedding, I re-enrolled in Cal State and finished the two courses required to complete my degree. Vulture capitalism left enough time and energy for a couple of courses. I graduated in December 1990, four months before my daughter's arrival. I wanted to set a good example for my daughter. Hopefully, she would be gifted without the behavior problems, or at least a typical suburban kid. In the end, I earned a bachelor of arts in psychology from the college of science with a minor in business administration. I had accumulated 270 quarter units out of a required 180, for a surplus of 90 units, with a final Cal State g.p.a. of 3.09. It's amazing what can happen with curiosity as the motivation.

My employers, the law-office automation consultant and the PC manufacturer, were both located in Fremont, an Alameda County city about twenty-six miles south of Oakland and twelve miles south of Cal State Hayward. Wynda and I moved into a modest rented two-story American colonial there just after I started with the computer dealer. Fremont was Wynda's childhood home. Her mother still lived there, and she was a big help with Aileen, almost like a third parent.

Fremont weathered deindustrialization better than the

other cities of the county. Formerly an agricultural area with roots in ranching and truck farming, the city of 173,000 offered flat, semi-arid land attractive for suburban housing and the warehouse-style industrial buildings favored by tech companies (much like Silicon Valley itself). The city's geography was characterized by expansive, open rolling ridges that filled the skyline to the east contrasted with dense suburban housing flowing west from the lower ridges into the flatlands that terminated in the wetlands of San Francisco Bay. Manufacturing and warehouse facilities were at the edge of the flatlands along the bay. Green high ridges of former ranches still emanated an aura of the areas recent rural history. The ridges formed an uptown of luxury housing and the flatlands a dense downtown concentration of apartments, condos, and bungalows. Our rented house was at the lowest edge of the ridges. Both Wynda and I worked in town. Ethnically and racially diverse, the city's residents lived within reasonable commuting distance of San Francisco, Oakland, Silicon Valley, Santa Clara, and San Jose. Access to tech jobs in Santa Clara and Silicon Valley was a big factor.

Fremont had retained a General Motors (GM) plant, which later became a NUMI plant (New United Motors Manufacturing Inc.), whereas Oakland had lost it. The grapevine says that GM pulled out of Oakland in the 1960s to avoid a predominantly Black and Hispanic workforce. Fremont residents were mostly Caucasian and Asian. Due to its easily-developed land, peaceful residents, and proximity to Silicon Valley, Fremont became a kind of borough of the tech sector. A few major computer-industry companies started in Fremont, including the PC manufacturer where I was a vulture capitalist. It had major assembly, distribution, and administrative offices right next to the GM plant. The PC company was the second largest employer in Fremont after GM.

Like most other companies in the area, easy highway access to the Port of Oakland allowed the PC manufacturer to import components manufactured in Asia, integrate them with other components, perform final assembly, and then package and distribute. Fremont's affluence stemmed largely from the Port of Oakland, the third busiest port in California after Long Beach and Los Angeles. Apparently, entrepreneurs found the Port of Oakland more attractive than the residents of Oakland. Interestingly, the founder of the PC manufacturer was a Chinese-American from Hong Kong who held master's degrees in electronical engineering and computer science from UC Berkeley—in other words, an Asian import.

Each of my employers—retailer, dealer, and manufacturer —was a small business, with the PC manufacturer on the large side of that spectrum. Each one had hit the point of diminishing returns, where a second or third round of investment was needed to stabilize current demand and surge forward into future growth. All failed to cross that threshold, and thus contracted into a plateau and then disappeared. Entrepreneurship was a complex phenomenon in the land of unlimited opportunity.

Turning Point

Toward the end of my three years as a vulture capitalist at the Fremont PC manufacturer, a sales rep in the Mid-Atlantic region, whose desk was next to mine and who I had become friends with over the years, offered to recommend me for a corporate sales position at one of the world's dominant software companies. Her husband started there during the archetypal start-up years, and had persisted through the growth surge before and after the software company's IPO. He availed himself of the stock purchase plan, a privilege afforded by his lucrative start-up compensation package, and the stock's steady climb was starting to pay off for him. The recently-married couple felt confident enough in the growth stock to simplify a bit by moving from Fremont to the Sierra Range to live the good life. They would still need to work, but in laid-back, mountain style. I could replace her husband if I passed muster with management. It's interesting to note that her husband had a business degree from Cal State Hayward. It was late summer 1993, and I was thirty-one-years old.

But there was a catch. My friend's husband left the company in mild protest of the firm's shift from lucrative start-up compensation to middle-of-the-road tech pay. This downward-mobile shift was in conciliation to Wall Street's demand for streamlining. Moreover, the stock's ascent was slowing—Wall Street apparently wanted to punish the company for its brash, lucrative pay. The husband wasn't disgruntled: a good half of the company's employees left at the same time. I was hired at the middle-of–the-road pay, which was roughly what I was making with the desperation compensation plan at the PC manufacturer. A horizontal move in pay, but I would gain stability, since the company had definitely secured a dominant position in networked database software and related business applications.

The company's database system maximized the networked approach to computing and that was the future of information technology. They had penetrated many of the world's largest corporations. The rule of thumb for finding customers was that any company outside the Fortune 200 was too small, and, in reality, the limit was closer to Fortune 100. We would try with smaller firms, but it usually didn't amount to much. As an inside account manager, I worked with corporate customers over the phone on deals under $100,000. A field-rep teammate handled the same accounts for deals over that amount, which frequently rose into the millions. I hoped to become a field rep someday, since they had higher pay. The structure of my territory dictated that my primary emphasis was existing accounts. I was part of the Midwest region, and I really did work with some of the world's largest corporations.

The dressed-for-success tradition at the PC manufacturer prepared me well for the similarly formal business culture at the world-leading database company. The demographics and social scene at the two employers were almost identical, although the twenty-somethings at the PC manufacturer had been more beautiful and stylish. Their culture had an element of celebration to it whereas the database company had a tone of begrudging compliance, like the way private school students wear their uniforms every day. Possibly the product's connections to data processing, quality control, and financial accounting were the cause of the less-glamorous atmosphere. If asked to identify each company with a political party, I would associate the PC manufacturer with the Democrats and the database company with the Republicans. But still, the workforce was predominated by the next wave of youthful social climbers from the twenty-somethings, with an increasing presence of thirty-somethings and young parents.

In my first fiscal year, my sales results were okay. I started late in the first quarter, but I came pretty close to meeting my annual goal. With that performance, my earnings rate was about even with the vulture days at the PC manufacturer. The benefits were the same, which included free comprehensive health care (The good old days!!). Because of the previous year's reorganization, I earned thirty percent less than my predecessor, even though I came close to my annual goal. Still, the compensation plan was pretty lucrative for the Bay Area and the times, especially for a psych-bus major. Maybe it was too lucrative, since Wall Street decided to take issue with it again. Looking for further streamlining, the company reorganized for the second time in two years, even though they had grown in revenue and market share.

My second fiscal year started with a $10,000 decrease in compensation plan. That meant a fifteen percent decrease in earnings, even if I hit my annual goal. This change was not considered a demotion. I had merely been assigned to a position in the reorganization that matched my experience with the company. Some sales staff fared even worse. They took an even bigger cut. If my year went perfectly, meaning I maxed out all commissions and bonuses, I would still be on par with my vulture years. But I would have to nail my sales goal: any shortfall would lead to downward mobility. As fate would have it, shortfalls would be the main theme of the year, and not just for me, but for the entire sales staff.

The company was doing well overall. They were meeting company revenue goals. But the reorganization was a failure. It left most of the inside sales force (like me) severely under-performing and underpaid, and most of the field force was in the same situation. Basically, the sales load had been unevenly divided, leaving almost all the revenue in the hands of a small number of key staff. The rest of us were subsisting on scraps. At the end of third quarter, I anticipated that my income for the fiscal year would probably be thirty percent, or $20,000, below the plan in place when I was hired, even though at that point in the year I was one of the leaders in inside sales. I was about thirty percent down from the vulture days.

I started planning my escape along with many others. A thirty percent pay cut from my vulture days was setting a personal debt crisis in motion. Wynda and I had viewed the vulture compensation as a sort of windfall, and we antici-pated some level of downward mobility, but the thirty per-cent reduction was cutting into our core finances. Debts were starting to pile up: big wedding, two late model cars (i.e. GEO Jeep, Ford Taurus Wagon), child birth, year of maternity leave, and preschool were the major ones. When we paid our debts on time, we were truly broke.

We were renting a modest two-bedroom Tudor bungalow about ten miles north of my office, so we didn't have a mort-gage or high rent to deal with. A few months before I was hired at the database company, Wynda had transferred up to a cor-porate accounting position in the West Coast headquarters of her national retailer, which was located in downtown San Francisco. She was commuting forty miles (one way) every day from Fremont, theoretically on BART (i.e. rail mass transit system). With my new job, I was commuting twenty miles dir-ectly across the bay to the database company's massive high-rise world headquarters in Redwood Shores, which was very similar to Fremont in economics and demographics.

With precocious private preschool for Aileen added in, our commutes reduced our lives down to an exhausting tedious juggling act. So we moved to Burlingame, a bungalow-based commuter town of tidy rectangular blocks and a bustling main-street shopping district twenty miles due south along the bay from San Francisco. The town reminded me of the modest lightly-wooded villages of Chicago's outer South Side where I grew up. In Burlingame, the White working class had cleared out of the distinctive Tudor bungalows in retirement and now the up-and-coming yuppies of technology were running up the rent. We were the fortunate beneficiaries of a retired working-class couple from Wynda's family who let us occupy the home at half the normal rent: they moved to their retirement cabin in the woodlands upstate. New-improved Burlingame was a bit metropolitan and toney for Wynda and me, basically two hicks from across the bay in semi-rural Fremont, but we still managed to enjoy the services targeting the affluent tech yuppies, including a very fine and somewhat expensive preschool for Aileen.

An interesting theme entered into our marriage. I should start making my way up to sales executive, by securing a senior field sales position in the computer-tech field, which would solve all the financial problems caused by Wynda's bad judgment, said Wynda. Wynda conceded that yes I had warned her that a used car might have been more appropriate than a new one, and that a small wedding might have been more fitting than a big one, and that maybe at some point her job should pay more than the expenses it generated. She also conceded that yes I had warned her of upcoming economic insecurity and uncertain times, and that a young couple like us couldn't be too careful. And yes she conceded that she had threatened to leave me every time I had tried to redirect her overspending. But still, she proposed, all things considered, didn't I see the virtue in devoting my entire existence to dealing with her overspending.

There was one major problem with Wynda's plans for my occupation. She wasn't me. Best not to rest your financial plans on taking over your spouse's occupation. At first, I tried to live up to her proposal. I started interviewing in other firms for senior sales positions. Alarmingly, their senior field representatives weren't making much more than the inside reps at my world-dominating software employer. I was looking at a horizontal move, although with a slight increase over the reorganization debacle. I might make some slight headway on our debts, but certainly no windfall. The only opportunity for a windfall would be at my world-dominating employer. Joining the field force there could bring an immediate $20,000 increase in compensation plan and within a year or two a total increase of $35,000. If I had some luck, my income would occasionally rise well into six figures.

The inside rep who sat next to me had just moved to Detroit to join the field force there. Escaping the reorganization was his motivation. After a month or so of searching, I started to think that holding tight and hoping for better times might be the best move. It felt a bit premature for me to pitch for a field position, but maybe I could switch to the field after a couple of years. In preparation for such a move, I tried to envision myself as a field rep. My product knowledge was sufficient: I definitely knew enough about core business software. In addition to product knowledge, the field rep must have a deep familiarity with executive culture: this qualification was paramount to all others. I sensed an obstacle. Could I become the dearest friend to the executive suite? A close confidant? A brother in the cause? No, I could not, especially not among the Fortune 200. I'm not a friend of the executive suite. But I'm not their enemy either. I'm a kind of an agnostic in their faith. It's just that executives are a bit paranoid and self-centered by my way of thinking. I'm more on the others-centered and open-minded side of things, so maybe their mission is different from mine—or maybe not, they might say if given a chance to speak. The wise man, the Buddha might say, respects his enemies above all and therefore has none.

My career ponderings led me to the realization that I had reached a dead end. It wasn't just the reorganization bothering me. I was burnt out on inside sales. I wanted out, and up wasn't looking like the way. My inside position required forty customer calls a day, which I again felt was onerous, and I repeated my habit of making twenty calls a week, mostly in response to incoming leads. I was considered hyper-productive among my peers. Contentment in inside sales revolves around the mild flaunting of work rules. At the headstrong age of thirty-three, my warrior's aspiration of refraining from deception felt seriously compromised. I wanted out and I started making plans.

In every plan, our family debts seemed an insurmountable obstacle. Yet I continued my research. My most serious plan was to develop websites that featured interactive learning experiences. I hoped to get a jump on online learning and maybe start some kind of small business. I was dreaming of a creative role in starting an early-adopter small business. Be careful with dreams. One might find oneself living them out—for better or worse. One morning, after a few weeks of researching in my spare time, I just quit when I arrived at work. I walked into my boss's office and announced, "I'm going quit at the end of the day." She set HR into motion immediately. I filled out the exit paperwork and left for good an hour later. I went from my office to my daughter's preschool. We had a nice day off in the park and at home playing with her role-playing toys in the mild, sunny spring afternoon. I never again worked in sales.

Trungpa might have referred to the day I quit as a moment of choicelessness. A seeker on the path of warriorship might encounter a time when self-abnegation gives way to authenticity. A warrior accepts the need to be genuine. I had no choice the morning I quit. There was no other option. Literally, it was pure reflex, like pulling my hand away from a flame. I was not wired for sales—on a metaphysical or psychological level. I ended my life as an imposter. I needed to work in a faith where I would be a believer. I had given corporate sales the old college try, but I experienced a complete absence of motivation, despite the potential for a high income.

CHAPTER FOUR

Living with Direction

Marital Credit Crunch

Wynda was also experiencing a career crisis during the time that I quit the world-dominating software company, exacerbating my somewhat rash decision. The difficulty in her case was not personal, though. Her employer, the leading national retailer, was bogged down in a threatened takeover fueled by junk bonds. To stave off the takeover, the retailer had imposed a wage freeze, even for employees seeking a promotion. Eventually, the austerity measures were cemented in a Chapter 11 bankruptcy.

A real-estate magnate on an acquisition binge eventually bought up my wife's retailer and a selection of other major national retailers. He then consolidated them into one holding company. The magnate issued junk bonds to pay for the acquisitions. In an act of incredible guile, the magnate convinced his newly-acquired employees that the holding company's financial problems were the result of their inefficiency and imposed austerity measures as a kind of consequence. My wife's managers saw the austerity measures as an once-in-a-lifetime chance to prove themselves—they were going to work harder than ever, despite the wage freeze.

Wynda received a promotion at about the same time the retailer's junk-bond debacle hit. After she returned from maternity leave, we had agreed that she would engage in a bit of overachievement to lift herself out of store-level hours and into corporate hours, which were basically regular nine-to-five. To her credit, she applied for promotion and was accepted into a junior executive position in financial security. With the promotion, she moved to the retailer's West Coast corporate office in downtown San Francisco. She received a nominal raise at the time of promotion and then joined her new managers in their debacle-driven zealousness, at all times working ten times harder than justified by her salary—obsessively harder.

The overachievement part involved Wynda working obsessively long hours with me holding down all the child care, morning and afternoon, even though at all times I earned eighty-five percent more than her. In my vulture years, I basically enjoyed the challenge of full-time parenting and full-time work—the quality time with Aileen was a fringe benefit. Wynda's promotion came at about the same time that I moved to the world-dominating software company. With my return to venture capital, I had to compel Wynda to share in the parenting. She could work late, but she had to at least lead in the morning. Not surprisingly, she worked just about as late as she could every night.

Wynda's corporate working conditions turned out to be even worse than the store schedule. She essentially was an auditor—a kind of internal affairs accountant. In this role, she travelled to far flung store locations, sometimes involving overnight stays. She was often assigned to monitor physical inventories at the end of the fiscal year, which were conducted on evening and weekends. Maybe worst of all, during the holidays, Wynda and the other auditors were assigned to work weekends in stores like temporary help. On top of all that, Wynda's department head was a careerist, with no sense of proportion: austerity was his chance to shine. He frequently put demands on her that required weekends—as overtime. Wynda was caught up in pleasing him.

At the end of Wynda's first year in the new job, a few months after I insisted she resume at least minimal engagement in parenting, she started having stress-related health problems.

Insomnia. Irritable bowels. Weight gain. Panic attacks. Three times at the end of that year, she called me from the emergency room to retrieve her after a panic attack. On those occasions, I had to leave work early to take care of Aileen and Wynda. She had never before experienced any of those symptoms. Sometimes in the morning, as we prepared to leave for work, she would break into an uncontrollable soliloquy about office culture—almost a rant. She was mad that caring for our daughter was going to make her a few minutes late (for her ten hour day).

One day, I interrupted her morning complaints: "Wynda, I want you to quit. I really want you to quit. This job is harming more than helping. We'll be better off if you quit." I meant it. Her pay was so low. It was at least thirty percent below what her workload justified. I wanted her to stay home, at least for a while. If she wanted to, she could return to work when she found a better situation. I had been looking into a career move, but with Wynda at home, attending to Aileen for a change, I could find a way to make sales work for a while longer. She acted insulted: "No. I won't quit. Out of the question. Forget about it." Thus began my fairly regular attempts at persuading her to quit.

I was frustrated by Wynda giving more of herself to a junk-bond magnate than to me. She didn't trust me enough to quit. She neglected Aileen and me, literally abandoned us, but she would stay faithful to the company to the bitter end (i.e. till death do us part). In the early years of our relationship, I paid Wynda's student loans, college medical bills, car payments, and clothing budget, and several other key items. I was debt free back then, but I didn't mind giving her a helping hand. I really felt that she should have trusted me when I asked her to quit. I never mistreated her the way the junk-bond magnate did, yet she loved him more.

My resentment of Wynda's infidelity peaked in the months leading up to my impulsive resignation. She was coming home late every evening. She would sit alone in the kitchen at the back of the house, get mildly inebriated, prepare a mediocre frozen dinner for me (I had already fed Aileen), prepare Aileen for bedtime, and then pass out in Aileen's bed. In other words, Wynda found an ingenuous way to drink herself to sleep, adding self-medication by wine to her growing list of stress-related disorders. Weekends weren't much better, with Wynda using gourmet cooking and gardening as an excuse to remain alone in the back of the house getting drunk—oh well, at least dinner was better. Life pretty much became Aileen and I together in the living room or about the town with Wynda hiding from us in the back of the house.

On our last getaway weekend, which was a belated fifth anniversary celebration, Wynda occupied our entire dinner with an encomium about her loveable boss, knowing full well what I thought of him. I didn't get one word in—she never even stopped to ask me how my day had been. She barely paused for breaths. A less patient man would have left abruptly. I indulged her and ate quietly, with fain attentiveness. We were at Lascaux on Sutter Street, one of our favorite gathering places in the city just down from her office. She drank so much wine that I practically had to carry her up to our room down the block in the Grand Hyatt Union Square. I was sober, having only had two modest glasses of the wine. When we arrived at our room, she immediately passed out hard. She awoke in the morning disabled by a killer hangover. We took a scenic coastal route home down the Pacific Coast Highway. She sat silent and sick the whole drive. Maybe her encomium was to placate my concerns about her working conditions, but instead it triggered thoughts of leaving her. It was clear to me where her heart truly lied.

When I quit the software company, I was not just dissatisfied and burnt out in my occupation, I was also a jealous husband taking a stand against my wife's infidelity. I was finally saying no to her. She had become all demands with no trust. My entire existence was being shaped by her judgment. I wanted to make some changes, which would require her to leave her abusive junk-bond magnate. She wouldn't extract herself from that all-consuming love affair, but I wasn't going to stop, so I quit my sales position to start things moving my way. Like most jealous lovers, I was only in limited possession of my faculties when I acted on the impulse to quit, but in the aftermath of the act, my intention solidified: "I'm taking a stand, Wynda, and you're just going to have to trust me. I'm going to do something my way for a change." I wasn't going to dedicate any more of my life to paying off the junk-bond magnate's bills. I find myself sounding incredibly similar to Betty Friedan's adherents. The Male Mystique? It was early May 1995. Marital relations were a complex phenomenon in the age of unlimited opportunity. Keen observers may recall that the nation's divorce rate experienced a resurgence in the early nineties, second only to the peak rate of the early eighties which had been followed by a steady mild decline.

Wynda's response to my quitting was to abandon the marriage within weeks, leaving her unfettered in spending all her time with the love of her life. Literally, the marriage was completely over in three weeks—we have not exchanged even one word since then. You might wonder about our daughter: Wynda eventually moved her mother in to take over for me, freeing Wynda for unlimited overtime in a partnership of feminist single mothers. As soon as I told Wynda on the day I quit, she started arguing with me. She wanted me to return to my job immediately. She didn't want to hear about any of my plans for a career move. After two days of her anger, which culminated with her calling the police to apparently arrest me for displeasing her, I asked her to go live with her mother for five days to cool off. She had been calling psychiatrists and police to have me detained. She claimed that I must have been crazy to leave such a lucrative job. Of course, they all turned her down. It's neither against the law or a sign of insanity to quit a job you don't like, even if your wife disagrees. Her attacks on me were raising my heart rate. I needed a break from her, before she gave me a stroke or heart attack.

After five days of living apart, with no contact, we met at our house on a Monday afternoon. Immediately after arriving, she asked me to leave. She had already rearranged our funds and accounts as if we were divorced, without my cooperation or a court order. I remember signing a few bank papers to complete her arrangements. She had planned the whole thing without speaking to me. I didn't mind leaving—I really needed to escape from her aggression. I left with a small backpack packed with just enough clothes to survive a summer out of work, our jeep, and a small bit of cash left in an account for me. I was ready to survive for months on those rations. I was in bodhisattva mode and no amount of physical hardship could intimidate me. There was no goodbye for my daughter, but Wynda arranged for me to visit Aileen on the weekend.

I drove to my parent's house near Mt. Diablo that afternoon, where I stayed for about nine months. In my first week there, I still held some hope of talking to Wynda about my career plans. We talked twice in that week. Each time, she simply patronized me, like I was a psychiatric patient. Our last conversation was on Sunday afternoon at her (our) place. I had returned Aileen after a weekend visit at my parent's house. I told her that I was going to start contacting employers in the next week, specifically major parcel shippers. I figured they were going to have a symbiotic relationship to mail order and even online commerce. I planned to look for a route into the operations-logistics side of business. First, I wanted to move out of sales. Then I would continue looking into online learning and commerce. She kind of pretended we could talk more and made a dinner date for Wednesday.

When I called Wynda to confirm our dinner date, there was no answer at work or home. Her office told me that she had taken a thirty-day leave. I called Wynda's mother, who still lived on her own. She said that Wynda had gone to a "safe place" and would not help me contact her. Wynda had taken Aileen with her. I'm thinking Amber Alert. The police tracked Wynda down and compelled her to return to our family home. They informed her that she must file a court order if she wants to control custody. The next day she filed a restraining order with the family court. As she typically did when stymied in one of her demands, she launched into an inflammatory soliloquy, setting off every one of the court's obligatory red flags and inaugurating a lengthy, acrimonious struggle.

Enter Mr. Hyde

Wynda's complaint about me centered on the insanity of quitting a lucrative corporate job: there was no mention of domestic violence of any sort. The statement in her application for the restraining order was a total fabrication, yet it was quite effective in accomplishing her aims. She started with a fact: I had quit my sales job at the world-dominating employer. I found it interesting that she named the employer. Then she went on to copy in the diagnosis for schizophrenia, like a fill-in-the-blank form, with the tacit implication that my quitting was some kind of psychic break: "He claims to have heard the voice of God," "He follows voices in his head," "He gets angry whenever I discuss his problems," etc. Not one word was true, and I'm not talking misinterpretation. I'm talking deliberate misrepresentation. The psychology major Wynda crafted a fantastical fiction as good as any found in Sherlock Holmes. It worked too, with the court therapists believing her every word, suspending disbelief, and setting out to apprehend the perpetrator, which was me, of course, since the therapists were always ready to believe the worst about *those men*. The real Sherlock Holmes at that point might have interjected the fact that the likelihood of an exceptionally healthy thirty-three-year-old male, known for sturdiness of mind and body, having a first experience of schizophrenia at that advanced age was nil. In other words, the discerning mind would have been suspicious of Wynda's motives at the outset.

From her statement forward, the entire case became a fiction, with Wynda as the damsel in distress and me as the unrepentant Dr. Jekyll. Apparently, Wynda and the court therapists felt that Hyde had finally emerged and was here to stay: only Hyde could do something as despicable as quit a job when it displeased his wife. Wynda had married the charming Jekyll, but the pressures of the world had turned him into Hyde and now she wanted out—before it was too late. The court therapists lived by the fiction and blocked any suggestion about scrutinizing Wynda's remarks. According to the therapists, Wynda's statements would be considered true, prima facie.

It only took me about a month more to figure out that I was better off without Wynda and her friends at the family court. That Sunday before she ran away was our last conversation ever, on any topic. I was stunned by the way she discarded an eight-year-long relationship in just one week. In our last conversation, Wynda told me that she could only love a corporate salesman—she could never love me in another occupation. She was really specific and emphatic. I felt she was being a little narrow-minded. I also thought it might have been the wine talking. I had been sober for four years at that point (and at all times clean), only drinking lightly on special social occasions, but Wynda was slowly developing a self-medication habit. A prime mover in my sobriety was the desire to set a good example for our daughter. Maybe Wynda wanted to drink on work nights and weekend days without the fetter of my sobriety.

I only met with the family court therapists on two occasions. I'm mentioning the therapists because they acted as evaluator and judge. The actual judge was just a rubber stamp, literally, which I found troubling but accepted as a fact of life. Apparently, jurisprudence in California conforms to the medical model now: we don't resolve disputes between litigants, we cure ourselves of the conflict through various psychotherapies. Wynda's tall tale activated their ambitions. They were going to cure me!

The first occasion was for Wynda's application for a restraining order after she ran away. The therapist met with both parents and made a report that became the judge's ruling. When I arrived at the therapist's office, he had already met with Wynda for a while. All three of us were going to meet. The therapist made a brief introductory statement about the purpose of the meeting: we would develop the custody part of the restraining order. Apparently the order itself was a fait accompli. I started rudely: "The first thing we have to discuss is Wynda's lying in her application." The counselor retorted, firmly: "*That* will not be discussed." So I stood up, walked out the door, left the building, and never went back. I didn't attend the hearing for her application. An order was issued for a year. Neither I nor my representative was present, but full orders were issued, including custody and visitation. The requirements of child support and spousal support were waived. I'm guessing Wynda wanted to maintain consistency in her plot line, meaning it would be inconsistent to ask Mr. Hyde for child support. I had no visitation or custody. I was content with the order. My goal was to stay completely away from Wynda, whatever it took. I wanted her out of my life. I had won that victory. In her order, Wynda had given me at least a year completely free of family responsibilities. In fact, she, for a change, had finally taken on a few burdens. I was looking forward to a really good year.

But my victory was short-lived. Mom and dad attended Wynda's hearing, without the benefit of my permission or our family lawyer. In the thirty days between the application and the hearing, I had stayed focused on becoming the healthiest person I could be. I basically had a daily regime of morning hikes, studying Buddhism and spiritual warriorship, formal meditation practice, physical fitness, and working on my writing skills. I focused on moving forward with my goals. My composure really got under my parent's skin. They wanted me to attack the vixen Wynda. They wanted action, aggressive action. "How are you going to get your child back?" they would demand occasionally when they lost their cool. "How can you just sit there and do nothing?" I informed them that Aileen was Wynda's child now and that I was just going to move on. So not only did I have to avoid Wyda's anger, I had to cope with my parent's aggression at home.

My mother wasn't going to settle for me just moving on. Neither Wynda, the family court, or I anticipated the intensity of Grandma Bartlett's Irish-Catholic loyalty to her granddaughter. This loyalty became the prime mover in everything that followed. As the husband of a workaholic, I relied on the grandparents for back-up parenting. My mom was still a homemaker in Aileen's toddler years, so I drew heavily on her support for the myriad days when neither Wynda nor I could care for Aileen: for instance, school holidays, sick days, and business travel. Wynda's mother worked full-time and mostly helped out only on work nights. In addition, my mom occasionally provided weekend respite care for Aileen when I needed a few hours to hike or bike or just catch my breath in general—sometimes mom would take Aileen for the whole weekend. My sister was the baby of the family, at eight years younger than me, the oldest. Aileen inherited the lavish girl-sphere left behind when my sister fled the nest. And it wasn't just hand-me-downs. Mom outfitted Aileen with new clothes, toys, videos, books, and all manner of toddler accoutrements. Aileen had no pets at home, but mom had a dog that Aileen really loved, a young male Shih Tzu, who loved her back. Mom wasn't always thrilled about her grandmother workload, but she and Aileen were definitely special companions.

In addition to the pragmatic connection, there was a mystical tie between mom and Aileen. They were born on the same date, fifty-two years apart. Mom's maiden Irish surname became Aileen's middle name. Interestingly, as Aileen matured, she developed a striking physical resemblance to my mother and her sisters. Aileen was my mother's only grandchild for sixteen years, and mom enjoyed spoiling her. Mom wasn't going to relinquish her grandmother's rights and she was quite adept at goading dad into court action. She couldn't move me, but dad leapt at her every demand. I didn't think grandmother's rights existed. Dad said he would make them exist.

Sure enough, the restraining order had visitation rights established for the grandparents. I have no idea how, but they got their grandparent's rights. The grandparent's visits included my participation. And a provision for phone contact between Wynda, Aileen, and me for family matters. I resented my parent's interference. I wanted no further contact with Aileen. That life was over. I wanted Wynda to have her way in everything. But I was obliged to participate in the visits since I was temporarily depending on mom and dad. The visits were approximately one day each weekend and eventually grew to include overnight visits every other weekend. One might pause to wonder at the prudence of coercing Mr. Hyde into unwanted contact with a child.

I dutifully attended the visits each week, which typically lasted from early morning to early evening on Saturdays. My parents mostly remained in the background. As a family with a workaholic mother, Aileen and I were already quite accustomed to occupying ourselves without Wynda, and mom's place was already a home away from home. In our limited time together, Aileen and I played games, read books, watched her favorite videos, went out to lunch, shopped for clothes, and explored nearby city parks and wilderness areas. On a few occasions, my parents and I pushed ourselves to squeeze in an outing such as the zoo or children's theater. There were no overnight visits during the year-long restraining order.

Aileen was able to relax and enjoy herself during the visits, probably because we were so accustomed to living without her mother. In fact, she was energized in my presence. I had to give her my undivided attention or she would redirect me with a move such as climbing into my lap or hugging me around the shoulders and neck. I noticed that Aileen steered role playing games toward the theme of a father rescuing his lost daughter. A couple of times, she asked me why I didn't rescue her from Wynda. I told her that Wynda had told some lies about me in court that I couldn't afford to disprove—I didn't have enough money to fight her. Aileen somehow made peace with that.

A few weeks into the visits, Aileen's psychotherapist requested a meeting with me. Apparently, Wynda had put Aileen into therapy. In the meeting, the therapist implored me to gain custody of Aileen. She said Aileen should really be with me, that she loved me deeply and needed me. I listened attentively, quietly. Then I concluded the conversation with a question: "Can you tell me how to get the family court to act on the truth?" The therapist gazed at me for a couple of minutes, trying to formulate a response. She ended with, "I know what you mean. But I just wanted to tell you that Aileen really needs you." I thanked her for her concern and left. I didn't like the way Aileen was being treated, but I figured she would adjust somehow. People are in fact robust and can adjust to just about anything.

Mr. Hyde Meditates

In the year of the restraining order, visits with Aileen helped me move forward by demonstrating that Wynda and her mother, who both now lived in the Burlingame house, were doing okay as a single-mother duo. As a precocious four-year-old, Aileen was healthy, attending school, performing well, and seemed to enjoy life. Wynda was still grinding along as an underpaid workaholic at the retailer in bankruptcy. There was no obvious need for a rescue mission. On the other hand, contact with Aileen was like playing with fire, and eventually I got burned.

Of course, my parents hoped that the visits would make me mad enough to attack Wynda in court. Consciously and logically, I had walked away from my life with Wynda. At that level of appearances, I was calm as a still pond. But at the physiological level, real panic was building, like how a soldier must feel when under attack. I started having nightmares about Wynda and Aileen falling into harm's way. My heart was elevated at least ten beats a minutes all day. My bloodstream was full of adrenaline and testosterone—I could smell them on my skin. It was a bit of luck that I was following a regime of rigorous daily exercise. That burned most of the anxiety off for most of the day. My parents were getting the outcome they aimed for, but I doubt they anticipated how powerful or tragic things might become.

At the time, I figured that I was under stress and that I had to endure the panic while things straightened themselves out. Upon reflection, I can see a powerful protector instinct at work. At some amazing level, my subconscious attempted to regain control of Aileen. I had protected her from Wynda's neglectful ways for the past three years: to see her have to live as Wynda's captive was just too much to handle. Logical posturing about walking away wasn't bringing the subconscious panic into abeyance.

In the first thirty days of the restraining order, I abided under its conditions with no struggle. I simply kept to myself. But after the visits started, I began to wonder if I shouldn't try to talk to Wynda again: the subconscious panic eventually made its way into panicky thoughts. I started to doubt my approach. Maybe I should try for some type of reunification for Aileen's sake. In that vein, I left a couple of voicemail messages for Wynda that were about marital matters more than family matters. They were peaceful, but technically outside the boundaries of the restraining order. Wynda responded by complaining to the local police department.

Her complaint triggered an arrest. Fortunately, the investigation was quite bourgeois. It was upper-class law enforcement. I was invited by the police to make a statement in my defense before the arrest warrant was sent by mail, and the entire investigation, trial, and sentencing were handled with me on my own recognize. Eventually, the charges were dropped, but only after I redeemed myself through a fine, seven weekends at hard labor, and three years of good conduct. In my statement, I apologized for transgressing the order's boundaries and promised to never contact Wynda again for any reason. The D.A. delayed prosecution for thirty days to see if I would honor my promise. At the end of this informal probation, the D.A. invited Wynda to drop her complaint, since it seemed likely I wouldn't contact her again. We were still married at that point. Wynda declined to withdraw her compliant. The D.A. and my fifty-something male Irish-relative lawyer worked out a probation deal, which the D.A. had Wynda sign off on (literally, in a handwritten note on the cover page of the complaint).

Wynda's complaint to the police and pursuing of the charges were disheartening, but they triggered a healthy commitment to never engage her in any kind of interaction. She was pure poison, and any attempt to appeal to her would be foolish. I wanted to never hear the sound of her voice again, and I never have. Her call to the police occurred approximately eight weeks after we split up. From that point forward, I was truly determined to move forward with my goals for a new occupation and to resist all attempts to pull me back into my old life. My parents were still badgering me to attack Wynda or placate her, but now I really knew better.

The surge of panic that welled up in me after the initial Aileen visits was my first lesson in Buddhist mindfulness. The powerful, panic-driven urge to do something now is called a klesha in Buddhism. In strict religious terms, a klesha arises from past karmic influences and current pressure from social conditions. On the karmic side, I was influenced by a growing family tradition of the pushy American salesman: the sales warrior can always persuade, threaten, taunt, tease, harass, flatter or beg the world into meeting his demands. Mom and dad were convinced that if I would just sell myself harder to Wynda and the court, the whole mess would clear right up, and they were relentless. On the social pressure side, I was troubled by Aileen having to rely on a mother who had spent less than four hours a week with her daughter for the past three years. I was used to sheltering Aileen, but now I had to trust in fate to save her.

Aileen seemed well during her visits with my family. She wasn't having problems at school, and she was quite attentive and energetic with me. She wasn't complaining about her mother. Social conditions indicated that there was no reason for drastic action on my part. Aileen would be okay with Wynda, at least for the near future.

Taming my inner pushy salesman would prove to be the real struggle, especially since there was an outer pushy salesman, dad, provoking me relentlessly. In the weeks following the break up, I committed to deepening my spiritual practice. I was going to find a new direction in life, and this time around I would start with a clear idea of virtue. This time around I would be my genuine self, with no hesitation. In that vein, I started reading Trungpa. First I reread *Sacred Path of the Warrior.* Then I went deeper into meditation, with Trungpa's meditation guides *The Path is the Goal* and *Meditation in Action*, and two guides recommended by Trungpa: *The Heart of Buddhist Meditation* by Thera and *Zen Mind, Beginners Mind* by Shunru Suzuki-roshi. These books are widely regarded as some of the greatest Buddhist texts offered to secular Westerners. I had dabbled in meditation ever since discovering Trungpa in college, but with no real technique. I typically sat cross-legged in a quiet, secluded space, usually a scenic outdoor setting, and let my mind soar. Now I wanted to meditate properly, with some guidance, so I located Trungpa's meditation center in Berkeley and received instruction in their meditation open houses and in a course on Introduction to Buddhism, which turned out be five weeknights of just a very-generous lay Kagyu meditation instructor and me.

I ended up staying out of work for three months after the break up in early May. After the few weeks of initial tussling with Wynda, those months became some of the most peaceful moments of my life. Every afternoon, I meditated for thirty minutes with good technique on the deck in my parent's spacious wooded backyard. Most mornings, I would hike up to a secluded spot on Mt. Diablo, where I would meditate and read. The sun-drenched hours spent in meditation on the grassy, wooded hillside baked every drop of hesitation out of me. The sun's warmth became my warmth. I hiked and ran with the mind of mediation too. I tried to bring that lucid state to every solitary moment.

In a nutshell, meditation puts one in touch with one's Buddha-nature, which basically means one's most lucid, ethical, and reasonable self. It typically doesn't connect to one's inner pushy salesman. While practicing meditation each day in the tumult of my conflict with Wynda, I became mindful of a kind of battle in my mind. As I sat following my breath, relaxing my mind and body, a felt sense of calm and confidence arose. For now, at least, I should let Wynda move forward unopposed and I should focus on changing my occupation—I shouldn't waste any energy attacking Wynda. I felt peaceful toward Wynda: just leave her be, that would be best for both of us. I abandoned all adversarial thoughts. Sometimes, you just have to let go. But amidst this peaceful abiding, the inner pushy salesman would intrude: "What if I did this? What if I told her that? What if we? What if…?." Over the three months of daily meditation practice, augmented with meditative hiking, I experienced Buddha-nature take over. When my pushy salesman arose, I labelled the thought "panic" or "impulsive" and simply let it fade away with the next breath. Eventually, those thoughts faded away all together, revealing the mind of peaceful abiding and self-confidence. I put first things first, moved my career change forward, and refrained from any contact with Wynda. I held firm with my parents, who eventually became more accommodating and less provoking.

In this experience of Buddha-nature, becoming mindful of the karmic inner pushy salesman and abandoning it in favor of my most lucid self, I learned a valuable lesson in paranoia and aggression. I'm pointing out a family tradition of the pushy salesman. But I could just call it the cultural tradition of the pushy American: the habitual cultural tendency of going one step too far, of ignoring signs it's time to let go. When we go too far, we get aggressive. Examples include nuclear escalation, stock market crashes, influence pedaling, securities fraud, banking crises, and crimes of passion. We pushy Americans have such difficulty heeding the call of restraint. Our presumption that our every wish should be granted leaves us paranoid and angry when we meet with the slightest obstacle. Sometimes the solution lies in giving up your demand, letting go, and moving onto the next thing...or making do with less... or making the most of what you already have... or doing the generous thing...or trusting in others...etc.

My peaceful abiding lasted for about a year. In that time, I dramatically enhanced my writing skills and began working as a copywriter in the PC industry. I started working in August, three months after the break up and at the end of the three months of rigorous daily meditation practice. I spent the next nine months focused on developing my writing skills and copywriter practice. But then, amazingly, temptation snuck up on me again. Seeing that my earnings were increasing and that I had indeed followed through on my career plans at least minimally, my parents resumed their badgering. They wanted me to petition for an improved custody order.

Clan Custody

During the peaceful year after quitting corporate sales, my parents continued to host weekly visits with Aileen. I moved into an apartment in the Mission District of San Francisco, so I had to commute thirty minutes out to Mt. Diablo to participate, although sometimes dad brought Aileen to visit me in the city. At first, they cajoled me into commuting out to their place for visits. I wanted my parents to end the visits. I wanted no contact, but they wouldn't honor my wishes. They developed a proprietary interest in Aileen, dictating to me what they would do for *their* grandchild. I wanted my parents out of my affairs, but I also felt sorry for Aileen. Visits with my parents would be depressing for her without my presence. I participated out of guilt and compassion, but the visits were actually a lot of fun. My vibrant ethnic-Beat neighborhood, city library, and city parks provided some new sights, and we continued our routine of movies, lunches, and shopping. Maybe visits were a good idea. Maybe I could endure minimal contact with Aileen (and by extension Wynda).

Toward the end of that year, Wynda petitioned for a divorce. I responded by asking my parent's lawyer, the middle-aged male Irish relative who had represented me in the misdemeanor case, to forward all the custody terms of the restraining order into a marriage settlement agreement. Custody was the only area of contention, which I resolved by simply giving in to Wynda's demands. The property settlement proceeded without any acrimony. The custody terms forwarded the grandparent's visits, which my parents coined "grandparent's *rights*," but my intention was to simply walk away and dare my parents to continue. As I mentioned, they continued with the visits and I wound up supporting their *rights* more than ever.

But those visits were limited to one day each weekend. My parents were pushing me to get typical overnight visits every other weekend, without their involvement, and eventually even holidays and vacations. Caving in to them, against all common sense, I filed a petition to modify the custody orders of the divorce. Not surprisingly, this second and final encounter with the family court therapists turned out as dismally as the first. In this meeting with the therapist, I was patient enough for the proceeding to end with a therapist's report submitted to the hearing, whereas in the first meeting I walked out in the first minutes. My meditation practice had brought the ability to engage with people even when I disagreed with them.

Unfortunately, the therapist picked up on the fiction of my

schizophrenia and ran with it, but with some interesting plot twists. She downgraded the diagnosis to bi-polar depression, apparently thinking that would help me suspend disbelief long enough to play along with a plan to placate Wynda. In the therapist's plan, I would submit to a series of elaborate observations and evaluations involving child supervision. The results of these assessments would be provided to Wynda, who would decide whether to modify the custody orders. I'm not being facetious. Wynda's role as judge was carefully laid out in the report. The therapist found no reason to limit my visits with Aileen, but she wanted to generate evidence to placate Wynda. My ex-wife's lawyer responded to the report by declaring to the judge that I was obviously a dangerous psychopath, a threat to self and others at all times, who should be prevented from ever visiting with his child. Astoundingly, just minutes later, that lawyer submitted a child support motion that included a large portion of Wynda's lawyer fees, with the order retroactive to the last day of the restraining order, which was the very order in which Wynda declared me completely, totally insane. The child support order, which followed statutory guidelines, was adopted unopposed. My parent's lawyer, ostensibly representing me, submitted the therapist's report as the next custody order. The judge approved. I didn't care. That was the last and final contact I had with the family court. I had already found the cure I needed: stay away from Wynda...for good. I finally and fully learned to trust my judgement. Now I had a real material reason to stay focused on my career change: a large child support bill, which included my wife's legal fees.

My parents saw that I really meant to walk away. I wanted no more contact with Aileen or Wynda. I even stopped attending Aileen's visits. They panicked. They wanted their rights, and if I wouldn't honor them, they would sue Wynda directly. Their lawyer filed a petition for grandparent's *rights*. I probably shouldn't have, but I signed their motion to acknowledge them as litigants in the matter of my divorce. My parent's got what they wanted, but by turning on me, even though they were litigating under my banner. My parent's established a visitation schedule with overnight visits on alternate weekends, and on holidays and vacations. In return for their grandparent's rights, they endorsed an order banning me from any further contact with Aileen. I was not at the hearing. I have no idea why or how my parents allowed that to happen, but it was characteristic of dad to go one step too far in trying to get what he wanted out of people. I didn't really care. I was done with Wynda, and I was moving forward. I shed not even one tear. As far as I know, those were the final custody orders—a ban on any contact.

My parent's lawyer suggested the possibility of a jury trial for me where he could question Wynda and present expert testimony. I wasn't going to spend that kind of money. That was just more of Wynda's overspending, and I was done with that. Besides, I was sure that the judge would let Wynda's lawyer dominate the trial—the court would lose too much face if the case changed direction in my favor.

The court never heard the one evaluation that I did submit to. About two months after the break up, I met with a psychiatrist from my healthcare provider, a leading California HMO. My healthcare coverage continued for about six months after my resignation. My parents badgered me into the consultation, thinking it might placate Wynda. The psychiatrist and I thoroughly discussed my situation. The doctor concluded that there was no evidence of mental illness and no need for treatment. My parents weren't satisfied. They wanted pills or some kind of other treatment to show Wynda. They urged me to seek a second opinion, which was allowed by the HMO. I met with a second psychiatrist, who concluded that there was no evidence of mental illness and no need for treatment. I asked about individual psychotherapy. The doctor advised against it. He thought the best course would be simply to move forward with my career plans, but he reluctantly made a recommendation when I told him that my parents were badgering me.

I followed up on the recommendation. It was a well-established family services clinic near Burlingame. I participated in thirty sessions with a marriage and family therapist at my expense, with the benefit of a subsidy from United Way. The therapist was an attractively curvy forty-something White woman with a full-round face, bright eyes, flowing sandy-blond long hair, and flower-child fashion statement with leather sandals or oxfords, long pleated cotton skirts, and handcrafted cotton tops and sweaters. She and I mostly had heated discussions in which she tried to convince me to follow her advice and I gently rebuffed it. She definitely wasn't a Rogerian. She would probably call herself an eclectic, which is the scientific word for mothering the client. I already had a mother, and they were amazingly similar in their approach. The therapy, which was based on my written goals, focused on making genuine choices in the future—living with some direction. To that effect, the therapist first advised me to move away from my father immediately: he was pushy and mildly psychotic. Second, she advised me to pursue my most genuine career ambition, which at that point would have involved renewing my past interests in child psychology. Third, forestall involvement with Wynda and custody matters until my most genuine career ambition had been realized. I would typically respond by saying that I could handle taking things in stages, that I could focus on making money while gradually working toward more genuine motives, and that I was getting better at containing dad's meddling. Occasionally, she would respond to my resistance with a mild shout: "Until you're a child psychologist, I'll consider you depressed. Do whatever it takes to make it happen! Don't compromise!" I guess she didn't go for nonjudgmental communications and empathetic listening. At home, mom was saying, "You must be depressed if you won't work in sales to please Wynda."

For all the years since that summer, I have followed the psychiatrists' advice. No treatment needed. Most of my crazy behavior can be attributed to metaphysical or spiritual causes, and I am on pretty good terms with the law and society. I could never say I was normal, and I don't intend ever to become so. But I am pretty clear about who I am and why I act the way I do, and that seems to be a sufficient substitute for normal.

Mom and dad expanded their visits with Aileen as allowed by the improved grandparent's *rights*. At first, I shied away, attending visits only intermittently and typically just part of one afternoon at their house. After all, I was technically banned from contact. But eventually, I arrived early each day for breakfast and left late each night after tucking Aileen in or saying goodbye when Wynda picked her up. I knew what my parents were up to. They wanted to draw me in, get me feeling guilty. That is why they were stretching the limits of their visitation agreement by including me. My parents, and probably Wynda, thought they were sucking me in, but this time I drew them in. I wasn't going to engage the court in the absurd proposition of proving that I was sane in response to Wynda's complaints. Once one heads down that slippery slope, I felt, there might be no end to the demands for various cures. Instead, I might triumph in the court of poetic justice, by living life with direction, as a warrior, and hopefully some of that would rub off on Aileen. I didn't yet have a plan for how to live, but I knew how I didn't want to live: I was saying no to Wynda's and the court's plan to cure me of my personality.

The result of my defiance was Aileen growing up in custody of the Bartlett clan as opposed to just me. Neither my parents nor I ever filed another custody motion. But over the thirteen years of the divorce agreement, Aileen had a nourishing and dignified relationship with my family and me. I continued to increase my involvement in my parent's visits, until gradually my presence and relationship with Aileen became the prime mover. Eventually, they became my visits, orchestrated and supported by my parents. By the time Aileen started high school, I had led everyone into forgetting that the court had ever been involved.

Aileen was the only grandchild for most of the visitation agreement. She was sixteen when her first Bartlett cousin was born. She was a petite and perky lass, with a trim yet athletic physique, lustrous short reddish-blond hair in a bob cut, creamy-fair skin, soft oval facial features with pronounced almond-shaped brown eyes, gently-broad brow and chin, ample lips, and expressive confident smile. In her school-age years, her fashion statement revolved around resurrected denim trends of the seventies with a variety of plain and designer flairs (especially embroidered), jean jackets, and all manner of designer cotton blouses, with leather boots or oxfords. She basically continued with her denim lifestyle as she grew to maturity. She loved pop music, Disney, Nickelodeon, all manner of cartoons and animated series, Dr. Who, anime, manga, choir, her notebook PC and the internet, her iPod, mammals domesticated and wild, her girlfriends, and her family on both sides. She was cute, and she could have easily joined the precocious cast of one of her favorite Disney Channel shows. She attended neighborhood public schools.

Aileen's visits became a natural focal point for my siblings and me to stay in touch with each other and my parents. My siblings were quite attentive and kind, supporting Aileen with valuable gifts such as clothing, electronics, and outings, and perhaps more precious, their companionship. Holidays with Aileen in attendance were celebrated by the whole family with maximum joy.

My parents developed a routine of traveling with Aileen once or twice a year. She joined them on trips to Seattle, Hawaii, Boston, Mexico, and Chicago. My siblings and I joined some of these trips. In high school, a week of each vacation visit was spent at an upstate summer vacation rental. The entire family gathered in a large waterfront house, at Russian River or Lake Almanor, for water skiing, canoeing, kayaking, swimming, barbecues, sightseeing, and just taking it easy in a serene setting. For the second week of the vacation, I spent time alone with Aileen in the Bay Area visiting our favorite haunts in Berkeley and San Francisco. Some of the grandparent trips were to big family weddings, adding to the clan dimension, and some included extended family. Aileen's loyal Irish grandmother made sure Aileen was included in the extended family.

My emphasis was on outings in the Bay Area: museums, theater, restaurants, cinema, books, music, scenic parks, beaches, zoos, city pools, restaurants, and others. When Aileen reached adolescence, we started to hold these outings alone more, but sometimes it was nice to have a family member along too. San Francisco and the Bay Area are incredible cultural, geographical, and educational playgrounds. San Francisco's Japantown was one of Aileen's favorite outings. She was a minor Japanophile. She liked finding manga and stationary supplies from the source, and of course the food. She really enjoyed the exotic multi-cultural city scene. At all times, and to this day, we have always been able to connect and communicate, probably because we spent so much time alone in her toddler and preschool years, so the outings were quite pleasant.

Our time together was a delight. I enjoyed watching her develop tastes, have new experiences, and mature with the passing years. I primarily tried to support and encourage her, and share a little wisdom without demanding anything of her. I felt it was best to let Wynda be the authority figure. I was authoritative and a proper role model, but I carefully left the micromanagement to Wynda. I basically convinced my parents to take the same approach. We were the visiting clan, and I was the visiting parent. Wynda was the boss. This sometimes caused a culture clash with my parents, who felt Wynda was a little casual in matters of manners and decorum, but I trained them to be more accommodating and less judgmental, which was no small feat. I think we did the best we could for Aileen, given that Wynda, a mildly pushy individual, was her mother.

At some point, after about seven years of informal clan custody, it might have been a good time to revisit the custody agreement and put the reality of the visits on paper, with me as the center of attention. But I was wary of the court and its plan to cure me. I figured they would pick up exactly where they had left off, regardless of how much I had accomplished since the last hearing seven years ago. In the last hearing, the therapist began her report with the sentence, "Robert quit his job at world-dominating software company," even though that event had occurred eighteen months prior. Despite the passing of seven years, I predicted the report would start with the same sentence: he quit his big corporate job without his wife's permission—he must be crazy!! I planned to live the rest of my life without my wife's permission. Besides, the court probably wouldn't have accepted losing face as a happy occasion.

I felt court was a Pandora's Box. I did pause in the middle of the clan years to assess the impact on Aileen. The clan was doing much more for her than I could have done alone. My parents and siblings rallied around Aileen to protect her from this conflict between Wynda and me. Quite often, my parents and siblings would fund an event that I felt was beyond my means and still include me in the event. Aileen and I were receiving a lot of support. My parents maintained a home away from home for Aileen—toys, games, crafts, video collection, private bedroom. It would have been the sofa bed at my place. Mom always made full, proper meals when Aileen was in town, often inviting guests. It would have been prepared foods and modest restaurants with me: I was strapped from paying child support and changing my occupation. Clan custody was almost like raising royalty—Aileen was treated like a princess. And it was nice to have additional influences in her life besides just mine—two hands are better than one, it takes a village, etc.

Clan custody was better than me alone, especially since changing my occupation was my priority. I just had to accept one difference from other fathers. I would never be the pushy American father. The decision to stick with clan custody had echoes of meditation: just let go of the impulse to control and dominate things that are essentially free....stop demanding that the world conform to your fantasies of conquest....embrace love and support without control and domination. Breath out the pushy American, breath in the tolerant, understanding American. Clan custody was working for everyone, apparently even Wynda, who at least was not complaining, so I found a way to keep my ego in check.

Keen observers might claim that I'm just rationalizing my passivity, that I'm just cheap and lazy, that pushy, domineering fathers are the best. I'll submit one more bit of evidence in favor of my inscrutable approach: single mother karma.

About four years after we split up, Wynda submitted a divorce document showing that she had received a $10,000 permanent increase in annual salary, which was a thirty-percent increase in one raise after three years of being grossly underpaid. She was still underpaid, but they were getting closer. Apparently, the retailer's bankruptcy was progressing, freeing up funds for selective pay increases. I was glad for Wynda and Aileen: with her mother's help, Wynda wasn't doing too badly at single motherhood. I was also glad to have divorced the junk-bond magnate—at least with the raise he was starting to pay his own bills.

Unfortunately, the raise came too late to bail us out of our own debt crisis. Wynda had prevailed on spending decisions in which she had pushed me into "doing the right thing": new car instead of pre-owned, big wedding instead of modest, etc. My resigning jeopardized her ability to pay those debts. I wasn't worried, because I planned to return to work in some other occupation than sales, as I told her. But to her, we were in a grudge match. Her basically kidnapping our child and sudden renting of our relationship, and eventual acrimonious divorce, virtually guaranteed a bankruptcy. In fact, I insisted on a Chapter 7 as part of the divorce settlement: Wynda was the petitioner in the divorce. Wynda and her junk-bond magnate could both get a fresh start in their blessed union. The troubling part of this debt crisis was that Wynda did have a way to continue paying those debts. All she had to do was stay loyal to the full vows that she had invested so much in at our big Episcopal church wedding. Instead, within just seven days of the slightest difficulty, which existed only in her impatient mind, she gave up on her vows. Until the slightest difficulty do us part?

A bit of anthropology might be instructive at this point. When Wynda was in middle school, her parents went through an archetypal seventies divorce. Dad continued on with his upper-middle class life as an administrator in federal civil service. Mom plunged into poverty with three of the family's four children in her sole custody. Mom took the daughters, and dad took the son, who was the youngest. The family lived in Fremont at the time. Mom and the three daughters moved from the family's single family home into an apartment in a working-class part of town. Mom found a job as an office assistant in an electrical contractor in town—it was a small family-run business. There she took up the life of the workaholic, serving as the company's general manager while still collecting wages appropriate for an office assistant. Mom worked there for most of her career, until the company's financial problems drove her back out into the workforce in the early nineties. The husband played rough in divorce negotiations, leaving mom with only nominal child support. That electrical contractor, on the other hand, supported mom as she got her children through high school and probably made her feel more important than the husband had. Husbands and fathers will leave, but exploitive bosses will love you and stick with you to the bitter end—just don't ever ask them to pay you what you deserve.

Following her mother's example, Wynda had more faith in the workaholic way than in me, her husband. Husbands leave, but exploitive employers will sustain you till the end. There was a general tone of distrust toward men in my mother-in-law's household. Even her male employer, a father figure who she was quite loyal to, was seen as incomplete and lazy. When I asked Wynda to leave her exploitive employer, I was asking her to give up the faith she had inherited from her mother, and thus she moved me out and her mother in. And this faith had deep roots. Wynda's mom learned it from her mother, who had been a single mother upstate in lumber country. You can't trust a husband, but you can count on an exploitive employer (just don't ask them to pay you what you deserve).

Wynda started our divorce by fleeing with our child. Her mother started hers by spiriting her children away to her upstate mother's place, in what was depicted as a blatant ploy to get the upper hand in custody negotiations. Wynda's father tolerated the situation until things were settled in court, mostly to his advantage. I, on the other hand, enlisted the police department to retrieve Wynda and Aileen: I was worried about Aileen's safety. Wynda reacted to this setback by smearing me in family court, but at least the disappearing act was over, and at least there was court supervision of her parenting. In just a couple of weeks after she ran away, I understood the change that had come over Wynda. She had succumbed to single-mother karma. Something in her mind had triggered a reenactment of her mother's life. She had become inspired to relive her mother's life, and there was no way to stop her. From that point forward, I would become just another one of *those men*. None of the things I had done in our relationship to refrain from being one of *those men* would be acknowledged. It was like she had amnesia. And she found a ready ally in the family court, who apparently viewed all men as *those men*.

By about three months after our separation, I had become resigned to the reenactment. At first, I was maniacally angry at being stripped of my individuality. I had been a good warrior in marriage: my approach was hard work, nonjudgmental communication, and generosity. Both Wynda and I had grown so much. We had done so many incredible things, with minimal contention or conflict. I had helped her materially get started in life, and she had helped me domestically, by modelling some sense of a household. But after her first day in court, it was like we were strangers, like her memory had been erased: no need to remember the particulars of someone who was just another one of *those men.*

My anger at being reduced down to a stereotype brought one of my first experiences in Buddhist mindfulness. It was a lesson in paranoia and aggression—my own. Having my life erased—all that I had learned, believed, and done—and replaced with a profile derived from *those men,* sent me into deep mental pain, a blind rage. At first, I tried to convince Wynda that she was thinking too fast by telling her about my plans. But she just ran away in response to that. After she ran, my parents kept exhorting me to sue, to start an expensive jury trial. They wanted me to save Aileen from the vixen Wynda. They wanted me to be an Anglo dominator. They were angry and wanted results. In the midst of these dynamic pressures, I made a deliberate decision to pursue my spirituality with some discipline. It was finally time to plant my own two feet firmly on this earth. I started reading Trungpa every morning plus hiking and meditating for a few hours. A wet spring at my parent's place near Mt. Diablo State Park provided many beautiful trails within walking distance or a short drive. I slowly perceived the insubstantial nature of my anger. It was the result of fixed, egotistical ideas about fatherhood and about how to handle conflict and loss. Let go of those ideas, or at least relax around them and question them, and the anger dissipates. In a moment of insight, I decided how to proceed. In my marriage, I had lived by nonjudgmental communications, generosity, calm, creativity, and patience: I committed to handling divorce in the same way. Once I had made this commitment, my mind and body became as quiet as a still pond.

Adversarial proceedings are antagonistic to nonjudgmental communications, patience, and loving-kindness. But those were the only solutions available to me, so I boycotted the family court. If there was going to be any justice, it wouldn't be had in the family court, where disposing of men's lives was a routine political expedient. I went for about a year with no contact with either the court or Wynda. I simply went my own way. I spent my time becoming my most-disciplined, healthiest self: studying Buddhism, formally learning to meditate, taking long solitary hikes in the weekday quiet of summer, running five miles a night, reading great literature, and working on my writing skills. Instead of vainly striving for control against the court's prejudice, like one of *those men* might, I gave up on control. Wynda was doing alright on her own, as I heard in updates from my parents, so no need to challenge her. My approach to this conflict would be to walk away from it, thus rendering it impotent: moving on as opposed to an egotistical struggle. I was focused on becoming the most authentic person I could be. That was the example I wanted to set for Aileen.

The Spiritual No

Starting in August 1995, three months after the break up, and continuing for three years afterward, I found a way to turn my interest in writing skills into a job as a copywriter. I was with a small marcom agency in Fremont focused on PC technology. When I began, I was a newly separated thirty-three-year-old father. When I left, I was a thirty-six-year-old divorcé with a child-support payment. On one hand, these were tumultuous years of acrimonious family court proceedings, painful separations, and family feuds. On the other hand, these were some of the most joyful and fruitful years of my life. What allowed me to thrive despite the struggles? This was the time of life when I discovered the power of No.

First, I was saying no to the snobbery and materialism of the suburbs. I moved into the Mission District of San Francisco. At that point, in 1995 through 1998, the neighborhood was still predominantly Mexican, augmented by other immigrants from Central and South America. It was a Latino neighborhood. Most of the residents worked in the city's service industries, especially hotels and restaurants located downtown about two miles north. The neighborhood's architecture was characterized by apartment buildings (tenement style), attractive row houses divided into single family, two flats and duplexes, and a minority of detached single family houses. There were a couple of thoroughfares that ran the length of the neighborhood, north to south, which hosted an incredible array of restaurants, cafes, bars, clubs, grocery vendors, and merchants of all sorts.

Most of the Mission's architectural style came from a turn of the century surge of Victorian forms in the late 1800s and early 1900s. In its heyday, it was a quite proper neighborhood of the Irish and Italian Catholic working class and emerging middle class. Interestingly, it was the south end of downtown and its political trajectory reminded me of Chicago's South Side. The blocks were dense with Catholic churches and schools, many abandoned in the nineties. The cultural landscape had been defined by White flight and immigrant opportunism. When I moved in, it was considered an area of urban blight and crime, but gradually the crime rate plummeted, gentrification set in, and as of this writing, it is one of the most expensive neighborhoods in America. In an interesting inversion of White flight, the corporate youth, fleeing housing inflation near their Silicon Valley employers, have flooded the Mission and now commute thirty to fifty miles *out* to the suburbs to work each day. The Latinos, still predominantly in the service industries, moved to towns thirty to fifty miles outside the city, and now commute *in* every day to work in downtown. So, everyone picked up a long commute, making the Bay Area one of the most traffic-congested and polluted areas of the country. Trickle down prosperity apparently isn't the simple phenomenon it might seem in the land of unlimited opportunity.

My move to the Mission was of course an affront to the paranoia of my White-flight upbringing, and that paranoia was very much alive in Bay Area suburbs too. I was in fact motivated by the higher-order challenge of living behind enemy lines. But on a practical level, I was making common cause with the Latinos. Both immigrants and I were refugees. I was a refugee on the run from the status-seeking, social-climbing ways of the corporate set. The Mission offered me a chance to go underground, a place where the limited means of my career change could support me. I was broke and needed cheap rent, cheap groceries, cheap transportation, cheap entertainment, and a refreshing bit of bohemian reverie.

I lived in a small one-bedroom apartment on Bartlett Street, near 24th Street and its BART station (i.e. subway). The street name was random chance. I walked into a neighborhood realtor and they had a vacancy that fit my needs perfectly. I believe the street was named after Mayor Washington Montgomery Bartlett of 1883-1887, who was not from my family tree but was from a cohort of English settlers similar to my ancient grandparent Puritans who landed in Massachusetts in 1640. It might be interesting to note that these Puritans were Methodists, the most egalitarian of the English Protestants. I, like my ancestors, landed in a new world, looking for opportunity, in the spirit of rebellion.

In another interesting parallel, Washington Bartlett's occupation before entering public service was printer and news publisher, and thus he was in the publishing and advertising game like my father. He never attended college, but he learned the printing business from his father who owned a newspaper. Washington Bartlett was also a California state senator from 1873 to 1877 and Governor of California in 1887 for nine months before he died prematurely from an illness. Amazingly, Governor Bartlett's inauguration speech contains almost all of the legislative controversies of our present elections: limits on immigration, the global workforce, education reform (extensively), regulating corporate finance, water districts, regulating utilities, state militia, national defense, and government finances. His views on education were focused on providing industrial workers with the skills they would need to hold their own in a marketplace increasingly shaped by international trade. He was with the Democratic Party when he ran for mayor and then governor. His campaign slogan had been "Honesty in Politics."

My three-story apartment building was basically an upscale tenement. It had about twelve units. It was on a quiet, residential street, and the façade was Italianate Victorian brownstone, with a sweeping arched center entryway. Most of my neighbors were Latino families, living with four or five members arrayed artfully in the same limited space I had to myself. Each family was typically a mother, father, a couple of children, and a grandparent or two. A main reason I took this unit was the political implications of the location. Immediately to the west, a mild influx of adventurous Whites (with some minorities interspersed) were creating an amiable bohemia or even a kind of working class renaissance. Immediately to the east, Latinos were trying to hold on to one of the best refuges they had left in the Bay Area, although immigrant flight was starting to gain momentum. Bartlett Street was literally a demilitarized zone between these two factions. I appreciated the middle ground, where I could honor and enjoy both sides.

I freely traveled both sides. For instance, the best grocery supermarket within walking distance was an independent local chain a couple of blocks into the Latino side. My late-night taqueria of last resort was on the east side, along with many other really pleasant eateries on Mission Street, the main thoroughfare of the ethnic culture. I would stop in the ethnic produce markets. When I first moved in, and was really poor, I shopped with Latinos in the discount stores and dollar markets on Mission Street. I even bought a few pairs of shoes at Payless. I had never been in places like that before, but I found what I needed and survived on very low wages in my first year. We all rode the BART every day, which carried me all the way out to Fremont, which was the last stop. The availability of public transportation—rail, bus, and taxi—was a big attraction for all of us, especially since it opened up all the resources of the city. I bought an old Dodge pick-up truck from a friend, since I had liquidated my autos in the divorce. The truck was only good enough for limited driving—I needed public transportation.

On the west side, which could be called the hipster zone, I traveled Valencia Street most often, just around the corner from my apartment. It was the major thoroughfare of the hipster side. I was a vegetarian in those years, as part of taking my spiritual life seriously. There were two nice small natural foods stores within two blocks of my place. The closest one, right on my corner, had a selection of fresh organic vegetables, a host of canned and packaged vegetarian foods, and a dairy case. Both of these establishments were on the vanguard of the organic foods movement—this was grass roots nutrition, before organic went upscale. The nine blocks running north from 24th Street on my corner up to 16th Street were the defining cultural niches of the neighborhood, both for Mission and Valencia. Valencia had the most incredible array of modest eateries in those nine blocks: Indian, Thai, Tapas, Vietnamese, Pakistani, Nigerian, Ecuadoran, Mexican, Peruvian, Greek, Italian, Mediterranean, California Nouvelle Cuisine, Diners, Pub Grub, Pizza, and Burgers. All offered modest prices, many were pretty good fare, and it was good hunting for a vegetarian. Hipster haven! I had many pleasant outings on Valencia with suburban and out-of-town friends, who were inspired to relax their paranoia and enjoy the reverie. Most of them lived corporate lives, but they still weren't afraid to indulge their free-spirited side.

Even in the gentrified Mission, this neighborhood has been the true home of coffee house culture. Valencia maybe has more coffee houses now than it did in my day. Two of my favorites were Muddy's at 24th Street and Café Macondo, which was at 16th and Valencia. Macondo was completely ramshackle. It must have outfitted itself from Goodwill. Or maybe they scrounged the classifieds looking for old dining room furniture. I loved the hipster rawness. It had a third-world quality to it. It was replaced by a sports bar for the corporate youth in the gentrification. My most favorite by default, meaning I frequented it more than any other, was Café La Boheme on 24th Street between Mission and Valencia— fifty yards from my apartment. The establishment's name and concept originated from the neighborhood's Catholic working-class era. In my day, it was recently taken over by a Lebanese immigrant who was raising school-age children with his wife. At first, he ran the place on a shoestring, and it had the Mission third-world quality, but he slowly cleaned the place up, mostly by working all the shifts himself, including evening hours. When you live in a third-story one bedroom of a wood-frame tenement, your living space expands to include certain essential services, the café being the most essential. It's the place you go when the hot (heat rises), humid quarters threaten to give you the jitters. Or you just need some place slightly less boring than your apartment while you recover from your last child-support payment. You read your novel in the café, because another hour in that apartment and you're going to lose it. You breakfast on your bagel and coffee (strong city brew) there on Saturday morning, because you know the congenial buzz of the room and the street scene will carry your thoughts away from that Friday deadline that you put off until Monday. At first, survival drives you to the café, and then it becomes a pleasant comfort zone.

I was probably one of the quieter patrons, but I got to know the proprietor and his small staff, and I made a few acquaintances among the patrons. Most of the patrons were aging Latino hipsters, and although bilingual, they often chose Spanish. They were hip: they read and even sometimes published poetry, kept up with politics, and enjoyed each other's company. Even though only thirty-three, I guess I felt more at home among the aging refugees than among the youth-oriented crowd on Valencia. It probably had something to do with child-support payments. In a way, the proprietor and I were on parallel paths, living the small-business life and supporting children. He had a quiet-amid-the-storm quality that emanated out to the space. At only eight hundred square feet, with about thirty-five seats, the café was an intimate, calm refuge of refugees, plus a few adventurous White youths.

Bookstores were an emblematic and enigmatic feature of Valencia. There were five bookstores in the nine blocks between 24th and 16th. Three were commensurate with the neighborhood's third-world tone, and two were actually somewhat typical retail establishments. They served English-speaking readers. This passion for reading contradicts the usual view of the working class. But the Mission was host to the uppity working class. It was a bastion of egalitarianism, where brain power had been liberated from the fetters of income and status. This was a most-American bohemia, where intellectual development was celebrated among even the most ordinary of denizens. Everywhere one looked, fellow travelers were embarked on various projects of self-improvement. Benjamin Franklin would have been proud. As a writer, I gravitated toward the bookstores, but there was also a budding alternative arts scene, with drama venues and galleries, all with the Mission's characteristically free-spirited approach.

Latino occupations were mainly in service areas such as janitorial, housekeeping, food service, and restaurants. A fair number of hipsters were in those occupations too. But there was also an upward mobile sector, in white-collar occupations such as university teaching assistants, grad students, school teachers, retail, nurses, health-care technicians, and information technology. Most residents were entry level, but occupation was not the defining factor. To be a Mission Hipster was primarily to be White without the Supremacist. We enjoyed the tolerance discount. We lived downtown in one of the world's most glamorous cities, with access to all the glories of cosmopolitan life, but at rent lower than the typical bar tab uptown. Hipsters were overachievers without the aim of snobbery or classism. On any given day, the cafes were full of writers toiling away at short stories, scripts, and novels, students grappling with texts, artists hanging their works, and other artistic collaborations—typically while maintaining a day job. Everyone was mad with youthful hopes and creativity. The hipster zone was the kind of neighborhood where the coffee houses were full at midnight but the bars had already emptied out. The bars had their place, but a quiet one, definitely not in the foreground.

One might envision hipsters wearing Member's Only jackets, satin gray slacks and shirt, and grey leather shoes. Not in the Mission. The hipster fashion unstatement was preppy New England. Levis, plaid shirts (often flannel), parkas, and boots for men. Women were exceptionally well covered, with cardigans, cable knits, turtlenecks, and parkas on top, fullish skirts with woolen or cotton tights or Levis below, with boots, most likely Doc Martins or hiking. Basically, preppy with modesty, decorum without chauvinism.

Crime was still a tangible presence for both Latinos and hipsters, but it had been pushed to the outskirts of the neighborhood. At the corner of Mission and 16th Street, an area once dubbed Heroin Alley, addicts, dealers, pimps, and prostitutes carried on with brazen candor. But that crime zone had been reduced down to less than a quarter block, and mainstream residents could easily pass through it undeterred. Deep in the ethnic side, about three full blocks east of my place, youth gangs were still present, and occasionally fell into violent rivalries. In that same area, the Mexican mafia had a drug wholesaling operation, observable to anyone who cared to notice their easily discernable routines. But both these groups, gangs and mafia, operated by stealth. They almost never came out in numbers before dark, and really only affected about a two square block area. Gentrification, both hipster and Latino, had cornered them and sent them undercover.

In my three years there, crime decreased rapidly in the neighborhood, especially drug dealing. The hipsters actively compelled the police to drive crime away from hipster territory. For instance, they successfully petitioned the District Attorney to remove all payphones from Valencia, a step that reduced violence related to gang rivalries, since the phones were used for peddling drugs. Gang and mafia activity were gone from nearly all hipster areas. I was never touched by crime or harassed in any way.

My main impression of Latino culture, where I came in contact with it, was mother culture. Mothers shopping for groceries, at the laundromat, on a stroll with the children and grandmother after church, preparing costumes for first communion, cooking for the family, working in the local businesses, and heading out to a shift downtown. Dad was at work, most of the time. But he could be seen cleaned up for Sunday or maybe taking the family out for a weekend meal in one of the neighborhood's restaurants.

The overall Latino scene was rural. One could easily mistake the neighborhood for a small town in agricultural San Joaquin Valley. Men wore jeans, button-down plaid shirts (flannel or western), parkas, and all manner of boots. My style was pretty much identical to theirs, making the neighborhood a shelter for me while I hid from expensive corporate fashions. At work, Latino mothers dressed like the men (depending on their job), but on the weekends donned dresses in rural style, tapered at the waist and bust, full at the hem line below the knee. When men dressed up, they sported crisply pressed boot-legged jeans, western shirt, fine polished leather cowboy boots, Stetson, and sometimes a vest or waistcoat. Some men started drifting toward the Anglo two-piece suit, but usually with some sort of Southwestern flourish such as wide lapels. Grooming was close-cropped hair and clean shaven for men, and long-straight hair with bows and light cosmetics for the women. Children pretty much followed their parents on issues of style. A block up Bartlett, at 23rd

Street, a middle school attracted families to reside nearby, so we had a lot of young children playing about the street. The mothers were a study in spiritual warriorship. Despite decrements in status and income, they never lost their grip on decorum and dignity. No joking, they made a strong impression on me, and on the dads too.

A few Latino nightclubs were located on Mission near 24th. They seemed to mostly serve out-of-towners looking for a night on the town. You could tell patrons were on the town by the way they were dressed up and by their inexplicable presence on a week night in a working-class area. The mafia was reputed to have a hand in the entertainment available in those establishments. I guess they call it the Wild West for a reason.

Latinos were hip. There was a major branch of the public library on Bartlett, practically next door to me, which was quite busy and vital for adults and children. They were politically savvy, and there was a theme of civic virtue and social activism. The mayor definitely saw the Latinos as an important constituency. Latino Christianity was flourishing, but with a twist. Pentecostal and other evangelical churches were springing up as fast as Catholic ones were retiring due to lack of participation. Every Saturday evening, hipsters heading home from work or out for the evening collided with Latino worshipers pouring into evangelical churches on Valencia; this weekly mob scene was a true culture clash, but peace was maintained. All things considered, the Latinos were just as energetic and resourceful as the hipsters, maybe more so. They were kind of hip too, and maybe there was a tacit common ground that kept everyone peacefully coexisting.

Keen observers may detect a remnant of the Beat Era. In fact, local media outlets and other cultural organs heralded the Mission District as the last refuge of Beat culture, or possibly a renaissance of youthful creativity. A key principle of Beat literature was to liberate intellectual activity from income and status, and the Mission was definitely home to that spirit, and maybe even a wholesome revision of it. But the hipsters unwittingly paved the way for White inverse flight. The safety of the hipster haven became the catalyst for an incomprehensible return of the White upper middle class. Now, there is barely a trace left of the hipster movement. The current neighborhood reminds me more of Manhattan's Upper West Side than of the Beat Era. I wonder what Benjamin Franklin would think of that. The Red Coats are coming! The Red Coats are coming! Hipster territory falls to invasion by global investor master race! Egalitarianism suffers a setback. Beer, burgers, pizza, and sports bars in. Intellectual development and self-improvement out!!

Developing Skills

After saying no to the social climbing of the suburbs by moving to Bartlett Street in the Mission District, I said no to living without the skills needed to live with direction. Specifically, I addressed my lack of confidence in my writing skills. In the three months of spiritual practice following my resignation from the world-dominating software company, I spent some of my time becoming a career changer. First, I inventoried my interests without too many worries about the pragmatic concerns of the moment (i.e. money). Second, I projected a path towards realizing those interests, with concerns about money added back in. I actually sat down with the book *What Color is Your Parachute* by Richard Nelson Bolles, which, even though it was first published in 1970, was still a ground breaking guide in that it openly acknowledged and empowered the desire for change that many workers were experiencing in the mid-nineties, like a career liberation movement. I worked through the guidance step-by-step. I considered that process a spiritual one: living with direction involves the sheer nerve to appraise your situation in the light of day without the shadows of wishful thinking or impulsive guesswork.

While inventorying my interests, the arguments with my

psychotherapist, the one my parents goaded me into seeing after the break up, echoed strongly, although I'm not thrilled to admit it. It was also probably all that meditation and time in nature—it tends to wash away the camouflage of self-deception. It tends to wash away everything but the real you. Given my druthers, I had to admit that I wanted to work with the raw material of my life as a gifted behavior problem. The ideas of accommodation and tolerance were present in my thinking, as I had experienced them in my Appalachian camp counselor days, and also the ideas of high expectations, routine, and time management. Moreover, the role of understanding, of how one's perception of an individual changes when you seek to understand them as opposed to merely impose your demands on them. Basically, I was thinking about becoming a psychologist, counselor, or teacher of some sort who could help young people experiencing problems in meeting expectations. I thought maybe I could find a way out for young adults who were feeling like a loser—a way of finding their Ashe, their instinct to thrive, the strength of their true self. And an occupation like that might help me investigate that question I seemed born with: Could there be more to manhood than status seeking and social climbing? Paranoia and aggression?

I felt that my experience as a gifted behavior problem was, in fact, pretty good raw material. I had progressed from being the worst student in my high school to studying at two pretty credible universities and graduating from one with above average grades. I studied most of the milestone U.S. Supreme Court cases and other aspects of democracy dharma. I explored a quantitative, rigorous view of business. I held a degree in psychology from the school of science. I worked in the groundbreaking fields of PC technology and networking. I didn't take them over, but I was a credible eyewitness. All launched from the humble perch of below average grades in high school. I knew a few things about personal transformation: what sparks it, what inhibits it, and what throws it off course.

Starting with the aspiration of helping those at odds with the demands of the master race, I formulated a strategy for changing my occupation. The change would have to be incremental, in gradual steps. Child support and visitation were in my life, and I needed to face squarely the need for income. I wasn't going to win Father of the Year, but Aileen, I thought, would fare better with me in her life, even if it was only from the metaphysical advantage of knowing her father loved her. Most occupations in psychology require training at the graduate-school level, and similarly in education and law, which were other areas I was considering. So, mostly for the sake of fatherhood, I would need to find graduate training that offered part-time or other modified study to accommodate working. Or, as a last resort, I could maybe settle for lower-status occupations that required less investment but still met the mission of my aspiration. In an analysis free of social climbing, settling for less isn't seen as a threat, and sometimes there is real efficiency in it.

My interest in improving my writing skills arose as a first step in this pragmatic scheme of change. If I undertook graduate study, I would need to write essays, articles, and exams— with speed and accuracy. In undergraduate courses, my writing prowess had come from a place of passion and audacity, with skills at about sixth grade. Early on, at Stony Brook, my advanced composition professor tried to warn me about the handicap this lack of skill might pose. In what now forms an auspicious coincidence, the course focused on reading American education theorists and then developing theses and essays in response to their arguments. For my final essay, I rejected Dewey's proposition that the public school could be the moral training ground of society. I argued that the pluralistic character of American society, especially in light of the immigration-driven multi-cultural reality of the eighties, which had actually evolved into *multiculturalism*, indicated that there would be no moral consensus for the schools to teach, and instead they would have to resort to a lowest-common-denominator view of culture based on science. In my grade, the professor commended me for an ingenious argument that hit the proverbial nail on the head, but closed with a scolding that my grammar, style, and spelling were atrocious. She urged me to come to grips with these important elements of scholarship. My grade was visually reduced from an A to a B to indicate the demerit.

I heeded the professor's advice. When I transferred to Cal State, I took a deliberate step backward to introductory composition. There, my professor excoriated me for trying to dazzle him with fanciful arguments. This class is about form, he imprecated while admonishing me, so you better get down to it if you want to pass!! I heeded his scolding too. I applied myself in his class, but more importantly, I kept the course text and continued to refer to it for years afterwards. I slowly built up a selection of writer's quick-reference guides for ongoing support. When it came time to take Cal State's graduation writing test, which I used as an occasion for further study, I passed with ease. My grammar and style were at about tenth grade when I graduated.

At Cal State, and then in the Mission District, addressing this deficit in a critical skill was part of my emerging warriorship. As Trungpa taught, and I have come to believe, the nonjudgmental and open-minded warrior sees setbacks and failures not as something to fear, but rather as information about what steps to take next. Besides this profound reasoning, my Mission years provided me with another, perhaps more powerful motive: the need for cheap entertainment. The written word became a hobby in those years, an effortlessly all-consuming one, which was less expensive than say rebuilding sports cars or bicycles. The hours of solitary pouring over the books suited the child-support paying lifestyle. Besides, I wasn't pouring over the books, it was more like discovering and interacting with them.

I started with self-help workbooks commonly published

for business professionals and students of English as a second language. One can typically find these in the reference section of popular bookstores. Then I progressed to books written for writers and other scholars of language arts, best described as scholarly books. You have to dig a little deeper to find those books, like in the "Writers" section of a major bookstore. Then I went on to writers' guides—professional advice for those who want to write essays, articles, and books for publication, and advice for marketing communications. Toward the end of the three years, I excelled in college-level courses in news writing, copy editing, and creative journalism. Inspired by warriorship, I followed a lu-nyen-lha approach to my autodidact grammarian studies, meaning that I followed a natural hierarchy, or taxonomy, of learning grammar and style. In other words, I went back to basics (lu) and carefully climbed (nyen) my way to craftsman (lha).

I learned so many aspects of grammar and style, with grammar being the favorite, as most writers will report. I would have to write my own book on those subjects to capture the breadth of the experience. I acquired literally hundreds of rules and axioms for working with English. But to give a general impression, one formative learning experience could be said to have really set the rest in motion for me. It was in the early years, the self-help phase, but the business writers' guide aimed to truly sharpen the practitioner's prose. The guide followed an unusual theory, at least to my neophyte sensibilities: Verbs Make the Writer. Writers, most of whom understand the underlying forces of our English language, are privy to the artistic and rhythmic aspects of language that may appear as simply prosaic to the amateur: in other words, they know how verbs energize the language. Basically, I was led into a thorough appreciation of direct active verbs, typically called transitive, and their nemesis, the passive, vague verbs, called intransitive. Mastering the transitive verb was prescribed as an essential step in capturing the essence of our Anglo-Saxon tongue.

I'll try to bring the dichotomous world of verbs to life. A report has been written and approved. The windy writer might say, "The report was approved by Mr. Smith" (passive). But the active, dynamic writer would say, "Mr. Smith approved the report" (active). As part of studying verbs, I became acutely sensitive to the role of compliments, which are the explanatory phrases that follow the verb. Active verbs, in simple direct sentences, carry phrases more efficiently than passive verbs. Thus one might say, "Mr. Smith approved the report yesterday, after I bribed him with a Starbucks at lunch." Powered by an active verb and its compliments, the formally simple sentence grew into a potboiler. Tuning into verbs led me to read with both my ears and eyes. Reading became about listening to the writer's verb choices and phrasing. I was hearing the writer's voice. I was hearing the voice of our ancient English tradition, which primarily emerged from the spoken word. I went on to hear all sorts of other verb forms, and all manner of grammar. No longer was language mere dashes and dots in a kind of code meant solely for achieving militaristic objectives—it was a living, human tradition of storytelling and enlightenment. The experience of awakening to language as an art of sound and meaning was a mild epiphany that energized me through countless hours of pleasant inquiry and study.

My reading habits in those years furthered my awakening. Like a typical new divorcé, I took up pursuits that I had put off during marriage, most notably reading great literature (and sometimes almost-great literature). I'm probably starting to sound like a workaholic, but without a child to care for, I found myself with almost limitless time on my hands, and reading novels was affordable sober entertainment. John Irving, Fyodor Dostoevsky, Tom Wolfe, Jack Kerouac, and Victor Hugo are leading lights in my memories of those times. Dostoevsky and Dickens, especially, gripped me with their democratic spirit and egalitarianism, the more so since they were from the mid-nineteenth century, as in the more things change, the more they stay the same. I read up on their backgrounds: they were characterized as spiritual reformers. They both had the courage to appeal to the reader's basic goodness, to let the truth evoke the reader's sympathies for those having trouble measuring up. They got past the stiff upper lip to activate the reader's tender heart.

Dickens became a role model for me. I loved Dostoevsky's rebellious insistence on equality for all and mild satirizing of the emerging bourgeois, but he lived a chaotic life on the margins of society. Dickens, on the other hand, had a steady, ferocious work ethic and raised a large family. On one hand, he so adroitly pointed out the blind spots in English morality, but on the other, he maintained his status in middle-class society. Dicken's works were energized by his clear, loving vision of Christianity, and, to their credit, the English almost couldn't help but respond positively. Dickens was true to his spirituality but still popular, and at least had a middle class income. He lived with direction, and I hoped that I might do the same.

Dickens and Dostoevsky helped me arrive at a decision I had been working up to since Stony Brook. Whatever impact I would have, whatever example I might set, would be a spiritual, moral one. I sloughed off any vestige of Marxist revolt or other sense of political upheaval: spiritual evolution wins over Marxist revolution. In the Mission District, I was more like Dostoevsky, holed up in the underground, living on the edge. I still take heart in Dostoevsky's long, fiery life. Dickens died of overwork at age fifty-eight, but he had lived a prosperous life. I have made steady progress in a Dickensian direction over the past twenty years. In the end, I'll probably wind up a hybrid of the two.

I developed a dim fantasy of writing a novel about the life of a gifted behavior problem, about a rich kid growing up at odds with the corporate set, about a young man who just wouldn't fall in line. But I was too earthbound to launch directly into that project. My writing goals were directed toward the functional requirements of holding a regular job. This ambition of writing a novel, though, still percolates in the back of my thoughts—maybe I'll get to it someday.

Renunciation

In addition to developing writing skills, the pragmatic phase of my career change would have to involve some sort of interim employment while I obtained training in psychology, education, or law. To that end, I called some contacts from my sales days. Some had become lasting friendships and some were professional acquaintances. I would need references for whatever job I would find next, so I did some networking. I found that my friends weren't too shaken by my decision to quit the world-dominating software company and that they were willing to help me move forward.

After checking in with a couple of close friends from my vulture capital days at the PC manufacturer, I called Peter, the owner of the small law-office automation consultancy where I started my business-to-business career as his marketing assistant. Remember that we had grown so fast that we outgrew our ability to live up to our commitments. Faced with that conundrum, Peter and I parted company as a way to avoid getting in any further over our young, inexperienced heads. Five years had passed, but we had talked once or twice a year. He wasn't surprised that I wanted to leave big business. At one time a software developer for a major corporation, Peter had made that decision long ago, he reminded me, and was still glad of it. He invited me out to Fremont to look at his new idea for a small business.

Peter had shifted the focus of his career from developing his legal billing software to marketing communications. In the year that I worked for him, and subsequent years, he realized that without marketing power, one's products and skills will likely amount to naught. His new mantra was "marketing is everything." In addition, he had enjoyed the marketing campaign we had created together in our efforts to expand his legal technology business. He was attracted to the creativity and power of marketing, some of which we had actually experienced. He had also experienced firsthand the way product-marketing executives rule over software developers: he was more than a little envious. Peter's plan was to serve as a marketing consultant and marcom agency to computer technology companies operating in the Fremont area.

He had established an office and small warehouse for this new venture. I met him there. The complex was like a strip mall for small businesses. One long rectangle, two hundred yards long, divided into five equal squares, each one with a front door, small lobby, carpeting, suite of offices, and a small warehouse with loading door in the back. Hardly the grand dream of the entrepreneur, but modern, functional, and affordable. He was fleshing out the office, and a network of PCs and printers were going up in the workstations and offices. He had furnished the few private offices with standard desks and hand-crafted an array of spacious designers' workstations in the large common area. Lithographs and other posters on tech themes punctuated the white walls. Things had a professional look about them.

While receiving a tour of the office, I was reunited with Walter, a creative director of Taiwanese descent. He had been our art director for the marketing campaign of my legal technology days. Remember that Peter was a Chinese Catholic whose family had fled to Taiwan and then immigrated to the Bay Area. Peter and Walter had become good friends while studying at California State University, Chico. Peter studied computer science and Walter studied graphic design. I sensed an auspicious moment. I had been the writer and Walter had been the art director. We had gotten results.

I didn't really know what a copywriter was, but as we wrapped up the tour I made a pitch: if they could use a copywriter, I was willing to work my way up and grow as the new marcom business grew (i.e. I would work for almost nothing). I told them that I was working on a book, and copywriter would be a great day job. My pitch caught their attention. I started a few weeks later, in August 1995, at roughly the same salary as my computer store days back in college. At that point, I wasn't paying child support yet, so I had the luxury of a head start, but the growth part of the pitch had to happen. When I started, the business consisted of Peter, who was the owner and general manager; Walter, creative director; Walter's assistant, a design student; and an administrative assistant in the lobby. The five of us cast off on our intrepid quest for marcom glory. I occupied one of the designers' workstations in the common area of the office.

Keen observers might recall the tension between Peter and me when we parted. I felt that Peter really just wanted me to be his sales guy, focused exclusively on soliciting new accounts. I, on the other hand, was mostly attracted to the more creative aspects of marketing, and I wasn't quite ready to accept a move from PC technician to sales. Some, my relatives included, sensed a trap. Peter might get up to his old tricks. But this time I was the one setting the trap. I developed a psychological fail-safe. I would continue to negotiate with Peter for what I wanted out of the position. If he declined or opposed, I would simply walk out and start again somewhere else. I was truly determined to live with direction.

We started on shaky ground. It was very quiet at first. In my first month or so, I simply moved my autodidact study of English into the workplace, but added the skills of a copywriter. I found *The Copywriter's Handbook* by Richard Bly. He was a retired engineer who built a second career as a freelance copywriter. I learned about concision, concept, layout, research, identifying the buyer's decision factors, and client relations. Bly put me on a solid footing. I also read *The Publicity Handbook* by David Yale, which gave a behind-the-scenes look at the role of publicists in news coverage. I wasn't interested in becoming a publicist, but I did learn how to write articles and press releases. Eventually, I read a couple of books by David Ogilvy, the renowned father of American advertising.

From him, basically, I learned the world view of the ad man. With these primers acquired into memory, I became a critical reader of advertising. I methodically started analyzing advertising that I felt was credible and effective; from this method, I probably learned the most. For a copywriter, I'm probably sounding a bit print oriented, but the computer industry was print and website heavy at that time.

I didn't feel too guilty about this dearth of activity, since I was earning almost nothing. I was learning a lot and enjoying myself. Then Peter came bursting into the office one day with a big idea. We could represent a Taiwanese television manufacturer at Fall COMDEX in Las Vegas. We would be creating a trade show presence for a pilot project: an MP4 decoding chipset for streaming audio and video content to various video devices. Since it was a pilot project, we would work from the ground up. That meant tons of billable hours and mark ups on materials: trade show booth, product literature, folder and folios, press releases, corporate backgrounder, etc. And we had an entire month to complete it! Oh well. No pain, no gain. Our little business could live for months on the fees.

But there was a catch in this Hail Mary pass. We had to actually represent the company in the trade show booth. I would be the press agent. We could bill for all the logistics, including our time on the floor. If I could tolerate this indignity, Peter pleaded, knowing my fastidiousness on issues of integrity, we could buy ourselves months to prospect for more clients. I agreed to play my part in the performance. Publicity Bunny! We embraced the plan. I studied the MP4 standard and the chipset. I wrote product literature, corporate brochure, and press releases. I worked with Walter to incorporate the copy into four-color layouts. Walter and Peter designed a trade show booth. We designed, printed, built, and shipped everything on time.

Staffing the trade show was familiar territory for me. I had staffed a few shows in my vulture days at the PC manufacturer. My suits were still in fighting shape from a career abandoned only six months earlier, so I could dress the part. I knew all about COMDEX, which, back in those days, was the nation's premier showcase for PC technology. It was a national news event. The booth was a kind of purgatory of extreme boredom. In the entire week, I had a handful of conversations with the trade press, most of whom weren't up to speed on this groundbreaking technology. We were ahead of the curve, especially as one of the lesser lights in Asian manufacturing.

The booth bunny quickly became the focus of my efforts. She served as the receptionist. She was no supermodel, but she could definitely hold her own with the Victoria's Secret crowd. She had been a dental assistant before traveling to Los Angeles to try acting. So far, she had some credits in children's theater. A friend helped her find trade show gigs. She was staying with another friend in Las Vegas. I kept trying to break free from Peter to flirt more, but he was treating me like a little brother, essentially confining me to quarters; we did everything together. The booth bunny gave me a card with her picture and phone number on it, but I never called her. Technically, I had only been separated a few months. I figured Peter was trying to keep me out of trouble.

We survived the ordeal, without damaging the client's reputation or our own, and collected the fees. We could hang on for a few months at least. This project was a pivotal moment for me because it gave me an opportunity to pull a switcheroo on Peter. In my first days, Peter had printed business cards for me. The title was Account Executive. I knew Peter was trying to convince me that I could both write copy and help him solicit new clients. But that, I felt, was chump change. I was only interested in writing copy. I didn't say anything at first. Somehow, I was going to convince him to leave me out of sales. We did make one solid sales call in my first month, at a manufacturer of video cards for PCs. At that point in PC technology, the display monitor required a plug-in card interface to the motherboard (i.e. central processing unit). At the end of the meeting, Peter and the client made plans to have me write copy and coordinate the design work for product packaging and a business-to-business sales kit. As part of that project, I handed my card to the client's marketing manager. In pen, I crossed out Account Executive and wrote in Copywriter, and then quipped that a mistake had been made at the printer.

My role as publicity bunny at COMDEX presented an auspicious opportunity to set things straight. I needed a believable identity in the COMDEX booth, so I convinced Peter to print new cards with the title Communications Manager. Then I discarded the original cards. Over the next few months, by subtly shaping certain strategic conversations, I convinced all key players that Communications Manager meant that I was an operations manager in charge of all client marcom projects, especially those involving copy, reporting only to Peter. Basically, I was the copywriter. And that is how the situation remained for all my years with Peter's firm.

My assertiveness in the matter of my role in the firm was an extension of warriorship. Trungpa, in several different teachings, pointed out how Americans crave infatuation in all their relationships. We want everyone to love us, and we get anxious if we think someone is displeased with us. This fear of rejection can become crippling and leave its victim without a sense of direction, since one's life becomes a madcap popularity contest. Buddhists might recognize the Worldly Conditions in these teachings—the vacillation between strong polarized emotions such as pride and shame. Trungpa advised that we don't need to be completely in love in all our relationships. We can survive a little conflict, especially when our cause is just. So, I was going to assert myself with Peter, even if things got a little rough on the emotional side. I didn't need Peter to love me; he was welcome to cast me out at his leisure, but until he did, I was going to assert my needs. I was renouncing the easy life of the popularity contest. I was going for what I wanted. I felt my spiritual aspirations were just, including my career goals, so I was confident in doing things my way.

I was there to practice skills in communication, because that served my career goals. Period! No compromising!

Ruthless

When we returned from COMDEX, the video-card manufacturer came through. They were ready to start work. Working with Walter for art direction, I would create product sheets, corporate brochure, and retail packaging for a line of five PC video cards. The cards ran from basic capacity to the most-advanced technology. The top of the line was aimed at gamers and home-video enthusiasts, who wanted fast, seamless processing of detailed video imagery. It had a video co-processor, dedicated high-speed video memory, streaming video, and even broadcast video. The client had manufacturing facilities in both Fremont and Taiwan. They sold their products through their own brand and by integrating them into other manufacturers' systems. Our marcom role was to create a retail brand that could be sold through regional superstores, regional wholesalers, and direct marketing.

I sensed an opportunity to prove ourselves. I worked ten times harder than justified by the fees or the stature of the client, but I figured it was an investment. Our fledgling agency would need samples for our portfolio. To ensure the potency of my copy, I studied other products in the video niche. I read up on media product reviews. I made sure that my copy covered all key sales factors. I labored through rewrites to bring concision and clarity. I pushed Walter to indulge me in rewrites and adjustments. When Peter would occasionally pressure me to spend less time on this client, I would work at home in San Francisco to buy another day or two to do things my way.

I was going to use this client to start our portfolio, and I was ruthless. In the end, we finished the project roughly on time. The work was approved quickly, printed, and shipped with minimal feedback from the client. Peter, Walter, and I were a little raw emotionally, but the result was impressive. The client brought the products to market and continued to engage our services. Over the next two years, Peter hired a couple of assistants to help him with client relations. They developed a marketing kit for our services, and it always prominently featured this video brand.

About this same time, just as we completed the video-card brand, Peter convinced a San Jose-based software developer to engage our firm in developing a corporate brand for products they had developed as an expert consultant. It was a family business, headed by a Taiwanese-American couple. They had developed and implemented security software that protected corporate computing networks from internet-borne threats such as viruses. Our firm's role was to package their previously expert-delivered software into an off-the-shelf product that businesses could install and operate on their own. They were ahead of the curve in the off-the-shelf approach.

From a branding perspective, we started from scratch, so lots of work in both design and copy. Walter developed their logo, brand identity, packaging, and all the layouts for marcom copy. The client had been promoting their services by means of publicity for a few years, so I had good source information in the form of articles written by and about them. My research consisted of their articles and my own competitive intelligence. With this solid start, I earnestly endeavored to convey their unique approach. The client viewed network security as a combination of vulnerable access points: internet access points, typically called gateways, and desktop computers. The client detected threats at both vulnerable points, at top speed, not just at the desktop. I strived hard to convey competitive advantages such as processing speed and the benefits of their holistic approach. Whereas the video-card project had involved generating a large volume of accurate information on fairly-mundane products, the security software required capturing the essence of a unique product.

This project was skill over volume, and we experienced less conflict and stress. But I still worked harder than justified by the fees, with the resulting being a potent brand that made a nice addition to our nascent portfolio. The products went to market, enjoyed some success, and the firm expanded its leadership role in the security field.

My obsessiveness on these early projects served an ulterior purpose. Peter basically left me out of sales activities. I hoped he would get used to it. After our first six months, about the time we completed the video brand, Peter hired Megan, a White twenty-something entry level account executive to help with sales and client relations. By simply refusing to cooperate with other options, I limited her to taking me to a client only after they had reviewed our portfolio and were ready to sign. She was a good sport and complied. With her help, we gradually grew for another twelve months on a stream of fairly respectable small-business clients. She was actually building on the video brand. A few notable clients stand out. A Taiwanese industrial-computer manufacturer hired us to make display advertising for U.S. trade publications; they were expanding into the U.S. after growing steadily all over Asia. A Fremont computer manufacturer catering to small businesses engaged us to make display advertising for a leading national magazine. A Fremont manufacturer and distributor of PC memory products hired us to establish a basic business-to-business brand, including advertising. We developed a complete U.S. brand presence—product sheets, corporate communications, product line brochures, display advertising—for a sizeable Taiwanese manufacturer of high-quality motherboards operating out of assembly, sales, and distribution facilities in Fremont.

With each new client, I worked ten times harder than justified by the fees or the client's stature. I was going to use these clients to build our portfolio, and I was ruthless. Sometimes Peter and Megan would get angry at me for slowing a project down to perfect it, but I was confident that quality had to be the priority. A growth trajectory was emerging. Substantial small businesses, with national presence, and even international presence, were giving us mission-critical work in their brands. I felt my theory of "quality or die" was working.

During this gradual expansion, Peter had bolstered our design capacity. He brought in advanced Macs with the latest design software, a variety of powerful color printers for proofing, poster and banner printing, mounted digital camera for high-res product photography, and computerized "film" output for full-color printing. All of the firm's users and resources were connected through the office network, which included productivity applications, e-mail, and high-speed internet access. Eventually we added the capacity to design websites. It was pretty advanced for 1997, and we were poised to hire more designers and account assistants. Essentially, we could take just about any marcom project from conception to production, quickly and efficiently. Peter seemed to have learned a lesson about diminishing returns: in other words, he sensed success and growth, and expanded his investment quickly to make room for more, thus avoiding that point where a successful business can exceed its capacity to a terminal degree.

Expansion brought a loss along with the growth. Walter quit at the end of my first year. Peter said that Walter didn't have the entrepreneurial spirit. At our goodbye dinner, Walter advised me to keep standing up to Peter. Walter was a gentle, quiet soul, and therefore easy for both Peter and I to wheedle things out of. Quitting was a reasonable act of self-preservation. His exit, however, opened up a new level of quality for me. Jack, his replacement, was an experienced, middle-aged creative director from a groundbreaking PC software developer. As with most early innovators in PC technology at that time, his pioneering employer, a prosperous small business, collapsed as a monolithic oligarch invaded its market share. There was a large population of displaced-yet-talented workers due to this downsizing effect of shrinking and disappearing pioneers, and Jack was one of them.

Walter brought a dreamy Asian quality to his work. His roots were in illustration. He could have worked in manga and anime. His design philosophy was "whatever looked good in the moment." I, of course, connected to his free spirit. However, our work might have looked a little off kilter to U.S. audiences. Jack practiced design discipline. He was a designer and not an illustrator. He knew a lot about layout, photography, and typesetting. Gradually, I incorporated my copy and layouts into his discipline, which made them more readable. Basically, our work started to have a kind of uprightness— a solidity that conveyed confidence, a restrained, industrial feel.

Working with Jack was an occasion for warriorship. Walter was 5'8", thirty-something, slim, a little slouchy, with slender facial features and infrequently-trimmed longish black hair, and habitually wore dark dress-casual pants, soft-soled shoes, soft cotton sport shirt, and cotton golf windbreaker. In contrast to Walter's easy-going nerdiness, Jack was athletic, White, 6'2" tall, middle-aged, and handsome. He was a confident professional with an impressive tech background. I couldn't just boss him around, nor would I tolerate him bossing me around. But I needed to continue my "quality or die" approach, meaning I needed to get my way. My nascent warriorship told me that this was an occasion for non-aggressive communication. To succeed in my agenda, I had to become an agent of Jack's desire for quality and success. Warriorship inspired me to refrain from asserting any kind of upper hand.

I learned to collaborate with Jack in a routine of draft and revision. At the start of each project, I fed Jack concept ideas, which means a basic combination of imagery and text, but I would try to leave the final word on the concept to him. We would usually have a meeting to discuss my draft. Then he would send me his draft concept. Occasionally, I would carefully give him feedback that he might want to try a different approach, but almost never. Typically, I would indicate my approval of his draft and return it with the final version of my copy. He would complete the layout (i.e. concept), which I would proofread. Since he always listened to my first proposal, I was comfortable giving him the last word.

Trungpa advised that the warrior learns to delight in the accomplishments of others. A wise leader spends most of his efforts supporting others. In this vein, one should not be too possessive of one's ideas: best to invest them in others' success, which ultimately becomes the ground of your own success. Ashe energizes this others-first approach—respect your co-workers' desire for self-actualization, and their instinct to thrive through connection with others will kick in. Keeping the peace with Jack, while doing good work, was one of my most-satisfying experiences of the three years. I'm pleased with the number of projects where the finished product reflected both of our influences, where teamwork had produced something better than we could have done alone, and where I was satisfied with the quality.

It might be helpful for me to explain my vision of quality in advertising, within the somewhat constricted view of the technology copywriter. Every product has a lexicon, a dialect that arises in advertising and the media. In addition, buyers have fairly predictable decision factors for purchasing a particular product. The copywriter should conduct sufficient research to master a product's dialect and concisely address the buyer's decision factors. Since I was working exclusively in tech marcom, attention to detail was essential in developing respectful materials. The writer should make sure that all technical specifications follow proper usage. All imagery should be relevant and address the buyer's decision factors. Finally, the layout should be readable. For instance, putting text over product images or colored type on a white background should be discouraged. To pull it all together, the writer should always finish with a thorough proofreading of every aspect—photographs, text, and layout. So, I emphatically insisted on working through all these steps of quality before releasing a finished product.

Sometimes Peter or one of his assistants would plead with me to apply a bit of obtuse sales patter and a short informal list of technical specifications to finish a project quickly. I just brushed them off, usually by promising to do my best—if you get my drift—and then did it my way. I made sure to powerfully address the buyer's decision factors and attend to details in everything I did. The result of my mad science? Growth for all of us.

Symbiosis

Amazingly, an epiphanic event came along to justify all my overachievement. We landed the big kahuna: an industry-leading client that we could attach to in a symbiotic, life sustaining relationship. The Pequod had Moby Dick in sight!! The Leviathan would be ours! As of this writing, the client is now the world's fourth-largest manufacturer of PC hardware. Peter's investment in technology and capacity, the credibility of our portfolio, and our efforts at self-promotion led this global company to give us a chance to handle a piece of their brand. It was toward the middle of my second year, a few months after Jack joined the firm.

The client, a Taiwan-based manufacturer gradually becoming a global presence, especially in the U.S., had haunting similarities to my vulture days. They manufactured complete PC systems and components and at that point sold them through a network of dealers. Most interestingly, our agency's role was to promote the components sold to small businesses, called value added resellers, who bundled the products into systems sold to commercial users for productivity applications such as...law-office automation! This market sector was typically identified as "build-your-own." In those years, it was actually the largest sector of the PC industry. Eventually, the company made its way into every major U.S. electronics superstore, but our role was the reseller channel and their build-your-own approach.

The Taiwan-based manufacturer was surviving and growing where my Fremont-based vulture employer, also a manufacturer of PC systems for value added resellers, had gone under. I was focused on my own survival and growth, but it's interesting to note that I needed Taiwan's help to do it. From a career perspective, this client was the literal culmination of everything I had experienced up to that point.

Our first project for the Taiwan-based manufacturer was five full-page ads to run concurrently in the leading trade magazine for resellers. Each ad covered a different component and included a rebate offer for large purchases. These rebate ads grew into a long-running campaign for a variety of components and were a steady source of business for us. My "quality or die" approach was well-suited to this campaign, since it was high-stakes direct marketing.

Peter helped the client develop a database for creating an authorized reseller program. New dealers who responded to the ads were typically enrolled as authorized resellers and existing dealers were added automatically. After a few months of the rebate ads, we developed a color four-page monthly newsletter targeting the authorized resellers. We printed 20,000 copies a month. Jack and I developed an editorial format in the first month that we converted into a template for the life of the newsletter. Each issue had a feature article on a product or corporate topic, blurbs about new products and corporate news, and rebate offers. I used the feature article as an opportunity to stretch my newswriting skills; sometimes my efforts at genius dragged on, but I basically kept up with deadlines. I saw this project as an opportunity for "quality or die." I compelled everyone to comply, and the result was an attractive direct-marketing program. After the first two issues, the client made a long-term commitment to the project.

The rebate campaign, which now consisted of magazine ads and internal newsletter, led to a steady flow of other projects for stimulating sales to the resellers: product line brochures, product data sheets, reference guides, direct mail, display ads for reseller and end user publications, and website content. We promoted a mind-boggling array of the client's products: video monitors, PC cases, power supplies, keyboards, motherboards, hard drives, and floppy drives. Their video monitors were a major force in the component market, for both retail and resellers, and generated a steady flow of lucrative projects for our firm.

In addition to the surge from the big kahuna, projects from smaller clients, existing and new, continued to flow in. We were juggling about fifteen projects at any one time. The growth part of my pitch to Peter at the start of this adventure was starting to come to fruition. In my first year and a half, my salary was at the same level as my store manager days just out of college at the retail PC store. At the threshold to my third year, my salary rose to the same level it had been at the start of my vulture years at the Fremont-based PC manufacturer. It was significantly below peak levels of the vulture compensation plan, but, then again, that wasn't really a healthy situation. Now, I was earning that salary to help my client and employer *grow*. Progress! In addition to salary, I earned free comprehensive health benefits: medical, dental, and vision (the good old days!).

Schism

With growth came complexity. We hired an editorial assistant to help with the newsletter and other copywriting projects. Eladia was a twenty-something recent grad in journalism and public relations from California State University, Chico. She was a body builder and a bombshell. Her Italian Mediterranean heritage showed in her smooth olive skin, long black hair, full cheeks and lips, and soft brown eyes. I appreciated her attractiveness, because you can't really be an ad man without at least a few bombshells on the staff. Megan was also a buff bombshell. They literally had the same trim-but-brawny physique: Megan was the Irish counterpart with fair freckled skin and short red hair. Surveying all the assistants hired by Peter, five were twenty-something bombshells, with four women and one male. Peter was no slouch either, at about six feet tall, athletic build, with handsome warrior bloodlines from his Manchurian heritage. At just five years older than me, Peter was still a relatively young man. We were a couple of thirty-somethings on a quest. Actually, everyone on staff, both designers and client relations, were quite attractive. We were a handsome dressed-for-success group.

To synchronize Eladia's work with mine, I created a schedule in a spreadsheet that I called the pipeline. I borrowed the term from my days at the world-dominating software company. Their sales management software created a spreadsheet of leads for each sales person, which listed each potential deal by priority based on factors such as projected close date and total revenue. I liked my new pipeline better, because it helped me sell products through marcom, which was essentially an educational process, a role I liked more than my inside sales days. We listed our projects by due date and complexity of the project. When a project migrated from the bottom of the list of fifteen to the top two or three, it meant that we had to finish it soon. My pipeline wasn't very sophisticated, but it truly inhibited procrastination and forgetfulness, and often facilitated a steady step-by-step approach.

At first, Peter's account assistants would ask me to forecast a turn-around time for potential projects. I would consult the pipeline and give them a proposed due date. The account assistant cleared the due date with the client. Finally, I entered the project on the pipeline and either met the deadline or kept everyone informed of any delay. So, I was in the driver's seat; the pace was based on my vision of the workload. This was the situation for Eladia's first six months. And then Peter tried to pull a switcheroo on me.

By the middle of my third year, Peter had amassed a group

of four account assistants. He added a designer too, for a total of three. The firm had twelve employees. One morning, I arrived a little late, like at ten o'clock. Eladia brought me a copy of the pipeline. "What's up?" I asked, puzzled. She had never done that before. "Peter asked me to make it." "Oh yeah," I snarled, "Then he can do the work himself. I'll be following my pipeline." I made a few changes. "Here. Take this to Peter. Tell him this is the pipeline, and that Robert sent you." I was a fair boss (some would say indulgent), and as I expected, my loyal assistant carried out my request. My intervention stifled Peter's ambition for about two months. But a rivalry started forming between Peter and me.

For about six months, we hadn't spoken but a few words to each other. Then Peter pulled the switcheroo where he tried to dictate the pipeline to me, even though it was my innovation. I felt he was really in my space. On the other hand, he was probably tired of taking orders from me. We had been properly absorbed in our respective responsibilities: Peter in business development and me in developing concepts, layouts, and copy. But I was puzzled by Peter. What were we doing with this huge staff? Every month of my third year brought a steady increase in the frequency of account assistants trying to push projects through the pipeline with less than a week's turn-around time. A kind of sweatshop was emerging, whereby Peter's numerous assistants were trying to push a high volume of low-stature projects through our tiny creative staff at top speed.

At first, before a pattern emerged, I indulged the assistants by accelerating a project now and then. But when these requests became habitual, I replied to the request with an upbraiding: "Get out of my office now. I might kill you with my bare hands. I mean it! I'll kill you. Go tell the client that we'll finish in two weeks." Sometimes the assistant would parry by saying that Peter had sent them. I would thrust: "Then bring Peter here so I can kill him too." That would usually inspire the assistant to ask the client for more time. By means of these soliloquies, I kept the pipeline under my control until my last two months. I had moved to a private office after my first few months at the firm, and I took advantage of the privacy to defend my territory.

I confess to becoming a passive presence. I saw Peter's empire building. But I didn't even bother to chat with him about his ambitions. By that time, I had developed my own working hours by fiat. I arrived at around nine thirty and left anywhere from seven o'clock to midnight, depending on the projects in the pipeline that day—typically seven o'clock. That fit my forty-five minute rail commute from San Francisco—providing quiet empty cars for reading, studying, or other personal pursuits. Moreover, I liked my hours to peak and ebb with the demands of each project, and sometimes I would just take a day off after meeting a big deadline. My pay was sufficient but minimal; I felt more than justified in claiming these privileges. I really felt we should keep the business small, so that we could continue to enjoy these free and easy conditions. And I would occasionally voice this utopian vision.

Peter, unfortunately, was moving in the opposite direction. He clearly wanted empire. He was going to be a man of business! I, however, was clinging to my Mission District hipsterism like a toddler refusing to give up his pacifier. In my vision of our agency, everything revolved around my talent and my ability to get others with talent to do good work: creativity and integrity bring riches (and the good life!!). In Peter's vision, everything revolved around the speedy exploitation of his human and technical resources. When I clearly comprehended this dialectic, of crass speed versus transcendental creativity, I felt my fail-safe heat up and threaten to detonate the ejection charge.

As part of his ambition, in early year three, Peter had initiated the morning meeting. He gathered all the account assistants and designers in a kind of roundtable at eight-thirty each morning. The firm had moved down the street into a fairly large converted warehouse. We occupied the entire building, and the meeting was held in a conference room large enough to seat the entire staff (ambitious!). The meetings went on for a few months before I attended one, so I'm not sure what they covered. I believe Peter went over his sales pipeline. It looked like wasteful group think to me, and I simply stuck to my flexible schedule, which allowed me to avoid the meeting altogether. No matter how much planning they would do in these meetings, I would assert my control over the project pipeline and make everyone follow my pace. I surmised that Peter wanted to mastermind these meetings, with the entire staff there, including me, to receive orders passively. My surmises were correct. Responding to Peter's persistent urgings, I attend one meeting, after which I told Peter, in not such positive tones, that I wouldn't attend any more, that I would continue with my flexible hours, and that he was invited to fire me whenever he felt like it. He didn't fire me.

Later, in a more positive setting, I told Peter in earnest that my flexible hours were important, especially given my commute, and that the morning meeting was a deal killer. Eladia could attend for me, and I would do my best—if you get my drift—to accommodate his desire for empire. He conceded to my conditions, but I could tell he was upset that I had escaped his trap. Then I pretty much continued doing things my way. That approach worked until about my last month, when Peter redoubled his Machiavellian maneuvers.

Suddenly, Peter and his assistants just couldn't get enough of me at client meetings. Typically, I went to a client meeting a few times a quarter. Now, practically every third day I was prompted to dress formally tomorrow for a client meeting. I truly only wanted to meet with businesses already committed to working with the agency, but now I was asked to meet with prospective clients and with existing clients contemplating a new project. They were dragging me into sales meetings!! I tended to not prepare or otherwise care about these meetings, and I must have sounded clumsy at times. Moreover, I maintained a rude posture toward the account assistants. For instance, on the way back to the office, I would launch into a soliloquy: "Could they be dumber? Could that project be dumber? Could we be dumber? Why do you waste my time in these meetings?" But despite all my protestations, I continued to be the star attraction. My fail-safe was red hot and ready to blow.

Most diabolical of all his Machiavellian tricks, Peter organized the women against me. Every time I walked into the office dressed in blue suit and red tie, cat calls and all manner of salacious innuendo issued forth from twenty-something female bombshells: "We're yours—all of us—together," "We're ready, just give us the word," and "Hot! Did someone turn up the heat?" Adding outright physical taunting to their verbal teasing, the lithesome bombshells executed well-timed provocative flashes of their tanned mini-skirted thighs from high heel to upper hip.

The most-provocative incident occurred at the Christmas party. It was our third, and the last one I would be a part of. Peter actually rented a small ballroom in a San Francisco hotel, near the financial district, and held a banquet and dance. I sat at the head table with Peter and his family. We could still keep the peace enough to share dinner at Christmas. I probably looked officious, dressed in a nice blue suit and sitting with Peter's family. While shuffling nonchalantly on the dance floor, I encountered one of my favorite bombshells. I occasionally flirted with her, usually without making much headway. Her daring high-thigh slit, low cut, open-back evening gown brought out her potent sensuality, and looked stunning against her tawny Latina skin and long black hair. She was actually a skinny nerd, a budding publicist, but with a sexy side. As I made eye contact to say a quick hello, she made a waltz-like step away from her twenty-something date and suggestively toward me, with arms outstretched in an obvious gesture of beckoning. With exquisite body language and facial expression, she made her demand clear: "Keep it up, and all this could be yours (i.e. her gorgeousness)." She ended her negotiation with a pouting frown and glided back toward her date. Such, apparently, was the magnetism of Robert in a blue suit at the head table.

I appreciated the pitch. But I saw a repeat of my marriage: another woman who could only love a corporate salesman. In reality, I was just a child psychologist working a day job. What would she do when she found out? This bodhisattva would resist Mara's temptresses too. As I have learned many times over, warriorship often involves tough choices. Farewell popularity contest!

One of the firm's temptresses had already succumbed to my charms, or maybe it was the other way around. I left her for the same reason I resisted the incredible Christmas temptress. But I was learning. Best to make these decisions before the love affair breaks out, then you don't have an angry rejected temptress itching for revenge. Warriorship, it seems, is sometimes a journey of trial and error—and broken hearts.

The final straw in this feud between founders involved a client meeting that blew up into a fracas of whining among the client's staff. Peter's newest assistant, Amy, a beautiful Taiwanese-American twenty-something woman with an early-development degree from UC Berkeley, was responsible for the account. She had no experience in marcom or technology. Peter, I felt, was really taking the bombshell approach too far; I actually was concerned that he had gone mad with ambition. The client was a San Jose-based telecom start-up that offered high-speed webserver hosting. Peter assigned me to write a proposal for developing the client's website. As part of the proposal, I quickly developed a mock-up of the website— a kind of trial run.

Amy and I drove to the client's office in her car (I always made assistants drive me around). My role was to back Amy up if her nascent knowledge fell short of the task. She started the meeting with introductions. The client had formed a committee consisting of representatives from various departments to guide the website (red flag!!). Right off, I saw that the twenty-something male techs wanted to flirt with Amy and even show off in front of her. I was in no mood to officiate as the grown up in this alumni mixer. Watching Amy posture like she knew what she was doing increased my irritation. I basically spaced out and ignored Amy's opening remarks. I think she reviewed the proposal. I just wanted to finish asap and leave—hopefully, I wouldn't be needed. Suddenly, the meeting was turned over to me: "And Robert will be developing the website structure and writing the copy. You have a draft done already, right?" "Yes," I replied curtly, trying to avoid further involvement. A petulant voice rang out, like someone who just discovered his roommate drank his last can of Coke in the midst of late-night cramming for finals. "I thought I was writing the copy. Why were changes made? I told Peter that I wanted to control the copy!!" This young man was shouting at the top of his lungs; he was having an episode. As often happens with young social climbers, he was gunning for resume credit or corporate cachet. Later, moreover, I learned that another marcom agency had already developed the website, but Peter had somehow insinuated our firm into the project as a rival. That was a low-quality way to conduct client relations. Peter and Amy hadn't properly established their relationship with this company, and so infighting broke out among the committee members. Peter sent me into a situation he had lost control of. Immediately after the outburst, I closed the meeting by assuring the committee that there was plenty of time to make changes, including letting one of them write the copy. Then I just rose and walked out, as in have a nice day.

When I returned to the office, I told Peter that I didn't appreciate being sent into a bullshit deal, and that I wouldn't work on the project anymore. He yelled at me that the client is always right, and that I *better finish* the deal, no matter what it takes. I told him he could "fuck off," and that he could just forget about me completing the project. "You better take that back," Peter shouted. "You can forget about it," I persisted. I straightened up my desk for a minute or two, with Peter glaring at me, and left for the day. The next morning, I called Peter, leaving him a voice message. I said that I would be taking some time off (i.e. paid) to consider my career options—a couple of days, weeks, a month—and I would let him know the time span in a couple of days. After about a week, Peter called and said that he needed to hear from me about my return. Another week passed before I finally contacted Peter. I met him at the office. I apologized for cursing him. Then I quit, explaining that I wanted to move forward as a copywriter, and that I was looking forward to finding work as a writer, without any competing demands. I told him, in simple terms, that I didn't want to help him with sales of any sort; I was done with that occupation. The fail-safe had detonated. Eject!!

CHAPTER FIVE

Growing Confidence

Pushy Copywriter

So I quit my copywriter job, without another one planned. Living with direction wasn't going to be as easy as "he made a change and then lived happily ever after, and never again did anything unpopular." My intuition told me that struggle would be involved. The key, I felt then, and have come to believe, is to embrace the struggle and not to run from it. I used the setback as motivation for further struggle, change, and accomplishment. The first step points to the next step, and on and on. To the wise warrior, setbacks are information rather than failures. I embraced the challenge of finding a new position on the basis of being a copywriter.

My three years with Peter's marcom agency brought information about strengths and weaknesses. On the strength side, I felt good about the Zen experience of singular focus, complete absorption in the task, with nothing held back. I acted on my heart's desire, with my vision of quality, and moved my goals forward in a fairly just way. I had a small file cabinet of samples, and I felt good about all of them. My portfolio could move me forward. Confidence in my ability to change grew. On a more mundane level, I discovered skills in time management and precision. I led well over a hundred projects in those three years, literally with no errors or mishaps of any sort. I surprised myself with my aptitude for detail-oriented tasks. Finally, my confidence as a writer grew. My autodidact grammarian studies were taking hold. I felt like I could communicate with the written word in just about any setting.

On the weakness side, my approach had been a bit egotistical for a Buddhist warrior, showing that I was really just a neophyte on that path. My summer of meditation and contemplation started to echo in my thoughts. I could literally sense the hardness and defensiveness in my thinking compared to my state of mind after that meditation summer. I had become a Pushy Copywriter! I hadn't transcended the Pushy American. Instead, I was becoming a master of it. I had used people in my success more than included them. I had been especially inconsiderate to the account assistants. Whatever I did going forward, I resolved, I would have to learn how to collaborate more than dominate.

In the hindsight of what now amounts to a lifetime of spiritual warriorship, I can see how I might have cut an opportunity short. Living with direction is about making peace with conflict. I had taken a one-sided approach: yield to my demand, or I cut you off. A confident warrior learns how to assert their desires in a non-threatening, win-win style. Gentle, nonaggressive communication will move your goals ahead more effectively than combative, defensive posturing.

Instead of shutting down in response to Peter's ambitions, I might have been able to present my personal goals openly and honestly, and entice Peter into a negotiation based on both of us reaching our goals. I enjoyed marcom, and saw the possibly of virtue and merit in it, but to truly succeed at it, I would have to learn how to communicate and negotiate like a warrior. But I wasn't that sophisticated yet. My focus had been to live with direction or die!! I had this idea of moving toward hallowed ground. When I arrived at right livelihood, all would be right with the world and me. I still hadn't learned that hallowed ground is always exactly where you're standing now. In other words, to succeed at anything, especially right livelihood, one has to learn to communicate and negotiate like a warrior. Despite the accumulation of some really life-transforming regrets, I felt the three years had been, all things considered, successful. By the way, regret is considered a healthy impulse in Buddhism and Shambhala warriorship.

Practicing with the Epicureans

My passion for extracurricular activities returned in the three years at the agency, but with moderation compared to my youthful excesses. I already covered my interest in literature. I branched out from novels to stage plays at American Conservatory Theater (ACT) in downtown San Francisco at Geary Theater. I even became a subscriber—that's a big step for a cheapskate like me. Every season, their resident directors and repertory company staged new and classic plays. Just about every great Western playwright has been explored to some extent by this organization. I came to see drama as a vehicle of insight. Because of the breadth of their offerings, it's hard to summarize. If I had to settle for one great influence, for me, it would be Tennessee Williams: *The Rose, Glass Menagerie, Cat on a Hot Tin Roof*, and *A Street Car Named Desire*. Moliere, a tough-minded French satirist, was another notable influence, showing ACT's breadth—his *Misanthrope* helped me curb my own tendencies.

My sister Mary often accompanied me to ACT performances. She was a single young twenty-something Irish bombshell of medium height and trim build, with a bodybuilder physique and a friendly, warm disposition. The chubby cheeks of her Catholic-school youth had grown into the firm commanding presence of an aspiring professional devoted to the loftiest hopes of feminism. She was working as the director of placement at an established private career college focused on computer technology in downtown San Francisco. Basically, she was responsible for meeting the job placement requirements of participation in federal student loans: she regaled me with numerous tales about preparing her typically-immigrant graduates for the American workforce. She met her placement quotas and placed many graduates in good infotech jobs. She was dressed-for-success at work and in touch with the hippest city trends in her free time, which was packed with friends and social occasions.

Mary was good company, since her undergraduate degree from California State University at Chico was in humanities—basically, western civilization. We kind of had a routine for attending plays. Typically, we would enjoy dinner after the performance. During dinner, I always liked to interpret the play's theme in terms of my own life. We could really talk. Mary could tolerate and even contribute to my ponderings. Dates, on the other hand, rarely understood my approach to theater —but a few indulged me anyway.

Both of my two siblings lived uptown in the Cow Hollow neighborhood of San Francisco, which ran along a broad ridge overlooking the Golden Gate area of the bay. I visited Mary on a regular basis, usually for a run along the Golden Gate and dinner in her neighborhood. There is nothing like a sunset run along Marina Green to the Golden Gate Bridge. It's all parkland along the bay. Free luxury!! I saw my brother Ryan less, but we would connect now and then. Mary would include us in her social occasions once in a while, so I made pretty frequent trips up to Cow Hollow, where I could still basically fit in with the corporate climber culture. Of course, we siblings had regular contact as part of clan custody, but that was at our parent's place out in the suburbs near Mt. Diablo.

In the second year of my agency days, Ryan renovated a Columbia 23-foot sloop he had purchased through a family friend. It had been languishing in a donation yard. Ryan was extending the mechanical skills he had developed working on vintage sports cars. He secured a slip for it in Berkeley City Marina, an incredibly well-located, affordable facility. The marina opens directly into a clear windward course that runs straight out to the Golden Gate. Yes, the winds often exceed twenty knots, and routinely fall between eight and fifteen knots, but that was part of the fun. By the end of five years with this boat, we could glide effortlessly through whatever the bay dished out.

Ryan was the sole tall and skinny member of the family at 6'1" and 145 pounds. Ryan and Bridget have the same gentle oval facial features with fair freckled skin, reddish-blond hair, narrow aquiline nose, and sparkly blue eyes. They could be fraternal twins, but my appearance is a bit more on the Norman side of our heritage, with ruddy complexion, green eyes, thick brunette hair, broad aquiline nose, wide shoulders, and broad brow. As he developed into adulthood, Ryan developed a passion for putting his skinny frame and wiry muscles to the test in sporting endeavors such as lacrosse, crew, downhill skiing, and sports car racing. In his barely thirties at that point, he was energetic and industrious, and, of course, clean-cut, dressed-for-success, and preppy in all fashion matters. He earned his degree in business administration with a concentration in management in his early twenties from California State University, Sacramento.

At the time a sales manager in a natural gas brokerage business, Ryan knew I was aiming for a life of good works, and he was very generous in sponsoring me as the sole crew member of his modest sailboat. He outfitted me with all the foul weather and flotation gear. He did a solid job of renovating the sloop, built in the 1970s, giving us a safe craft. We both were diligent in learning about the dynamics of the boat and navigating in the bay. I leaned toward navigation and Ryan favored the mechanics. Neither of us was complete on our own, but we did really well together.

The Golden Gate area of San Francisco Bay is basically one of the wonders of the world—a truly grand physical geography. We conducted about a hundred voyages, covering every aspect of the region: Raccoon Straights, Treasure Island, Alcatraz, Golden Gate, Delta. Most voyages took from five to six hours. We could tack straight up the twenty-knot slot to the Golden Gate Bridge and then jibe right back—with mast and crew still intact, or meander around Raccoon Straights in the lighter airs of the Bay proper. Ryan named his boat Rumblefish, for warrior training ground (inspired by the warrior fish of our aquarium days). We learned a lot about patience, nonjudgmental communication, thoroughness, respect, and concentration on our voyages, and filled our minds with the incredible nurturing beauty of the land. We weren't good enough to race, but we had a lot of safe, sober fun in our little cruiser.

In addition to the supportive companionship of my siblings, my Mission District days were marked by lots of fun with friends. Simone, a fellow student at Stony Brook and one of my closest friends from Long Island, and I had stayed in touch through an incredible series of coincidences. I already mentioned Simone in my account of my life at Stony Brook. About a year after I moved to California, Simone called me. He was living nearby, stationed at the Defense Language Institute in the coastal city of Monterey. He had enlisted in the U.S. Army, completed basic training, and was preparing to work in surveillance. In my school years before marriage, Simone and I would connect about twice a month. He bought a late-model Volvo sedan and I had my MGB. Sometimes I would drive down to Santa Cruz on Highway 1, where we would catch a live world-beat music performance at the Catalyst or join in the youth culture in the downtown bars. We went on a couple of incredible hikes in the back county of Big Sur. Other times, Simone drove up to my parent's place and stayed for a day or two—our favorite pastime was waxing metaphysical in the Beat bars of San Francisco's North Beach. Simone shared his passion for locating obscure bookstores with works of metaphysical significance. He passed me a lot of books in those days. Most memorable were *Confederate General in Big Sur* by Richard Brautigan and *Post Office* by Charles Bukowski. These books were mind-altering experiences. I became a Bukowski fan—although I confess that I probably shouldn't be. I tend to appreciate creativity, even when it causes me to digress from my typically bourgeois trajectory. Thus Simone got me hooked on The Grateful Dead and Jimmy Hendrix. We had lots of gentle fun traveling up and down the central coast—you could almost call it pristine territory in those halcyon days of under population. Mind-inspiring natural wonders dominated the landscape.

Our friendship had an instructive and nourishing tension to it stemming from our diverging spiritual paths. Simone was proposing the quest for power as an end itself. The enlightened individual seeks power because his pursuits energize all the myriad occupations of modern society. Fair play is of course needed, but any transcendental notions of ethics or wisdom were fetters to the enlightened power seeker. I, on the other hand, saw transcendental notions of wisdom as the end in itself—you could say I was a Transcendentalist or a Romantic. I saw the quest for power as a fetter on the highest end, which was the development of oneself into an agent of compassion and Buddha-nature. Ends are just gateways to the next means. One might engage in all manner of risk taking and entrepreneurial zeal to reach a particular end, only to be confronted with the fact that it's the next beginning. There are no ends. Take care with means, and the anxiety over ends will fall away.

The Buddha might say, "How can there be ends, when there was no beginning?" Our plans can be shaped by modest ambitions, but those goals must be tempered by the knowledge that only by disciplined means can we relieve suffering and bring prosperity. We only have means to work with, ends often degenerate into destructive fantasies. "In other words," Simone might exclaim, "You're afraid to take risks. You're a slacker!"

I'll offer a practical example of this tension at work in society. To address American dependency on foreign oil, the power seeker might propose expanding domestic oil exploration (i.e. find more). The romantic will propose research into energy efficiency (i.e. use less). In the end, society will probably adopt both approaches together (i.e. try a little of both). To Simone's credit, he might form a goal to spearhead a world-leading energy-saving technology—thus combining power and discipline. Basically, he wanted to make things happen and get rich doing it.

Simone saw shyness as the greatest impediment to power. All his intellectual wanderings, everything he did, was aimed at wearing away the habitual hesitation that prevents one from making the contacts, asking the questions, and pitching the proposals that will bring one to where the actions is, to where the great deals are made. The trick was to slough off suburban shyness and self-doubt and emerge into the world of possibilities. We were joined in this desire to shed shyness and self-doubt, although I wanted to become a bodhisattva and he wanted to be an entrepreneur, and so each seeking power in our own way.

We drifted apart a bit after Simone was deployed on his surveillance assignment. Simone could always reach me at my parent's place or through my parents, and he called once in a while, but we basically lost touch for a couple of years. After I got married and started working in the PC industry, we reconnected through another incredible circumstance. When Simone moved on from the Army, he moved to Arlington, Virginia. He secured a position there as a communications specialist with a defense contractor in the Beltway.

The defense contractor was involved with information-technology projects. Peter parlayed his English degree and military experience into a position as editor for the contractor's business communications. Peter didn't really know what he was doing, but he was excited at the prospect of all the free training. He was convinced that technology was where the action would be in coming decades. I was in my vulture days at the PC manufacturer. My territory was the Mid-Atlantic region, which included Maryland, parts of Virginia, and DC: in other words, the Beltway. My company had extensive business in the area, including a few government suppliers, and so I enjoyed a couple of occasions to travel to the DC area.

We were able to visit extensively on these business trips. We pretty much picked up where we left off in San Francisco, but maybe tamed slightly by the cautious denizens of Arlington and DC—everyone there seemed to talk in hushed tones like they were afraid of eavesdropping. In his social repertoire, Simone always cultivated a few pubs, music venues, organic markets, eateries, authors and poets of a metaphysical bent, and musicians. He was a true Epicurean. I really enjoyed sharing his interests. We relaxed, but we didn't just make small talk. We mulled over decisions about our future. We allowed a modest amount of shop talk, mostly wondering about our next moves in the technology market. My contributions to these discussions typically consisted of various schemes for escaping from the sales force—I hope that I didn't sound too one dimensional. Simone's contributions had that euphoric peal of the recently converted zealot—entrepreneurs and their technologies would lead us to the promised land. I tried to help Simone move forward with his feet on the ground instead of his head in the clouds. "Technology, my friend," I would offer nonchalantly, "is a manifestation of greed. And the struggle against greed will be the force that shapes our future more than any other."

We held many verbal ping-pong matches on the topic of libertarian capitalism versus social democracy. At that point, Simone's interests laid with the entrepreneurs and their promises of a capitalist utopia—with the best of intentions. I felt that once the ruination of the Reagan years, including the rapid deindustrialization of American cities, came to light, the baby boom would turn to socialist approaches to right their course. Remember this was the early nineties, the peak of one of the worst recessions since the Great Depression. Unemployment had gone over seven percent nationwide. Going all the way back to college in the eighties, I had predicted that libertarian capitalism would leave the baby boom unable to put their children through college, protect their health, or retire before their final resting place. Libertarians had feasted on the heart of the country, leaving it on the brink of collapse, with its vital organs in tatters. We both threw volleys and kill shots, but we kept the match friendly. This intellectual rivalry lasted for about ten years. I confess that by the end of the Clinton presidency, I was more receptive to the entrepreneurs. Maybe their New Economy was possible. Or maybe not. We'll be answering this question for decades. Does the New Economy have to be on the entrepreneurs' terms? Or can it usher in a broader perspective? Will the echo boom answer this question?

Simone and I continued to visit on a fairly regular basis for ten years, but we travelled mostly on our own initiative starting in the mid-nineties. Actually, Simone was able to combine business and travel in a few trips to San Francisco in his new role as director of business development for the same government contractor. Simone had started making the kind of incredible moves he had dreamed of in his metaphysical period. First, he negotiated with Stony Brook to enter their master's program in technology policy studies, which was a branch of the Harriman School for Management and Policy. Next, he negotiated a consulting position with his Beltway employer, which allowed him to attend school and continue working. Finally, upon graduation Simone pitched a proposal to his employer whereby his occupation would involve helping the contractor expand their business.

The defense contractor was a small business founded by a Korean-American businessman who had started with minority set asides. The founder's goal was to expand beyond the set-aside business into regular government contracts, non-defense projects, and even commercial projects. That expansion became Simone's full-time occupation. He became an entrepreneur! He didn't really know what he was doing, but he took advantage of the free training. Simone's first attempt at expansion went pretty well. He focused on the Year 2000 Crisis. He formed a partnership between his contractor and a software developer, and the joint venture developed off-the-shelf solutions for detecting and resolving Year 2000 issues in large computer networks. They enjoyed substantial success and made a profit. Of course, that venture had an expiration date, and Simone had to find the next opportunity.

Simone finished his master's degree and became an entrepreneur in the years immediately following my divorce. We both experienced interesting aspects of social mobility. I left a software company and became a communications specialist. He moved up from communications specialist and started a software company. I got divorced. He got married. I moved into a one-bedroom apartment. He moved out of his one-bedroom apartment and bought a house. It's hard to argue with these entrepreneurs when they're getting results. Suffice it to say, I felt I was getting results too, but just more in the spiritual direction. Simone might argue with me over the definition of spiritual.

I really appreciated Simone's friendship in the early years of my divorce. I never interrogated him about the bottom line of his software venture, because it really didn't matter. I was impressed by his ability to extend himself and develop relationships. At that point, the doing was in the trying. We reflexively pursued our Epicurean ways, and we continued our discussions on the merits of various political and economic positions. Observing Simone's progress helped me develop the inner resources for my own next moves.

I spent some time by myself on my visits to Arlington. As a student of democracy dharma, I appreciated the opportunity to tour the Capitol building and the Supreme Court. I went to all the usual patriotic sites, but my favorite destinations in the Mall were the Smithsonian's Hirshhorn Museum of Modern Art and the National Museum of American History. I visited those as often as I could. They were more than mere artifacts, they were active institutions that maintained relevance. On what turned out to be my last visit, I drove east to Shenandoah National Park and looked down on the Shenandoah Valley from atop the ridgelines on Skyline Drive. I crossed paths with one of the park's elusive black bears when I took a short stroll into the woods. I also drove along the Potomac to Mount Vernon and visited George Washington's plantation. You don't really know the story of early America until you see the verdure of northern Virginia and the Appalachian Range in fall—the dream of self-sufficiency takes on a new meaning. You get to perceive the word "opportunity" the way the pioneers did.

Simone and I lost touch at the turn of the century. I fell out of favor with all my entrepreneurial friends within a year of my decision to truly drop out of corporate life and attempt right livelihood. I'm not sure why they dropped me. I enjoyed several nourishing friendships in my computer industry years, including the Mission District phase. Partly I fell out of fashion. My friends were, in fact, fair weather Beats. Brushing up against the real thing is probably a little unnerving. Maybe most significant, I unexpectedly experienced a period of maniacal overwork and overachievement in my first year as a teacher—total absorption. The Buddha didn't have drinking buddies and love affairs after he left the castle, so I guess it makes sense that I shed mine too. I recently saw Simone's profile on a social media site—he was coordinating sustainable manufacturing projects for a major defense contractor—a perfect expression of his metaphysical and materialistic ambitions.

By focusing on Simone, I'm might be short changing a few important friendships. Two love affairs transpired in my Mission hideout, with proper middle-class women (one at a time, monogamously). Maybe I should say failed in my hide out. A pattern emerged. Despite my lovers' obvious generosity and enthusiasm, I secretly harbored the reservation that they would drop me once they realized I was just a child psychologist working a day job as a copywriter. Growing weary of me hesitating when it was time to leap into marriage, they dumped me. So I learned the hard way that I needed to establish my own authenticity, in other words put first things first, before attempting a new relationship.

Finally, I'll briefly mention Adam, my best friend from my vulture years at the PC manufacturer. We became friends when I transferred into selling all the company's products, not just networking offerings, into the Northeast territory, which included New York at that point. Adam was a major accounts manager in those territories. We had both been SUNY students in the eighties—Adam was at the Buffalo campus. He had grown up in the Chelsea neighborhood of Manhattan, and his father was a merchant in Greenwich Village. We had both spent a lot of time in NYC in the eighties. Adam had a degree in journalism and I had studied democracy dharma. We enjoyed political sparring.

My time with Adam was intriguingly similar to my friendship with Simone. Adam was a great Epicurean, and I enjoyed being included in his tastes. We were both thirty-somethings, with Adam a few years senior. I wonder if my birth cohort, the tail end of the baby boom, will amount to more than their Epicurean ways. Adam was a fan of the Beats and other kinds of avant-garde art. He and his best friend from SUNY Buffalo had packed up in the late eighties and made the classic clunker-powered journey to San Francisco—they were inspired by the Summer of Love. The two friends were roommates in San Francisco's Fillmore District until Adam moved in with his fiancée in San Jose in the early nineties. I was a determined bohemian, but Adam was more of a retired hippy. Yet he projected the warmth that was still emanating out from many summers of love.

When Adam and I were students in NYC, Ed Koch was mayor and Mario Cuomo was governor. While we were co-workers, Bill Clinton unseated a Republican presidential regime of twelve years, and his first year unfolded. These charismatic leaders energized our faith in the Democrats. We experienced a kind of liberal hubris: we were proud to identify ourselves as Democrats. But I experienced the same kind of schism with Adam as with Simone: Adam the rising libertine entrepreneur

versus Robert the stubborn, growingly steadfast spiritual dissenter. Our friendship arose in the peak years of venture capital activity and foreign investment in the San Jose-Silicon
Valley region. Adam felt I needed to get on board, to join in
the gold rush. He felt I was letting family and friends down
by indulging in ideas such as right livelihood when there was
so much money up for grabs. I felt any growth was a mirage,
and the true repercussions of predatory investing would be
revealed eventually. America would have to turn to democratic socialism if only just to keep the peace; and for that
transformation to occur, we would need the values of spiritual warriorship. Besides, my motives for right livelihood
were not rooted solely in political dissent; they were mostly
driven by personality factors. In response, Adam would call
me self-indulgent. Whereas Adam and I had some really tough
talks over the years, Simone and I didn't touch on politics very
often, we mostly pondered the proper outlet for our spiritual
ambitions.

Adam's affiliation with the Democrats was mostly tied to
the protection of civil rights and civil liberties. In this way,
he was true to his NYC Jewish heritage. He wanted the government to guarantee civil liberties and equal opportunity, but
he was wary of central planning, because it creates the possibility of wide-scale religious intolerance and other kinds of
bigotry. I, on the other hand, identified with the Democrats
because of their support for central planning: for instance,
Clinton's combination of a technology investment tax credit
for businesses and high tax rates for individuals, and the familiar example of The New Deal. I thought our New Economy was
falling short of our needs, and it was going to need an intervention eventually.

Our friendship basically spanned the nineties. In that short
time, we both got married, had children, moved our careers
forward, and got divorced. Wow! Fast living. Adam was a hard-
charging businessman. In the waning days of our friendship,
when I went my own way to become a teacher, Adam was vice

president of sales for a trade-show company in the infotech market space, a position he had risen to internally by making sales. Like I said earlier, it's hard to argue with these libertarians when they're getting results. I was a naysaying antagonist, but in those peak years of venture and foreign investment, even a dissenter like me could make a living. But still, I felt, there was an undercurrent of collapse that would have to be addressed.

Adam and Simone were quite similar in physical stature and fashion statement. Both were about 5'8", medium athletic build verging on slim, with friendly intelligent eyes, shapely oval face with attractive features, fair to tawny skin, close cropped dark hair and clean shave, and strong shoulders and trim legs. Dressed-for-success in all phases of life, they both had an impressive collection of stylish two-piece classic suits, coordinated separate jackets and dress pants, attractive and sometimes even creative ties, and leather shoes in oxford and loafer styles. Their causal wear hewed to the preppy, with cotton oxford sport shirts and dress shirts, designer jackets and sweaters, tasteful jeans and chinos, and a variety of outdoor and casual fine leather footwear. They dressed with enthusiasm, and they looked youthful and motivated. They both had the same burly confidence mentioned in my description of my father, and keen observers may have noticed similarities in physiognomy. Like my father, they were life-long learners. Both Simone and Adam considered my father their friend, and Adam even received guidance from dad on a business project.

As I already mentioned, I lost track of Adam and Simone as well as all my other friends. The Buddha walked away from his ascetic friends in the forest to meditate alone and eventually discover the way of moderation—the middle way. I walked away from my Epicurean friends in the city to discover??

Drala Power

The Buddha exhorted disciples to withdraw from worldly affairs and to embrace a moderate level of austerity. In the Shambhala view, on the other hand, the warrior artfully engages in sensualistic and physical pursuits. The senses are seen as gateways to drala, meaning energy that exists in the world beyond the enemy, beyond the struggle to satisfy or avoid demands of the master race. In my Mission District years, my life seemed to fill up with drala. I ran from four to seven miles a day, five days a week, often in Golden Gate Park and adjacent Ocean Beach. Ocean Beach has a trail running for about two miles along the dunes—really inspiring at sunset—I went on many runs there after work. GG Park closes to car traffic on Sundays and thus opens up to every other kind of traffic: roller skaters, inline skaters, bicyclists, joggers, and walkers. I ran the circumference of the park, which was about eight miles—starting at the big lawn in front of the Conservancy of Flowers, downhill to Ocean Beach, and then back uphill on JFK Drive. It was pure joy gliding among fellow worshipers. Skillful creation of a beautiful physical setting such as the layout at GG Park is a great source of drala, and San Francisco overall is a truly drala-rich environment.

Drala practice involves taking care with your physical life from the grandest physical settings to the minutest details of personal decorum: wardrobe, grooming, physiology, speech, home, belongings, diet, friends, and entertainment. And the standard is taking care, applying attention, more than living up to a particular style or trend. For my Mission years, an appreciation of physical geography and its energizing properties made the biggest impact on me. I arranged my one-bedroom into an orderly, clean refuge for work, study, relaxation, friendship, and even romance, and that is no small challenge in a tenement. So I made the most of my modest domicile by taking care with it, but the real drala power came from two oversized pane windows in the middle of the living room—almost floor to ceiling, occupying the middle three-fifths of the wall. They formed a ten-square foot wide view of the skyline over North Beach—basically the view over the Golden Gate area of the bay. My third-story apartment was in the middle of the top floor, and the window sills were level with the roof of the building next door. I could see over the rooftops to the northern horizon. I didn't install window coverings. I let the azure majesty of the Pacific sky pour in every day, all day, and then the chill indigo brilliance of the starry nights. Those windows formed an opening to the cosmos that filled my mind with a lightness of being that will stay with me forever.

I spent an enormity of time in the outdoors under that azure brilliance. Whenever a gap would arise in my regime of daughter visits, work, socializing, study, and exercise, I would head out for a solitary hike. Solitary hikes typically originated with me in the café growing tired of reading after breakfast and not wanting to search for companions. I would hastily stuff supplies into a daypack and head out without much thought, and therefore Marin County became a favorite destination since it was a relatively short drive northward across the Golden Gate Bridge. Point Reyes National Seashore, Marin Headlands, Golden Gate National Recreation Area, and Mt. Tamalpais State Park were my favorites—basically coastal mountains and forests, and true wonders of the world.

Hikes typically lasted three to six hours. I seemed to have a knack for getting off the beaten path and avoiding crowds. Towering redwoods form a canopy to capture the fog and sunlight hundreds of feet above the trail. Massive oaks and firs bend, twist, and blossom into expressionist masterpieces. Creeks cut through steep ravines with winter rainfall rushing through stony waterfalls. Neon-green natural fern beds illuminate moist, humid passageways through groves and canyons. Wildflowers burst forth in spring with iridescent orange, yellow, and purple petals in the vivid green grasses of grand hilly meadows. High ridges with sweeping vistas of the azure Pacific waters leave you speechless. Breaking waves on sandy expansive beaches remind you of the rhythms of life.

When alone, the drala of these magical parklands starts to speak to you, to teach you the way of mindfulness. The mind stops racing, and starts opening, expanding, and awakening. It's about learning how to notice the enlightenment that is already there. Some Buddhist teachers might scold me for meditating in this wide-open way, but I'll just say that the Marin coast was an important temple in my path.

I also occasionally took solitary urban hikes, with the same routine: jump up, fill a pack, and go. My favorite walk was from the Mission District to Union Square through Chinatown to North Beach for lunch and shopping at City Lights Bookstore, a great bookstore in the most ordinary terms and a historic citadel of free speech. On these walks bristling with city life, I kept my mind relaxed and watched for the enlightenment that was already there in the environment.

Essentially, drala is about noticing the enlightenment that is already inherent in the world, about bringing it forth with skill. I stopped gobbling life up while stomping on it, and instead started living with life, in life, as part of it. It's about living in life without needing to conquer it. Connecting with the nourishing energy of the Bay Area's beautiful physical geography brought me in contact with the energizing power of drala. I felt healthy, good, and glad to be alive, despite struggling with issues of family and career.

With my vegetarian diet, emerging cooking skills, and regular exercise, in addition to time in the outdoors, I was lean, fit, and strong. I should mention that drala is best realized when sober. I confess to the occasional bender with a drinking buddy, but I was totally free of intoxicants at least twenty-seven days out of every thirty. I never used drugs. I was a warrior, or at least a warrior trainee.

Setbacks

My Mission District years ended during my search for a way to continue my career change after leaving Peter's agency.

After about a month at home in the Mission, a time of mostly just reading and hiking, the reality of my situation settled in. I had never looked for work as a writer. None of my friends could provide any leads, so I had no familiar contacts or other kind of network to tap into. It was going take some creativity and audacity to pull this off, and maybe some time. Living with direction wasn't going to be easy, but I felt it was worth the struggle.

It was the spring of 1999, and I was almost thirty-seven-years old. The business climate was defined by the shrinking government deficits and mild, wide-spread growth of the Clinton years, and nine consistent years of the bull market of the nineties. The bull market created unwarranted optimism, but that worked to my advantage as a job seeker. The economy had experienced six fairly-peaceful, growth-oriented years (although still falling short of prosperity). The New Economy was taking hold, fueled by the advent of the World Wide Web, and this was creating a lot of jobs in the infotech-oriented Bay Area. Given these favorable business conditions, I felt the odds for my career change were pretty good.

Business conditions were favorable, but my lack of experience and nascent skills were risk factors, so I moved into the guest room of my parent's place in the Mt. Diablo area. They had been empty nesters for about five years, yet they were still in the prime of middle age and both working hard at their careers. I was more of a housemate than a child. Living with them rent-free protected me from going totally broke before reaching my goal—it allowed me to draw out my savings gradually. In addition, I extracted unemployment benefits from Peter by underhanded and ruthless means.

I argued that Peter had laid me off by changing my role without my cooperation, through heavy-handed methods. I was careful to be truthful about all the details. The state appeals board liked my argument enough to let me get away with it, while not actually condoning it. I had learned about that kind of victory in political science: the one with money in hand is the winner. My defense in this matter was an awakening to the power wielded by my newly-developed writing skills. The pen is mightier than the sword, and sometimes it's the best way to stand up for yourself or get what you need. This was the first of several maneuvers conducted by means of pen.

Dad's story had changed a bit since his country-club mansion days back in eighties. The impetus for moving to Long Island had been dad being kicked upstairs and then eventually fired by a world-leading publishing firm in his hometown of Chicago. Dad had switched to that company to gain a promotion to sales manager denied him by his previous employer of ten years. At first, dad brought record sales to his new position on a worldwide publication. But his aggressive ways started to offend his preppy bosses. They promoted dad to publisher of a smaller publication, so he could run his own show, and thus kicked him upstairs. Dad's pushy ways were too much for the smaller publication and he was fired.

Scrambling to find a job after being fired for cause, which was a new experience for dad, he followed up on a lead from a friend who used to live across the street in Buffalo Grove. They had been neighbors and essentially coworkers in the publishing field. The lead involved dad moving from his homeland Chicago to Long Island, which was tragic, but dad was desperate. Once again, the position was with one of the country's most powerful publishers. In all the years of my youth, dad always worked on one of the nation's premier trade magazines.

This new Long Island employer saw dad's aggression as an asset they could use in growing their recently-acquired business publications. These publications were small fry compared to dad's typically world-leading roles, but they were in the office-automation area, which seemed like a promising situation in the emerging age of infotech. As publisher of two modest publications, dad found himself in one power struggle after another with his staff. It was pushy corporate dad versus small-fry stubbornness. The small fry won, and dad was kicked upstairs again by his new firm. Just three years after arriving as a publisher, dad was stationed as a regional vice president in Santa Clara, just outside of Silicon Valley. That is when he moved to his mansion in the Mt. Diablo area, and then later I followed him.

In his California role, dad would not manage a publication. He would use his big-company experience to help the small-fry sales staff make contacts with major advertisers. Basic-ally, he would be a sales advisor with no direct reports. The acquired business publications were not making it, and dad's role was a last-ditch effort to make the acquisitions work. The publications weren't positioned correctly for the New Economy, and they failed. The publishing firm closed the pub-lications and laid dad off without making any attempt to re-employ him. It was 1988, and the economy was heading into the savings-and-loan crisis and the junk-bond scandals.

Dad couldn't find suitable work, at least not in California. Dad's country-club lifestyle was spiraling out of control. He found work in Santa Clara as a sales rep for a trade publication on data communications, but that was just a temporary stop gap. Dad was just fifty-two-years old, but it looked like he had not just been kicked upstairs, but kicked out altogether. In a maniacal attempt to remain in California, where his youngest child was finishing high school, dad developed a business plan and started a publication of his own addressing office automa-tion. He actually enlisted qualified consultants and raised pri-vate-placement capital.

But developing a plan and raising money are not necessarily predictors of skill in running a company. As you might have discerned, management wasn't exactly dad's strength. When on your own, you don't have the luxury of getting kicked up-stairs for a few years on your way out. You're kicked right out onto the curb, typically with nothing left but the clothes on your back (paid for with the last of your credit cards). After just one year of running his own company, dad had lost every last dime of his wealth and was deeply in debt. He was totally busted and would never again enjoy any accumulation of money.

Now dad was really in dire straits, because it was 1991, the first of three peak years of one of the greatest recessions since the Great Depression. He left two of his three children, my brother and sister, stranded in college. I had been living with Wynda for a few years by then. Both siblings resorted to California State University, with my brother actually transferring out of a private university in New York. I would like to think that my career in public universities paved the way for my siblings to survive dad's reduced means.

Up isn't always the best way out, and ironically it sometimes leads to a decidedly downward trajectory. My ambition to be *not dad* was rooted in more than just abstract experiences such as learning the truth of the Nixon Administration or witnessing Wall Street abandon the working class and the domestic economy. It was rooted in my father's pain. Social climbing and status-seeking are powerful forces—of self-destruction.

My mother will occasionally excoriate my father by saying, "Everything went downhill when you left your stable sales rep job back in Chicago. You could have retired comfortably from that position. Those were the nicest people." That was her oblique way of telling dad that he didn't know his place, that he shouldn't have been so ambitious. Dad could never see the possibility of people skills—people are for stepping over on the way uphill. Charge!! Sergeant Advertising only charges one direction—uphill!! Keen observers may detect an element of Sisyphus. I wonder how dad's life might have turned out if the Irish Catholic Corporate Climber culture had embraced ideas of contentment and restraint.

When I moved in with dad after leaving Peter's agency in 1999, dad was living in a nice two-story, three-bedroom American colonial townhouse about three miles to the south of his mansion days. This rented home would be the resting place of his reduced years. It was located in the town of Danville. The townhouse was part of a small planned community nestled into the lush ranchlands of the Mt. Diablo foothills —appropriately scenic and appropriately above dad's means (Sergeant Advertising never surrenders!!). Dad sold his mansion in a panic a few years after his company collapsed, and then travelled through a series of three rented homes before landing in this modest-but-scenic community. It was very quiet and pastoral.

When the dust settled from the business collapse, which was followed by five more years as a magazine-advertising sales rep, dad found his way into the direct-mail coupon business. These coupons targeted home owners with direct-marketing offers. Dad solicited the small businesses that advertised in the coupons. At first, he was a sales consultant to an entrepreneur starting a coupon business. Eventually, he became a sales consultant to the nation's largest publisher of coupon direct mail by teaming up with the franchisee who sold the advertising in the Bay Area. It was an uneasy alliance with this franchisee, who had a knack for harnessing dad's aggressive energy while not succumbing to it. Dad sold a lot of advertising for the franchisee, and the relationship lasted fifteen years, but dad's income was still slightly below his first management position back in Chicago: in other words, he was back at sales rep.

Dad working with the small businesses of the Bay Area had an auspicious dynamic to it. Grandpa Bartlett's occupation had been local banker and loan agent serving the small businesses and homeowners of Chicago's South Side. Now dad was doing business with that same constituency, but in advertising. The more things change, the more they stay the same. Apparently aware of this auspiciousness, dad started incorporating the name "Bartie" into his e-mail address, which had been my grandfather's nickname.

When I moved into the Danville townhouse, it was 1999, and Dad had been making pretty good way in the coupon field for a few years: in fact, he was on the threshold of ten prosperous years. The emphasis on home building and home remodeling (driven by low taxes and aggressive mortgage bankers) that culminated in the Great Recession of 2009 was a healthy source of expansion for the Bay Area and dad's regional advertisers, who were selling goods and services directly to homeowners. He rode the crest well.

Unexpected Opportunities

My return to the suburbs created unexpected opportunities. Technology companies, especially software firms that in the eighties might have resided in Silicon Valley or San Jose, were now establishing major offices and even headquarters in areas near Danville, such as Pleasanton, San Ramon, Walnut Creek, and Concord. The firms were attracted to the lower rents and lower wages of these still-partially rural areas. In addition, Danville was within workable commuting distance of Fremont and San Jose. Once I got down to looking for work in a determined way, it quickly became apparent that these were the cities to watch.

The dot-com boom was starting to ripen in San Francisco, but after just a couple of interviews at dot-com startups, I knew my prospects in that field were limited. I just couldn't communicate in their buzzword dialect. "We're looking for someone to expand our presence on the network," said a cheerful twenty-something young lady who might have been from the cheerleading squad at Ohio State. "Who would this network bring together? Who would be connected?" I replied in the reflexively literal way of the tech copywriter. "We're mostly thinking of the community." I sat silently for a few seconds, probably looking nonplussed. "And who would this community consist of?" "The net, of course," replied the interrogator, with a look of growing consternation. "Hmm. The net. I see. Well, I'm a net man all the way," said me giving up on the interview. This conversation occurred at a dot-com site providing contact-management tools to small businesses. I had been fishing for an answer like, "We'll be targeting small businesses in the b-2-b sector with sales under 200 million." Instead, I was referred to "the community."

An unsuspecting visitor to San Francisco in those days might have thought they stumbled into a massive insane colony offering inmates an incredible array of services, such was the widespread use of incoherent vagueness and puffery among the populace. Clearly, the prime mover in the dot-com movement was the passing of investor's money to friends from old alma mater until the adults caught on. The adults (i.e. investors) did catch on after a few years, withdrawing support in a sudden, sweeping move, leading to an exodus among the cultists of the buzzword. This exodus was so swift that it caused one of the few real-estate deflations in San Francisco history. Even though I was only thirty-six, and a bona fide Mission District hipster, I was aged out by the dot-com crowd.

Luckily, I had moved to an area where industrial, mission-critical software companies had set up shop. I felt truly blessed by this opportunity to avoid the dot-com field. Even in those industrial companies, however, I could seem outdated. The way of the buzzword had taken hold everywhere: everyone seemed to be "increasing their presence" on "the net," even in companies focused on back-office applications such as personnel and payroll. Interestingly, my strongest leads and ultimately my next job were in the banking and financial-services sector. I guess money matters are serious enough to require the use of literal language.

First, I landed a job at a financial-services firm, one of the nation's leading mutual-fund managers. My role as copywriter was to polish the quarterly statements sent by fund managers to investors. My pay would only be ten percent higher than at the agency, but I was attracted by the opportunity to be a writer without the marketing side. My autodidact studies had elevated my writing skills to the point where I could function as a copyeditor. The firm had reviewed my samples, interviewed me, and administered a skills test: I passed all those challenges and they hired me. I was a writer! But alas, I wasn't quite mutual-fund material yet, and the job fell though in the first few days.

My first day was spent in orientation. Mostly we watched films on decorum. My main memory of that day is a solid two hours of reviewing every aspect of a woman's appearance, right down to what type of straps a brassiere should have. I had never seen such paranoia. It's like they hated sexuality —like they assumed women were vixens to be kept in line. As I was pondering the implications of their hyper prurience, the personnel office called me in for a meeting. A background check had revealed a misdemeanor charge. On my application, I had stated that I had a clean record, which was true since I had honored the terms of the plea agreement. I told them I would check with my lawyer to clear up this error.

From my lawyer, I learned that I had to file a perfunctory motion at the municipal court wherein a judge would issue an order to formally dismiss the charge and enter a plea of not guilty. This was the charge of contempt of court from when I left Wynda a peaceful voicemail that wasn't exactly, perfectly within the terms of her restraining order. The mutual-fund firm declined to wait for the motion. It was only a misdemeanor charge of contempt of court—it wouldn't disqualify me from the state licensure required for the position. But it was my impression that they were spooked by the whole sordid affair. I was kind of peeved about the fact that neither my lawyer nor the court had informed me of the necessity of this step. On the other hand, I accepted that this motion was just one more step in disentangling myself from Wynda's anger. Living with direction was going to take some struggle.

I put my job search on hold, filed the motion, and waited the thirty days to appear before the judge, who issued the verdict in a quick minute, and then I had a clean record (i.e. plea of not guilty, charges dropped, case dismissed). I had found the mutual-fund position within three months of leaving Peter's agency. The motion had cost me a month, but I was encouraged by the fact that I had found a solid lead in just three months. I resumed my search, which yielded an even better opportunity a couple of months later. A bit of adversity turned into a better opportunity, one that was more of a culmination of all my experiences. To the nonjudgmental warrior, setbacks aren't failures, they're information about what steps to take next.

I found a position as product-marketing manager at an established software company focused on core banking systems. Core processing describes a network of computers that provide sales, customer service, online banking, accounting, and management functions, and integrates them into one unified system. The firm mainly served community banks and credit unions, meaning the small-business side of banking.

A successful small business itself, with national reach, the firm had about $100 million in annual sales; they were on NASDAQ at $20 a share. They were located in Pleasanton, which was growing into a kind of "software ranch." They occupied a modern two-story rectangular glass-and-steel building with 65,000 square feet of office space, lightly-wooded grounds in a quiet office park, and its own parking lot. My commute was twenty minutes southward on back roads. The mutual-fund lead had offered a ten percent increase in salary; the core software position yielded a twenty-seven percent increase, plus retirement matching. Of course, both positions offered free, comprehensive health benefits (the good old days!). Core processing drew on all my tech experiences since college—PCs, open-systems networking, UNIX servers, client-server database applications, and accounting applications. I had significant exposure to all these elements of the core-processing view. Even with all this relevant knowledge, my pay merely equaled the peak compensation of my vulture capitalist years back in the late eighties.

Online hiring was the cause of this precise matching of qualifications to the task. This was my first job search in the online era. By applying careful attention to the keyword structure of online recruiting, I found a position I was qualified for with no help from my usual network. A new kind of network was involved, and it looked a little more like a meritocracy. For middle managers and staff, it seemed like finding a job might become more about what you know than who you know. For executives, though, things would probably remain business as usual. I was actually encouraged by the emerging meritocracy of online hiring.

This is the software firm where the present story started, the one where I was thrown out unceremoniously just months after receiving a merit raise, after being rendered obsolete by an acquisition that was meant to rescue a previous acquisition that had occasioned the need for a high-priced copywriter like me.

I was hired to help a stalled acquisition. The grand $100M enterprise that I described a couple of paragraphs ago was the result of a larger software company (parent) in Portland, Oregon, acquiring a smaller firm (acquisition) in Pleasanton. My role was to help integrate the two entities into a new, unified brand, almost as if the parent had started over again. At the point of my arrival, Pleasanton had sabotaged nearly all of Portland's efforts for a year. Pleasanton refused to shed their old identity; they were actually harboring fantasies of defiance and an eventual return to independence. My strengths would be project management and the ability to compose and edit my own materials: in short, my agency years proved I could pull people together and makes things happen. The parent company thought that my strengths would allow me to clamp down on the rebels and force them into line with the acquisition's grand vision. In a thrust of authoritarian rule, I would simply grab power—parent dominates child!

I already mentioned at the start of this journey that I facilitated the miraculous integration of these warring factions into a new, glorious brand. Yet the parent had squandered too much money and time fighting the rebels, and so put the new expanded entity up for sale to raise cash for their lenders. That rescue operation left me stranded in Pleasanton, where the personnel redoubled their efforts at independence, in an act of monumental backsliding.

Peacemaking Copywriter

Even though the product-marketing position didn't end well, I gained a beneficial insight about warriorship. I made serious strides away from the pushy way of accomplishing things and toward more of a peacemaking, empathetic approach. My formation of a project pipeline for marcom projects provides a pivotal experience for explaining this insight.

In my first few days, the social climate was a bit chilly in Pleasanton. A personnel assistant, who reported to Portland, showed me to my spacious corner office and attended to connecting me to the company network. I was encouraged to be online by my second day, which contradicted the office gossip that predicted weeks of delay: Portland was in a hurry. For the first week, the personnel assistant was my only real contact with the staff. But I didn't mind, because my pushiness was kicking in—I would move forward alone, silently almost like a spy, and then draw the staff in. I knew how to stand alone from my agency days—Pleasanton wasn't going to bog me down in a popularity contest.

On my own initiative, since no one gave me any direction, I did a little reconnaissance. The cabinets and shelves in my private office held a collection of past and present marcom materials. I strolled around the office complex brashly picking up and requesting all kinds of materials. I had the web on my PC, which gave me access to competitors. In about two days, I had amassed an impressive collection of source material and competitive intelligence, without even introducing myself. I crammed hard for the rest of the first week. I probably knew more than any other person in the company at that point. I was ready to take over—and hardly anyone had said hello yet.

The second week I flew up to Portland to meet the marketing department and just about everyone else. I was briefed on the brand identity that they were ready to launch. The layouts for marcom materials were ready, and they had already been applied to Portland's products. My first task would be to translate Pleasanton's marcom info into the new layouts. When I was done, there would be a sales kit under the new brand. Pleasanton's core processing software products were the prize possession of the new entity. Portland's specialty was computerized documentation for lending (i.e. the contracts and disclosure forms). By acquiring Pleasanton's products, Portland hoped to enter the big leagues of core processing. So, developing a sales kit under the new brand would be Portland's way of finally taking possession of the acquired products.

When I got back to the office, I settled into the task. Pleasanton's extant marcom info consisted of a kind of essay for each product, with basically letterhead at the top of the page for branding. The copy was rambling, nearly-incoherent puffery, with no subheads or other organizing marks. Using the new branded layout, I developed one sheet for each product, with a header, bulleted key-features column, and a column of body copy with subheadings. I adapted this same layout to write a couple of system-level overviews. In the sales kit, the sheets could be organized with overviews first to create a seven-page booklet describing the entire integrated system. My week of cramming really paid off, since it enabled me to cull key features from the rambling text of the original info. My cramming also supported a matter-of-fact, detail-oriented tone for body copy. I lean towards journalism in my approach to marcom, but that doesn't mean that I don't know how to compete. I made sure the bulleted key features went toe-to-toe with the competition. Pleasanton was transformed from a wishy-washy amateur to one of the most powerful brands in the industry.

Since I was kind of a lone wolf, I was able to resolve a few problems left unattended by Portland. First, no one had attended to product names for Pleasanton. This oversight was my first opening for peace negotiations. Following my own intuition, I turned Pleasanton's former company name into a product line, and then just carried the individual product names forward unchanged. So, Pleasanton's products became *The Pleasanton System by New Brand*. Portland would have liked to rename the products to reflect only the new brand, but I convinced them that reputation-sensitive software buyers would appreciate the explicit continuity with a proven system. From an emotional perspective, Pleasanton seemed comforted by the acknowledgement of their past leadership and good reputation. I didn't help either faction dominate; instead I mingled their interests.

Second, Portland hadn't considered the scope of Pleasanton's products. They would have been happy with one overview sheet for Pleasanton, with a list of bullets covering all their products. But each major function of the core-processing system was sold as a full-fledged product on its own (i.e. data processing, lending, tellers, online banking, etc.), and lucrative upgrades and service contracts were sold for each product. By covering all the products in detail, and thus accommodating Pleasanton's existing marketing strategy, I prepared them to increase sales to new and existing customers —the smiles reappeared around Pleasanton, and staffers even started to greet me.

Finally, I initiated an alliance with Pleasanton's sales tech, Melanie. She conducted sales demonstrations, helped the sales staff prepare bids, and managed the user's group. In peaceful times, she would have been the natural counterpart of my position. Our NYC connection provided a good basis for collaboration. Melanie went to Catholic school in Queens and graduated from Long Island University with a degree in accounting: a Catholic Corporate Climber! She was a working mother of one young child, and she was really materialistic and ambitious. Dressed for success every day, Melanie's daily two-piece classic suit with nice blouse, leather pumps, and stockings distinguished her as a leader in an office that had converted to business casual. She identified her ethnicity as "Persian," which I interpreted to mean Iranian. Her tawny Mediterranean complexion was complimented by expressive soft eyes, trim styled short dark hair, cheerful smile, curvy-yet-sturdy frame, and petite physique. She was perky and formidable, and essentially the heart of the Pleasanton operation, even though technically she was just a specialist at that point.

I enlisted Melanie as my fact checker for the new sales kit. Portland was miffed about my investment in the sales kit. Once when I told them that I was waiting for Melanie to check one of the product sheets, they said, "You know, this is taking longer than we planned," meaning I should send it up without her involvement. They clearly wanted me to treat Pleasanton staff as subordinates, but I knew better—my plan was to coexist more than dominate. Melanie was conspicuously pleased with *our* new sales kit and helped me disseminate it throughout the organization.

When the sales kit was completed, I was left alone in the office again with no direction, but I was starting to take a stake in Pleasanton's progress. I noticed that they were maintaining an old website completely out of compliance with the new brand. I set about to convince Portland to develop a new site and Pleasanton to take down the old one. I wanted to integrate the website with the sales kit. I developed a marcom project pipeline (spreadsheet) and showed it around Pleasanton. Melanie and the general manager thought it was a good idea. I contacted my boss in Portland and established a running weekly conference call with my boss, Melanie, and the general manager to plan the pipeline. This pipeline and our weekly meetings became the prime mover in my peace-keeping maneuvers.

My first entry in the pipeline was a new website, even though no one had asked me to deal with it. As I had hoped, the first meeting resulted in a new website incorporating my approach to the sales kit. With the pipeline, over the course of the next year, we meticulously worked through every aspect of integrating Pleasanton's products into the new brand.

My peacemaking plans actually came to fruition, starting with these weekly meetings. They required Portland to listen to Pleasanton's concerns in real time, through personal interaction. In conversations with Portland management, I dropped the suggestion that they should deliberately visit the Pleasanton office just to connect, to get some face time in. In other words, Portland should try selling the acquisition instead of the failed approach of threatening and dominating. Portland followed my suggestion. The management visits were well received. Pleasanton's smiles grew even brighter.

The healing power of listening is a key principle of warriorship. In facilitating opportunities for listening and dialogue, I was trying to improve over my agency job, where I had stymied dialogue whenever I thought it might not lead to my position prevailing. Increased personal contact between the divisions led to genuine teamwork. By the end of my first year, there was fluid and meaningful interaction between the two groups. They had actually become one company. A sense of vision arose, and people were energized throughout the organization. I've never forgotten the experience of watching the ice break between these warring factions, and I carry this lesson of listening into everything I do.

Across that first year, I used the Pleasanton marcom pipeline to keep myself well-employed. I resurrected and refined a monthly newsletter sent to customers, who essentially functioned as a user's group; we started moving to an online format. I helped the sales force develop their PowerPoint sales presentation. I edited sales proposals. I wrote copy for the new website. I wrote product and corporate announcements, and I continued to refine and expand the product literature. Both divisions often included me in meetings for sales, product strategy, and even corporate functions. Compared to my agency days, it was easy living. I went home almost every night in time for a run or a trip to the gym before dinner. My hours were pretty regular, with very few late nights or weekends needed to hit deadlines. I was respectably busy. At the end of my first year, I received a positive evaluation and a modest merit raise.

The organization had welcomed me, but I still felt slightly marginalized, so I started wheedling my way into strategic decisions, testing my limits. By means of dropping hints at auspicious moments, I moved Pleasanton to intensify the marketing of current products to existing customers. We even developed discount offers published in the monthly newsletter. My approach worked. We exceeded that goal for the year, making up for softness in sales to new customers. I subtly nudged Pleasanton into selling consulting services to existing customers. But I couldn't really claim credit for those things, since they weren't my direct responsibility...yet. I was starting to wonder if copywriter was enough. I pondered returning to school to expand my qualifications.

But about the time I started sidling up to power, the bad news hit. I recall that the announcement was made at a grand sales conference held in a resort hotel. It was the spring or summer of 2000. The new, unified company meetings had become truly grand, once we got everyone on the same team. People were actually looking forward to a bright future as a major software company. Despite progress in integrating the two organizations, said the CEO from the podium, sales were soft and creditors were hard. The new company would be sold in an acquisition to raise money for the lenders.

At that point, the CEO promised to urge the acquiring company to keep the new brand intact. He couldn't really promise anything, but how, said the CEO, could the new investor disrupt the incredible progress made so far? There was a collective gasp, psychic and physical. Most people, in a predictable state of denial, believed the investor would keep everything intact. The investor, in fact, did just the opposite, starting with the firing of the CEO and COO, which cleared out the two executives who had hired me. I probably should have figured on a similar fate befalling me, which it did, as I mentioned at the beginning of this story. For a couple of months after the preliminary announcement, we followed the marcom pipeline in a perfunctory way, pretending that everything would continue uninterrupted. Then in the summer of 2000, when the final, formal announcement came, Pleasanton was informed that the unified brand would be broken up, with Pleasanton's products cast off on their own. But there were no plans for how that divestiture would proceed.

Doubt

After the acquisition announcement, I was actually the first and only one to wonder exactly how Pleasanton would operate autonomously: in other words, to attend to details. Literally, everyone was sitting around the office thinking big picture. I prepared a task list for Pleasanton's general manager, showing what it would take to get a sales operation moving fast. Somehow, he located some cash and gave me the green light. The process was disturbingly informal. I developed a quick and thrifty brand, and the new investor basically acquiesced to it out of indifference. I also handled many of the corporate announcements related to the acquisition. But then came the mad scramble for power.

When the Pleasanton managers noticed that I had brought some substance to the autonomous entity, they saw the opportunity of a lifetime—a renewed chance to truly shine!! A return to the halcyon days of yore!! I, on the other hand, couldn't care less; I was truly downhearted and burnt out. "Pardon me. Could somebody tell me how many months 'till the next debacle?" A stream of superficial projects issued forth from the eager beavers at top speed, but it was like my brain had blown a gasket and seized up. Literally, I had writer's block, which I never experience. The unified brand that hired me was going to be a national leader, but Pleasanton on its own was small fry. I just didn't feel like pushing myself for them. My main mistake at that point was in not initiating a job search immediately.

Launching the spin off brand took about three months. Then I tried to play along with the eager beavers for another three months. Then I stopped communicating with my co-workers and respecting deadlines. Human Resources warned me a couple of times. Then finally, one morning, the HR manager called me into her office. "Robert, you're not responding to your supervisors." "Nope." "Then we're going to have to conclude that you don't want to work with us anymore." "Yep." "Okay then, here is your last check." I didn't bother to argue that I never agreed to work for Pleasanton's management: that was how I felt, but it was a moot point.

And that was the end of my involvement with corporate life. It felt really good to walk out of that office and just goof off for rest of the day. I stopped for a nice breakfast. By some intuitive force, I knew I was done. It might be interesting to note that the first acquisition, with Portland acquiring Pleasanton, had occurred primarily because Pleasanton had squandered the proceeds from its relatively recent IPO.

I had no specific thoughts of a new occupation on that day. It was more like a numb sensation in the frontal lobes. Whatever it was that one needed to survive in the war-torn landscape of the investment bankers' war on the human race, I was missing it. Maybe I had a case of battle fatigue. Nearly all of my jobs since college were shaped by volatile forces outside my direct control, typically the influences of Wall Street hegemony. My expectations for meritocracy were more noble than just being tossed about as a pawn in one investment ploy after another.

When I started college in the early eighties, the Federal Reserve interest rate was relatively high and the Dow Jones was just below a 1000 (it had been below that level since its inception in 1896). Slowly, incrementally, the interest rate went to rock bottom and the Dow Jones went skyrocketing. By the mid-nineties, a business could only raise money on NAS-

DAQ or NYSE, since banks were not motivated to make long-term strategic loans at low interest rates. This shift in the availability of funds gave investment bankers unprecedented power; they were suddenly the center of attention, and they established themselves as gods over all business activity and eventually all human endeavor. Every business of any merit had to take their shot at getting in on the gravy train, and thus many small businesses, like my last employer, jumped into the stock exchanges and started dreaming big.

I've been talking about the role of lenders, but Portland's business plan was to expand using strategic loans and then issue new shares in a kind of grand reopening: the proceeds of this public reoffering would repay the loans and fund even more growth. Sounds magnificent, but neither Portland nor Pleasanton, says me with crystal clear hindsight, had the talent or resources to bring their vision to fruition, and thus they stalled in the middle and went broke. Portland planned to sell its online documentation customers the Pleasanton core-processing system, but that proved to be a hornet's nest. They just took too much on at once.

Before Wall Street hegemony, these two small businesses would have diligently stuck to long-term borrowing and careful, incremental growth. But in the frenzied rush to the stock exchanges, they were lured into taking wild, speculative chances. The bull market of the nineties was in part driven by this kind of dreamy activity. Keen observers might remember that the Dow Jones went over 10,000 during my years in Pleasanton, and the leading source of income at major national banks shifted from commercial lending to consumer loans such as credit cards, auto loans, and mortgages. The same major banks also increased their activities in investment banking.

The Bay Area economy looked pretty good from the satellite view during my corporate years, but from the zoom view things were pretty rough on me and almost everyone I knew. This disparity based on viewpoint creates an interesting quantitative dilemma. How can macro-level growth wind up as individual human misery? The misery happens the way water boils over or metals break down. If you apply too much energy, the molecules burst into hyperactivity until the substance changes form or breaks down. From a molecular point of view it's quite violent, but from the macro view you get a nice cup of tea or a finely-honed tool. I was one banged up molecule, a fuselage panel about to give way.

Everywhere I went, and all over the Bay Area, investment bankers were turning up the heat in their rush to get their cup of tea. But we molecules were just being consumed and vaporized, in a business climate characterized by occupational upheaval, workforce churn (i.e. wanton, indiscriminate turnover), and transient organizations. Even major innovators came and went, rendering the corporation a flimsy and insubstantial institution. It became clear that very few of my generation would experience the pride and stability of the company man (or lady). Instead, we would be "rugged individualists" in the "creative economy" (i.e. inmates in the asylum).

I was, in fact, one of those rugged individuals in the creative economy, in a very literal sense. Keen observers might describe the experience as more chaotic than creative. Once again, I found myself an agnostic in a faith in which I was a doubter. In the weeks after I left, I reflected on my next move. I wondered if there was a way for me to move past agnostic in corporate life.

On the strength side, I had markedly increased the professionalism of my approach to marcom projects. I left the pushy copywriter behind. Instead, I had grown into the peacemaker copywriter. I completed many mission-critical projects without any of the interpersonal conflicts that I had inflicted on the agency. In Zen, there is the principle of "staying upright" under duress, meaning the practitioner remains thoughtful even when all around him are enthralled in destructive emotions such as resentment, jealousy, and hatred. I had stayed composed and positive in an atmosphere awash in destructive emotions. And I had even played a central role in helping everyone regain their composure. On the day-to-day level, I was actually an upbeat and even-handed presence. From this experience of positivity, I gained confidence in my people skills, energizing my thoughts about what to do next.

On the weakness side, I was still writing about topics that I didn't truly care about. The experience felt a little mercenary. I mentioned numbness in the frontal lobes. Actually, they had grown progressively numb every month until they just seized up. I figured a new employer or project would probably perk me up, but I was starting to worry about motivation.

My reaction to the politics of the second acquisition was the major weakness. At the risk of exaggerating, I proclaim myself the single greatest reason the company avoided bankruptcy. My decision, from my first days, to emphasize the marketing of Pleasanton's extant products to their existing customers saved the company, says me. And it truly was just me against insurmountable odds. But I didn't put any energy into claiming credit, and, not surprisingly, no one else put much effort into giving me credit. Interestingly, though, when the new investor arrived in the final acquisition, Pleasanton started claiming credit for all kinds of accomplishments, but I just sat back.

When the new investors were in Pleasanton for a meeting, managers would crowd around them, "Mr. Smith. I would really like to sit down with you for a few minutes. I've got some ideas for the new company that I know you'll want to hear," exhorted one manager after another as they diverted an executive to a nearby office. The executives couldn't make it down a hallway without being accosted at least two times. I, on the other hand, never took the trouble to meet even one of them. I went passive. When I wasn't busy on a project, I found a few books and websites on marcom topics and occupied myself with some informal professional development. I kept out of the way, while everyone else feverishly asserted themselves. Of course, that was just the wrong move on my part. With me as a passive presence, sooner or later, some Pleasanton manager looking for power would want to put my salary and budget under their jurisdiction by moving me out of the way. I'm guessing that is what happened. I had reverted to uppity hipster mode. I just couldn't play the eager beaver to the investment banker's domination. I had been through too much upheaval in my young life.

That experience of passivity really got me thinking. If I'm going to make it in marcom, I thought, I have to assert myself as a professional. I have to stop working the back office, and I have to start networking and selling myself as a professional. I needed to develop my own brand, either on my own or on the inside as an employee. Passive in the back office wasn't going to cut it in the creative economy—that was just a fact of contemporary life. So I had a tough decision to make. Was I prepared to give marcom my all? To really make it work?

In my last months at Pleasanton, after the second acquisition, when I developed yet another brand, I acted as an internal agency. I secured a budget from Pleasanton's general manager and then managed all the projects independently, like a director or vice president of marketing might do. I hired a design firm (i.e. art directors and designers), developed concepts with them for print, online, and other materials, wrote the copy, and then arranged printing and other aspects of production. I didn't need oversight from executives in Portland. My skill level allowed me to handle things on my own. Put another way, I acted as an internal agency when I probably should have been starting my own agency. I was finally the account executive that everyone in my life wanted me to be.

At that point, I might have replaced myself with another writer, formed a partnership with the design firm and printer, and gone on to hire or partner with whatever talent was needed to handle my clients. For my part, I would spend all my time communicating my vision for marcom to regional and national executives and selling them services. I was a skilled and creative writer. But my most marketable service was becoming the marcom pipeline—the ability to define projects, set deadlines, commit resources, and bring plans to fruition... with real quality. That last sentence reads like a job description for an agency's account supervisor.

But to even think that thought felt like giving in to temptation. Eject! Live with direction or die!! Yet people were right about me. The real money, power, and glory in marcom go to the account executives, especially those who can attract new clients. Conventional wisdom says that inside marcom staff are always the first thing to throw overboard in a crisis. If I wanted to stabilize in marcom, I should shift my career to developing accounts in ways that would allow me to ride the crests and avoid the ebbs in the stormy seas of the creative economy: in other words, work with a list of clients instead of just one. That approach would make a lot of sense, except that it just wasn't me.

I meditated on the possibility of starting my own agency or forming some kind of alliance with an existing one. First, economic conditions didn't look favorable for small business, which probably would have been my target. I saw the conditions of the Great Recession brewing, plus the characteristic corporate transience of the tech sector. A credit crunch seemed to be on the horizon as a chain reaction to a crash on NASDAQ, which plunged its composite index from an all-time high of 5000 in year 2000 to a plateau at 1200 in year 2001, where it would stay for the next two years (i.e. the dotcom crisis). Second, I would have to start on a small scale and scramble my way up. That felt like too much salesmanship for me: I might give up in the middle, with clients, employees, and partners depending on me. Third, I was an agnostic and doubter in the faith of the libertarian executive. Say I actually had the skill needed to make it big. Before that could happen, I would have to prostrate to the gods of the global investor master race. I didn't hate executives, but I was really disappointed in their lack of loyalty to the workforce. I didn't want to be a champion of the executive suite, yet that is exactly what it would take to make it big.

Despite making some impressive headway in marcom, I was still really just a child psychologist working a day job. I decided to not embrace marcom as a career. I might hold one or two more jobs in marcom, I decided, but it was time to end the day jobs and somehow get into graduate school. Moreover, I was getting older. It was the spring of 2001, and I was thirty-nine-years old. The time had arrived to bring this mid-life identity crisis to a conclusion.

So within a couple of weeks of being laid off (i.e. fired), I pulled my online job search together and resumed where I left off when I was hired at the core-processing company. I knew that I should be networking like a real marcom pro, but I figured that I could squeeze at least one more day job out of my writing skills. I identified myself as laid off, and even listed Pleasanton as a reference, because I believed that the separation from Portland constituted a de facto termination due to circumstances beyond my control. I even successfully applied for unemployment benefits.

As described in the first chapter, my online search received no responses. No inquiries. No interview requests. Only a year and a half earlier, I was virtually swamped with inquiries with basically the same resume and pitch. In this new search, it was summer, which is typically a slow time for hiring, so I thought maybe inquiries would pick up in the fall. Then came September 11, 2001—9/11. Expansion was already slowing down in the computer sector. A credit crunch was looming. And then the attack on the World Trade Center intensified these subtle factors into something ominous. I started to worry that this mid-life change would not be as glamorous as one more high-paying day job with some graduate study fit in around it. Austerity, struggle, and even desperation may be involved. I was anxious and energized at the same time. Maybe it was time for some bodhisattva activity.

Another New Beginning

Despite being "laid off," my personal life at that point was in a good space for making a change. The year and a half at my parent's place since leaving the Mission District had been very quiet. Occasionally, I would connect with Simone or Adam, my Epicurean libertarian friends pursuing their will to power as men of business, but these occasions were becoming rare. They were growing tired of my self-righteous resistance of the executive suite. To them, I had become a naysayer. For my part, I became a saver. I banked almost my entire disposable income for the year and a half. Between my penny pinching and their irritation with me, we just seemed to connect less frequently. No love affairs, although one brief fling that didn't do too much damage to either participant.

Back then, in summer of 2001, the Mt. Diablo area still had remnants of its rural roots (the population has now doubled). In downtown Danville, our town, you could grab breakfast at the diner and then put your feet up at a street-side, oak-shaded patio with a cup of coffee and a book and pretty much feel like you were in a quiet small town. There was still a shade of the old west on main street—just a shadow—but it was a relaxing change of pace. Occasionally, the town's peace would be disrupted by a local Ferrari GTO or Porsche Carrera roaring through, but they don't call it the Wild West for nothing. What the heck, I was even driving a late model Miata, maintained by a local mechanic, by the way. No more jack stands in dad's garage.

Mt. Diablo seems to have a magical influence on me. Recall that my summer of meditation unfolded there six years earlier while staying with my parents. The gentle, rolling aspect of the volcanic mountain and foothills convey a feeling of hospitality and accommodation, as opposed to the jagged, uprooted impression conveyed by some of the more tectonic mountains of coastal and central regions of California. Back then, there were ample open spaces in Mt. Diablo with rolling hills populated by lush grasses, an incredible variety of oaks, and a smattering of alder, ash, walnut, pine, and cottonwood, among others: orchard and cattle country.

I mostly filled my free time with workouts and reading great books. Downtown Danville featured the Iron Horse Trail, a converted Southern Pacific rail right of way that runs north to south through the former agricultural towns of the region. It wound through commercial and residential zones beautifully, making a park-like setting for walking and running. I ran about four to five miles a day there: it was good drala. I also joined a fitness center, adding circuit training with weights to my running. I was in peak condition and free of any health problems.

I stated a sobriety rating of twenty-seven days totally sober, meaning no intoxicants of any sort, out of every thirty for my time in the Mission District. In Mt. Diablo, my rating improved to forty-two days totally sober out of every forty-five. I felt clear-headed, with the direction of my life set by my values more than by my drinking buddies, lovers, or other peer influences. Yet I still enjoyed the occasional outing with Epicurean friends and family.

I continued to work on my writing skills, mostly by reading great books. My grammar skills were becoming second nature, and I didn't need to invest much more time in them. Dickens provided the kind of total absorption needed for taking my mind off the fact that I was stuck in my parent's place: Nicholas Nickleby, Hard Times, Great Expectations, Bleak House, and Little Dorrit. The total absorption into nineteenth-century London really moved me—after a while, it's as if you actually lived there. It makes Dickens very memorable. I read many authors while at my parent's place, contemporary and classic, but I have a panoramic memory of Dicken's London. Dickens had me feeling moralistic and high-minded as I prepared for my next beginning.

So, when I entered the teaching profession in July 2003 with pre-service training, I was fit, strong, and high-minded, and feeling very young for forty-one. I've pretty much already described the intervening two years between my last corporate job and my first day in the credential program: research on the teaching profession, locating a special-education credential program, applying to a program, acceptance, and finally securing a teaching contract at Mt. Diablo Unified School District.

In the middle twelve months of this research and application process, I held a couple of hourly jobs to help stretch out my savings and to keep the child support flowing. I worked swing shift to leave room during the day for research and interviews. I chose laboring positions to avoid corporate employment of any sort: I was determined to never return. No backsliding! Live with direction or die!! First I was a delivery truck driver for a major national news organization. We moved the morning edition from the printer to regional distribution centers. Then I was a gas station attendant for a franchisee of a global refiner.

After I had worked at the gas station for six months, the franchisee fired me, out of the blue, because, I say, they had to pay me time and a half for overtime when immigrants were willing to forgo that privilege. In any case, newly-arrived immigrants were routinely working sixteen hour shifts. The franchisee trumped up a concern that I had shoplifted a food item (i.e. no evidence). I applied for unemployment with a scathing report on working conditions at the franchisee—they promptly dropped their opposition, and I collected the benefits. The pen is mightier than the sword, and sometimes it's the best way to stand up for yourself or get what you need.

By the way, although Sikh immigrants from India managed and staffed the station, the actual franchisee was an affluent White Danville resident. On applications, I listed the reason for leaving this position as "laid off." The franchisee never objected. It's interesting to note that the franchisee contributed to record profits for the global refiner on their income statement: macro-level profits often add up to individual human misery.

In spring of 2003, when I was confident in my plans for the move to teaching, I stopped looking for temporary work and took a few months off. I resumed my regime of exercise and reading, brushed the dust off from my brief return to basic labor, and psyched myself up for changing my life, so I was in a pretty good state of mind on my first day of pre-service training in July.

Exiting corporate life, I reflected on my philosophy at the start of my business major years: I wanted to be a business rebel. I would be a businessman who wasn't a snob, who wasn't materialistic, who wasn't a workaholic, and who balanced the needs of customers, workers, and country—and I guess investors had to fit in their somehow too. I was going to transcend the authoritarian ways of Wall Street.

I hadn't quite lived up to my fantasy of business rebellion. I evaluated my performance on the fantasy rubric. I wasn't a snob ("A"). I wasn't materialistic ("A"). I was a workaholic, especially at the agency, but I had managed to keep pretty regular hours in Pleasanton, so I almost hit that one ("B"). I favored customers over workers, country, and investors: my integrity-based, trust-based approach to marcom could get oppressively customer-centered and out of balance ("C+"). I'll give myself credit for transcending the authoritarian ways of Wall Street. My peacekeeping work in Pleasanton lifted an authoritarian parent company out of a stalemate with its acquisition ("A"). Maybe I could move forward as a peacekeeping educator or just more of a peacekeeping person in general. Significant realization in my meditation on the pushy American had occurred. I looked forward to the possibilities of transference.

CHAPTER SIX

Living the Challenge

Highly-Qualified Educator

Becoming a teacher in California involves a series of background checks. You can't just become a teacher by applying to a school district or signing up for a credential program. First you have to establish your identity and basic qualifications with the state's licensing agency for teachers, the California Commission on Teacher Credentialing (CCTC). To do that, you apply for the Certificate of Clearance. The application has two elements: a basic skills test and a criminal background check. Both elements made me nervous.

As I already established, I never really went to school, at least not in the way typical students did, and especially not during the years of basic skills. However, I did have a college degree, so I figured there was a small chance of passing the clearance test, which was called the California Basic Educational Skills Test. To overcome my jitters, I bought a prep book at a local bookstore and studied assiduously. As a result, I got a near perfect store. Maybe I had overreacted in preparing so well, but I actually enjoyed the process.

With the test accomplished, I could submit my clearance application, which would trigger the criminal background check. This was the part that really made me nervous, because it forced me to once again deal with Wynda's anger, manifested in the form of a misdemeanor contempt of court charge. As part of my research into the career change, I submitted my clearance application early, in fall of 2002, because

I wanted to confirm that the misdemeanor charge would not disqualify me. For almost all clearance purposes, I had a clean record, since the probation agreement rendered a verdict of plea of not guilty, charges dropped, and case dismissed. But under California state law, a licensing agency such as the CCTC can ask for the details of the case and decide for themselves if they want to honor the probation agreement: in other words, they can ignore the court's verdict and render their own. The finger-print based background check uses a Department of Justice database containing a record of every crime committed in the U.S. The CCTC would have a record of the charge whether I provided it or not. But their process afforded me an opportunity to explain my situation. To complete the application, I contacted the municipal court about the now seven-year-old case and secured a copy of the entire case file, which I included in my application along with a brief statement per CCTC instructions. My clearance came through without a hitch. With clearance in hand, I proceeded to apply to credential programs and school districts, a process that led to acceptance into Project Pipeline Teacher Credential Program and a teaching contract at Mt. Diablo Unified School District.

But a credential program and teaching contract were still not enough. Before I could start my credential courses in July, I had to establish my subject-matter competency. As early as the seventies, California declared itself a "reform" state. Under the umbrella of reform, the state government launched a series of initiatives, some legislative and some bureaucratic, designed to improve the quality of instruction in public schools. Established by the state legislature in 1970, the CCTC and its credential process were formed in that spirit. The CCTC sets the standards for teacher education in university and non-university settings: only organizations chartered by the CCTC can recommend teacher candidates for credentials.

No Child Left Behind, which officially entered the scene in January 2002, connected with many California reforms already in place. NCLB aimed to put a highly-qualified teacher in every classroom. Once NCLB was in effect, the CCTC defined what a highly-qualified teacher would be for every role in the school system, and by limiting schools to hiring only credentialed teachers, California implemented NCLB in a forceful and rapid manner. Even though the CCTC had been at work for thirty years, only about eighty-six percent of California classrooms were taught by a credentialed teacher when NCLB went into effect, and estimates indicated that between five to ten percent of those teachers would not be considered highly qualified. The new law put the CCTC into low gear, finally (i.e. where all the torque is).

A cornerstone of the CCTC's efforts was the content area competency exam. When NCLB arrived, the CCTC had already been working to put a content expert in every classroom. So every credential candidate, which meant every new teacher, had to submit evidence of expertise in the subject they were going to teach. Before NCLB, teachers could submit a relevant degree from a CCTC-approved institution of higher education: for instance, a math teacher could submit their math major from Cal State. But after NCLB, the CCTC would only accept a subject matter exam as evidence of competency—so then a math major had to prove that she had actually learned what Cal State had tried to teach her. The subject matter exam must be taken at the teacher's expense, before applying for a credential. The exams aren't cheap, running from $300 to $500.

For my credential as an Education Specialist, the CCTC term for special-education teacher, I was required to pass the Multiple Subjects Teacher Assessment (MSAT) published by Praxis, an expert organization dedicated to teacher preparation. Special-ed credential candidates had been required to pass this exam for many years, but NCLB inspired the CCTC to shake things up, so I would take a new CCTC-designed test called the California Subject Examinations for Teachers (CSET). Keen observers might be experiencing acronym fatigue syndrome. Welcome to education reform!!

The new test was a refinement of the MSAT designed to

reflect California's subject-matter standards and information unique to California such as state history. Essentially, the test assessed basic competency in the core subjects of the k-12 curriculum: language arts, social studies, sciences, math, health, and child development. Teacher candidates were responsible for knowing any topic that might be taught within the k-12 range, but not in extraordinary depth. It was a wide-ranging-yet-shallow examination. For instance, the candidate only needed math skills in algebra I, geometry I, basic trig (functions), and basic statistics: no advanced math was covered. It required short essay and multiple-choice responses. Once again, I was vexed by my lack of education. I never studied the k-12 curriculum. I felt the test might be a deal killer, so I investigated ways to prepare for it. Amazingly, I found a prep course at Cal State.

At this point in NCLB's trajectory, the CSET was the qualification for two classes of teachers: elementary school (k-6) and special education. Upper-grade teachers, meaning grades seven through twelve, were required to pass single-subject tests in their area of specialization, such as social studies, chemistry, etc. Cal State's prep course supported their elementary-level credential candidates, but they were happy to include me. The course, which met on weekends, was based on a popular prep book for the MSAT. In addition, the professors, who were from Cal State's teacher-ed department, threw in some of their own material.

I enjoyed the prep book, which was a little over three inches thick. I read fast but thoroughly, with underlining, every page front to back. Finally, I was getting a high school education. And my study habits had dramatically improved! I took the prep course in the winter of 2002-2003, with the goal of completing the CSET exam in the spring of 2003, meaning ahead of starting credential courses. I met my goal, scoring a near perfect score on every section of the test. I probably overreacted a bit in preparing so well, but the intense studying was great preparation for entering the k-12 environment. The study sessions for both the CBEST and CSET (acronym overload alert!!) really put my head in the game. Teaching is about delivering academic content more than intervening in behavior problems, and my mind was full with content when credential courses began that summer. And the studying kept life interesting in my last few months of day jobs driving a truck and attending a gas station. Most important, I experienced the self-esteem that comes from having a high-school education. I'm serious about that. I started to think that maybe I had made the right career move. My confidence grew a bit.

But my confidence was slightly diminished by a growing controversy over how NCLB would affect the subject-matter requirement for special-ed teachers. NCLB's emphasis on the term "highly-qualified" had set off a round of hand-wringing and perfectionism among school administrators. NCLB left it up to individual states to flesh out the definition of highly-qualified. California's education specialist credential would authorize me to teach any subject in any school to any student, but was the CSET (i.e. multi-subject approach) a sufficient authorization for special-ed teachers who were specializing in a subject area such as math? Should those teachers also be asked to pass a single-subject exam? Historically, neither the state nor districts had required that. But with the advent of NCLB a debate had been unleashed on the grapevine. Watch it special-education teachers! You might be asked to earn an additional credential if you're specializing in a subject area, said the gossips. This discussion never rose above rumor, and the CCTC gave no indication of added requirements, so I decided to rely strictly on information from the CCTC and take things one step at a time.

This controversy had another dimension to it that directly affected my upcoming position as an upper-grade resource specialist. If I succeeded in my credential studies, I would be one of the state's very first education specialists trained under the latest requirements. It was a brand new credential path and one of the CCTC's responses to NCLB. On one hand, I was lucky. My credential and my job were considered the van-guard of post-NCLB school design. Previously, most resource specialists in the upper grades taught their students in small-group settings to accommodate modification of the curriculum. This was known as the pull-out approach. So, special-ed students struggling in math would study that subject in a small-group classroom with their resource specialist as the teacher. In other words, they were "pulled out" of the general classroom for math and possibly other subjects. For the most part, parents, students, and faculty were content with this arrangement.

But a new dawn was rising in the egalitarian age of NCLB. Pull-out instruction was seen as undemocratic by some reformers. First, it stigmatized the students by segregating them unnecessarily. Second, pull-out classrooms tended to rely on modified curriculum, which meant that students would fall short of the coveted "proficient" in school accountability tests, which were based on the state's subject-matter standards for each subject. To rectify these undemocratic conditions, education specialists would be trained as educational psychologists who could advise mainstream teachers when pull-out students were reintegrated into their classrooms. From now on, the reformers projected, only severely handicapped students would be pulled out of the general classrooms. All mildly handicapped students, according to this camp, should be educated among their age-group peers in the general classrooms. Students with mild learning disabilities, meaning my students and the preponderance of students in the mild category, historically have comprised five percent of the total student population.

Education specialists would be experts in assessing student learning needs and recommending classroom-level and individual-level accommodations for classrooms based on flexibility and tolerance—a new era of ability-level diversity. Working alongside the general faculty, sometimes even as co-teachers in the same classrooms, education specialists would bring leading-edge, research-based strategies to this new reality. At this point in my credential studies, my knowledge was limited to the publicity coming out of the California Department of Education (CDE), and that is what it sounded like. As an unsuspecting reader of this inspiring P.R., I was impressed. I was ushering in an era of expanded democracy. Democracy dharma! I even knew how the thirteenth and fourteenth amendments supported this dream of diversity.

My new job, my first experience teaching in any public school, was to walk the dream, literally. I was the vanguard. I was to be the resource specialist for the seventh grade of a middle school that would be reintegrating all of its pull-out students. An announcement had been made to parents over the summer alerting them to the en masse reintegration of all the school's mildly-handicapped students. I would co-teach in my students' mainstream language arts, social studies, and math sections. This was formal co-teaching duty, and I would be on a special teaching team that brought all affected seventh-grade teachers together for joint planning and professional development.

The controversy over subject-matter expertise arose in my role as co-teacher in single-subject classrooms. Theoretically, the single-subject teachers would be content-area experts as established by CCTC examination. Should I also have a single-subject credential in each of the three subject areas: language arts, social studies, and math? Watch out special-ed teachers! You might have to get an additional credential for each content-area classroom you work in, said the gossips. Four credentials, at my own expense, really? Again, the discussion never rose above rumor, and I strictly adhered to CCTC guidelines and took things one step at a time.

Under the education specialist model of co-teaching, the special-ed teacher views lessons from the perspective of educational psychology, which cuts through subject matter to identify the best instructional strategies for a given type of lesson or student. So, in theory, it's not a matter of matching the single-subject teacher's content knowledge, but instead it's about bringing a unique behavioral and cognitive perspective, said the publicity release.

Teacher Education

In July 2003, I arrived for my first day of credential courses in good shape for the journey that lay ahead. My diligence in passing the subject-matter competency exam before starting classes meant that I didn't have any contingencies hanging over my head, whereas a number of the candidates hadn't taken the exam yet. My savings had held out fairly well over the two years of un- and under-employment. I had some cash in the bank to tide me over until my salary from the teaching contract began in September. And I had a teaching contract in place, which I had secured in June—some candidates still didn't have a job. I was forty-one-years old.

Internship-based credentials required the candidate first to apply for an intern credential and then upgrade it to a "clear" credential (i.e. permanent). Project Pipeline was very supportive and walked candidates through the application process expeditiously. The greatest significance of this step was becoming one of California's licensed teachers, which meant that I had become a public figure. From that point forward, any criminal activity in the community or serious disciplinary matter in a school setting would be reported to the California Commission on Teaching Credentialing (CCTC). In addition, any member of the world could report any kind of suspicious conduct to the CCTC. Every time I changed school districts, and every five years when I renewed my credential, my criminal history would be checked. Defending credentialed teachers against accusations is one of the union's key functions, and one of the main reasons for the intense loyalty of its members. I had always been a pretty stable, lawful person. I felt up to the challenge of being a public figure.

As I approached my first day of Pre-Service, which was the

CCTC term for the battery of summer cram classes, I actually felt a little tired. The two years of researching, studying, and working day jobs had been a bit of an odyssey. But with deliberate mindfulness, the tiredness inspired me to vow privately to give my best effort to all credential courses. I had the insight that this might be the only opportunity in my busy life to review the teacher-ed material in an organized way, and I was going to take the privilege seriously. Such was my state of mind when I arrived at the newly-launched professional development center for Mt. Diablo Unified School District in a middle-class residential neighborhood of Concord, California.

Located about fifteen miles north of my Danville home, the neighborhood was a pleasant arrangement of winding, quiet streets populated with one-story ranch houses and bungalows on modest manicured plots. The district had converted a modern elementary school into a conference center for training teachers, and the building offered all the amenities: central air conditioning, wall-to-wall carpeting, adult-sized conference tables, dry-erase boards, and projection screens. It was as comfortable and decorous as any corporate setting. In Concord, where July temperatures routinely reach one hundred, the climate-controlled environment was definitely a blessing. Keen observers might note a definite upgrade from the typical California school facility. NCLB had arrived, and Mt. Diablo's new training facility showed their commitment to making it work.

All Project Pipeline courses would be held in a library converted into an oversized meeting room. Ten circular or square conference tables supported candidates working together in small groups and created a congenial, social environment. Furniture could be moved easily to accommodate a speaker, projection screen, or rolling boards. A few floor-to-ceiling windows gave a spacious, open feeling. It was an attractive space that you could take yourself seriously in.

Our first day started with ice breakers conducted by Wendy, our program administrator from Project Pipeline.

These activities were meant to simulate the kind of lessons that teachers might use to break the ice with their own students. This was the age of reform, and teachers were encouraged to break the ice with students in the first days of school as opposed to the old authoritarian approach of preaching to students that there was no time to waste and to open their books to page whatever. We actually spent the entire morning on ice breaking. Some activities were cerebral, like interviewing the classmate to the right, writing a quick profile, and then introducing the classmate to the group. Some activities were kinesthetic and physical such as a water balloon relay, with the balloon held under the chin and handed off in a predictably awkward maneuver. Participating in these activities, which most of the candidates embraced with delight but I suffered through demurely, alerted me to just how much ice would have to be melted before I would be a teacher.

Wendy was a firm and demanding leader, and that helped propel me past my doubts, or at least to forget them long enough to make it to lunch. A short, athletically-built Japanese American, Wendy had the power and perkiness of a gymnast who had stayed in shape into her thirties. She held a master's degree in special education from University of the Pacific, and she had been a credentialed primary grade teacher and administrator in the Mt. Diablo district for ten years before leaving to manage our credential program. It was Wendy's first year with Project Pipeline, and you could tell it from the first minute. She was definitely out to prove herself, and she had the quality-or-die mentality. She believed in herself, the credential process, and in special education, and those facts of her existence were established within the first few hours.

She would be leading a cohort of thirty-five candidates for the education specialist credential, specializing in mild to moderate learning impairments. Many of the candidates had already been teaching for as many as five years with an emergency credential. In fact, most of the candidates were already established in a school, but without proper qualifications: NCLB forced them to finally invest in a special-ed credential. That left a few candidates who were special-ed classroom aides advancing to teacher, and then me, the only candidate who had no recent experience, and no experience at all in a public school. It's amazing what a copywriter can get himself into with the right pitch.

The cohort's age breakout was roughly twenty-somethings 10%, thirty-somethings 40%, forty-somethings 25%, and fifty-somethings 25%, with each sex at 50%. As a cohort, the thirty-five candidates would do everything together over the three years. At school, we were on our own as regular contract teachers, but in the credential program, especially during class time, we worked together. And not just by being in the same room at the same time. The format of almost every course was candidates teaching each other, with the instructor providing only the content and oversight. It was active learning, no more sitting back making the prof do all the work.

Pre-Service consisted of one hundred and fifteen hours of training, divided into six courses, running from early July to mid-August. Instruction consisted of class meetings during the work day and homework in the evenings. As a sign of our devotion, we interns paid cash tuition for the privilege of this rigorous initiation. Instructors were experienced leaders from various Mt. Diablo schools. They all had graduate degrees and a record of success on the job.

Amazingly, the pre-service program was designed to serve me, the only candidate with little to no experience, since the alternative credentialing path was meant for recruiting individuals from outside the teaching profession. And with all things run by Wendy, she went by the book—so pre-service fit my needs perfectly. Courses both prepared the candidate for surviving their first few months on the job and served as a preview of the subjects to be covered over the next three years. The course topics reflected the hoped-for movement toward including nearly all mildly-disabled students in general classrooms. Three training themes emerged for unifying the education specialists and the general-ed faculty: teaching special needs students in the general-ed classroom, reading and writing intervention, and classroom management. To add weight to this unifying effort, our instructors for these topics were from general education.

As I mentioned earlier, the education specialist views the classroom from the perspective of educational psychology. So, the specialist doesn't just see a history lesson, she sees a reading, writing, or group-work lesson. The specialist looks at the skills needed for processing the content, and these skills are needed for every subject. Essentially, we learned about the underlying practices that should be adopted by every teacher: how to design a classroom, how to plan an academic unit, how to plan a lesson, how to start and end tasks, how to run a discussion, how to make visuals, and the list goes on for three years (and to infinity). We thoroughly studied the research-based elements of effective lessons. An effective lesson is one where an assessment at the end of the lesson shows that students accomplished the learning goal stated at the start of the lesson.

In this unified vision, the unique aspect of the education specialist was training on how to adjust lessons to accommodate learning disabilities: for instance, how a reading lesson could be structured to improve retention for learning-disabled students. In addition, we learned about how learning disabilities affect the apprehension, processing, and recall of academic information. Ideally, education specialists and general-education teachers would jointly apply their knowledge of classroom management and lesson planning, with the education specialist advising on how adjustments might be made to accommodate students with learning disabilities. Keen observers might sense a harbinger in the term "ideally."

Two additional training themes focused on matters that were the sole jurisdiction of the education specialist: IEP law,

IEP planning, and behavior intervention (including school disciple). IEP stands for Individualized Education Plan. I mentioned the evaluation and eligibility process in an earlier chapter when I discussed my psychology degree. Special-education services are a federal entitlement program, authorized by an act of Congress called the Individuals With Disabilities Education Act (IDEA). This law defines the eligibility criteria and establishes guidelines for administering the services. Since it's a federal civil-rights program, states must follow it, and typically, state legislatures will build on IDEA by adding a few guidelines of their own.

We studied the text of the law and the underlying principles for eligibility and service delivery. The IEP process is actually a legal proceeding and has rules of civil procedure much like a court case. It's a kind of litigation, sometimes with disputes involving real law suits and verdicts. Education specialists are responsible for knowing and carrying out these procedures on their own, and we were actually given a thorough briefing in case law, which was as involved as anything I had seen as a legal scholar at Stony Brook.

Special-ed law has three major components: evaluation, placement, and planning. Evaluation revolves around assessment and team decision-making. The IEP team consists of the education specialist, school psychologist, a general-education teacher, parents, and a district administrator with decision-making authority; for students over eighteen, the team includes them too. The eligibility evaluation establishes services, the three-year evaluation thoroughly checks student progress, and the annual evaluation provides basic data for the yearly update of the IEP. In the evaluation process, education specialists are responsible for the academic aspects, which consist of standardized assessments of academic skills (administered one-on-one), classroom observations, work samples, report cards, and interviews with teachers. Education specialists are trained in administering the academic assessments and conducting other aspects of the evaluations.

School psychologists are the other key players in the evaluation. They conduct assessments of comprehensive intelligence (i.e. IQ), cognitive processing in auditory and visual domains, and emotional functioning. The team might also include a speech therapist, occupational therapist, and psychotherapist when the team suspects that these services will be needed for the student to make progress in school; eligibility for these services is also based on the evaluation process (i.e. formal assessments).

Evaluation leads to placement. Before placement can occur, the IEP team must reach a consensus on eligibility. The education specialist and school psychologist present their findings to the team in a formal report called a psycho-educational evaluation. Then the team discusses the evaluation data as well as subjective information such as the student's feelings about school. If the team decides that a significant learning-impairment exists, they assign the student to one of the eligibility categories: in my upcoming job, almost all of the students would be in the category of mild learning disability. When appropriate, the therapy providers (speech, occupational, or psychotherapy) also present their findings at this point, and they also shape placement and services.

Once an eligibility category has been established, placement commences. And the sparks fly. The crux of IDEA is that every child is entitled to a "free appropriate public education" and that school services must lead to a "quantifiable educational benefit." The phrases "appropriate" and "educational benefit" are provocatively vague, and they have in fact led to incomprehensible levels of litigation in school districts throughout the country. Litigation typically involves a dispute over which placement (i.e. school services) will be "appropriate" as determined by the likelihood of an "educational benefit." To begin special-ed services, the IEP team must decide where and how the student will go to school now that they have been identified as learning disabled, to refer to my type of student. In every IEP meeting after initial placement, the questions of appropriateness and educational benefit are revisited to ensure that the student's needs are met in a flexible and responsive manner.

There is a wide spectrum of school services administered by special education. In the case of my students, meaning those with mild learning disabilities, three basic settings define the placement options. One, the student studies in a specialized classroom with all learning-disabled peers, typically with fifteen or fewer students. Two, the student studies in general-education classrooms with minimal accommodations specified in the IEP, in sections with only one or two other learning-disabled students. Three, the student studies in inclusion classrooms that are a hybrid of general-ed and special-ed, with each classroom comprised of roughly ten learning-disabled peers out of a total class size of thirty-five students. Experts will notice that I'm writing with broad strokes and without discussing gray areas, but these are the three main options in California. Most litigation stems from parents disagreeing with the other IEP team members about which of these three options is right for the student.

Planning is the ongoing implementation of the placement decision, and it's the educational specialist's forte. Planning occurs in annual IEP meetings, where the education specialist is asked to hold court, and it's typically free of controversy since the initial eligibility and placement decisions have already been made. School psychologists usually don't attend annual meetings: their specialties are initial evaluations and triennial re-evaluations. But all other members of the IEP team should participate.

To prepare for the annual review, the education specialist conducts an academic evaluation that will serve as the data for the planning process, including standardized assessments, teacher-developed assessments, teacher interviews, classroom observations, grade reports, statewide testing scores, and parent questionnaires. Progress on the goals of the previous year's IEP is also considered, in terms of quantifiable educational benefit. Using the data, the education specialist establishes the placement, goals, and accommodations, which the IEP team will approve as the services for the next twelve months.

Goals can be academic, therapeutic, or behavioral. A behavioral goal might set the expectation that the student will complete their homework planner independently in every period, starting with tutoring from the teachers and then gradually fading to independence. Students with speech impairments, who usually flow into the same mild placements as learning disabled, will have speech therapy goals, presented by the speech therapist; occupational therapists also offer services to eligible students, but that is rare in mild placements. Academic goals focus on a quantifiable increase as measured by the taxonomy of a skill area: for instance, a student who mastered subject-predicate sentences in the past year will demonstrate a paragraph with topic sentence in the upcoming year; the goal includes step-by-step objectives for achieving the desired skill.

Accommodations involve modifications to the classroom environment. An increasingly popular accommodation is the availability of a word processor for writing assignments. For my students, typical accommodations might include a seat near the teacher or board, a copy of the teacher's visuals and notes, extra time for long writing assignments, and test questions read aloud. Accommodations are almost an industry in itself. Students with serious speech impediments are entitled to computerized assistive devices that will turn keystrokes into the spoken word. Assistive technology is where the true special-ed practitioner's heart lies, although the public mostly hears about time spent on behavior intervention. Deaf and blind students especially benefit from these services.

Behavior intervention will conclude this brief orientation on the IEP process, saving least for last. Theoretically, my upcoming role would be mostly about accommodations, behavioral goals related to study habits, and occasionally an academic goal for remedial math or reading. Keen observers will once again note the appearance of "theoretically" as a harbinger. For the education specialist, behavior intervention consists of the formal, data-driven identification of a problem behavior, meaning one that clearly impedes time on task, and the methodical development of a plan to teach a replacement behavior that will eventually supersede the disruptive one. The aim of intervention is the teaching of healthy behaviors as a means of extinguishing self-destructive ones. So, raising one's hand for help replaces throwing one's book at one's classmate.

Teaching replacement behaviors is where the controversial issue of reinforcement comes in, since the intervention plan often includes a carrot on a stick. The old school seeks to change behavior through punishment (i.e. negative reinforcement), but the special-ed way relies on incentives (i.e. positive reinforcement). Under the law, if a student is deemed eligible for behavior intervention, the school should emphasize incentive-based means of conditioning over punishment-based intervention—this only applies to special-ed students identified in a formal intervention. Punishment is just fine for the rest of the student body. An incentive-based plan for our book-throwing student might pair ten minutes on a favorite personal computing device for every fifty minutes of hand-raising without any kind of outburst.

It might be helpful at this point to recall the example in an earlier chapter of a third grader who threw his book at his teacher. First, he was suspended a couple of times (i.e. punished), and then an IEP with behavior intervention plan was developed. To the education specialist, a mild learning-disabled student caught in a pattern of punishment and relapse indicates the need to initiate a formal behavior intervention. Or maybe not. Maybe the student is a juvenile delinquent who has been punished justly. The decision to expel or intervene was one of the major topics of the credential. Intervention should be the response when the cause of the misbehavior is clearly rooted in the learning disability or other eligible condition: for instance, a learning-disabled student only experiences outbursts during remedial algebra I, where the rookie teacher loses control of the class every day. On the other hand, if a learning-disabled student is repeatedly caught peddling illegal drugs on or near campus, while displaying gang paraphernalia, I'm going to support expulsion (although mom might want to change the eligibility to emotional disturbance and the placement to a specialized classroom as a kind of settlement with the superintendent). Ideally, special-ed shouldn't be a resource for managing delinquency. I'll just say that this was a highly-relevant area of the credential.

A behavior intervention plan is an aspect of IEP legal procedure. The development and implementation of the plan flow with other IEP procedures, and the intervention becomes part of the planning. In educational psychology, behavior intervention is a branch of Applied Behavioral Analysis. It's an area of extensive scholarly and professional activity, producing countless books, seminars, and articles, yet it's just one aspect of special education. In addition to formal behavior intervention, education specialists are expected to master informal counseling (i.e. old-fashioned scolding) and other unscrupulous forms of behavior mod applied in school settings.

In most specialized classrooms, the teacher will create a system of behavior intervention that applies to all students, meaning all activities will be guided by an incentive-based motivation plan that reduces misbehavior and minimizes the need for punishment—an ounce of prevention is worth a pound of cure. From the parent's point of view, the prevention-oriented environment is one of the main advantages offered by a specialized classroom, since it keeps their child out of the principal's office. Moreover, if a formal, individualized intervention is still required, it's easier to administer in a specialized classroom. The prime mover when placing a student in a specialized classroom is the presence of a cognitive impairment serious enough to require individualized modification of the curriculum, but it's especially appropriate when the student also needs a behavior intervention plan.

Education specialists are renowned for "writing" the IEP. All the information described in this orientation, now that you've joined me in pre-service, must be entered into the appropriate forms. Evaluation summary, placement info, goals, and behavior intervention had to be hand written (in those primitive years of the fin de siècle) onto the district forms in triplicate. Then the forms had to be reviewed, approved, and signed by the IEP team during the annual meeting and any other occasion requiring a change. Signed forms had to be distributed to all faculty members involved with the student, entered into the student's cumulative file, and archived into the massive district vault. In my new job, all the steps of writing the IEP would be my responsibility for twenty-four students in the seventh grade, a challenge for which I had no preparation. My heart was in the right place, but my head was about to explode.

On the Front Line

Teachers are first responders. Credential training on this topic was a startling introduction to the life of a public figure. As mandatory reporters, we learned the details of all forms of child abuse. We also learned about the teacher's legal responsibility to report abuse even if it requires going against the school administration: there is no exculpatory circumstance. We studied the dilemma of the requirement to defy an immoral order, and we learned about bystander laws. The teacher is responsible for being an autonomous moral agent, no excuse can be found in following orders. We had to be certified in certain aspects of first aid, especially in the transmission of blood borne pathogens. And at the school site, each teacher plays a vital role in evacuation plans and drills for earthquake, fire, and security disasters. I'll report that the candidates took these responsibilities in stride. I, however, started to realize what a grave matter it is to be the guardian of hundreds or even thousands of school age children every day.

Teachers are front line warriors in the battle against bigotry and discrimination. In pre-service, in a course entitled Diversity, training on this area primarily involved the sociological aspects of classroom instruction. Our instructor started the class with data showing that middle-class White women were the culprits in many of the school-achievement problems of minority and disadvantaged children. It was easy for me to believe her, since that same group had been such a challenge in my own life. That is why I didn't stop to ask if maybe that impression was more a factor of California's faculty being seventy-three percent female, and that White women were the first to attend college in the seventies and eighties at levels high enough to create that situation (the ethnicity demographics of the California teaching force were approximately 63% White, 18.6% Hispanic or Latino, 5.4% Asian, 4% Black, and other categories below 3%). I can't recall the exact dimensions of the data, but I do remember wondering if "White" and "women" were the causal factors that they seemed at first glance. In any case, minority students, especially Hispanic and Black students, and most especially boys from those two groups, experience punishment more often than other groups in the school setting. This trend was blamed on White women and their pushy Protestant work ethic (i.e. their high—inflexible—standards for all students).

In my opinion, this situation might have been more-properly blamed on liberal White women and their union-organized resistance to any demand on them to alter the curriculum or other aspect of the classroom to better accommodate minority and disadvantaged students. In short, it's about a dispute over working conditions, a term all union members will recognize. "Union" and "working conditions" might be better causal factors for the instructor's research. To go just a little further on this topic, another causal factor might be school administrators' lack of direction on just how to modify the curriculum or other aspect of the classroom. So, "administrators" and "lack of direction" might also contribute to the problem; this angle would bring the male dimension back into the discussion.

Despite my reservations about the statistics, I was energized by my credential program introducing this data up front in its most controversial form to a room where the majority of candidates were middle-class White women. Black liberal woman confronts White liberal women. One might experience hope for common ground. Our Black instructor, though, didn't seem very liberal. Her Protestant work ethic was much in evidence, looking as smashing as a supermodel from Talbots in her two-piece suit. A diversity expert and administrator from Mt. Diablo school district, she was tough-minded and successful. She made a strong impression and the candidates attended to her presentation well, which consisted of sensitivity training based on a portfolio of statistics broken down by ethnicity and sex, including college attendance, graduation rates, suspension rates, expulsion rates, school attendance, proficiency scores, and economic background.

The other statistic that really grabbed my imagination was a correlation between family income and student achievement. Family affluence is the most reliable predictor of student achievement, said the data via the instructor. Inversely then, improvising a bit, one could conjecture that a lack of family affluence is a predictor of a student experiencing punishment in school. If one surmises a little further, one could conjecture that residing in a deindustrialized town as a child of a working class, working poor, or welfare family increases the likelihood of experiencing both punishment and underachievement in school. Then, of course, we should include the race factor too—or have I already covered that. My improvising was purely a private matter.

There have been some creative challenges to the affluence

bind. In training on how to teach reading and writing, candidates learned about the causes of reading deficits. Students from homes with a book and reading culture are more likely to read at grade level by the third grade; students from homes without books and reading are more likely to fall behind. On a corollary point, I've heard at least one study that showed the home's skill in preparing their child for reading was more significant than their economic status. On this point every teacher will agree: a child's success in school depends on the parent's skill in preparing them for the tasks of reading, listening, and following adult directions, and economic disadvantages aren't necessarily an impediment to a skilled parent, although one can imagine how ample disposable income and free time (i.e. affluence) can make it easier to bring books and other preschool activities into the home and to continue providing them through the school-age years.

Pre-Service diversity training was mostly about raising awareness through data, but other pre-service courses and many courses over the next three years would cover in detail the modifications to the curriculum and other changes to the classroom that might make school a better experience for minority and disadvantaged students. We actually covered the solution more than the problem. I was in this field to help students with behavior problems, so I really appreciated this training. For instance, when assigning a term paper, the teacher can include instruction on locating source material in the library that will support a topic relevant to the student's race or ethnicity; teachers can learn methods of intervening in classroom misbehavior that don't lead to punishment so quickly (i.e. tolerance); teachers can learn to deliver information through visuals and other support materials that increase engagement for struggling students; and teachers can follow best practices to minimize misbehavior in general (i.e. an ounce of prevention is worth a pound of punishment). I believe in all these methods, but keen observers may notice an altering of the teachers' usual working conditions, so now we revisit "working conditions," "union," "administrators," and "lack of direction."

At this point in the history of the struggle for civil rights, outright bigotry doesn't seem to be the main cause of problems of diversity, at least not so much in contemporary Mt. Diablo or even the rest of the Bay Area. The root of the problem is a lack of direction and resources for dealing with diversity in an honest, realistic way—teachers insist on a fair workload on one hand, and aren't really sure what people want from them on the other hand. Teachers basically go by their gut, egalitarian instincts about right and wrong, meaning they treat every student the same way, with no flexibility for accommodating struggling students. In other words, teachers resist discriminating in favor of minority and disadvantaged students.

In teacher education, a subtle suggestion has been insinuated into the conversation. Research clearly indicates that proficiency in reading, which is considered the gateway skill to all other academic subjects, corresponds to the academic skills and affluence of the home. Many disadvantaged and minority students experience reading deficits in the early grades due to this skill deficit in the home. So, reformers suggest, typically in a sidling, oblique tone, the teacher should endeavor to supplement child rearing in ways that will make up for the deficits at home, and therein lies the genesis of the conflict between authoritarian-leaning teachers and the welfare state.

NCLB cranked up the intensity of this conflict by demanding all students reach proficiency by 2014. In response to this challenge, reformers increased the intensity of their suggestion that teachers should adopt practices to supplement child rearing that ideally should have occurred at home, since that will be the only way all students could reach proficiency. Predictably, authoritarian-leaning teachers objected by replying that parents need to live up to their responsibilities and to not expect teachers to engage in excessive levels of stress and uncompensated tasks (they say in the teacher's lounge when reporters and parents are occupied elsewhere). Authoritarian-leaning-yet-unionized-Democratic-voting teachers reply further that NCLB just seems like a ploy by President G.W. Bush and his libertarian supporters to push teachers into uncompensated activities as a sideways approach to dealing with the failure of their conservative economic philosophy to respond to deindustrialization and the global workforce.

So, teachers are steadfastly resisting both the welfare state and the libertarians at the same time. Caught in the middle!! Teachers, for the most part, do not single out or persecute students based on their race or ethnicity, and they are now monitored closely by the school administration. But many teachers steadfastly resist giving special treatment to any group or individual: teachers consider that a breach of their job description. Amazingly, NCLB exacerbated their resistance by necessitating a pacing guide for every subject, giving teachers a set benchmark by which to measure where every student should be. Teachers teach to the pacing guide: if a student falls off the pace, it's their family's fault—no special treatment!!! A teacher can go the extra mile for a struggling student by developing rapport, reasonable modifications, and even a good relationship with the family, or she can methodically and mechanically remove the student to the principal's office when he is disruptive (i.e. punishment). Both options are legal. But the kind option puts the teacher to a lot of uncompensated effort.

Now I'll give my opinion on how to decrease underachievement among minority and disadvantaged students, with the aim of reducing the reader's pulse rate to a sufficiently low enough level for reading the rest of the present story. I must have set off at least a few political nerves. In key neighborhoods of underachievement, as measured by statewide testing data, I would implement small schools with small class sizes, extra staff, modified curriculum, modified assessments, and hybrid discipline procedures: in short, I would apply a structural solution, one that didn't involve increasing the workload for teachers or requiring any other kind of heroics. Of course, this method would require state legislatures to increase funds flowing to these neighborhoods without decreasing funds flowing to more successful neighborhoods—a net increase in investment. Now we can expand my causal factors of "workload," "union," "administrators," and "lack of direction" to include libertarian legislators. There. I've finally worked racism back into the discussion. Or maybe I hit on the elitism. It's hard to distinguish one from the other.

Most Americans have a cartoonish vision of teachers as saints, superheroes, priests, or nuns. In reality, they are ordinary workers, whose minds are mostly on the day's first cocktail, preparing dinner for the family, a couple of hours of television before bed, and their next vacation. You're not going to make much progress against underachievement expecting them to be your heroes—I would like to see our legislators take their turn at heroism for a while.

Okay. I clearly sided with the welfare state. Now everyone can roll out their stereotypical defenses and pour a nightcap. Except that I call it the bodhisattva state—an empire of wise ones who know how to keep the peace in a free world. Bodhisattva-warriors rule by keeping their greed and paranoia in check and by bringing generosity to the fore. It might seem like I digressed from the narrative to indulge in speechifying, but in fact I captured the collective state of mind of the California faculty as I approached my first days as one of them. I've drawn fairly black and white battle lines on the topic of diversity, but actually I was headed for a school that stepped into the gray area of making structural changes to support struggling students with me dead center in the middle of it all. Grey comes from black and white.

Pre-Service set a grueling pace in amount of material and speed of processing that would prevail for the next three years, although we did get summers off from that point forward. During the school year, the credential cohort met every weekend on Friday night and all day Saturday at the professional development center, plus a heavy load of independent work to complete in one's free time. Each course was instructor-led by an experienced educator with an advanced degree, under Wendy's watchful, perfectionist gaze. Over the three years, we would complete thirty courses accomplished in five hundred and fifty-three hours of instruction yielding forty-eight semester units of post-graduate semester credit. Hours of instruction were divided between class time (emphasizing active learning and candidates teaching each other), textbook readings, reflection papers, essays, case studies, and classroom practicum. One of the courses involved a yearly requirement of five classroom observations with written score and professional feedback, with the last observation of the year on a pass-fail basis. Observations were conducted by Project Pipeline supervisors, and sometimes school principals would conduct additional observations of their own.

After pre-service, the candidates who worked in the Mt. Diablo district had to spend one more day in the professional-development center before moving on to their schools. Despite ending pre-service with a six-hour course on planning for the first few days of school, the candidates would spend one more day learning about Mt. Diablo's vision of that same topic.

First Days

Most of the credential candidates would lead at least one course each school day, and almost half would be leading a specialized classroom, so pre-service's first-day training focused on the candidate's need to engage students as quickly as possible upon their arrival on the first day. I've already mentioned ice breakers. Candidates also covered teacher-led writing lessons and discussions that would help students explore what they already knew about the course's subject matter, literally warming up students' memories for challenges to come.

Research had shown that the first two or three days of class often determine the teacher's ability to direct their students in the first few months. With the advent of NCLB, and its pacing guides designed to lead to proficiency in May, Mt. Diablo wanted instruction to move fast in the first few months so that students would be ready in the spring. Good first days would be essential to setting the pace. In the credential course, we emphasized the need to set a positive, interactive tone in the first days, regardless of the pace of instruction. Good first days prevent behavior problems in the first few months.

Mt. Diablo's first-days training was for new teachers only, so all the district's first-year teachers were gathered in the professional development center for a day of passive learning at the hands of district administrators. I was ready for the passive approach, since I was a little worn down from uber-active pre-service. Many of the teachers knew each other from credential programs, substitute teaching, and even from high school. The overwhelming majority were women. They really enjoyed seeing each other. It was like a reunion, of well-dressed, meticulously-groomed preppy women—we're talking about the children of the eighties after all.

The event started with a general assembly wherein teachers were given a rousing pep talk on the district's ambitions for living up to NCLB—first days and every day would be essential to keeping up the pace. After the general assembly, the teachers were broken out into small groups for instruction on initiatives the district wanted to implement throughout the year. Teachers were grouped into cohorts according to their specialty, so special-ed teachers went through the day together. Each cohort participated in three 1-hour seminars. Our cohort studied first-day activities, culturally-responsive strategies for writing projects, and writing standards-based academic IEP goals.

The first-day activities were similar to those described in the earlier section on the first days of my pre-service training. The two primary goals of the first days were to establish rapport with your students and to set expectations (i.e. lay down the law). Rapport-oriented activities break the ice with exercises like the balloon rely and partner interview of my credential cohort. Some readers might remember telling classmates about the most interesting aspect of summer vacation as an ice breaker. In a quieter approach, the teacher can pass out art supplies and have each child create a graphic "I am" diagram as a way of introducing themselves to the teacher; the teacher can then post the finished artwork on an oversized wall display for the class to share. Students are more likely to attend to an adult who shows interest in their lives, the theory goes, and they are less likely to suffer from anxiety and other inhibiting emotions.

Setting expectations involves teaching the course rules to students in explicit direct lessons over the first few days. These lessons are the next step after establishing rapport. Rules shouldn't be taught through punishment in "gotcha" fashion. In education reform, punishment is seen as the weakest motivation and least-effective lesson. Teach rules thoroughly at the start of the school year, and students will follow them in pursuit of adult approval, peer recognition, and good grades, says the theory.

Punishment-oriented rules are replaced by positive discipline, which views the student as innately goal-seeking and positive. To engage the student's organic goal-seeking nature, the student needs clear directions on the expectations for performance. Explicitly establishing expectations for performance at the start of tasks is the main feature of positive discipline. To create an orderly, focused learning environment, rules should cover expected conduct in detail with dos and don'ts on issues such as taking turns in a discussion, attending to the teacher, retrieving and storing supplies, completing assignments on time, assigned seats, and the list goes on. In accord with the positive theme, dos are better than don'ts.

In the first days, the teacher covers only the essential expectations, but then is careful to establish expectations for the day's lesson at the start of each period. Effective teachers will type up all the major expectations in a welcome kit and send them home to give parents a preview of conduct expected from their child. The classroom should have visual reminders for rules, and it helps to post a few proverbial gold stars in recognition of student cooperation. Positive discipline doesn't eliminate trips to the principal's office or calls to parents, but it should reduce them and other kinds of negative events associated with misbehavior.

The training on culturally-responsive strategies for writing projects was an extension of improving performance by explicitly and thoroughly setting expectations at the start of the task, and then recognizing progress on those expectations at each step of the project. Culturally-responsive refers to the need for the teacher to anticipate a high percentage of English Learners in the class. English Learners typically know English fairly well, but come from households where it is a second language. There are several angles to the culturally-responsive approach, including topic selection, social learning, and setting expectations. At that point in their reform efforts, Mt. Diablo was emphasizing the setting of expectations, which kind of made the point about suburban White women and their Protestant work ethic. Topic selection and social learning are the really innovative elements that tie into the inspiration of ethnicity, but Mt. Diablo wanted to show that teaching English Learners doesn't have to involve much more than the same elements of good teaching for any student. Interestingly, my credential program taught me all three elements in detail.

Mt. Diablo wasn't completely off course, though. Reform theory says that much of the underachievement among students from disadvantaged and minority backgrounds comes from American teachers, who are mostly from affluent or middle-class backgrounds, assuming that underachievers will comprehend information at the same rate as typical students. But language barriers, cultural differences, and the effects of poverty often conspire to make the disadvantaged students less attuned to the values of the academic environment. By simply being explicit and thorough in setting expectations, the teacher will help the disadvantaged students, and really all English Learners, better connect to the academic task and environment. Better communication about expectations will lead to broader and deeper levels of student engagement on academic tasks, especially the challenging ones involving higher-order processing of language like writing projects.

In the seminar, we studied Six Traits Writing, a strategy that prescribes teaching the traits of good writing along with subject-matter issues such as the history topic to be covered, for instance. The teacher shouldn't expect performance on expectations unless they have been first taught to the students. The six traits of good writing are ideas, organization, voice, word choice, sentence fluency, and conventions. In themselves, these terms are kind of vague. Teachers must assess the proficiency of their students on these traits and then give instruction to fill in the details for each trait as needed. In addition, the teacher should apply relevant examples of each trait for the subject-matter assignment. Finally, visual supports such as a handout should be given to the student to help them focus their work around the traits.

Grumbling about working conditions breaks out in the back of an imaginary break room: "That adds a lot of time to subject matter lessons when we are already being pushed by the pacing guide. My seventh graders should have mastered that in fifth grade. Why should I have to slow down for students who didn't listen to their teacher?" once again kind of making the point about suburban women and their Protestant work ethic. In my numerous years of training in education reform, I noticed that two spiritual factors might have enhanced the impact of the dozens of strategies: accommodation and tolerance. In fact, the reformers are asking teachers to indulge the nation in a little bit of tolerance: please go back and review the six traits in middle school for the benefit of those disadvantaged students who just weren't ready in fifth grade.

In nearly every underachiever's life, there will be a list of skills that they should have acquired in fifth grade. The old-school teacher says that they flunk seventh graders to teach them a lesson about not paying attention in fifth grade. That'll teach'em to disobey. But from that point forward, the seventh grader fails at many tasks and becomes the next dropout. What if the teacher could find a way to reteach six traits in middle school, and even through high school, for students from disadvantaged backgrounds, English Learners, and even those with learning disabilities. Might more students succeed? Might the teacher save a few underachievers? Punishment is the weakest motivation and the least-effective lesson. Keen observers can draw their own conclusions.

Writing standards-based IEP goals was an intersection of California's broader reform initiative to standardize subject-matter instruction in its schools and NCLB's requirement of uniform proficiency in annual statewide testing. California implemented its subject-matter standards in the late nineties. But districts had not uniformly implemented those standards, and some clung to their own vision of standardization. With the inception of NCLB, and its requirement of proficiency on annual statewide testing, the districts finally threw all their weight behind the state standards, called at that time the California State Content Standards, which were the direct source of the annual tests. The California Standards Tests (CSTs), the name for the annual content tests, were initiated in 1998, but took center stage as the evidence for NCLB's school accountability requirement in spring of 2003, a few months before my first day. Other statewide tests, such as those for general ability, were essentially discontinued.

The annual content tests were not common core but instead comprehensive subject-matter examinations covering social studies, language arts, math, and science on a strategically-staggered basis though eleventh grade, exceeding NCLB requirements, which were focused on math and reading. Keen

observers might grow concerned that this subject-matter approach might limit teachers to teaching strictly content matter appearing on the tests for all subjects and at a certain
pace (i.e. a fast pace). Working conditions alert! Libertarian
alert? Wall Street hegemony adds up to education hegemony.
It's interesting to note that California had been implementing
various forms of statewide testing for a little over a decade
when NCLB was passed.

Writing an IEP goal based on a content standard involved
two steps. First, the teacher assesses the student's present
ability level using a norm-referenced test of general ability,
and then matches the ability level to a content standard without regard to grade level. Second, the teacher develops an annual goal that uses short-term objectives to form a task list
that starts at the present level and moves forward to grade
level. The goal will include a format for measuring progress
on the task list in roughly quarterly increments. If the student
completes the short-term objectives on time, they will arrive
at grade level and thus will be ready to score proficient for
that skill on statewide testing. That is the strategy in a nutshell, ideally.

Often, however, the IEP will have to implement goals that
plot reasonable yearly progress but still fall short of grade
level. The main thing is to start where the student is at. The
actual writing of goals involves a lot of subtlety and negotiation, and it's more like an art than a science or strategy. But
it's always nice to spend a few minutes with the ideal at the
beginning of the school year.

My students would be taking the CSTs in the spring, with no
modifications, which means that they would be tested on the
same content as their age-group peers studying at grade level.
At that time, that was considered the NCLB-appropriate test
format for mildly disabled students. Modified content standards and corresponding statewide testing had been developed
for eligible special-ed students in 2003, but my students were
too capable for those standards. Five years later, in 2008, a

modified version of the CSTs would be developed for mildly-disabled students like mine. But in my first year, 2003-2004, the goal was for my students to achieve proficiency on the CSTs with their typical peers in general education.

This one-day professional development meeting for new teachers was an example of NCLB in action. Several schools in the Mt. Diablo district were entitled to Title I funds, which were federal funds meant to subsidize programs that benefit disadvantaged and minority students. The funds stem from legislation dating back to 1965 and the Great Society, and NCLB was actually a 2002 reauthorization of that legislation, signed into law by President G.W. Bush, and a Republican House and Democratic Senate. NCLB expanded the subsidy and accountability measures to include English Learners and special education. Title I funds were typically used to expand professional development activities for the affected schools.

My school, El Dorado Middle School, was a Title I school, which means that there was a high percentage of students from disadvantaged backgrounds as determined by the rate of participation in free and reduced lunch. To receive Title I funds, which was really just another name for NCLB subsidies, a school must have at least forty percent of its students eligible for free or reduced lunch. Schools receiving Title I funds can apply them to schoolwide programs that serve all students. NCLB school accountability requirements (i.e. statewide testing) were tied to Title I funding in that any state accepting Title I funds had to comply with the accountability measures. I'm ready to conclude this briefing on my first days as a teacher and NCLB's first days as the law of the land. Now onto the real thing, my first actual day as a teacher. Not just yet. I still had to undergo a couple more days of NCLB-fueled and -funded training at my school site with the faculty.

Teamwork Trouble

Most of my first two days at my school site, El Dorado

Middle School, were spent in professional development meetings that occupied about half of each day. The remaining time was available to move into my classroom and get acquainted with the faculty and the facility. These two days are best characterized by two very unpleasant surprises.

First, I learned that I would be teaching a section of intervention reading for struggling readers in seventh and eighth grade, with a mix of both general-ed (i.e. typical) and special-ed students. A section in this case meant one period a day with twenty-five students. No one had told me that I would be heading a classroom during the hiring process. At hiring time, I was told that I would be a co-teacher in general-ed sections all day, which, given my total lack of experience, was an opportunity to be a kind of apprentice.

Ideally, as a formal co-teacher, I should have been as accomplished as the general-ed teacher, but as a new teacher, I offered the principal naiveté in a situation most special-ed teachers thought was beneath them. At that point in reform, the special-ed teachers opposed the move from small-group instruction headed by them to including almost all mildly-disabled students in the more populous general-ed classrooms. In fact, my experienced predecessor had transferred to a different school and role in opposition to the change.

I was pretty comfortable with handling an apprentice role in classrooms headed by experienced general-ed teachers. I felt my peacekeeping experience from my last marketing job had prepared me to maintain composure amid the hostilities, and my camp counselor and intern counselor days gave me some familiarity with leading youngsters through various kinds of activities, academic and recreational. But I had never taught even one academic lesson, not even as a student teacher, not even as a substitute. The principal had pulled a switcheroo on me by adding on teaching responsibilities without getting my consent. On the surface, I took the news in stride. In my mind, I decided to embrace the challenge as a learning experience. I would strive like crazy to make the reading course work for that year and then move on to another school next year when the aftermath hit. I doubted if I could actually succeed at the task.

The unexpected challenge wasn't made easier by the school's lack of preparation. Apparently, the principal had added the course to the schedule on the spur of the moment. No preparations had been made: no classroom, furniture, curriculum, or instructional aide had been arranged yet. And the first day was only two days away.

The second surprise was disappointing but easier to handle, since it involved only a minor deviation from my job description at hiring time. Remember that my resource specialist position would involve supporting mildly-learning-disabled students in the seventh grade as the school changed their placement en masse from small-group specialized classrooms led by resource specialists to hybrid general-ed classrooms with a mix of special-ed (1/3) and general-ed (2/3) students led by general-ed teachers. This scenario was sometimes referred to as push inclusion, since it was characterized by pushing as many students as feasible out of specialized instruction. From an ethical standpoint, push inclusion represented the democratic value of giving every student the greatest chance of studying with the general community in a typical setting: equal protection of the laws. From a policy standpoint, the district was pushing the school into following the *least restrictive placement* provision of federal special-ed law, which was defined by the Individuals with Disabilities Education Act (IDEA), legislation that had been continuously reauthorized and refined since its inception in 1975. The least restrictive provision requires the IEP team to develop accommodations in the IEP process that will enable the disabled student to study with their typical peers in the general-ed setting whenever it's reasonably probable that the disabled student will succeed. In short, the IEP team should always be considering whether the disabled student might be able to study with typical peers—and they should push everyone involved, especially general-ed teachers and principals, to go the extra mile for the disabled students in this effort (i.e. the real implications of "push"). Pushy Resource Specialist! Maybe I was qualified after all, from my years as both a pushy and peace-making copywriter.

The least restrictive provision has been a source of almost incomprehensible amounts of litigation, including landmark Supreme Court decisions, with disputes typically centering around the defining of reasonable probability of success, reasonable extent of accommodations, and exactly how far to push principals and teachers. Parents typically take issue with the rest of the IEP team (i.e. teachers and district administrators) in disputes, with the parents seeking inclusion or greater levels of accommodation. Parents usually want to push more, and principals and teachers want to give less. Recall from earlier sections that the IEP team must include as fully-vested members a district administrator, school psychologist, special-ed teacher, general-ed teacher, parents, and representatives of therapeutic services such as speech therapy, with parental consent for all team decisions being the pivotal legal issue.

In the case of my new job at El Dorado Middle School, the district felt inspired to push teachers more, the parents were indifferent and even a little dubious, and the teachers wanted to give less, a lot less, as I learned from the grapevine in my first days. Working conditions alert! District administrators wanted to be on record as embracing the *push* toward total proficiency mandated by NCLB, in an incredible interaction of NCLB and IDEA. Pushy Administrators!

To support teachers in going the extra mile, in doing the truly democratic thing for mildly-learning-disabled students, the school had taken an innovative step in organizing teachers into teams for professional development and continuous joint planning throughout the year. Each grade level was to have a teaching team consisting of the teachers leading the hybrid inclusion classrooms; that team would include the grade's resource specialist. This scenario would maximize communication between the resource specialist and general-ed teachers for developing accommodations and other kinds of joint planning, and it would also allow the general-ed teachers to share experiences and advice. Remaining teachers would be organized along similar functional lines.

The push inclusion effort would be a challenge to students, teachers, and even parents, but the team teaching approach was considered the best possible method. The main teaching assignment for my job was formal co-teaching four periods a day, which meant that I had to report at the bell to the general-ed teacher's classroom and teach with them for the whole period. Basically, I would support the students on my caseload in their language arts and math sections. This was a radical approach, the vanguard: the district administration would be on record as pulling out every stop to make push inclusion work in the first years of NCLB. Team teaching unified by grade level was the key to this radical approach, especially the daily joint prep time during the school day when all of the team's teachers would have a common period to plan, prepare materials, and meet with the resource specialist to discuss the academic and behavioral interventions that would undoubtedly arise as the disabled students adjusted to the larger class sizes and more-demanding curriculum.

But, on the spur of the moment, for a reason not disclosed to the faculty, the principal abandoned the team approach in the first days of the school year. There would be no common prep period during the school day and no unification by grade level. Instead, I would be supporting disabled students by subject matter rather than grade level, teaching language arts for two periods with seventh graders and two periods with eight graders. Another resource specialist would have a similar subject matter focus in teaching math to two sections with seventh graders and two with eighth graders.

The subject-matter approach sounds reasonable until one hears that the IEP caseload would still be assigned by grade level. So I would only support my seventh graders in language arts; they would study math with the other resource specialist, who was not in charge of their IEP planning. The strength of the team approach was the opportunity for the resource specialist to develop rapport with each student, intensive familiarity with their strengths and needs in key skills, and a relationship with their parents, but those advantages were abandoned. There would be no common prep period during the school day, meaning the best time for me to work with my seventh graders' teachers would often be during after-school hours. Keen observers might guess at the reception that fact received. Working conditions alert! Moreover, the eighth grade teachers and students in the two language arts sections would technically not be part of my IEP caseload.

A scenario that was supposed be streamlined and uber-effective was reduced to a complete muddle. Keen observers might wonder at the motive for such backsliding. Indulging in a bit of time travel forward, and assuming the role of Sherlock Holmes, I will share with readers that the principal had made this adjustment to accommodate a favored veteran teacher at the site, the teacher who was supposed to be the resource specialist for the eighth-grade push team. That resource specialist didn't like teaching language arts, so she convinced the principal to organize the seventh and eighth grade co-teaching load by subject matter instead of caseload, despite the obvious debilitating consequences to the team approach, and despite the increased burdens on after-school hours for all affected faculty members. It might be relevant to note that the principal and resource specialist could best be characterized as middle-aged feminist friends and working mothers, both tastefully attired in business wear from Talbots or similar brand, and that the resource specialist had no credential and no intention of earning one. Teacher-first education! By the way, the sixth grade remained properly organized by grade level and caseload, with push team teaching and the resource specialist with her students in both math and language arts.

Expanding the muddle to maximum outrage, the seventh grade push team would remain intact for the sake of appearances, and we were assigned to participate in professional development as a team, even though we wouldn't work together very closely any more. The general-ed team members would still be the teachers for my students in language arts and math. So there was some value in occasionally training as a team, since I would have to interview team members in developing the seventh graders' annual IEPs, and I would be teaching language arts with two of the members. But the loss of common prep got everyone feeling downhearted and disenchanted, especially since the consensus coming through loud and clear on the grapevine was that push inclusion was bound to fail, just you wait and see.

My presence on the push team was met with diffidence and minimal engagement in my first two days at the site, which were primarily dedicated to orienting the faculty to the team approach. My teammates and I never got past exchanging pleasantries and faking our way through whatever teambuilding exercises were demanded of us as we sat stiffly around a circular table in the school library, which doubled as a meeting room for professional development. My five teammates (four female, one male), who all had credentials, significant experience, and all but one tenure, made it clear that they thought I was doomed to fail: "Can't you see, Robert, how they screwed it up already, before school even started?" The professional development aspect of those two days was a total waste of time—a bummer. I received no direction on how to proceed with the year. In response to this chilly reception, drawing on my peacekeeping experience from my marketing days, I reflexively resorted to stealth in making connections, gathering intelligence, and securing resources in order to get ready for the students' first day. After professional development in the morning, the afternoons and even the evenings were left free for maneuvers. From a warrior's perspective, it was clearly an occasion for inscrutability—don't worry too much if one isn't infatuated with one's teammates at first.

Downstairs

El Dorado Middle School was located in the suburban city of Concord, which lies in the Delta region of the San Francisco Bay Area, about a thirty-minute drive inland from downtown San Francisco or Oakland, with a population of 121,000. The Delta is both a region and an actual major body of water and related land masses formed by the intersection of the Sacramento, San Joaquin, and American Rivers into a kind of inland sea that pours into the famous Golden Gate. Delta waters are dark, brownish, muddy, sedimentary, brackish, and cool. Originating from alpine sources in the Nevada Sierra mountains, the winter rain and snow fueled water, dense with sediment and mineral runoff, moves forcefully with currents and tides in its speedy descent though northern California's inland mountains and vast agricultural plains. In warm months, the interaction of the relatively-hot, arid landscape on the banks of the Delta and the cool sea breeze from San Francisco Bay produced daily bracing winds of up to twenty knots at the school in the afternoons; the school was about five miles inland from the junction of the Sacramento and San Joaquin rivers. The school's climate was hot, humid, and windy in summer and fall, and cold, humid, and windy in winter and spring.

At that time, August of 2003, Concord and a few neighboring cities on the Delta where more like remnants of agricultural and industrial eras than full-fledged suburbs of San Francisco. The terrain was distinguished by grassy hillsides, rolling plains, and valleys that ran from the north side of Mt. Diablo down to the Sacramento River, with numerous oak groves spread throughout the landscape. There were actually ranches and a coal mine in parks memorializing the area's history as an outpost of the old west and industrial revolution.

In fact, the gold rush had unfolded about a hundred miles up-river. The large Mt. Diablo state park and regional wilderness preserve abutting the city preserved a touch of its former wildness.

From an agricultural perspective, the city had been part of a farming region that included ranching on the Mt. Diablo foothills and the banks of the Delta, extensive orchards for fruits and nuts, vegetables and seed crops, and even grapes. A smattering of ranches still penetrated into the borders of the landscape, and one was pretty likely to see some cattle on any given day while going about one's normal business. In addition, the region was still a significant producer for a variety of crops. The two-square-block Old Concord part of downtown, which was characterized by mission-revival-style architecture, could have easily been located in Santa Fe, New Mexico. There weren't many cowboys or ranchers around town anymore, although there were still a few, but parts of the city retained the windy, dusty, slightly-ramshackle quality that many agricultural towns have acquired in the New Economy: El Dorado Middle School was in one of those parts.

From an industrial perspective, Concord was halfway down the transition from deindustrialized rural area to infotech outpost and bedroom community to the New Economy in San Francisco and other modernizing cities in the Bay Area. The deindustrialization mainly resulted from the loss of a major steel foundry, a division of U.S. Steel, in the neighboring town of Pittsburg, the downsizing of agriculture, and the base closures of the 1980s, which had actually been occurring gradually since the 1950s; the Delta region had been a major area of military bases, ports, and manufacturing.

As with most deindustrialized areas in the Bay Area, the White working class progressively and somewhat rapidly abandoned the city in search of better prospects, depressing rents and housing prices, and immigrants and minorities moved in to take advantage of the low rent. Thus El Dorado Middle School, opened in 1980, arrived at its Title I status, with a student population comprised of 21% Hispanic, 5% Black, 5% Asian, 5% Filipino and other Asians, and 64% White, with many of the White students coming from homes led by single mothers and blended families. Further illustrating this trend of demographic shift, the current demographics (i.e. 2018) are Hispanic 59.4%, Black 4.6%, Asian 2.7%, Filipino and Pacific Islanders 6.7%, and White 18.4%. Recall that I mentioned immigrant flight in describing my years living in the Mission District of San Francisco. Concord was one of the suburban low-rent refuges the immigrants headed for in escaping rising downtown S.F. rents.

The industrial situation wasn't all downward mobility in Concord. Four major global refiners had gasoline refineries in cities within short commuting distance around the Delta; the refiners also had marketing and R&D in nearby facilities. One refinery was located on the Sacramento River about a mile from the school. A major independent energy company had two power plants (electricity) just upriver, and a top multinational chemical company had a plant in the same vicinity. There was some minimal activity in the steel industry.

The New Economy was penetrating Concord at a fairly brisk pace as an outlet for urban-flight homeowners and corporations seeking relief from inflation within commuting distance of San Francisco and the greater Bay Area, of which Concord was becoming a tangential part. For a while, Concord was home to the most eastward stop on the BART, the Bay Area's rail transit system; the system has since expanded eastward to Pittsburg, the next town over. In the downtown area near the BART station, a pleasantly-arranged collection of mid-sized corporate towers hosted data-processing facilities looking for industrious-yet-humble-rural workers to toil for modest wages. The BART also supported the commuters of immigrant flight on their daily trip into the city for work in the service industry.

Concord culture was about pockets of emerging affluence avoiding remnants of its deindustrialized and agricultural past. El Dorado Middle School was in the part of town leaders would rather just forget about for the time being. Keen observers might speculate that NCLB could inspire El Dorado to train disadvantaged students well enough to work downtown in the corporate towers, for slightly better wages than their parents, who mostly worked in entry level jobs in the service industry. Maybe the upward mobile students could purchase and renovate the old working-class one-story bungalows and ranch houses (before the yuppies escaping inflation get to them). That would be the ideal interpretation. This would be an opportune moment to toss in the mortgage crisis and its role in the upward-mobile students' efforts to gain ownership of the working-class bungalows and ranch houses, but that is beyond the scope of this narrative. The Great Society is apparently not the innocent dream one might wish it to be in the age of unlimited opportunity.

Upstairs

Concord was on the north side of Mt. Diablo, the windward side. Recall that I lived on the south side of Mt. Diablo in Danville, which would be the pastoral leeward side of relatively gentle, temperate breezes. Like Concord, Danville's terrain was distinguished by grassy hillsides, rolling plains, and wide valleys, with numerous oak groves spread throughout the landscape. In Danville, the hills were gentle, vast rolling masses that gave a feeling of openness whereas in Concord ravines were a little steeper and gullies deeper.

In Danville, the Mt. Diablo foothills ran for seemingly countless miles to the south along a vast valley with the dimensions of a savannah. In Concord, the foothills terminated into the dark turbid waters of the Sacramento River or into the steep cliffs of Mt. Diablo. Whereas the housing stock in Concord was characterized by sizable tracts of humble one-story bungalows and ranch houses, Danville featured spacious, even luxurious ranches, two-story colonials, and stately townhouses on winding streets and lots from a quarter to five acres. In general, the physical geography in Danville and neighboring towns seemed a bit more hospitable.

In large part due to its hospitable landscapes, the small town of Danville, at 42,000 souls, had become a suburban-rural outpost of the corporate set and all manner of beautiful people in general. Danville had the same agricultural roots as Concord. In fact, it was principally and intensely an agricultural area, with no other industries, until it started to attract commuters from San Francisco in the sixties and seventies, who eventually became the main commodity.

As described in earlier chapters, I moved from Long Island to the Danville area with my parents in the mid-eighties. Back then, Danville's main street looked like many tiny towns in the Sierra foothills, where mining, logging, and ranching had been the prime movers; the Mt. Diablo foothills were interestingly similar to the Sierra foothills, in physical geography and economics. Some Danville buildings even retained their authentic old west facades. Frankly, the aesthetic of the town was a little dingy, right down to the rundown, out-of-date Safeway supermarket in Alamo, that might have looked downward mobile in Concord.

Now, at the time of this writing, the town's main street looks more like Wilshire Boulevard than Danville Boulevard, and the term "city" seems more appropriate than "town," with numerous upscale restaurateurs, clothiers, gift shops, and grocers, as well as an increase in more middle-class versions of those same services. A couple of old timers hung in there on Danville Boulevard like Primos Pizza, Valley Medlyn's Fountain & Coffee Shop, and Elliot's Bar, but they are increasingly overshadowed by newer, glitzier establishments. This trajectory toward modernization and affluence was about half underway at the time of my first day at El Dorado Middle School. Danville is where the elite meet to relax, do business, and avoid Concord.

Danville's ranchers found a real cash commodity in commuters both heading home to Danville and to work in massive-yet-tastefully-park-like office complexes in neighboring San Ramon. A new elite region was forming, the Diablo Valley, consisting of Walnut Creek (southern neighbor to Concord and host to a BART station), Alamo-Danville, and San Ramon. The region stretched about fifteen miles north to south and had a population of 150,000. Amazingly, all three towns still shared one 2-lane main street that ran down the center of each town. Most households were headed by a corporate executive, manager, or specialist, spanning the full variety of fields from high tech, biotech, infotech, low-tech, and finance; mothers tended to work full-time but earned less than dad and enjoyed slightly less status.

Alamo-Danville's main commodity was affluent home owners, but Walnut Creek and especially San Ramon became major outposts for urban-flight corporate development—plus affluent home owners. The Diablo Valley was only minimally impacted by the White flight of the sixties and seventies, but the region really cashed in on urban flight driven by the inflationary forces at work in Silicon Valley and San Francisco. New Economy Flight! The psychology of the region said that it was the last bastion of affordable housing for the upper middle-class, but that, predictably, sounded like an invitation to the rich, and the area experienced a dramatic expansion of upper-class refugees with mansions, luxury housing, gated communities, country clubs, exotic cars, etc. The upper-middle class now has to strain to keep up with rising prices, but housing and other costs are still modest compared to Silicon Valley and its neighboring cities, which are located about an hour's drive south. Real-estate development is apparently not the predictable linear phenomenon one would wish for in the land of unlimited opportunity.

NCLB was partly responsible for Diablo Valley's boom years at the fin de siècle. The San Ramon Valley Unified School District unified all three towns of the region, but especially Danville-Alamo and San Ramon. Those towns were the heart of the district: in other words, nearby Concord and the rest of the Delta region were totally excluded. The increased attention on statewide testing and the concurrent rating of schools on a points system called Academic Performance Index quickly identified San Ramon and Danville-Alamo as the last bastion of top-performing schools combined with affordable-yet-suitably-spacious-and-stylish housing, a family culture, beautiful physical geography, and what used to be a manageable auto commute to most centers of the New Economy. There wasn't even one Title I school. Despite the region's middle-class tone, their schools were holding their own with the traditionally-dominant, more-expensive suburbs closer to San Francisco. As a result, the region was teaming with children, one had the feeling one might be stampeded. This reform-driven effect was underway before NCLB, and it really took off after NCLB's inception. Ranchers of Diablo Valley had done quite well in their response to the New Economy, but in northern Concord, just fifteen miles and a twenty-minute drive to the north, the fortunes of the workers of the service industry hadn't improved much in the neighborhood surrounding El Dorado Middle School, and thus the school had settled into its Title I status.

Keen observers might wonder how a progeny of Diablo Valley would relate to the gale-force winds, dusty surroundings, and working-class values of northern Concord. Actually, I was just picking up where I left off in the Mission District where I lived peacefully among my fellow refugees, most of whom were of Latino descent. Now I would be working with those very same refugees in Concord. I went from living next to a middle school on Bartlett Street, a street named after an ancient fellow traveler of English-descent who was a mayor of San Francisco and even briefly governor of California in the aftermath of the gold rush years, to being a Bartlett teaching in a middle school of immigrant flight along the Sacramento River—in the aftermath of the New Economy.

El Dorado Middle School

Despite the neighborhood's modest housing and working-class economics, the campus at El Dorado Middle School was not without charm. Courtyards and walkways were enhanced by well-tended gardens throughout the school, which featured flowers and shrubbery, and a smattering of tall pines and oaks added grandeur and connected the school to the Diablo Valley. The Delta breezes, California big sky, and park-like setting could be quite pleasant and soothing at times. Mt. Diablo's north face filled the skyline when you looked toward the rear of the school.

The architecture was similar to many California schools built since 1960. All the buildings were one-story rectangles with flat roofs. Exteriors of buildings featured sturdy vertical wood siding, board-and-batten style, or painted plaster, with all surfaces painted light gray, and with banks of paned, rectangular windows. A short turn-around driveway led to the main office, which was a small rectangular building that formed the nucleus of three longer rectangles arrayed around it. The longer rectangles were classroom buildings, with two buildings behind the office, parallel to it and equally spaced apart, and one building to the right and parallel to it. This atomic layout reinforced the fact that life for the faculty in a public school revolves around the main office. It typically houses the principal and other members of the school administration, conference room, attendance clerk, office manager (i.e. school manager), faculty mailboxes, teacher workroom (i.e. copiers and ditto machines), office supplies, faculty restroom, and faculty break area. The spacious parking lots were in front and to the side of the campus, so they were aligned with the street more than the campus; the campus was well isolated from traffic.

The main office was separated from the other buildings by broad walkways on the sides, and there were spacious courtyards behind it and between all the other buildings, which provided a kind of plaza for the campus, like it was a small village in the Southwest or a ranch. The impression was like the classroom buildings were the living quarters and the office was the big house. In the Chicago area, where I went to school, the entire school was typically in one multi-story, long, rectangular building. Students entered and exited through one main entrance in the center, and then remained inside the entire day, except for maybe P.E. and recess for younger children. At El Dorado Middle, and most schools in California, especially in the suburbs, the upper-grade students go outside five to six times a day between academic periods.

During these passing periods, the plaza was buzzing with adolescent energy, to the extent that the school supervisors (i.e. instructional aides) had to make a concerted effort to prompt the students into their classes at the bell. Tall shady oaks in the plaza areas between classrooms were a favorite resting spot. As Californians, the students loved to be outdoors, rain or shine, and only reluctantly yielded to the task master's bell. Northern Californians are a hearty, rugged people, and the students tromped right though the rain and cold of winter with hardly a care, and, in the warmer temperate months, they put up a fight before returning indoors.

Classroom entrances all faced the plaza, so egress and exit between classes occurred outdoors, and most of the classrooms had oversized windows facing the plaza. In a way, it was somewhat elegant, and did not convey the impression of poverty or blight. Inside the classrooms, however, the facilities were starting to show signs of wear. Just about every classroom was a long rectangle with a board at the front and a couple of bulletin boards on the sides. Most floors were hard clay white tiles.

Most classrooms had fresh paint, which was applied to nearly every surface, since the teachers ritualistically painted using their own resources over the summer. If it wasn't for their efforts, everything except the dry erase board would have been faded and grimy. Teachers also applied board paper, supplied by the school, to spruce things up on the bulletin boards. The furniture was up to date and appropriate for the young adolescent students. But at thirty-five students each class period, conditions were cramped when class was in session. The dimensions of the classrooms seemed to be built for a more prosperous era of small class sizes. Each classroom was equipped with a teacher desk and personal computer with printer, which was connected to the district's network. There was also an overhead projector and screen.

The greatest sign of wear was in the heating and cooling systems, which didn't exist. The air intake ducts seemed to be missing or without proper grates. They seemed like they were under repair but then the project was abandoned. Heat was somehow delivered in the winter, but there was no clear evidence of how, and occasionally the classrooms grew oppressively warm. Air conditioning was not available anywhere on the campus, despite predictable daily temperatures in the nineties for much of the late summer, fall, and spring. Students and faculty worked up a sweat on a regular basis, until midday when the cooling Delta breeze arrived in the afternoons. Teachers had to master the art of working the classroom windows at the front of the room to get the breezes in. But, like I already mentioned, Northern Californians are a hardy people, and there was almost no complaining about the classroom climate.

The campus included a spacious multipurpose room, which functioned as a gym, cafeteria, and performing arts center. A well-stocked, up-to-date library, including a bank of PCs with internet access, was available for book reports and research projects. The kitchen featured hand-cooked fare, and even served the faculty, and the food was lovingly prepared and a cut above the usual ready-serve offerings in a Title I facility. The kitchen went a long way toward creating a welcoming environment for the school's working-class students. Classroom trailers have become ubiquitous in California's population explosion, but there were none at El Dorado Middle. Overall, El Dorado Middle managed to prop up the faded glory of its facilities to the point where it provided a feeling of middle-class stability. Renovation would be an issue soon, but the situation was okay for now.

CHAPTER SEVEN
Teaching on My Own Two Feet

Fight Crazy with Crazy

As reported in the previous chapter, my first day on-site at El Dorado Middle School brought an unsettling surprise: I was assigned to teach a section of intervention reading on my own. At this point, keen observers may be anticipating the introduction of a supportive mentor, say a master teacher, who would give me a plan, a blueprint, that would enable me to succeed at this task with effectiveness and grace. But no such assistance was provided. In fact, I was given no information but the simple facts that there would be a daily class, of twenty-five students, consisting of a mix of general-ed and special-ed students, from seventh and eighth grade, selected on the basis of their below-proficient scores in language arts and reading in last spring's statewide testing. That was the extent of the directions: no room assigned, no curriculum, no period, and no roster. Students would arrive for their first day of school in two work days.

I interpreted this lack of support as an extension of the faculty's disdain for the push inclusion initiative. Their sadistic indifference to my well-being was apparently one way of venting their anger. It was time for me to fight crazy with crazy.

Over the years, in my quest to change my career, going back eight years to the breakup of my marriage and my leap into copywriter, I had developed a mantra that helped me prevail in situations where my progress was hindered by someone else's crazy decisions: fight crazy with crazy. Typically, these situations involved an employer stuck in some kind authoritarian rut wherein they wanted me to follow orders even though those orders would likely lead to harm: habitual tendencies versus creativity and problem-solving. Instead of passively complying with the harmful orders, as most of my generational peers would, I intensified my efforts at creativity and negotiation in a confrontation: my crazy versus their crazy. Sometimes my crazy efforts succeeded, and other times they didn't, but those times weren't a problem, since they provided information about which step to take next.

The faculty's mildly-sadistic resistance to push inclusion, which mirrored other faculties throughout the state, I would learn later, was a situation of reflex reaction to having one's comfort zone threatened. They were bogged down in habitual tendencies. Their minds were closed, they were afraid of the pain, and they didn't want to think of the possibilities. They were pessimists whereas the state officials who wrote the publicity were optimists. For my part, I was totally self-interested, driven by my desire for success in my own ambitions, and thus inspired to transcend the confusion of both camps, pessimists and optimists. To fight crazy with crazy, I adopted the posture of a spy on a mission to gather whatever intelligence would be needed to at least survive passably as teacher of the reading course.

Surviving the faculty's pessimism would be an occasion for the warrior's value of outrageousness. Faced with a challenge, the warrior remains fearlessly firm in their commitment to compassion and non-aggression. I wasn't going to trade harm for harm with the faculty, or even start making accusations about them. Nor was I going to join in their sabotage as a conspirator, as some new teachers might have. By some outrageous and defiant means, I was going to help them put their fears aside, to open their minds, and to consider the possibilities of inclusion. But first I had to survive my first days as reading teacher to the lowest-performing adolescents in a working-class neighborhood where sixty percent of the students came from disadvantaged backgrounds (i.e. parents who worked in the service industry or single mothers).

The first two days on-site consisted of mornings of professional development and afternoons for teacher prep, which could consist of informal meetings with colleagues, decorating and organizing the classroom, and preparing lessons and curriculum. Most teachers had gained early access to their classroom, and their furnished floor plan was already in place. Only I was still walking around in search of a classroom, but that was somewhat good news, since my co-teachers might have a few minutes free to talk. With their classroom layouts in place, teachers were intensely focused on decorating and preparing lessons; any attempt to gain information would have to be quick and inconspicuous. Every teacher was in their room, alone, gripped by the solitary struggle to get as much done as possible before the students arrive, but I summoned up the nerve (and audacity) to hold a quick conversation with each of the four teachers with whom I would co-teach language arts.

Basically, I made the rounds, so to speak, which was literally as basic as getting the teachers' room numbers and a map, and as sophisticated as the pitch and planning meetings of my copywriter days. I just made small talk, offering a brief background on my intern status and intention to complete the credential, and a few statements about my motives for the career change. But in these neighborly chats, I was able to subtly make key inquiries about how to locate resources for opening a classroom. I was consistently directed to the custodian as the pivotal authority on everything to do with buildings and furniture.

I tracked down the custodian by circling the campus until I bumped into him, since no one could pinpoint his location for me. When I found him, I introduced myself as the new resource specialist for the seventh grade, and then I told him that I needed a classroom for a reading section that had just been announced. He led me to a disused large octagonal building at the edge of campus and opened the door to an obviously inactive classroom: dusty, musty, and littered with out-of-date books and papers.

I informed the custodian that I would need enough furniture for twenty-five to thirty students. The custodian led me to a large inactive classroom used to store extra furniture. I located a number of matching rectangular two-student tables and matching chairs. Veteran teachers might anticipate trouble in using tables, which would require pairs of students to sit in close proximity. The preferred seating for an intervention section would be individual student desks spread out in grid format (i.e. rows and aisles), with each student a solid four feet from their neighbors. This militaristic arrangement inhibits impulsive conversations. Senior teachers had been diligent in securing all the individual student desks before the end of the previous school year. But the tables were attractive stained wood veneer, with minimal wear. My luck was turning, at least a little.

My classroom was a wedge that occupied one-fourth of the octagon. The spacious, well-lit room with high-angled ceiling had a row of tall windows facing the school yard and main campus, which was fifty yards away across the blacktop yard. The plaster-exterior building, erected in the eighties, was starting to fade in the trim, but still retained some of its original luster. The interior featured high-quality indoor carpeting with minimal wear, attractive retractable dividers that allowed expansion into neighboring rooms, and ample dry erase boards at the front of the room, which was the raised end of the angle that fanned out and widened toward the outer walls. There was no damage from vandalism or excessive wear.

The custodian gave me some small help moving the furniture across campus. I was tasked with cleaning the room, moving the furniture, arranging it, and locating any supplies that I would need, since no one talked to me unless I talked to them first. For supplies, I started with nothing. I had to inter-rogate sources for everything: stapler, dry erase markers, pens, post-its, legal pads, trash cans, paper towels, etc.

But once I got the room cleaned, and furniture moved in and arranged, I could see that it was a pretty attractive space. The oversized windows facing the school yard provided fresh air, a cooling breeze, and natural lighting. The building and room entrance were ensconced in strategically-arranged tall trees: I remember fir and oak. The front boards, accentuated by a raised angled ceiling, created a natural center of attention for visuals that could support time management and instruc-tional prompts, and a built-in overhead screen could display detailed visuals for leading discussions (if I could find a work-ing projector). I even found a teacher's desk, which might eventually hold a PC, which was conspicuously missing.

I arranged the tables into group seating. Floor plans are actually a major area of research and training, but I hadn't learned that yet. My inner gifted-behavior-problem karma took over. By pairing the two-person rectangular tables, the floor plan consisted of eight four-person rectangles, aligned perpendicularly to the front board, such that students would turn slightly to the left or right to see the front board, which was easily viewed. If viewed from above, the arrange-ment would look like one large rectangle, perpendicular to the front board, running to the back of the room, broken up into smaller component rectangles. Students weren't facing the front board, since I was envisioning a workshop format wherein the students would work mostly on their own, some-what independently, and I was actually thinking of defying the teacher-led style. The front board would be for basic time management and occasionally a simple writing prompt: no lectures or demonstrations. This floor plan could be charac-terized as welcoming, independence-oriented, and even a lit-tle corporate: in other words, a real step up for intervention students. Keen observers may remember that senior teachers had already absconded with the site's inventory of individual student desks.

I wasn't just thinking of student autonomy, though. A sense of strategy was forming even at that early date. For supplies, each student pair of a rectangle's length could share a resource such as scissors, colored pencils, or glue. Or possibly the entire four-person group could share. I could also check the understanding of four students at each table when monitoring progress. By arranging the rectangles with the length perpendicular to the front board, I could see each student's face by positioning myself at the front of the room, thereby gaining maximum advantage in detecting off-task behavior the instant it breaks out. I wasn't totally naïve. But master teachers would have recommended against such a liberal arrangement for intervention students in favor of the traditional grid of individual student desks.

By the evening of my second day at the site, I had a hospitable, welcoming classroom with an innovative, bold floor plan. I had enough supplies to write a few instructions on the dry erase board and make a few notes on a legal pad. The lights worked. I didn't know how to control the climate, but I could at least get a breeze through the windows in the next few days, which would undoubtedly be over ninety degrees. I would at least have a place to seat my students, take roll, and maybe talk a bit. After that, I wasn't sure what I was going to do. I didn't have any curriculum or other learning-objectives to follow, a student roster, a computer, an overhead projector, or any kind of mentor assigned to advise me.

At no point over those first two days at the site did an administrator check in with me or ask me to check in with them about the reading course or any other aspect of my duties. They literally had no awareness of my activities. Essentially, I was given the silent treatment. It would have been hard for them to find me, since no preparations had been made for my arrival, even though I had been hired in mid-June: no voice-mail account, no e-mail account, no computer, no desk or cubicle anywhere, not even in a shared space. Actually, people looked surprised and even annoyed whenever I approached them to introduce myself, especially the office staff.

Probably the principal had hired me to keep up appearances, to show the district that she was going to pull out all the stops to make both NCLB and IDEA work for the people at maximum speed. But in actuality she probably figured that she could sabotage me in a few month's time (my intern contract had no right of appeal) and bring in a substitute teacher that couldn't give the principal any feedback about the neglectful conditions everyone predicted would arise for push inclusion students at the hands of resistant general-ed teachers. The last thing the principal needed was a bombshell overachiever from Diablo Valley like me sticking my idealist aquiline nose into her faculty's habitual tendencies. Whatever the cause, the administration, which consisted of a principal and two assistant principals, turned its back on me and persisted that way for most of the year.

At the end of my first three days on the job, including my first two days at the site, with all days spent primarily in professional development, as per Title I, I went home to work on my personal PC, using my desktop-publishing software and an inkjet printer, to create some first-days curriculum using recently-acquired knowledge from first-days training and my extant copywriter skills. I also stopped at an office supply store to buy some colored dry erase markers, colored pencils, and a few other supplies at my expense.

This reading course was exactly what NCLB aspired to: a supplementary period of reading instruction, meaning in addition to a period of grade-level language arts, meant to increase the number of hours spent on reading skills for students who had struggled with proficiency in statewide testing, in an age range previously thought too old for reading intervention. The age range for NCLB monitoring of reading was grades three through eight, and tenth. I was actually inspired to be part of this momentous thrust of democracy. But the school administration apparently couldn't have cared less.

Introductions

The first day of the school year finally arrived and that meant the first day of my intervention reading course, a task for which I had no experience to draw from. I recall that it was third period, after one period of co-teaching eighth grade language arts and one period of co-teaching seventh grade language arts. I had to rush from my second period classroom to unlock the door to my classroom and let the students in, and then I had to get my bearings quickly as they filed in from a fifty-yard walk across the school yard. A tentative roster had been given to me upon my inquiry that morning, after I tracked down the assistant principal working on the site's scheduling. It had over thirty students, but I was told that it would be honed down as the semester progressed.

My roster included five special-ed students from my seventh-grade caseload, a few special-ed eighth graders from that grade's caseload, and the remaining twenty-five students were general-ed from seventh and eighth, about half each grade. Keen observers may see poetic justice and a cosmic sense of fair play in this inclusive configuration of students. I, like my co-teachers, would be tasked with teaching language arts to a hybrid mix of special-ed and general-ed students. But, unlike my co-teachers, I would be on my own. The demographics of the class pretty much mirrored the school's, with 35% Hispanic, 5% Black, and 60% White, with the sexes at fifty percent. I never looked into socioeconomic status, but single mothers, I would learn as the semester unfolded, were amply represented.

I allowed the students to find a seat of their choosing. Assigned seating would have been better, but I didn't know that yet. On the other hand, the students had a chance to chat with friends on the brief intervals of down time that arose (said the gifted behavior problem). I confess to hoping that the students might be able to form some friendships during the course (said the g.b.p.). Fortunately, the students seemed to be giving me the honeymoon period most new teachers enjoy in the first few days of class. Students were curious about the course and me, and sat quietly with relaxed attention, following me with their gaze, waiting for me to make some kind of announcement. They were middle schoolers, in a general school, and thus relatively well-trained from their seven or eight previous years of schooling. Adolescents are receptive and know what is expected of them. They will go where you lead them. I was relieved to see the students fall into familiar patterns of decorum.

The image of a hall pass bursts into consciousness. From this moment forward, I would be the guardian, the first responder, for these students during this period every day, and I would be part of a faculty supervising the school's one thousand students from first to last bell. Teachers don't have the luxury of focusing just on lessons, they have to shoulder the burden of guiding and monitoring all physical aspects of the student experience: attendance (i.e. cutting class, running away), late arrivals, movement to and from the restroom, illness, aggression, suicide, theft, and accidents. To succeed, a teacher must embrace public safety to a degree similar to a police officer. Yet guardianship is trade craft: it can only be learned on the job, from experienced teachers and administrators.

I could write a book on the various strategies that I have been exposed to for administering student access to restrooms. If there is one part of instruction on which every California principal is focused, which gets their undivided attention, it is movement to and from restrooms. Keen observers might wonder why a mundane aspect of life such as elimination should be the main focus of a principal's efforts in a middle school. Drug and alcohol abuse, and weapons would be the answers to your wonderment; illness, suicide, and sexual misconduct are also factors. I managed to acquire the required skills and endure the public-safety aspect of teaching, but I never embraced it, and I have frequently been accused of too freely giving students the benefit of the doubt (said the g.b.p.).

I started my year in the most mundane, least controversial way possible. I slowly conducted roll call, asking each student to raise their hand and announce their presence with a "here." That gave me at least some chance of memorizing student names, for purposes such as hall passes to the restroom, plus the office would want attendance in the first ten minutes of class to support tracking down truants. Assigned seats would have been a quicker way, but I didn't know that yet. Students were quiet and attentive, and appropriately indifferent and a touch passive. I hadn't yet fully appreciated the humbling aspect of being a student assigned to intervention reading, but I was starting to get a clue.

Another mundane move helped establish rapport with the students. In the morning, before school started, I wrote my name in bold, oversized letters in the upper left-hand corner of the front board, where it remained for the rest of the year. All students are a bit intimidated by first days, especially underachieving ones. They're a little disoriented. Posting my name declared my intention to lead the class and to be accountable to the students, and it allowed them to address me by name, especially when they needed something such as a trip to the restroom or an intervention in bullying.

To the same permanent location, I added the name of the class, the period, and the day's date in long form. When the course started rolling, I added an agenda to the middle of that board to help students anticipate the period's activities. Reform research indicates that students will concentrate better in environments with minimal anxiety. Posting the facts of each class period can reduce anxiety by acknowledging the student's desire to be dealt with in an upfront and predictable manner. It might be kind of deflating for some reformers to hear this fact, but at this point, by having a strategy for posting key facts, I was as much the teacher of that classroom as I would ever be. In some respects, teaching adolescents is that simple.

With the basics accomplished, I will move on to the subtler art of curriculum. I launched right into the day's lesson, with almost no small talk. I did introduce myself, in a literal way, with full disclosure: "Hi. I'm Mr. Bartlett. I'm a resource teacher for the seventh and eighth grade. I'm a new teacher in a training program. Some of you have already seen me supporting your language arts section. I'll be teaching this course all year. We'll be working on your reading skills. You can choose your seats for now. We'll see how that goes." Then I called roll, as I already described.

With middle schoolers, direct and concise speech is best. Over time, my principle for all adolescent students became less is more: simple, concise directions, explanations, and demonstrations. Let the lessons teach the lessons, and save your speechifying for the pulpit or dinner table. As a gifted behavior problem, I knew just how ineffective and tiresome teachers can be in their soliloquies about self-respect. I also learned to not answer questions off topic, at least not during class time. Underachievers love to bog their teachers down in metaphysics.

After roll call, I announced the day's assignments: filing out a few surveys about your reading interests, your attitudes about reading, and your experiences with reading. I explained that this information would help me plan the course. Students should work quietly in their present seat, on their own. Students were probably relieved to have a simple task that required them to merely be themselves and to not have to listen to another rule-laden welcome kit. They embraced the task with a satisfactory level of rigor and there was no misbehavior worth attending to: no wisecracks, no leaving seats, no teasing or taunting, no pranks, and no bullying. The honeymoon was still in effect, and I was grateful for this unexpected bit of luck.

When I made the rounds and met my four co-teachers of language arts, they shared their welcome kits and a few of their first day's activities with me. The seventh grade teachers were going to teach book reports, so they included reading interest inventories in their first day's activities. These were generic formats that were downloaded online or found in inexpensive teacher's resource books. I started by giving my students one of those. But then I went on to conduct some attitude-and-opinion research using self-authored documents, which I had created the night before using my home-computing resources and a late-night trip to the copy shop, since I couldn't trust the school copier's reliability under the first day's deluge.

My surveys asked students about their reading preferences. Do you like to read? If yes, why? If no, why? What kind of story? When do you read? Do you have a favorite author? What would you like to read in this course? Is there any kind of story that you don't like to read? How do you feel about the course? And a few other similar questions. Then I asked about their experiences with reading. Do you feel like you are a good reader? Do you want to learn how to read better? What is your favorite part of reading? Your least favorite part? Do you have a difficulty in reading? What was reading like for you last year? Do you have a favorite school subject? Least favorite? And other questions meant to divine students' feelings and expectations about reading. My copywriter skills helped me adjust the layout and other aspects of readability.

The main goal of my research was to have an excuse for occupying the period with students filling out the surveys, since I couldn't think of a better alternative. I got to relax and observe, while the students did all the work; that opportunity to observe was a blessing, and it helped me to develop confidence in the students and in their latent reliability. Honestly, I was following my nose, without a good hypothesis to guide my research. I was just being nosey. On other hand, I was following the principle of education reform that said students will attend to a teacher who takes an interest in their lives. The students worked diligently on the three surveys and then handed them in toward the end of the fifty-minute period. At the start of the assignment, I had announced that I would grade the surveys and return them the next day.

That left about ten minutes of down time at the end of the period. I assigned the students to remain in their seats but talk quietly amongst themselves. They complied, luckily, since downtime is always the riskiest time for outbreaks of major misbehavior. I decided not to teach a welcome kit, in other words, the classroom rules and procedures, at the start of the semester. One, I wasn't sure how I was going to proceed, and, two, I hoped to make the course a reading workshop more than a reading penitentiary (said the g.b.p.). I aspired to transmit my passion for lifelong learning, as one behavior problem to the others. In that vein, I hoped to introduce procedures and rules with each assignment.

Power of Choice

I started the second day of intervention reading with some listening, in a strategy reminiscent of my peacekeeping copywriter days, when I brought together an authoritarian parent company with its defiant acquisition in weekly joint-planning meetings, a move that facilitated a lasting peace between the warring entities. After school on the first day, I carefully read and marked each student survey from the first day of reading class. I wrote in a few words of encouragement here and there to show that I had really read each survey, so my listening started with taking time to carefully review them.

I experienced some pleasant surprises while reading the responses. Nearly every student had preferences for reading, including a favorite book and type of story. Some students even had a favorite author and had read a few of the author's works. Nearly every student wanted to become a better reader and thought reading was an important skill. Students had favorite subjects in school and subjects that they didn't like. When it came to preferences, student responses reflected a preference for fiction books, which is typical for that age group. Only a few students had negative views of reading, and gave reasons such as it's boring or television was more interesting. Most special-education students had relatively refined preferences and clear expectations about reading; on the experience and expectations level, at least, they were in line with their grade-level peers.

After taking roll and making a few housekeeping announcements, I returned the graded surveys to the students by calling out to each one. The honeymoon was still in effect: students were quiet and attentive, and appropriately indifferent and a touch passive. Returning the surveys one student at a time was a tedious procedure, since I didn't have assigned seats, but it provided the benefit of connecting faces to the survey responses. Then I launched into my first classroom discussion.

I wanted to have students share some of their responses with the class. Seeing is believing. By calling on students and taking an interest in their responses, I would show them that I was focused on their well-being and that their opinions mattered. And they would discover something about each other. This would be the final stage of listening.

Not surprisingly, some of the best responses came from students with negative views of reading. They tended toward the class clown, and thus were better at speaking out in front of the group. On the other hand, I did ask students with negative responses to volunteer, and they were merely cooperating. These doubters gave me an opening: I was careful to listen nonjudgmentally and to refrain from any kind of correcting or scolding of their views, and I didn't try to convince them to change. It's rude to ask someone for their opinion and then put them down for it. I calmly received their response, in a deliberately nonchalant fashion, thanked them for their participation, and moved on to the next student. The class was nonplussed and then kind of awed. Disruptive students, who love to taunt moralizing teachers into hours of soliloquy, were not going to have any fun with me, and we may even learn to respect each other.

The avid readers tended to be a little shy, predictably. The most memorable responses were from students who showed me the books they were carrying in their backpacks. Seventh-grade teachers had assigned book reports, meaning their students had to read a book and turn in a corresponding report at regular intervals throughout the year, and some had to take a computerized test. Students were expected to carry their book with them every day, so teachers could assign silent reading time when the timing of a lesson fell short of the period or students needed a break from the pressures of grade-level curriculum. A few of the avid readers asked if they could use books from home or books of their choosing from the library.

My listening indicated that I had a room full of readers. They were already life-long learners, but somehow they hadn't rated proficient in last spring's statewide testing. My research results reminded me of the school's library. There was a full-time librarian, in a spacious structure that rivaled college libraries, with a huge collection of fiction and non-fiction books in a color-coded system of reading levels, the same level system that was applied in the district's elementary schools. Computerized reading-comprehension tests were available in the library that matched the leveling system; the tests helped the student rise through the levels. Nearly all of El Dorado's students had been trained using the leveled reading system and book reports in elementary school, and most of El Dorado's seventh-grade teachers were using book reports.

My students were pretty well-trained, even if I wasn't. Might there be a way to tap into the students' present levels of knowledge and training, such that their existing motivation and preferences would drive them forward (and relieve me of the burden of inspiring said motivation). In response to this question, the library started to look like a source of free curriculum that might last for months. One of my co-teachers of language arts (7th) had given me her materials for teaching book reports in our first meeting. As an avid reader, the materials immediately caught my attention. First, it reminded me of fourth and fifth grade. But then I remembered the critical thinking skills that I had gained even as an adult in analyzing stories; I had become an active reader.

Intervention guidance recommends extending instruction that should have been mastered in earlier grades. I could use the first months of my course to reteach the book report, which ideally would have been mastered in fifth grade, with the goal of helping students become active readers. Student could use books of their choosing from the library or home as source material for book-report assignments that I would create. The assessment and motivation system would be choice, since the students would select books based on their preferences and experiences. At first, I could observe which books the student chose, and if needed, I could intervene in situations where a student went above or below their competence level. There would be some overlap with seventh-grade language arts and their book reports, but my reports would be different and they would be taught like a lesson, so I didn't see a need to worry if the student used the same book for both courses. The extra depth might even help the student's comprehension.

Choice was definitely a good system for motivation, but slightly imprecise for establishing a reading level. Technically, I should have administered a couple of classroom assessments of reading-comprehension ability. But I didn't really have the skills for that yet. In general, students want to be seen as keeping up with their peers, so I figured social pressure and personal preferences would lead the students to the right choices. Generally, students take pride in facing a challenge and will stretch themselves in a supportive setting. Mostly, I was mad at the principal for not having a curriculum prepared. I liked the freedom and respect for individuality of my plan, even if it wasn't totally precise. It had the counter-intuitive quality of resting on the innate positivity and desire to learn of intervention students. I felt the principal didn't have much regard for me and even less respect for my students. Underachievers unite! The workshop scenario based on student choice appealed to my inner disestablishmentarian karma.

I went home after the second day of school and developed curriculum for my choice model for running a reading workshop based on the book report, once again using my personal desktop-publishing resources. Keen observers would probably like to know that no administrator or any other kind of mentor or supervisor had approached me about curriculum or any other aspect of the course. I wasn't being defiant in developing my own materials. I was scrambling for survival in an environment that defeats at least fifty percent of new teachers every year.

Workshop Rules

By the end of the second day of intervention reading, I had decided to use books of the students' choosing as reading material for my first unit, which would hopefully occupy a couple of months. Books would come from the school library or home. Then I had to develop the learning products that students would work on and submit for a grade: in other words, the curriculum. A lot of new teachers might have dived straight into creating the handouts students would use to develop their book reports. But my psychology background and business experience told me that I would need a motivation and time-management system to compel students to attend to those materials with some vigor. I didn't want to just hand out the materials and then demand that students respond to me as an authority figure (i.e. do what their told). I wanted them to develop some self-direction and autonomy, so I had to develop curriculum integrated with a motivation plan and time-management scheme. As previously mentioned, all this would be accomplished on my own time using my personal desktop-publishing resources.

To develop a unit, meaning a coordinated system of work that lasts about a month, I envisioned a packet system of curriculum for using the book report to show students how to find meaning in a story. The student would complete a packet for each book. The packet would be a study guide that helped the student analyze the story in incremental steps. For instance, the student can predict what the story might be about by studying the cover and title, so that was step one, the first increment; predictions, meaning thinking ahead and anticipating, are an aide to comprehension and a trait of the active reader. For the second step, the student would identify and describe the main character after reading twenty or so pages. Being clear about the main character early in the story gives the student a frame in which to build memories about the other story elements. Active readers typically have a collection of such mnemonic strategies. Step three would be another mnemonic: summarizing the plot of each day's reading rather than writing one long summary after reading the entire story. This page of the packet would have ten or so lined text boxes to hold each summary. Ongoing summarizing is a key trait of the active reader. In general, reform methodology encourages the teaching of mnemonics such as timelines for history texts or main-idea-supporting-details organizers for articles.

Each page of the packet would be one of these incremental steps in the book report. Remaining parts of the book report would be time period, setting, themes, moral of the story, identification with a character, and relevance to the reader's life, moving from literal to evaluative kinds of thinking. Reform methodology says that evaluative thinking improves retention and recall.

Time management and motivation would be built into the packet. Each incremental step of the packet, which typically took up a page or two, contained a checkbox in a header. The student had to locate me when a step was completed and have me enter the date and my initials into the header. I gave feedback and asked the student to correct errors at that point, instead of waiting for them to complete the entire packet.

For time management, each checkbox header included directions on when to complete the task. When all the sections were done, the student handed the packet in and received their grade, which covered the quality of each step, conformity to the directions, and overall timeliness. Motivation had two factors. First, when the packet was viewed as a whole, the checkboxes in each step formed a checklist, with visual feedback at each step. Checklists are believed to be an effective motivator for underachieving students. Second, I rewarded speed. A student's grade was based on the quality and compliance factors already mentioned and the number and pace of packets handed in: in other words, speed. When given a room of laborers, speed them up! I was the Henry Ford of reading. Actually, the speed bonus was meant to reward stronger students for pushing themselves into greater levels of achievement when they might have tried to sit back and make a little mischief. To set a minimum pace, I put an agenda on the front board every day reminding students of the minimum pace required to pass the unit, shown in terms of due dates and elapsed time. Keen observers may have noticed that I created a small business that produced book reports, in an act of subliminal transference driven by desperation. The interesting part of this business was that it offered workers a flexible pace based on their ability level and a chance to pursue their interests. Creative economy meets Title I.

When I developed this unit, I was guessing wildly, but I landed on a few reform strategies that would later be introduced in my credential training. Study guides were a recommended format for training young readers to be more active and think critically. To prepare students for upper-grade writing tasks, my study guides required short written responses for each step, instead of less-demanding multiple choice or fill in the blank. In upcoming statewide testing, and in high school, students would have to respond in essay-length writing to reading passages as established by the state content standards for literature response. Writing tasks in my study guides such as describing the main character in two or more sentences and generating ten sentence-length summaries prepared students for proficiency in literature response. Most importantly, reading books of their own choosing was widely regarded as one of the best ways for students to expand their vocabulary—that is why the seventh-grade teachers taught the book report as homework in addition to the state-content standards for language arts.

Workshop Curriculum

On the third day of intervention reading, I passed out a sample of my book-report packet to each student and briefly went over the format that I described in the previous chapter. The honeymoon was still in effect and students were at least minimally attentive. Students would choose their own reading material, complete a packet for each book, and the packet would create a book report. Grades would be based on completeness and accuracy of the short writing assignments in the packet and the number of packets completed. A schedule for minimum number of packets would be posted. I would be the supervisor and tutor to help keep students on track (and to quickly detect and correct any misbehavior). Middle schoolers are still more obedient than philosophical, so I didn't deliver an oration on the underlying methodology of the study guide.

After that brief introduction to the study guide, I assigned the students to walk to the library, check out a book with my assistance, find a seat, read silently when they had their book, and return to the classroom upon my prompt. I gave students a few parameters for selecting a book: fifty to a hundred pages, at your reading level, a narrative fiction or non-fiction book (i.e. *not* jokes, Ripley's, book of world records, how to) and a few others. The mob scene of thirty- two wasn't as bad as it might have been, but I definitely had to provide some high-speed tutoring. The librarian, a perky business-casual middle-aged woman, gave a quick briefing to guide students in their selections. About half the students were pretty well trained. They found a book on their own, showed it to me, obtained my approval, checked it with the librarian, and sat down to quietly read (and slip in a hushed chat) at one of the library's round tables. A quarter were slightly-less-trained but often more ambitious: "Mr.Bartlett, where can I find a book about sports?", "Mr. Bartlett, is this book too long, too many pages?" Some students needed help using the library's computerized card catalog. They needed tutoring before they could locate a book, but still they were enthusiastic and focused on the task. Roughly a quarter were disorganized. They couldn't check out a book because they had library fines from last year, or hadn't returned textbooks from last semester, or had never established a library account. Even when they found a book, and demonstrated an interest, the librarian became an impediment. Ultimately, I prevailed upon the librarian to allow me to check out the disorganized students' books on my faculty account, which meant I accepted financial responsibility for any lost, damaged, or stolen items.

Every student found a book by the end of the period. The speedier students had maintained pretty good decorum while waiting for needier students to find their way through the assignment. All the students seemed to have reverence for the library and librarian, and although the class was a bit chatty for the library, they had actually showed some respect, staying in their seats and talking in hushed tones, which was good for me, since I really had no strategy in mind for handling misbehavior.

Now each child had a book to use for source material, but I wasn't ready to jump into the book reports with students reading and completing assignments on their own. In accord with intervention methodology, I stopped to check the students' understanding of the key concepts involved in the book report. So, I wasn't going to assume that students should know what a main character was. I was going to quickly teach characterization and then have students apply the concept on a sample assignment. Technically, I was reteaching information that should have been acquired in fifth grade, so I was going to move fast, like a refresher course. Plus I would be available for tutoring for students who still had questions after the refresher.

To provide a foundation for this refresher course, I modified my study guide for books into a movie report. I would lead students through a study guide a step or two a day while watching a popular movie for the source material. The class would watch about fifteen or twenty minutes of the movie each day, simulating the reading of a book. Then I would guide them in completing a portion of the study guide for that day: summarizing, for instance. For the movie, I chose *Spirit*, the contemporaneous and popular animated full-length feature. The film embodied the human drama of adolescence in the lives of a herd of beautiful wild horses in the American West. Good, clean family fun but with poignant psychological themes that middle-school students could connect to: desire for autonomy, rebellion, first love, the struggle for justice, and dealing with elders—plus a primer on the cultural conflicts of the old west. The film was just right for seventh graders, but a touch juvenile for eight graders; yet I felt the mature themes of adolescence would still engage them.

I figured this movie format would provide an opportunity to focus on the book report while avoiding the anxiety that reading sometimes elicits. In addition, the class could work together for a week or two. All students would work at the same pace, roughly, and each day's lesson would easily fill the entire period. Even after only four days of co-teaching, and observing the push inclusion sections, I could sense that allowing my reading students to work on their own, workshop fashion, would be a real stretch for my limited discipline skills. Starting with a warm-up unit in which my reading students could probably handle the demands without too much stress, and work together under my leadership and watchful gaze, would give me a chance to develop rapport and skills in a scenario with minimal behavior challenges.

So, on the fourth day of intervention reading, I started the period with a preview of the movie report, launched into the first ten minutes of *Spirit*, and led the students in the first step of the movie report, which was writing a short prediction for the story's content based on the title and first ten minutes.

Innate Positivity

The movie report went well. The lessons went according to plan. Each day, the class watched fifteen or twenty minutes of the movie, *Spirit*, followed by me leading students through a relevant section of the movie report: prediction, main character, plot summaries, and so on. The movie report unit occupied six periods, which meant that I had survived my first two weeks as the teacher for reading intervention. Those periods had been blessedly uneventful, and the students had actually followed the lessons and completed their movie report.

Now it was time to set the students free to read a book of their choosing and complete their book-report packet. In my co-teaching classrooms, I observed that every period began with a starter assignment lasting from five to ten minutes. These assignments typically involved relatively simple tasks such as diagramming a sentence or summarizing the previous day's homework. The starter assignment had two purposes. First, it gave the teacher ten minutes to enter attendance data into the district's new software, which triggered automated phone calls to parents for truants; this hypervigilant approach to attendance was one of the district's key responses to NCLB. Second, the starter helped students calm down from the adolescent-energized chaos of the halls and warm their brain up for academic tasks.

Initially, I felt the starter was a superficial waste of time and thus an infraction on the student's right to learn. My reading periods started with a few announcements from the teacher at the head of the class, typically a preview of the period's activities. But then I started to worry that fifty minutes of working independently was more than my students could maintain without lapsing into impulsive conversations and other bits of mischief toward the end of the period. So I implemented a starter assignment in my classroom, but with a twist. My starter would be a fifteen-minute drill on a language skill with intervention value: in other words, not superficial. Language skills would include subject-verb agreement, pronouns, figurative language, and other linguistic and grammatical conventions. I obtained the materials for these starters in a conversation where I received some mentoring from one of my seventh-grade co-teachers of language arts. I collected each day's drill and returned the graded work within a few days. The fifteen-minute drill left thirty-five minutes for reading and working on book reports.

With the starter in place, I launched the book report unit at the beginning of my third week as teacher of intervention reading. After working with co-teachers for three weeks, I had some idea of the challenges involved in engaging students and keeping them on task. I was a little nervous about my reading students being able to resist peer attention during the thirty-five minutes of working independently. Side conversations with peers are a major source of time off task in middle school, even though they aren't typically that disruptive to the classroom as a whole. In addition, struggling students will sometimes drift off into daydreams and other kinds of idleness when not being prompted by the teacher every few minutes; these idle moments are often the result of neurological deficits in attention span, but I didn't know that yet. Consistent, sustained engagement was the main behavioral challenge at El Dorado more than suppressing extreme forms of misbehavior such as defiant speech directed at the teacher or violent rivalries between peers. My book-report unit might turn into an experiment in using an open format (i.e. sustained working independently) with underachievers.

On the other hand, I had seen students in action in my co-teaching classrooms. Most periods involved students working independently for at least some part of the period. In any one period, a fair percentage of the students engaged with the material and demonstrated progress on the spot. Other students struggled with sustained attention. Some of those seemed to be procrastinating, planning to complete the assignment as homework. Others were struggling with the content, disconnected from the lesson; they seemed to have lost the thread of the discussion. Gradually, I became more adept at offering tutoring to the struggling students, which suited my role as co-teacher. The procrastinators usually completed the assignments somehow, without requiring much support. Misbehaviors during times of working independently were typically minor and consisted of hushed side conversations, surreptitious procrastination, and distractions such as doodling. Engagement was a challenge, but the classrooms remained sufficiently calm during these times to support learning. I figured conduct in my classroom would be about the same.

My motivation and time management schemes for the book-report unit were designed with engagement in mind. Well-structured curriculum with clear expectations for performance and a checklist format would give all students a definitive path to success. The speed bonus would spur overachievers on to consistent, sustained effort, and actually distinguish them as leaders with higher grades. The daily agenda on the front board with posted minimum expectations would mildly prod underachievers to put in a minimal effort each day or at least expect me to intervene in procrastination. Such were my optimistic predictions at the start of the unit.

I'm glad to report that most of my predictions came true. The book report unit lasted about a month, meaning four weeks of instruction, meaning twenty periods, running from mid-September to mid-October. Each period began with a starter on English language conventions, followed by a few quick reminders about the expectations for progress on the book reports. Then I spent the remaining thirty-five minutes of the period attending to individual students by answering questions, initialing completed sections of the packet, and occasionally tutoring students who were struggling with sustained attention or with interpreting the instructions on the packet. Just after I launched the unit, the principal assigned an instructional aide to the period, and she basically mirrored my actions when students were working independently.

Julia, the instructional aide, was a young forty-something with a petite, slim, and shapely body, delicate oval facial features, clear creamy skin, and styled brunette bob. Consistent with most of the school staff and faculty, her fashion statement was business casual, anchored in high-waist cotton dress paints, fashionable cotton blouses, and leather loafers or other comfortable dress shoes. She was shy, retiring, and soft-spoken, even with the children, and she tended toward one-on-one tutoring as opposed to leading the class like a surrogate for the teacher.

Over the twenty periods, student performance on the book reports gradually stratified into three categories. In the top-performing group, which consisted of about ten individuals, students were relatively independent and completed multiple book reports; some of these students even completed three books. Almost all of these overachievers were from general education. The next group, which consisted of about fifteen students, was the minimalists. They completed one or two book reports, but without much tutoring or other kinds of intervention. Their working style was to balance hushed side conversations and a bit of procrastination with intermittent periods of reverent compliance. Most minimalists were from general education , but a few were the strongest from special education. Then came the underachievers, who required near constant prompting and tutoring to complete the minimum of one book report. Almost all of the seven under-achievers were from seventh-grade special education.

Keen observers might note a disturbing inversion of the warrior's organizing philosophy of lu, nyen, and lha described in earlier chapters, with the greatest effort being applied to the lowest achieving group instead of the highest achieving. But upon closer reflection, one can see how the philosophy still applies. The overachievers comprise lu, since they are the foundational workers who toil compliantly, driven by intrinsic motives. Nyen forms the sales force, if you will, intermittently flaunting work rules on one hand and assertively pressing the company's cause on the other. The people of nyen are basically true believers but wary of full devotion; in America, we would call this the middle class. In devoting at least some of our best efforts to lha, the underachievers, we establish our greatness as a nation. A warrior's nobility is measured by how skilled they are in including everyone in society's blessings.

In those twenty periods, the overachievers were a delight to behold. Several of the overachievers were English Learners reading and writing in their family's new language. They were energetic and even showing off a little. The minimalists were experts in staying off the radar; sometimes it seemed like if I hadn't noticed them during attendance, I wouldn't have remembered them at all. A couple of the assignments in the book report involved creating visual representations. The main-character assignment required the student to draw and color a poster of the character in addition to listing out a few personality traits. I artfully wallpapered the room with these colorful, vibrant, and precise 2' x 4' rectangular posters. They were fantastically detailed and indicated a surprising depth of perception. The plot-summary assignment included a requirement to draw a favorite scene from the plot on an 8.5" x 11" sheet. Whereas students easily excelled at the posters, many struggled a bit with this more analytical task; most students did a relatively detailed drawing, but some had to resort to stick figures.

Most of the seven underachievers were struggling with attention deficits, learning disabilities, and gaps in prior learning. Typically, I would try to help these students with short visits to their desk in which I would ask a few questions and tutor them on the instructions for the present step of their packet. Often these visits would be timed to intervene in mildly disruptive behavior such as joking with a nearby peer or flirting with the young ladies. If I was lucky, the student would maintain attention to the task for ten minutes before the next episode of misbehavior. These students basically never made it through a period without needing some kind of redirection. But, step by begrudging step most of these students made it through a least one packet with satisfactory responses to the assignments.

Occasionally, I could conduct an intensive tutoring session of ten or fifteen minutes with an underachiever. Those were enjoyable sessions for me. I really got to know the students. I also gained first-hand exposure to the effects of attention deficits and learning disabilities, sitting right next to the distractible student when their gaze jumped this way and that when it should be focused on the text or me, the speaker. I would also have the student read to me as way of helping them focus; I learned about slow decoding speeds, pronunciation problems, and vocabulary deficits. Helping a student plan their response to an assignment aloud such as summarizing improved their written response, which was still halting and full of improvised spelling and omissions. Julia the classroom aide kind of migrated towards specializing in these intensive tutoring sessions, leaving me free to move from student to student in brief bursts of support.

The underachievers were responsive to these tutoring sessions and even seemed to enjoy them. They basically expected them, since they were frequently available in the small-group settings they had studied in before push inclusion. But in my intervention reading course, in the large mainstream class, these tutoring sessions sometimes came at a serious cost to classroom climate. The more focused that the aide or I became on a tutoring session, the more likely disruptive behavior was to break out somewhere else in the classroom.

If both the aide and I tried to conduct tutoring sessions simultaneously, it was almost a sure thing that side conversations would grow to a discernable din, meaning that only the most-determined students could continue on task. Basically, the minimalists sensed an opportunity for a bit of mischief when they saw that both teachers' attention was drawn away and gave in to temptation. Amazingly, if I left the tutoring sessions and resumed making brief visits to individual students, the disruptive chatting would usually subside. And if I deliberately stationed myself at the head of the classroom and glowered at the class, maybe even making the rare announcement that I might need to send a student or two to the office if the noise doesn't subside, then the misbehavior would markedly decrease and work would resume. This response to the level of monitoring was a dramatic introduction to the strategy of constant visual monitoring, which says that when teaching students who experience attention and motivation problems, constant visual monitoring will improve focus and time on task.

Student conduct during the book-report unit was about the same as I had observed in my co-teaching sections. Misbehaviors during times of working independently were typically minor and consisted of hushed side conversations, surreptitious procrastination, and distractions such as doodling. Maintaining sustained attention from day to day had been a challenge for about half the students, but most of the time the classroom remained sufficiently calm to support learning. Despite this modest success in teaching my first major unit, situations like the students' response to the level of visual monitoring were alerting me to the need to be even more strategic in creating a classroom climate that supported high levels of sustained attention.

Blind Spot

Student conduct during the book report unit had conformed to my predictions. Most of the time the classroom had remained sufficiently calm to support learning. Students' training from six or seven previous years of schooling was evident, and they generally showed a healthy level of reverence for school and learning. A few had even demonstrated exemplary levels of intrinsic motivation. But for two of the underachieving students, the honeymoon was definitely over.

These two students could best be described as defiant. It was two eighth grade girls who epitomized the problem of defiance. As ascertained through observation, their goal for intervention reading was to engage in as much socializing with peers as possible while giving the scantest appearance of compliance. These peers were often of the minimalist type described in the previous section. They were inclined to at least comply with the minimum pace and expectations for decorum, but when enticed by the opportunity for exchanging confidences of the dearest nature with a potential girlfriend, the minimalists lapsed into underachievement. This contagion effect of defiance is why so much research has been done on the topic. It's rare to get through a job interview for a teaching position without at least one question on how you will intervene in defiance.

Defiance usually arises from some type of adjustment problem in the child's life. Typically, the net effects of these adjustment problems manifest as depression and corresponding attention deficits. The depressed student seems inattentive and unmotivated; they just can't put socializing away and concentrate on academic tasks. Even when sitting quietly, they doodle or daydream the period away. They typically feel isolated and alone due to adverse circumstances at home such as a traumatized upbringing due to an abusive or addictive parent, economic hardship related to breakdown of the family, or hardship that led to the breakdown of the family. Whatever the cause of the adjustment problems, the symptoms of depression, attention deficits, and school underachievement are what the teacher encounters in the classroom.

Defiant students often use aggressive behavior toward the teacher as a means of escaping academic tasks. My two defiant young ladies were no exception. When I approached minimalists to check in with them about progress on their book report, they would show me their progress or stop socializing and apply themselves, frequently even moving to a quieter location to avoid a distracting peer. Basically, the minimalists weren't defensive, and they showed reverence for the setting, even though they had gone mildly off task. Underachievers were similar in their reverent response to redirection. But defiant students attempted to scare me away when I would visit their seat to check on progress.

My two defiant young ladies had a precocious fashion statement that set them apart from their peers, who pretty much stuck to the school's unisex uniform of hoodies, t-shirts, jeans, and athletic shoes. The two Caucasian rebels almost always dressed in a loose plaid flannel shirt or jacket of heavy cloth, jeans that tended toward designer, sometimes with boots, and sometimes with black leather jacket. They might have been a couple of teenage runaways headed for Woodstock in a different era. They had long brunette hair, worn simply and naturally, with almost no styling, with trim figures and mildly sexualized auras for their age. They were precocious aspirants to the ranks of granolas, thrashers, tree huggers, and stoners endemic to the teenage scene of Northern California.

When approached, even in a neutral, nonjudgmental tone, in the nonjudgmental positive environment of my classroom, the defiant ladies would hurl an epithet at me like "Why don't you just fuck off?", or "Just leave me alone. I don't want to do your stupid report," or "Get the hell away from me." With these oppositional bursts, the students sincerely hoped

I would follow directions. Most readers would imagine an immediate removal to the principal's office. But teachers are encouraged to apply some sort of progressive warning and maybe even some problem solving before removing a student from the classroom. The principal might immediately return the student to the classroom if no warning process has been applied.

For my part, I would just give a nonchalant response such as, "That's fine. Just remember the schedule up there on the board," and I would move to a cooperative student. This bit of planned ignoring worked since most of the overachievers, minimalists, and even underachievers weren't depressed and were sufficiently motived to ignore the defiant students and remain successful. My motivation, time management, and tutoring schemes worked for most of the students. The first intervention in defiance is well-structured lesson plans and classrooms, since those factors will almost always keep nearly all of the students on task, creating a kind of quarantine to the defiance contagion. My first responses to defiance were mild warnings about progress and planned ignoring. That kept the class sufficiently calm, with most students making pretty good progress. But I was genuinely worried about the three or four minimalists being disrupted and the mild generalized disruption of the learning climate.

Eventually, after two weeks of persistent defiance during the book report unit, I warned the two ladies that the next outburst of oppositional speech would earn them a referral to the principal and a parent conference. The two students had not been that disruptive to the classroom, being careful to conduct their socializing in hushed tones, but I was concerned about their impact on their minimalist peers and in the precedence of defiance going unchallenged. A lot of teachers would not have intervened, but I owed it to the defiant girls, their classmates, and even the taxpayers of California to intervene in the defiance and try to address the root of their inattention.

In response to the referral warning, one girl immediately

intensified her oppositional speech to the point where it was almost a threat of a violent outburst. I followed through on my warning and sent the student to the office and followed up with a detailed referral, which basically means a brief written description of the problem behaviors and attempts to intervene. In response, the student stopped attending school for multiple weeks, which might have included a short suspension. When the student returned, the principal moved her to a different course for the period, so her defiance was no longer my issue, but her problem of underachievement, and obvious depression, went untreated, since no formal therapeutic intervention was applied. Eventually, the student changed schools in the middle of the year.

The other girl grew more skillful in her defiance, strategically avoiding peers but still failing to engage in the unit. This less-disruptive defiance lasted for about a week until she intensified her oppositional strategies to include vandalism and pranks. She had taken up the habit of sitting quietly in a rear corner of the room, where the classroom aide typically sat while tutoring the underachievers. I mistakenly figured the aide would be able to monitor all the students in that area.

One day, despite the aide's objections, the defiant girl walked around a sliding divider and into a neighboring empty classroom, where she secured a fire extinguisher. She sprayed the dry-powder extinguisher around the neighboring classroom and the edge of mine. The aide immediately sent the student to the principal's office and I followed up with a detailed referral about the student's persistent defiance. The aide was completely traumatized by this outburst, not because the extinguisher had done much damage, in fact it hadn't harmed anything, but because the student had totally defied the aide's commands and imprecations. Of course, the student anticipated the aide's trauma and hoped it would lead to expulsion. Instead of expulsion or even suspension, the principal immediately moved the student to another course for that period. Once again, the student's defiance was no longer my issue, but her problem of underachievement, and obvious depression, went untreated, since no formal therapeutic intervention was applied.

After the fire-extinguisher incident, the principal called me to her office for a conference regarding the two defiance referrals from my reading course. She was concerned about statements made to her by the classroom aide. The principal reported that the aide felt that the students weren't listening to her because I was too considerate of the students' feelings. The aide felt that defiance was breaking out because I didn't reprimand and scold students enough. I seemed unwilling to put students in their place. The principal said these things in a pensive way, like she was testing me for my response. She knew, I'm guessing, that what the aide was saying went against the philosophy of positive discipline that I would learn through my credential training in accord with special-ed law and reform methodology: IDEA mandates that all attempts at intervention should be based on the evidence-based practices of positive behavioral intervention.

The principal knew that if she told me off, my credential supervisor and professors would hear about it afterward. She maintained a sideling glance while she presented the aide's concerns. The tenure-track maneuver would have been to apologize for my naiveté and promise to give students a firm scolding whenever they failed to meet my expectations, especially in situations of disruptive behavior. Instead, I defended my positive methods. Fight crazy with crazy! I informed the principal about the book report unit and the outstanding progress of the overachievers, satisfactory progress of the minimalists, and begrudging progress of the underachievers. I told her about how students followed their choices in tackling the intellectual challenges of my study guide. Overall, I had accomplished a great deal with this class, especially given the lack of support and direction from the administration (insert principal frowning). Note that the first time the principal or any other administrator spoke to me before I spoke to them was on the topic of defiance. I expressed my belief that the aide was overreacting to relatively minor outbreaks of mild defiance, which had been soundly outweighed by major outbreaks of engagement and positivity.

But then I kind of conceded to the principal on a few points. I shared that I had been thinking of adopting a highly-structured format like those I had observed in the classrooms of some of my co-teachers for language arts. That would mean reorganizing my classroom's floor plan into rows and aisles, with all students facing the front board and overhead screen to receive direct instruction from the teacher, who basically remains at the head of the class for the entire period. I further shared that the individualized tutoring and feedback sessions of my workshop format had kept me literally darting around the classroom at a barely-composed pace. My legs actually ached at the end of each day. I had started to wonder if the workshop was the best format; maybe direct instruction could work for both students and faculty, whereas the workshop mostly worked for students. Finally, I acknowledged that the workshop format mildly exacerbated the engagement problems of chronically defiant students and some other students with mild proclivities to misbehavior. By the way, the two defiant girls of my reading course had a history of defiance and suspensions in previous years, and they had been identified as students with chronic problem behaviors. I concluded my part of the conversation by informing the principal that I would convert my classroom and course to a highly-structured format in the next few weeks. She responded to my plan with a regal nod of approval and a begrudging "Okay. We'll see how it goes."

Shortly thereafter, roughly a week later, the principal called me in to begin an evaluation cycle for that school year. She basically intended to evaluate me as if I had a tenure-track contract even though I was just an intern. My credential (i.e. internship) supervisor would be conducting five classroom observations that year, consisting of four formative observations for instructional purposes and a final summative assessment for a course grade. The principal would probably hold two formal classroom observations for her evaluation. I felt that performing for both evaluators comprised an onerous burden, especially for a first-year intern, but at least the principal had acknowledged my presence in the school and tacitly conceded to the progress of my students. My decision to convert my reading course to the highly-structured format had been serendipitous: that format would be a lot easier to manage during the classroom observations held for the evaluations.

Mr. Chips Gets Tough

After my conference with the principal regarding her concerns about outbreaks of defiance in my reading class, I dedicated myself to adopting a highly-structured format for at least the rest of first semester. It was the end of October, which meant that I had survived past the mid-point of first semester. The principal's evaluation cycle, which is controlled by both state law and collective bargaining, typically begins with a classroom observation and follow-up conference in early November. I had a couple of weeks of instruction, meaning about ten periods, to get my highly-structured approach in place.

In adopting direct instruction over the workshop format, I wasn't attempting something for which I had no preparation. In reform methodology, direct instruction is touted as an effective strategy for promoting engagement for students with deficits in prior learning, motivation, attention deficits, or learning disabilities: in other words, the students in my reading intervention course. My credential program anticipated that NCLB would likely lead to a near universal switch to direct instruction for below-proficient students and appropriately started the year by thoroughly training the credential candidates in the reciprocal approach to direct instruction.

In a nutshell, the reciprocal approach follows a lesson design in which the teacher starts the lesson by delivering new information to the students, followed by the teacher briefly checking students for their understanding of that information and guiding them in some application of it, followed by a time of students independently applying the information, and concluding with an assessment that measures the student's ability to apply the new information on their own. This lesson format can be adapted to any subject matter. As the teacher masters this format, they acquire subtleties of craft such as creative ways to invoke students' prior knowledge of a topic before delivering new information at the start of the lesson; research indicates that invoking prior knowledge at the start of the lesson will improve performance on the assessment at the end of the lesson. There are myriad levels of expertise to be acquired in reciprocal instruction. The lesson's effectiveness is measured by how well student performance on the assessment phase reflects the learning goal stated at the beginning. An interesting aside: As far as statewide testing, each lesson should ideally be a stepping stone to the knowledge required to complete the assessments in May.

My credential training on reciprocal direct instruction included writing lesson plans to support a principal's classroom observations. In fact, the credential course explicitly walked candidates through the process of earning a proficient rating in a principal's evaluation. Candidates also planned and taught a mock reciprocal lesson to their peers in the cohort. My mock lesson was on the reading skill of identifying main idea and supporting details.

In addition to my credential training, I had observed my co-teachers teach reciprocal lessons in language arts more or less effectively for the past nine weeks. Some of those lessons were textbook readings of grade-level content. Most of my co-teachers were applying reciprocal direct instruction to the entire language-arts curriculum. On one hand, I was nervous about having to perform for a classroom observation on a task that I had no experience with. On the other hand, I probably had enough knowledge to pull it off, a thought which brought the energizing force of outrageousness. Fight crazy with crazy!

So, I had ten periods to prepare for the observation. To get started, I had to rearrange my classroom floor plan to focus students on the teacher, front board, and overhead screen. I separated the four-person rectangles of group seating back into the original two-person rectangular tables. Then I connected them in pairs at one end (i.e the width) that ran parallel to the front board. The two students of each rectangle sat on the length opposite the board, facing straight ahead toward the board and screen. Two of these pairs formed a row, with space for entering and exiting provided between each pair, such that each row had eight students facing the board. Four of these rows, all similarly parallel to the board, from front to back of the room, contained the thirty-two students such that each one faced the board, and each was in an aisle of four others. Reminiscent of the long shared tables of university lecture halls, the floor plan had an attractive linear feel, with parallel lines reinforcing the focus on the teacher and delivery of new information. But it was a little cozy for intervention students, who would still be sitting shoulder to shoulder with peers. I hoped the change of focus to the front board and overhead screen would be enough to support reciprocal lessons and elicit higher levels of engagement, and two of my co-teachers, the untenured youngest two, used similar configurations of rectangular tables. Keen observers will recall that senior teachers had absconded with the individual student desks, which would be optimal for direct instruction to intervention students, at the end of the previous school year.

After rearranging the floor plan, I located a working overhead projector. I literally conducted reconnaissance until I found a dusty projector in some shadowy disused space. In my co-teaching classrooms, I had observed that overheard slides provided an engaging visual support for focusing students' attention on the curriculum, and reform methodology recommends visual supports to improve the performance of students with attention and motivation problems. Visual supports especially aide the teacher in guiding students in applying recently acquired information in the phase of a reciprocal lesson called guided practice.

With floor plan and overhead projector in place, I needed a curriculum that would support direct instruction. The grapevine had started to indicate that a curriculum called Reading Rewards should arrive soon, including professional development for teachers, but no one had notified me of any solid plans, and thus I still had to draw on my own resources. I visited a couple of nearby learning stores that featured curricular materials for teachers and families. I purchased Reading Detective, a curriculum designed to promote active reading for struggling middle and upper grade readers.

Reading Detective was a book of reproducible stories and reading comprehension exercises that strategically taught readers how to identify the elements and patterns that arise in expository texts (i.e. non-fiction). Reproducible means that the book provides masters that the teacher uses with the school copier to make handouts for each student. The curriculum was organized into a unit each on main idea, supporting details, chronology, inference, and cause and effect. Active readers enjoy better retention and recall because they actively search the text for these elements and patterns when they read. Most school systems assume students have mastered these elements of expository text by fifth grade. But reform methodology recommends continued teaching of them to struggling readers in middle school. In addition, the focus on comprehension of expository texts would prepare students for the textbooks and other expository texts that they will increasingly encounter in middle and high school. Each unit was organized into introductory, intermediate, and advanced levels of proficiency for the particular topic. Direct instruction would give me a way to mildly lead students to higher levels of mastery than they would have accomplished on their own. This master-apprentice effect is considered one of the main advantages of direct instruction.

Now I had a floor plan, overhead projector, and curriculum. Next it was time to make a plan for instructional delivery, which is what experts call the process of actually conducting the lesson. Every period began with a starter on English language conventions, but now I could use the overhead to streamline and improvise, and even make up my own quick mini lessons. The agenda for each period's activities was posted prominently on the front board, with elapsed times in a checklist format. Each day's lesson started with me handing out the reading material and comprehension exercise and concisely introducing the topic—main idea, supporting details, etc. Then I led the group in reading the passage aloud, alternating between calling on students and reading myself.

After the passage was read, I moved on to leading the students through the first few questions of the comprehension exercise, which typically had five questions. I displayed the questions on the overhead. Sometimes I modeled the proper thinking and response and let students copy me. Other times, I asked students to attempt questions on their own and then led them through self-correction. The extent of my modeling depended on the place in the unit and the difficulty of the exercise. For instance, I might strongly model the first two items of an introductory exercise and then ask students to complete the remainder on their own. For an advanced exercise, I might have students attempt each question one at a time and immediately lead self-correction for every question, with almost no independent time.

My motivation plan for the reciprocal lessons consisted of letter grades for each day's comprehension exercise, which was handed in and returned with a grade, and participation points for reading aloud and answering questions aloud. I kept track of the participation points on a clipboard that held an adapted copy of the class roster serving as a tick chart.

After I gained momentum with the reading-skills lessons,

I interposed reciprocal lessons on English language conventions. I focused on basic semantics and syntax, including prefix-suffix, pronouns, tenses, subject-predicate, adjectives, synonyms, homographs, homonyms, and other forms of figurative language. In the last weeks of the semester, I spiced things up with two movies reports: *Willy Wonka and the Chocolate Factory* (1971) and *West Side Story* (1961). It was nice to have the lesson design of the movie report in hand. It gave me a good means of coasting a couple of weeks in the classroom while I crammed credential courses and my IEP writing responsibilities, which started to pick up momentum in early winter. One part of my study guide for *Willy Wonka* was noticing and summarizing Oompa-Loompas ethics. This immigrant workforce in Willy Wonka's factory had truly assimilated to the Protestant work ethic. I wonder what Dahl and the scriptwriters were trying to say with that. This Eggducator wanted to find a way for everyone to be a good egg, as opposed to most Anglos, who are merely content to divide the population up into good eggs and bad eggs.

The direct instruction phase of the semester actually went well. Student participation evened out. Overachievers, predictably, hovered at eighty to one-hundred percent accuracy on the comprehension assignments; they did well, but they might have been better working on their own, possibly at a faster pace. The minimalists experienced fewer opportunities to engage in side conversations and thus applied themselves in a more concerted, rigorous fashion; direct instruction is primarily aimed at these centrists. Their accuracy was also at eighty to one hundred percent, and they now worked at the same pace as the overachievers. The level of misbehavior among the minimalists was reduced, which meant that I had improved my productivity by the principal's standards.

The underachievers experienced a dramatic decline in misbehavior, but they experienced the same problems with inattention and focus. Their accuracy averaged around forty percent. To bring an underachiever to higher levels of mastery, I had to visit their desk and do some tutoring. In fact, I had to visit their desk almost at the same frequency as in the workshop format of the book report. But the improvements in minimalists' conduct left more resources for tutoring underachievers. Moreover, the principal's reassignment of the two defiant young ladies greatly calmed the classroom climate.

For underachievers, direct instruction created new risk factors related to problems with attention and language processing. An underachiever will seem quiet and compliant from the head of the room, but if the teacher visits the student's desk they will likely find a notebook full of elaborate doodles and the assignment tucked into the student's backpack. When a teacher doesn't visit underachiever desks on a regular basis, the teacher won't notice the skipped assignments until grading, well after the period is over. This idleness is not defiance, but rather a manifestation of a learning disability or attention deficit or both. Remember that the underachievers were almost all seventh grade special-ed students.

Clutch Play

When the day came for the principal's classroom observation in mid-November, my direct instruction skills had progressed to the point where all the students were settled in their seats, eighty percent of the students were paying attention to a significant degree, and twenty percent were feigning attention or otherwise skipping the assignment by means of some ingenious covert strategy. If a passerby looked at the classroom through the door for a few minutes, I could at least claim the appearance of delivering a lesson.

Miriam, the principal, sat at the back of the room, in an empty seat at the end of the back row, giving her the same perspective as the students. A petite White middle-aged woman, she wore her daily uniform of cotton formal dress in frock cut, loosely trim at the bust, waist, and, hips, in a demur blue grey, with stockings and matching leather pumps: strictly business and a touch puritanical. Jewelry was limited to a tastefully demure gold watch and her sandy blond hair was in a professionally maintained bob. Her proper formal wear tastefully hid her expanding weight. Judging by the pictures of past occasions on her office wall, the attractive, perky, slim physique of her forties was giving way to the huskier dimensions of middle age. Her soldierly gate and sad gaze as she moved about campus implied to me that she experienced the transformation into old age as a kind of punishment. On this day, she entered the room emanating her typical world-weary countenance and intransigent nonchalance.

For the observation, I followed my usual routine for a reciprocal lesson on a reading skill. First, students completed their ten-minute starter on an English language convention. Then I led the students in a Reading Detective assignment on identifying main point and supporting details. The principal entered the room at the point where I had distributed the handout for the comprehension assignment and had started to lead the students in reading the short expository passage aloud. She had my lesson plan and a copy of the handout, so she knew what to expect. I was standing at the overhead projector in the center of the room, about five feet from the front board. I called on a few students and read some of the passage myself. Then I used the overhead projector to discuss each of the five comprehension questions. For this lesson, I decided to preview the question, let students attempt it on their own, provide immediate self-correction, and then collect the assignment to measure student involvement and compliance. The principal left the room when I had finished self-correction on the last of the five questions.

The students followed along well, at least considered from my vantage point at the front of the room. My delivery strategy kept me at the overhead for the entire lesson, with minimal student independence, and thus minimal circulating and tutoring. From the principal's vantage point at the back of the room, she was probably catching the twenty percent of the students with attention problems and their mild bits of off task mischief. I saw her frown in the direction of a Black boy who snuck in a quick side conversation in her vicinity when he should have been attempting one of the questions. Maybe he was asking a neighbor for help or maybe he was saying something about the principal or maybe he was cheating. I couldn't hear him from my position, but at least he spoke in a hushed tone.

As far as behavior, I didn't make one intervention during the lesson. I stayed at the overhead and led students in completing the worksheet. Basically, there were no interruptions, although I could perceive some slight fidgeting from the underachievers near the principal. I actually believe they were trying to impress her by keeping up, but since I didn't do any tutoring, they probably tried to get help from peers. I looked good standing there, poised like a CEO dazzling the investment press, but really I should have included time for independent work and tutoring. The principal made a "not bad" remark and gesture on her brisk way out the door. I was pleased with that feedback and felt that it was better than I deserved.

I really only covered the guided practice part of a reciprocal lesson. I was in the intermediate level of the unit on main point-supporting details. I probably should have let the students finish the last two or three questions on their own, independently, but I was afraid that when I did, the overachievers and most of the minimalists would race ahead and break into side conversations while I somewhat maniacally tutored the underachievers. That kind of mild chaos might have been okay on an ordinary day, but I wanted to look poised and even a little dominant in front of the principal, so I settled for guided practice, which kept all the students under my proverbial thumb. Ideally, I should have finished guided practice and then had students complete one more five-question worksheet on their own in class or as homework as the independent phase of the lesson.

I met with the principal a few days later for my post-obser-vation conference. I would receive one of three scores: satis-factory, needs improvement, and unsatisfactory. I received a score of needs improvement, which made sense, if you were comparing me to a master teacher; I was just a first-year teacher on an intern contract. On the other hand, it wouldn't be reasonable to make it to satisfactory in my first lesson, in my first three months ever in a general school. Under state guidelines, I would have two years, and possibly even more, to make it to satisfactory, but the principal insinuated that she was looking for improvement within the next three months.

As part of the needs improvement score, the principal wrote a brief Performance Improvement Plan (PIP). The plan focused on my role as co-teacher, which was kind of annoying since I had just put so much into my lesson plans for inter-vention reading. The performance objectives focused on the team teaching process: establish rapport with all co-teachers, involve co-teachers in the IEP process, and finish IEPs on time. She mentioned that my lesson was "pretty good, not too bad" and gave me a couple of pointers on how to teach from the front of the classroom. It wasn't bad advice: try using quick non-verbal prompts to discourage side conversations, and avoid verbosity when delivering directions—direct more than sell. In other words, take a slightly tougher, more au-thoritarian stance toward the students.

The difficulty with the PIP was that my future as a teacher rested on the activities of others (i.e. co-teachers) over whom I had no authority and not much influence, at least not yet. An increase in authority wasn't available, but maybe by some outrageous means I could increase my influence. I was re-lieved to at least have a plan in place that projected my pres-ence in the school into early March. My intern status basically meant that the principal could walk me off campus on any given day, on any given whim, with no repercussions to her or the district and disastrous consequences to me. I had survived this first milestone comprised of my first lesson observation and evaluation conference.

I stuck with the reciprocal direction instruction format for the entire second half of first semester, delivering lessons on reading skills from Reading Detective interspersed with occasional lessons on English conventions and ending with entertaining movie reports on *Willy Wonka* and *West Side Story*. The periods passed amiably without much struggle or serious behavior problems among the students. I turned in my reading intervention grades for first semester. Then came two weeks of winter break: finally a fringe benefit. Two weeks to rest and recuperate.

Welcome Kit

I spent the two weeks of winter break in the most ordinary fashion at home in Danville: reading, watching television, Christmas shopping, visiting with Aileen, and celebrating the holidays with siblings. My daughter Aileen flew down from Seattle and visited for a week of the break. As devout practitioners of both Catholicism and the pleasure principle, my parents really loved Christmas. My mother's holiday décor easily rivaled downtown department stores. Her holiday home was a shrine to home, hearth, New England culture, and the merciful savior (in that order). My parents held a luxurious holiday celebration on the two days of Christmas, and it was always a joy to have Aileen join us. My family still thought I was having some kind of episode in switching my career to education. They quickly showed impatience at any more than a minute or two of shop talk, and I basically just played dumb about the whole experience, which was probably good, since I didn't have much good news other than I somehow survived the gauntlet resulting from the principal's indifference.

I was looking forward to the fresh start coming up with the first days of my intervention reading course for second semester. Credential training had taught me that the second semester can be an opportunity for new teachers to restart the year with more structure. The site administration had reworked the student schedules over winter break, partly to accommodate changes to the team teaching program for push inclusion. As a result of the changes to student schedules, I basically had a new intervention reading roster for second semester. Roughly eighty percent of the students were new to me, rotated in from the other intervention reading course held in first semester, and the roster had been reduced down from thirty-two to twenty-five students. I decided to start second semester as if it was the first days of the school year, but these first days would benefit from all that I had learned over the course of first semester.

The demographic breakdown of the roster was similar to first semester. My roster included five special-ed students from my seventh-grade caseload, a few special-ed eighth graders from that grade's caseload, and the remaining seventeen students were general-ed from seventh and eighth, about half each grade. Once again, keen observers may see poetic justice and a cosmic sense of fair play in this inclusive configuration of students. I, like my co-teachers, would be tasked with teaching language arts to a hybrid mix of special-ed and general-ed students. The ethnic demographics of the class pretty much mirrored the school's, with 35% Hispanic, 5% Black, and 60% White, with the sexes at fifty percent. There would be no aide this semester; in fact, the aide was reassigned about the same time that I switched to direct instruction in first semester.

I arrived at the first day of second semester with a welcome kit that I had prepared during my free time over break (i.e. free to the district); ample free time is an essential resource for the new teacher. On the first day, I greeted new students with my name, date, and course name prominently displayed on a permanent location on the front board and the same brisk matter of fact bio about being a new teacher in training. I administered the same surveys on reading interests, attitudes, and experiences as first semester, but this time around I marked and returned them without holding a class discussion. I was eager to get to the curriculum, and I wanted to spend significant time teaching the course rules and expectations. In other words, I was becoming as pushy and self-centered as the rest of the faculty. I'll give myself some small credit for marking the completed surveys with words of encouragement and returning them.

My welcome kit was a two-page handout describing the course's learning goals, course rules, expectations for performance, and grading-motivation plan. I spent the second two days of class teaching the welcome kit through reciprocal direct instruction. I based my welcome kit on examples provided to me by my co-teachers of language arts, strategies learned in credential training, and my ancient disestablishmentarian heart. The learning goals were simple bullets: improve reading comprehension, improve writing skills, and get smarter, because the smarter you are the happier you'll be. From that point forward, I have always included the individualized objective of getting smarter in my learning goals for the year. School should train lifelong learners to live the best possible life given their neurological and cultural background: political demands for universal entrepreneurial genius should never diminish our ardor for individualism and each American reaching their full potential.

For course rules, I didn't repeat the dos and don'ts covered by schoolwide discipline. Instead I focused on rules that applied to the direct instruction format that I was going to continue with from last semester. For instance, I started the first day with assigned seats, by putting a post-it note with the student's name on each seat. Students were required to remain in their assigned seat unless given express permission to move by the teacher, who could be summoned by raising one's hand and waiting patiently. To gain the teacher's attention for any purpose, whether in a discussion or asking to use the restroom, the student will raise their hand and wait quietly.

Students should remain silently in their seat unless given permission to speak by the teacher. Basically, I presented a short list of rules that set explicit expectations for movement and communication.

Consequences for breaking a rule were a verbal warning and semi-private talk with the teacher, a call home to parents on the afternoon of a serious violation, removal to the principal on a referral for persistent, seriously disruptive misbehavior, and a low citizenship grade on one's report card for a pattern of chronic misbehavior.

My expectations for performance were a simple code of making one's best effort and seeing the teacher as a supportive person. Students should strive for the right answer in every task, either by trying on their own or asking the teacher for help: requests for help were invited. Accuracy matters, even in intervention reading, because it helps you get smarter. The main point was that accuracy matters for its beneficial effects on learning and it will be monitored, graded, and reported to parents. From a brain-based perspective, the learning task has to engage and mildly stress the memory before it will experience growth, and striving for accuracy elicits the necessary stress.

The grading-and-motivation system, which I will hereafter refer to as the motivation plan, was primarily based on handing in all assignments for a grade based on accuracy. The final grade for the semester was based on the average mastery for all assignments. I used a basic five-step scoring system to give students feedback about performance on each assignment, but I kept each step a little vague so I could skew the grades toward encouragement. A score of five on an assignment would mean that all questions were attempted, almost all answers were accurate, workmanship was neat, and the assignment was done on time. A score of three would mean that most questions were attempted, half the answers were accurate, workmanship was neat, and the assignment was done on time. A score of one meant that only a few questions or less were attempted, only one or two answers were accurate, workmanship was poor, and the student needed intervention to finish the assignment at the last minute.

Notice that the accuracy of student responses was only one item in the four part rubric of performance: attempted, percent correct, neatness, and timeliness. I taught this rubric of performance to the students in the first few days. If an assignment was particularly difficult, such as one of the advanced assignments in a unit from Reading Detective, I would give a five to students who attempted all the questions, answered half correctly, showed neat workmanship, and finished in a timely way. Since accuracy was only one aspect of the quality rubric, I could relax the accuracy demands if it was clear that the student was among the leaders of the class; thus I could give an effort bonus to those I knew had made their best effort on a difficult task.

The overachievers set the standard for the curve: the breakdown of overachievers, minimalists, and underachievers typically generated a rough approximation of the normal curve, giving me statistics that told me when to relax the accuracy standard. When all the overachievers got three out of five questions accurate, plus a significant proportion of the minimalists, then it was time to give a score of five for three correct answers out of five questions. In a situation like that, I might give underachievers a score of three for sitting in their seat with minimal side conversations, trying a few questions, maybe getting one correct, and not stuffing the assignment into their backpack.

In teaching the four-part rubric of performance, I was following the reform methodology that says learning how to learn, typically referred to as metacognition, should be part of an intervention for disadvantaged and working-class students, who don't acquire this knowledge from college-educated parents like affluent students do. Report cards at the end of the semester required a letter grade. To determine each student's letter grade, I averaged the numerical performance scores for the semester, with weekly checkpoints: average score of five earns an A, four earns a B, three to two earns a C, one earns a D, and frequent skipped assignments or poor attendance earns an F. The report-card scale was also included in the welcome kit and taught briefly in the first days.

I graded each assignment in first semester, so I had already seen that positive feedback about performance would keep a fair number of students on task. But I wanted to draw the minimalists into higher levels of engagement and maybe even lift a few of the underachievers up, so I added routine posting of grades by adapting my grade book into a classroom visual chart posted on the wall. I hadn't provided students with incremental progress monitoring toward final grades in first semester (although I did return graded work on a regular basis). The chart visual looked like an accountant's ledger book. It showed all of each student's performance scores such that the student could see the trend that added up to their letter grade, which was reported in weekly updates. One of my seventh-grade co-teachers of language arts, a trim, determined middle-aged lady, who was the department chair, a tenured master teacher, and taught university-based credential candidates, used a similar reporting format in her classroom. I noticed that all her students checked their progress regularly, even my inclusion students, who typically weren't seeing much good news.

In addition to a grade based on accuracy for assignments, I included a simple letter grade for participation in the chart. Participation credit was collected on a tick chart during reading aloud and discussions. When a student read aloud or responded to a question, they received a tick on my clipboard chart, which I tallied for each weekly checkpoint. I also added informal visual feedback such as stamps and stickers to reward timeliness. Students who finished the day's assignment with good accuracy and within the suggested time limit earned a timeliness sticker placed on their handout, which would add to their participation grade. I hypothesized that visual supports in the form of timeliness stickers, the partici-pation tick, and progress monitoring chart would decrease mild misbehaviors such as side conversations and increase the attention span and focus of all students, but especially the minimalists.

Attention to the task is the goal of all motivation and grading strategies, because attention is the precursor for the formation of new long-term memories. Attention and obedi-ence typically look the same to the principal, so I was hop-ing to impress her too. A teacher can intimidate children into obedience but one has to inspire them to attention. The reason frequent feedback about performance typically improves attention levels is because most children want to please their parents and join with peers, in other words enjoy the blessings of society. If you give students an explicit path to success and help them monitor their progress, they will typic-ally embrace the challenge (and so it's essential that the path to success be based on a realistic assessment of prior know-ledge and present ability level).

To emphasize the importance of the of the welcome kit, I administered a multiple-choice quiz of about five questions at the end of each of the two periods, with questions on the learning goals, course rules, expectations for performance, and grading-motivation plan. I graded the quiz at the end of the day and handed it back the next period to support a brief discussion of the correct answers. Mastery was high, and the students had clearly comprehended most of the informa-tion. This was challenging material, and I read it at the stu-dents more than with them, but the honeymoon factor was in effect, and the students indulged me in this brief outburst of authoritarianism. At the end of the brief unit on the welcome kit, the kit was sent home with the student. A signature page was signed by a parent and returned to the teacher.

For lesson design, I planned to deliver daily highly-struc-tured lessons using the same reciprocal direct instruction for-mat that I launched in the second half of first semester. Each period begins with a quick starter supported by the overhead, moves to the teacher introducing the day's topic and delivering new information, followed by the teacher leading students in applying the new information like apprentices, culminating in students applying the information independently, and ideally concluding with some form of quick test. Keen observers will note the presence of the term "ideally." The floor plan was the same as the second half of first semester, with four rows of eight students, making eight aisles, with each student squarely facing the front board and overhead screen, except now the back row was mostly empty due to the decrease in the roster from thirty-two to twenty-five.

As opposed to first semester, when I started the semester without even an iota of curriculum, now I had three curriculums to teach. The first curriculum of the semester would be Reading Rewards, which was the reading intervention program finally provided by the district toward the end of first semester. The goal of the program was to increase the student's ability to decode academic language, defined as multisyllabic words describing complex phenomena: for instance, long, meaning-rich words such as disestablishmentarianism (a difficult word but one vital to the understanding of U.S. history). The intervention theory behind this curriculum said that low-achieving students often come from homes where multisyllabic academic words are rarely spoken, so when they encounter them in middle school, they freeze and give up on the text rather than striving to understand the unfamiliar terms. Reading Rewards aimed to decondition students out of this anxiety by simply practicing these complex words with guidance from the teacher. The district had put a group of teachers, including me, through two days of off-site training to prepare for the curriculum. My reciprocal direct instruction strategy dovetailed nicely with the teacher-led format of Reading Rewards, so I was confident that I could teach the curriculum with at least minimal effectiveness.

Reading Rewards was a fast-paced intervention focused on

a narrow skill, decoding of unfamiliar complex words, which only required about a month of instruction. That left with me plenty of time in the semester to teach Reading Detective and other reading-skills lessons, like I had in first semester, and I was actually looking forward to improving my direct instruction skills. I also planned to intersperse lessons on English language conventions for a change of pace. With three curriculums in place, I looked forward to five and a half months of direct instruction with modest anticipation. If things went well, my lesson delivery would be sharp enough to satisfy the principal in her second, meaning final, classroom observation of the year in late February or early March.

In the Groove

Second semester lived up to my modest expectations for improving in teacher-led instruction, referred to so far as reciprocal direct instruction, and in realizing increases in student attention levels and decreases in mild misbehaviors such as off-topic side conversations, doodling, and skipped assignments. Teaching the welcome kit with learning goals, course rules, expectations for performance, and grading-motivation plan in the first few day of the semester, and then applying them consistently, definitely led to enhanced student engagement in the daily lessons, especially among the minimalists and underachievers.

Reading Rewards, the short-term curriculum on decoding unfamiliar complex words, was named "rewards" to call attention to its points system, which was integrated into the curriculum. The curriculum provided a workbook organized into daily lessons. After peer correction led by the teacher, students filled in their points for the daily lesson in a header on the workbook pages. Teachers were encouraged to create some kind of reward system, at their own expense, that corresponded to the points system. I decided to skip the curriculum's reward system and instead apply the grading-motivation system taught with my welcome kit.

Basically, I taught the Reading Rewards curriculum in my framework of reciprocal direct instruction. For each lesson, I previewed the day's expectations, conducted oral call-and-response drill on the word-attack strategy for the day's unfamiliar multisyllabic words, led a read aloud of a short passage that included the day's words, and then previewed each of the five comprehension questions followed by students answering independently and culminating with self-correction, including an opportunity to earn participation points by sharing an answer when called on. A correct answer earned a Jolly Rancher in addition to a point; suddenly the underachievers were vying with the overachievers for my attention.

At the end of each day, I collected the workbooks and gave each student a numerical score from my four-step rubric of performance taught with the welcome kit. Those scores, plus the participation points, were posted in the weekly progress chart, including a weekly update on progress toward the semester letter grade. The daily lessons went quite well, especially at Jolly Rancher time. The overachievers and minimalists thought the candy was a little passé for their age group, but the underachievers couldn't get enough of it. Following a strict analysis of reciprocal instruction, I probably should have let the students answer the comprehension questions completely on their own, as a kind of assessment. But I felt that for my students, in this intervention course, extra guided practice was probably a better strategy. Reading Rewards occupied about a month of instruction, meaning twenty periods.

Whereas I hesitated to conduct the independent phase in Reading Rewards, I found a way to include more independence in Reading Detective and other reading-skills lessons. I taught expository reading, meaning the active-reading skills of identifying patterns in a text such as main idea-details, chronology, and cause-and-effect, the same way that I had in first semester (i.e. with reciprocal direct instruction). For each lesson, I previewed the day's expectations, introduced the reading-skills topic (chronology, etc.) and any new information needed to understand it, led a read aloud of a short passage that incorporated the day's skill, then previewed two or more of five comprehension questions, followed by students answering independently, and culminating with self-correction. But in second semester, when I got to the independent phase, after correcting one set of questions, meaning one assignment of the unit, I would occasionally extend the independence phase through the end of next period, making time for students to complete from one to two additional assignments totally on their own. This extended independent time gave overachievers an opportunity to shine by going deeper into a skill by completing up to three assignments and underachievers on opportunity to get some tutoring on maybe one assignment.

Basically, for each skill unit (i.e. chronology, inference, etc.), I conducted two to three days emphasizing guided practice followed by one day of independent practice. Since I collected, graded, and posted all assignments, the independent practice sessions served as an assessment of the effectiveness of the guided practice. The overachievers really excelled in independent practice, and I was pleased to witness their competency. The minimalists' mastery was solid, within twenty percent of the overachievers. I enjoyed tutoring the underachievers, who I praise for their exertion but worry about regarding their mastery. I discontinued the Jolly Ranchers after Reading Rewards; maybe I should have kept them going.

When early March arrived, and with it the day of the principal's final classroom observation, I had taught twenty periods of Reading Rewards, and roughly twenty periods of reading skills, meaning forty periods of reciprocal direct instruction in second semester. For the observation, instead of a Reading Detective lesson on an active-reading skill, I chose a self-authored reading comprehension lesson based on Bloom's

Taxonomy, which is an instructional strategy for moving students from literal kinds of recall to evaluative processing of the information. For reading material, I used an abridged news feature of about a thousand words from a non-fiction reader of high interest-low readability stories for middle and high school. High-interest refers to compelling, newsworthy topics, and low-readability refers to the deliberate modifying of the text to below grade-level vocabulary and sentence length.

The story was a short news feature on the Triangle Shirtwaist Factory Fire. On March 25, 1911, the Triangle Shirtwaist Company burned in the eighth, ninth, and tenth floors of its blouse-sewing factory in Greenwich Village of New York City, near Washington Square, a neighborhood I had actually frequented on many occasions while a student at SUNY Stony Brook. I must have passed the building many times, which was still in operation, but not as a factory. I recall seeing an anniversary story on PBS, or maybe I heard it on NPR, that inspired me to select this particular topic.

One hundred and forty-six of the company's five hundred workers died in the fire, which is remembered as one of the most infamous incidents in U.S. industrial history, as the deaths could have been prevented if the city government and the company had been more vigilant in protecting the factory's workers. Many precautions considered routine today were missing in the ten-story building of 1911, in which Triangle Shirtwaist occupied the top three floors. The excessive fatalities were largely a result of failed escape routes and sloppy working conditions: the sole rickety, narrow fire escape collapsed and it only reached to the second floor, doors were improperly mounted or permanently locked, elevators collapsed during the fire or were already out of order, telephone communication broke down, scraps, fabric, and other materials were indiscriminately stored, the sole fire department rescue ladder only reached to the sixth floor and water from hoses couldn't reach the building's top floors, no sprinkler system, water delivered on the factory floor only by hand in buckets and no other kind of fire retardant available. For ninety years, this fire stood as NYC's deadliest workplace disaster, surpassed only by September 11, 2001, at the World Trade Center, commonly referred to as the 9/11 attack.

The non-union factory, which in the previous five years had attracted intensive organizing efforts from the International Ladies Garment Workers Union, was widely known as a sweatshop. Mostly teenage and young-adult women, recent European immigrants who did not speak English well, worked at sewing machines arranged in lines in cramped spaces; they toiled twelve hours a day, seven days a week. The terrible tragedy elicited widespread concern about the dangerous sweatshop conditions of many factories and led to the enactment of city and state regulations that protected the safety of workers.

Scholastic Press, a prominent source of reading curriculum, published the reader that I found the article in, and they used an editorial angle that emphasized the positive developments in city government that arose in the wake of the disaster. The tragic loss of innocent young lives was described, but not in gory or sensationalistic detail, so I felt comfortable reading the article with middle schoolers. One of the learning goals of my lesson was for students to reflect on their awareness of fire safety practices at school and home, and Scholastic's approach dovetailed nicely with my goal.

I made a master copy of the article, wrote a five-question comprehension assignment using my desktop-publishing resources, and used the school copier to make handouts for the class. I taught the lesson using reciprocal direct instruction. I introduced the expectations for the period, introduced background info on the Triangle Shirtwaist factory and fire regulations, led a read aloud of the story text, previewed each of the fives questions aloud supported by an overhead slide, called on students for suggested answers to each question, modeled the answer on the overhead, and collected the assignment with student answers written in.

The first three questions focused on literal information including the date and location of the event, the type of business, and the number of fatalities. These questions were included to emphasize the active-reading habit of getting the facts straight before moving on to evaluate the information. For the last two questions, the student was asked to reflect on ways fire safety and precautions had touched their lives. The first question asked students to recall or observe a few fire safety measures at school. Student responses included follow the teacher's directions during an emergency, fire extinguishers, and fire alarms. The second question asked students about a few precautions that they had taken or should take at home. Answers included have an escape route planned, keep living spaces neat, smoke alarms, and flashlights. Most students could generate at least one precaution for each setting, and a fair number generated the required three for each question.

The lesson went well, with students complying readily to my prompts for participation during the read aloud and guided practice. Students were proportionality attentive for intervention reading and there was no misbehavior, except possibly for surreptitious side conversations, which would have occurred outside my awareness and probably for the purpose obtaining a peer's assistance on the sly.

None of my lesson's questions were very deep. The story was weighty material, and my plan was to let the students experience it simply while just touching on some skill development. On the other hand, the story was a cautionary tale, and I asked the students to assess their own situation regarding fire safety; I had led them one step closer to developing a self-directed adult outlook, which should be the aim of all reading instruction. Regarding the technical merits of my reciprocal lesson plan, I had abandoned the independence stage in favor of extending the guided practice. I had planned on the students answering the last two questions, the evaluative ones on fire precautions in their lives, by working independently at their assigned seats. But I lost my nerve in front of the principal and led the students through the two questions as guided practice. The guided practice looks really good, with students practically following the teacher's every word, but theory says that the independent phase might have yielded higher rates of retention and recall, especially among the overachievers. If I had an entire class of students at the same level as the overachievers, I might have continued the lesson into the next period with a writing prompt asking students to describe three ways that they might react if they found themselves subject to unsafe working conditions. For my actual class, I was pleased that students had been able to follow along with the complex historical content and maintain sufficient attention levels to complete the five questions with guided practice.

The principal arrived in the first ten minutes of class and observed the lesson from a vantage point at the back of the room. She had a copy of my lesson plan and handout; part of a classroom observation is the principal's assessment of the teacher's fidelity to the lesson plan. As with her first observation, she was studiously unimpressed and exited the room with a nod and some phrase along the lines of "Not too bad. Pretty good." I interpreted her nonchalance as positive, since she hadn't demanded that I meet her after school because this kind of buffoonery had to stop immediately, as was her right under my intern contract.

My credential supervisor Sheila also observed the lesson, basically on the same basis as the principal. Sheila was a middle-aged Anglo-Irish lady who groomed and dressed formally in a two-piece business suit for classroom observations, was of medium height, trim and energetic, had retired early from a distinguished career as a credentialed California elementary teacher, held a master's degree in educational leadership, and taught some of my credential courses. She was every bit as professional as a principal, but her management style was skewed toward encouragement rather than nonchalance. Sheila's evaluation of the lesson was delivered on a form based on the California Standards for the Teaching Profession, which was a rubric of desired traits in a lesson. The standards were developed by the California Commission on Teacher Credentialing. To summarize, Sheila noted how I had organized the subject matter and delivery method (i.e. direct instruction) to give access to all learners. On the subject matter side, the use of high interest-low readability reading materials gave intervention readers access to a historically-significant event that might otherwise have been beyond their reach. On the delivery side, the teacher-led format with introductory background info, read aloud, and guided practice provided intervention students with adult modeling to help them understand the challenging information. The combination of a high interest-low readability materials and teacher-led instruction gave students access to this anniversary-inspired civics lesson, meaning students encountered the information the same way PBS viewers or NPR listeners had done earlier in the month. I had given the intervention readers a taste of life as an adult lifelong learner (i.e. my life).

Sheila also noted the strategic floor plan that focused students' attention on the overhead screen, the well-prepared overhead slides, the effect the participation points had in eliciting student responses, and the overall attentiveness of the students, who she felt respected and followed me throughout the lesson. Her evaluation was delivered in a meeting during prep time on the day of the observation.

Sheila's background as a general-education teacher showed through in her evaluation, since she didn't chide me for not getting around to tutoring or otherwise checking in with the underachievers. I had stayed at the front of classroom with the overhead for most of the lesson, which had been mostly guided practice. Her evaluation emphasized the lesson from the perspective of the overachievers and minimalists. If I had done the observation, I would have asked for a seating chart with a mark stating overachiever, minimalist, or under-achiever by each name. Then I would have walked around looking at each underachiever's assignment throughout the period (i.e. what it must be like to have a co-teacher in the room). I have to admit that I didn't mind that she was from general education; it was in fact a general-ed course after all, even if I was a special-ed teacher.

In addition to the basic importance of a current anniver-sary story, my choice of the Triangle Shirtwaist Fire as the topic for the principal's observation had mildly subversive overtones. Sweatshops have not disappeared from the U.S., although they are probably safer. Sweatshops in New York and Los Angeles have been identified as violating minimum wage and overtime laws, and some put the health and safety of workers at risk. El Dorado Middle, including my reading class, had many families with at least one member working as entry-level labor, and those families probably have relatives in the same situation. I wanted to show students that read-ing can be the route to informing oneself about exploitive working conditions and even taking action. Reading can be the difference between life and death, even for intervention students, and this relatively-rich Anglo bombshell thought his working-class students' lives were worth the trouble of teaching them the skills they would need to be informed and assertive workers. I hoped the principal might learn a thing or two from me on that front too.

Reading Wrap-Up

On the day of the principal's observation in early March 2004, I had taught about forty periods in second semester, at roughly one lesson per period, with some lessons lasting two or three periods. I had thirty-five or so more lessons to teach in the remaining months of the semester. In credential training, candidates were taught planning strategies to break this requirement of mass lesson production into manageable chunks. Teachers actually sit down with a planner, often borrowed from the corporate world, to plot out lessons for each day that add up to units that last for weeks or a month and that form a curriculum for the year, typically referred to as a grade level. "Plan you work, and work your plan" is the teacher's mantra.

With Reading Rewards, Reading Detective, and English language conventions, I had plenty of raw materials to support the seventy-five lessons needed to keep students well-engaged each day of the semester. With ample raw material and emerging skills in teacher-led instruction, I spent the second half of second semester in the zone. My motivation plan consisting of grading all assignments, frequent posting of student performance data, and participation points kept students attentive and engaged on a consistent basis. It's fair to say that students experienced lower than normal levels of misbehavior. Problem behaviors were within the typical range of mild challenges at El Dorado Middle, which consisted of inattention, hushed side conversations, and attention deficits.

I made just a few phone calls to parents per the consequences established in the semester's welcome kit, and those calls were mostly for persistent mild inattention. The calls worked and the students improved their performance. One of my seventh-grade inclusion students was severely struggling with his peers and teachers in his new general-education placement. He attacked a classmate with a flurry of punches one day while in a manic state. That was the only removal to the principal's office that I can remember. From a student conduct perspective, it was a blissfully uneventful semester.

As far as student performance on the lessons, the overachievers were once again a delight and a joy to behold. The consistent implementation of independent practice in each unit gave overachievers an opportunity to learn each reading skill in depth. After teaching the introductory level of a skill such as identifying cause-and-effect through guided practice, a period or two of independent practice provided overachievers an opportunity to attempt the intermediate and advanced exercises at their own pace and thus complete more assignments than their classmates. The minimalists also responded to independent practice by completing one to three assignments, but typically settling for the intermediate level. Minimalists definitely engaged well during independent work and their accuracy was on average between sixty to one hundred percent. Underachievers needed tutoring to reach sixty percent accuracy when working independently and completed at most one assignment per period of independent practice.

Since I collected, graded, logged, and posted every assignment, my course became a kind research project for tracking the effectiveness of my curriculum and reciprocal direct instruction. In a statistical break out similar to first semester, seven individuals emerged as consistent overachievers, which means about twenty-eight percent of the students, with accuracy consistently between eighty and one hundred percent, and advanced levels of independent practice. Nearly all of the overachievers were eighth graders from general education.

Eleven minimalists emerged, meaning forty-four percent, who responded well to instruction, but were a little less energetic, possibly less skilled, and slightly more prone to side conversations. Minimalists included both seventh and eighth graders, general-ed and special-ed . They averaged between sixty to eighty percent accuracy and responded strongly to independent practice but not with the same depth as overachievers. The seven underachievers, who comprised twenty-eight percent of the class, were all seventh graders from special education. They averaged between forty to sixty percent accuracy and really couldn't benefit from independent practice without at least some tutoring.

So, seventy-two percent of the students, meaning overachievers and minimalists, were well served by the curriculum and reciprocal direct instruction. Overachievers stretched themselves with extra independent practice on intermediate and advanced skill levels. Minimalists, who definitely experienced less side conversations and more earnest effort, showed signs that they were mildly challenged by the curriculum with peak accuracy hovering at eighty percent, and thus they had studied in the growth zone. The minimalist experience improved the most over first semester. Underachievers were slightly more compliant, with less-boisterous side conversations and fewer assignments stuffed in the backpack, but with about the same limited accuracy without tutoring. Their compliance was probably the result of positive peer influence exerted by the improved minimalists.

This persistent distribution of individuals into consistent performance trends of thirty-forty-thirty was my first encounter with the relationship between task difficulty and student performance when teaching a group of students with heterogeneous ability levels. If I had made the tasks easy, markedly below grade level, the mastery curve would have been flat, with all students at one hundred percent mastery. That might have looked good to the uninitiated, but savvy observers would know that the overachievers and minimalists would have studied under the growth zone; they would have been underserved and denied an educational benefit. If I geared the difficulty level to the minimalists, the overachiever would have been underserved at least part of the time and the underachievers would also have been left out occasionally, but the growth curve would have a nice humped shape to signify that the majority of students were served.

What I actually did, and what most educators do, is cater to the overachievers and let the rest hang on the best that they can. Trickle-Down education! This trickle-down scenario usually results in overachievers and minimalists being well-served with the underachievers poorly or minimally served. Some philosophers might point to a natural tendency of society to take a utilitarian and even evolutionary approach to education, whereby educators steer learning programs toward serving those students who show the most strength. I'm more spiritual than utilitarian, so I worry that whatever we do to the least of us, we in fact do to all of us, to interpret the Prophet's words a bit. The utilitarian approach sounds like yet another American quick fix, and fails to account for the effects of a poorly-educated child on his family and neighborhood.

The stratification of individuals into discernable, consistent performance levels is not endemic to the student or the task. It's an interaction of the students and the task, and since the difficulty of the task can be manipulated by the teacher, the performance of the students can also be altered. Task difficulty is not the only factor in student performance, and instructional methods can also be manipulated to see if the same students can perform better on a task previously considered difficult. The main point is that the teacher controls student performance by choosing the difficulty of the task and choosing instructional methods, and the teacher monitors the effectiveness of their choices by grading and collecting data. Through this experience of making choices, I learned just how difficult it can be to reach all students in a class with heterogeneous ability levels. I settled for trickle-down education for this year, but I vowed to figure out ways to reach the underachievers in the future.

The biggest lesson of intervention reading for me was the humbling realization that I like every other teacher had to develop a disciplinary-motivation strategy that yielded sufficient levels of student attentiveness to support the formation of long-term memories. In other words, I had to keep order. I had to be a disciplinarian and motivator. Or could that be disciplinarian or motivator? Just the act of asking that question shows my gifted behavior problem karma and my ancient disestablishmentarian heart.

With the term "disciplinarian," I am referring to the stereotypical authoritarian teacher: reprimand the fidgety boys in front of the class, send some of the more charismatic students to the office for minor infractions to make an example of them, call the girls' mothers about the zippers getting a little too plunging on the hoodies and replace those tank tops with t-shirts or blouses, and fail students to teach them a lesson about overlooking or forgetting a direction (i.e. gotcha as motivator). Authoritarians basically believe that humiliation, pain, and intimidation are effective motivators.

The authoritarians will do well with the overachievers, but they might lose the minimalists and underachievers to resentment, frustration, and depression. They will almost always lose the underachievers, because they start to wonder why they're getting the lion's share of the scoldings and resulting humiliation. Both NCLB and special-education law were asking teachers to stop losing the minimalists and underachievers, especially in schools with high percentages of students from disadvantaged and minority backgrounds.

This mandate of inclusion led to a surge of research on how to elicit student attentiveness without intimidation or other kinds of fear-based tactics. This research is generally described as the positive discipline movement. In positive discipline, fear is seen as an inhibitor of performance rather than a motivator. Students are inherently goal-oriented and optimistic. Intimidation and fear interfere with these organic qualities, and thereby decrease the level of attentiveness. Positive discipline aims to compete with the authoritarians by generating data that proves student attentiveness will be at higher levels the positive way.

With the term "motivator," I am referring to me, actually. Among the positive disciplinarians, including me, the prime mover is the motto stating that "all disciplinary systems should be for the purpose of eliciting sufficient levels of student attention and not for the purpose of propagating a moral or spiritual demand for obedience in children." An obedient child may not be an engaged child, as any experienced California teacher will tell you. Many urban districts of our state have legions of obedient students on the non-graduation rolls.

There are many aspects to positive discipline. In my reading intervention course, I emphasized clear expectations at the start of the semester and each lesson, timely explicit feedback about performance, curriculum modified for intervention purposes, adult modeling of skills though reciprocal direction instruction, visual supports for time management, frequent checks for understanding with underachievers, tutoring, and concise directive-oriented speech by the teacher. Essentially, I controlled student conduct by taking positive strategic steps that I predicted would both motivate students to engage in the lessons and minimize the kind of distractions that might lead to misbehavior. The positive disciplinarian anticipates the possibility of misbehavior and implements strategies that research has shown will minimize it.

I just listed the strategies that I actively implemented to minimize off-task or disruptive behavior. For positive disciplinarians, actions they refrain from can speak as loudly as those strategies that they implement. In my reading course, I didn't scold the underachiever boys, or any other boys, in front of the class to humiliate and intimidate them: in fact, I didn't scold anybody. I didn't remove charismatic students to the office to make examples of them. I didn't call a parent without giving the student a few warnings and a second chance. I didn't grade students on their attitude but instead stuck to performance data. I didn't launch into any soliloquies about student or generational deficits in self-respect when my students struggled or drifted off task. I refrained from any kind of angry outburst and maintained unconditional regard for students, even when they engaged in troubling behavior. Because of all the things I didn't do, most observers felt I was a friendly, supportive presence, even though I felt like a task master. Authoritarians, predictably, were concerned that I was a little weak on sin and wanted to see more fire and brimstone.

When I started the school year, I had absolutely no conception of a classroom, especially how to lead one. I had never spent even one period as a teacher. Skills learned through my credential training and the school district's professional-development initiatives gave me an introductory view of positive discipline. In addition, I observed my co-teachers of language arts adopt similar strategies.

Through training and observation, I developed a method of motivating my reading students while avoiding disciplinary tactics rooted in intimidation. I had become a positive disciplinarian, which suited the view that I had arrived with, which was that students are organically optimistic and want to join their peers and family in the blessings of society. They just need the right path. By the end of the school year, I had a view, meaning organic optimism or goodness of the student, and a method, meaning positive discipline, that formed a path for becoming an effective teacher. I might just be able to make this teacher thing work out. Fighting crazy with crazy was slowly evolving into fighting crazy with view and method.

I knew that I could never be an authoritarian. One, I'm not in this world to intimidate, subjugate, or oppress my country's children in any way. I want to liberate them from ignorance not inflict it on them. And I'm a gifted behavior problem and ancient disestablishmentarian. I don't have the background for authoritarianism; my efforts reflexively drift toward sympathy for students with learning challenges.

My co-teachers were minimalists when it came to positive discipline. They adopted the positive strategies of setting explicit expectations, modifying curriculum, and using frequent feedback about performance, but when misbehavior arose, they tended to resort to the authoritarian tactics of scolding students in front of the class, making an example of charismatic students, and failing students rather than supporting them with reminders and other accommodations. Some of my push inclusion students were starting to react negatively to these intimidation tactics. They were growing inattentive, depressed, downhearted, and even defiant in a few cases. For them to succeed, and for me to succeed, I had to find some outrageous means by which I could lead my co-teachers into adopting all the principles of positive discipline and thus fully embrace the aims of IDEA and NCLB.

CHAPTER EIGHT
Team Teaching

Dream of Inclusion

My reading intervention course introduced me to the demands of teaching a heterogeneous grouping of students. The twenty-five students were diverse in age, grade level, ability level, and prior learning. In response to the diversity, I tried to provide the overachievers a way to study deeply, the minimalists a supportive path to satisfactory performance, and the underachievers tutoring to help them minimally engage in the material. At first, I attempted individualized curriculum by allowing students to choose their own reading material in the book report unit: each student could read material that fit their past experience and ability level. But after a couple of months of that workshop format, I switched to the popular approach of teaching all students the same curriculum while addressing individual differences through differentiation (i.e. reciprocal direct instruction). For instance, I created time for independent work in each lesson, allowing overachievers to complete additional exercises, minimalists to complete the basic requirements independently, and underachievers to receive tutoring. As is often the case in intervention courses, I faced the most-difficult challenges posed by heterogeneous grouping. I rate my performance as okay for a beginner. Ideally, I would have found more ways to individualize the curriculum for each of the three performance strata, especially for the underachievers.

My co-teachers and I would be facing a slightly-less challenging form of heterogeneous grouping. Our language arts courses of thirty-five students would be unified by grade level and age but diverse in ability level and prior learning, due to the introduction of learning-disabled students at thirty percent of each course's population. In the prior year, most of the learning-disabled students had studied a modified version of the grade-level curriculum in small homogeneous groups taught by special-ed teachers. Now those students would study the grade-level curriculum in heterogeneous groupings with minimal to no modifications and the special-ed teacher as a co-teacher. All my co-teachers had chosen to use reciprocal direction instruction, so all students would study the same curriculum and the teaching team, meaning the general-ed teachers and me, would follow the principles of differentiation to accommodate individual differences, ideally.

Despite my status as a neophyte teacher, I did have basic preparation for the challenges of differentiation. My credential program was both a crash course in differentiation and eventually a thorough examination of it. Essentially, it was a credential in differentiation. My credential authorized me to deliver instruction as the head teacher, and it included sufficient training to do so, but I was really being trained as a co-teacher. This emphasis on inclusion was a response to NCLB, which was interpreted as a mandate to extend full inclusion to the greatest number of appropriate students—to leave no stone unturned, to pull out all the stops.

The requirement of considering the possibility of inclusion had always been a part of IDEA, the special-ed law, but the arrival of NCLB, said most California districts, had turned this guideline into a *mandate*. Parents at El Dorado Middle had been told that their children were placed in push inclusion because of this mandate, as if the district had no choice. This was an interpretation on the district's part and not part of any law. In my credential program, we were told that full inclusion was the future and any teacher planning a career as an SDC teacher (i.e. Specialized Day Class) might see their occupation ending prematurely. The push was on!

Personally, I was intrigued by the democratic spirit of inclusion and differentiation. I appreciated the goal of giving each disabled individual the greatest possible access to the curriculum studied by their typical age-group peers. Spiritually, I appreciated the fact that inclusion asked us to love all of God's children, the way he does, even when it puts us to some extra trouble to do so. From a humanistic point of view, one might appreciate my axiom that what we do to the least of us, we do to all of us (i.e. what goes around, comes around).

From a formalistic point of view, the school district had decided that a "free appropriate public education" for my students meant in the same classroom with typical age-group peers led by a single-subject expert: in other words, a general-ed teacher credentialed in the subject area for grades seven through twelve. The grade-level curriculum for each course would be defined by California's content standards. The goal for my students would be proficiency in statewide testing based on the content standards without modification. So, measurable educational benefit, which should always be the outcome of the IEP, would in large part be measured by progress on grade-level statewide testing—or possibly some other measure of mastery still based on the same content standards. Previous to push inclusion, educational benefit for these students would typically have been based on a norm-referenced test of general ability and a portfolio of modified curriculum.

The unilateral nature of the district administration's definition of appropriate public education for my students marked a unique moment in legal history. Parental consent and team-based decision-making were the prime movers of special-ed law. At El Dorado Middle, neither teachers nor parents were included in the decision to move the students into the push inclusion scenario. It was a top-down, unilateral decision, which is normally considered grounds for legal opposition by parents and generally off limits. A federal appeals court provided criteria, often referred to as the Holland Test (after Sacramento City School District v. Rachel Holland, E.D. Cal. 1992), for use in evaluating an inclusion decision in the team-based decision-making process. The Holland Test identifies decision factors such as impact on teacher, impact on classmates, difficulty of the task, and ability level of student. Basically, the inclusion decision should consider these factors in reasonable proportion to the parent's desire for inclusion. Holland is typically invoked when denying a parent a desired inclusion placement or a parental demand for an accommodation within an inclusion placement.

By leaving teachers and parents out of the inclusion decision, the district administration created the ground of cynicism. If these students had not been placed in full inclusion previous to NCLB, why should they move now? What had changed about the student, or curriculum, or teachers, or classmates? Nothing had changed. District administrators may have considered the Holland factors, but since teachers were not consulted, they lost faith in the administration and adopted a pessimistic outlook on the district's push inclusion initiative. Surely, a strategy based on a pseudo mandate and unilateral administrative decisions can't last more than a year at most. Maybe it will even fall apart as soon as second semester. We'll go through the motions, teachers of El Dorado Middle said to me in a hundred subtle ways, but this inclusion thing is doomed to fail.

As I mentioned earlier, I was intrigued by the political, spiritual, and humanistic aspects of full inclusion. I was ready to fight crazy with crazy, and I was not surprised by the faculty's reaction. Back in my days of studying political science at SUNY Stony Brook, I took a course in organizational decision theory. A significant theme of the course was how bureaucracies respond to top-down decision-making. Typically, top-down decisions are met with defiance in a kind of first-wave response, even when the authoritarian is Congress or the president.

The district administration's linking of NCLB and push inclusion was creating this kind of defiance at El Dorado Middle, and the defiant mood was exacerbated by the authoritarian tone of NCLB's provision of penalties for underperforming schools. I planned to draw on the peacemaking skills developed during my last corporate position where I brought a parent company and newly-acquired defiant division together through careful proactive communication and joint planning activities. Increased contact and non-aggressive communication between the warring factions led to a cessation of defiance. The keys to success, in the present case of inclusion, would be maintaining empathy for the challenges and stressors faced by my co-teachers, listening to them as much as presenting my own concerns, non-aggressive proactive communication and joint planning, and being organized and timely.

Sabotage

My effectiveness in my first semester as co-teacher was hampered by the principal's decision to align my teaching load by subject matter instead of grade level. As I described in earlier chapters on my first days at El Dorado Middle, the push inclusion initiate was conceived as team teaching, with each grade level supported by a team consisting of a resource specialist and the general-ed teachers handling the grade's mildly learning-disabled students. My role, as one of the resource specialists, would be co-teacher and consultant to the seventh-grade general-ed teachers who would have to incorporate the principles of differentiation into their courses. In theory, I was the expert on differentiation and the gen-ed teachers were the experts on subject- matter instruction. By working as a team, the gen-ed teachers and I would create differentiated subject-matter instruction on grade-level content standards, theoretically.

As the resource specialist for seventh grade, I was supposed to support my caseload's students through the essential periods of the day by serving as co-teacher in their language arts and math courses. For other subjects, such as science and electives like woodworking, art, or Spanish, I would only consult with the teachers. By spending nearly all day with my students and supporting their essential subjects, I would really know my students' strengths and needs. But instead of that ideal scenario, I spent half my day with the eighth-grade caseload and their teachers in language arts and the other half with my seventh-grade students in their language arts courses.

Despite this schizoid teaching load, I was still the seventh-grade resource specialist with the primary responsibility of case manager for the teaching team's IEP students. The eight-grade general-ed teachers had their own teaching team and resource specialist for push inclusion. The eighth-grade resource specialist was in the same bind as me since her teaching load was focused on math only and she spent half her day with my students in their math courses (but, as described in an earlier chapter, this outbreak of disorganization was in response to her desire to teach only math).

In eighth-grade language arts, the real relationship was between the general-ed teachers and the students. I wasn't a teammate of the teacher or the IEP case manager for the learning-disabled students. I had no stake in the situation. If I consulted with a student's parents or advised the teacher, I would be in the other resource specialist's territory. Moreover, I was yet another source of stress for the teacher, who would surely be pushed to the limit of endurance by push inclusion. Despite the organizational limitations, the eight-grade general-ed teachers welcomed me into their classrooms, and we even managed to collaborate on a few strategies for differentiation. Mostly, though, I focused on tutoring students during key points in each day's lesson. In other words, at least I could serve as a glorified aide.

I was co-teacher to two general-ed teachers in each grade (i.e. four total), seventh and eighth, with each gen-ed teacher leading a two-period core course that strategically integrated language arts and social studies. These two-period courses were called blocks. So, I co-taught in four blocks of language arts-social studies each day: two in the morning, and two in the afternoon. In accord with my assigned schedule, I was only present for the first half of most blocks, and in the part of the block in which I was absent, an aide assigned by the principal replaced me (to add yet another stressor to the general-ed teacher's day). In addition to the four blocks, my duty assignment included the period of reading intervention already covered and one period of prep time.

So, basically, I co-taught in four blocks of combined language arts-social studies, two in eight and two in seventh. An example of a combined lesson would be teaching a reading-skills lesson using a text from the current unit in social studies. The combined format was slightly deficient in reading skills and language conventions. On the other hand, combining the two subjects ensured that the students covered key standards of social studies. The trade-off was not without merit, since historically special-ed students have often missed significant parts of the academic curriculum due to greater time spent on essential skills.

In seventh grade, we studied academic subjects such as the seven points of geography, the Eurocentric worldview, medieval periods in Asia and Europe, Greek and Roman Empires, formation of world religions, and early Western Civilization. In eighth grade, we studied U.S. history, including the colonial era, formation of the U.S. Constitution, and civil liberties. The language arts aspect of the blocks was emphasized in a couple of major writing projects for each semester. In first semester for seventh grade, the major project was a three paragraph essay describing the student's prototype for a robot to explore other planets. The format was main idea with supporting details, and the project was integrated with the science teacher. In first semester for eighth grade, each student proposed an improvement to the school in a persuasive essay with a thesis and supporting arguments of three to five paragraphs.

The team teaching model, which aimed for a high-degree of collaboration between all team members on issues of differentiation, meaning how to accommodate the unique needs of learning-disabled students as they attempted the grade-level curriculum without modification, was basically sabotaged by the principal's decision to align the resource specialists by subject and thus across two different grades and two different inclusion teams. In first semester, the realignment reduced the inclusion initiative down to a muddle: too many chefs in the soup make for a bitter, foul brew. One major consequence of the realignment was the elimination of a common prep period for each push inclusion team: this joint planning time was considered key to collaborating on issues of differentiation. The net effect of the realignment was to reduce the resource specialists down to highly-qualified aides when they should have been full-fledged co-teachers and consultants. As long as the resource specialists confined themselves to supporting the teachers like aides, the deficiencies of the realignment remained hidden. Professional development activities reflected this diminished capacity as well. My seventh-grade teammates humored me with an occasional knowing nod or gesture as I played dumb about the lack of potency in my role. The team teaching model existed on paper only, although my students were expected to perform on a very real basis in the domain of the general-ed teachers, as evidenced by their frequently failing grades on assignments and tests.

Fifth Wheel

In my first five months as co-teacher, I was definitely hobbled by the principal's decision to align the resource specialists by subject and thus across two different grades and two different push inclusion teams. The realignment positioned the resource specialists as highly-qualified aides instead of full-fledged co-teachers and consultants. There were just too many chefs in the soup to properly influence the general-ed teachers, leaving the resource specialist with almost no choice but to withdraw to a passive role. On the other hand, I was less qualified than most aides at that point due to my total lack of experience. Before I could address organizational problems faced by my students, I had to at least develop some skills as an aide and tutor, which were in fact significant parts of my job.

In class when co-teaching, I often felt like the fifth wheel, with the real relationship in the room consisting of the general-ed teacher and the students. This sense of isolation was especially dramatic during my first months. Since the general-ed teachers were following reciprocal direct instruction, a significant part of each period, typically half, was occupied by the teacher at the head of the classroom delivering new information to students in their assigned seats. It was hard to know how to support that scenario, since movement on my part might create a distraction. In addition, I had no experience with how my students would react if I approached them during these teacher-focused times.

At first, I stood quietly at the back of the room or to the side, out of the way. My thinking was to minimize the potential disruption caused by my presence. I probably spent about three weeks that way. I literally did nothing. It was often a struggle to stay awake. The classrooms were organized in the same fashion as my reading intervention course after I moved to reciprocal direct instruction, with students facing the front board and overhead screen, with seating arrayed in a neat rectangle of rows and aisles. There was essentially no misbehavior during these weeks, especially when the teacher was addressing students directly. These weeks of passivity weren't a total waste for me. Although I didn't do much good for the students, I was able to observe the flow of the lessons and to envision ways to intervene at key moments. By the way, the general-ed teachers made no attempt to involve me in the lessons in any way.

My relationships with students in my reading intervention course started to pay dividends in my co-teaching work. Eventually, I felt comfortable offering my reading students assistance during transitions and independent work in the general-ed teacher's lesson. I focused my offers of help on the special-ed students who were also my reading students, but a few of my general-ed reading students would occasionally reach out to me too. At the end of my first month, I had established a cohort of students who were comfortable with me approaching their desk, checking their understanding, and offering assistance. The cohort of about five students in each course began with my reading students, but gradually grew to include all special-ed students and a fair number from general-ed. My careful interacting with students familiar with me broke the ice, and then day by day the remaining students grew comfortable with my presence in classrooms previously ruled by general education.

Strategically-timed prompting was my first attempt at intervention in those weeks. At first, I wasn't very strategic. I would scan the room for special-ed students who showed obvious signs of being off the pace or other indications of being off task: doodling on their notebook's cover, for instance, instead of following the teacher at the overhead. To intervene, I approached the student's desk quietly, moving stealthily among the rows and aisles, crouched down semi-kneeling, and repeated the teacher's directions that the student had apparently not comprehended: "Johnny. Let's turn your notebook to the next blank page. The teacher is starting a new page and she wants you to copy the details on the overhead onto the new page. I'll help you catch up. Put the date there. Title there..." And so on. In short, a quick reteaching of instructions probably missed due to attention deficits or auditory processing disability. I tried to provide quick interventions that restored the student to independence rather than letting the student depend on me. That quick style prevented dependency and also allowed me to move between students faster.

Over time, I observed that off-task behaviors arose in patterns and at predictable times and frequencies. Transitions in the lesson elicited the most wide-spread and predictable outbreaks of misbehavior, which were almost always rooted in attention deficits. The misbehavior could be described as missing the transition and failing to start the new task. In the example in the previous paragraph, Johnny didn't respond to the teacher's direction to open his notebook to a new page, prepare to receive new information from the overhead, and to transfer that information on cue to the notebook. My tutoring helped Johnny process and act on those instructions whereas his own attentional and processing resources had faltered. In behavioral terms, this intervention is sometimes referred to as the student borrowing my stronger attention span, since I had comprehended and acted on the teacher's directions.

Another major category of predictable misbehavior was failing to sustain the task once it has been initiated. This misbehavior mostly arose in times of independent work during the lesson. Reading lessons were particularly difficult for my students and elicited high levels of misbehavior. Typically, the teacher had led the class in reading the text aloud, but afterward some of my students would just sit and daydream when it was time to answer on their own the five or so questions of the comprehension exercise. The student's book or text would be at the right page, but the student basically wasn't engaging the questions. In that situation, I would visit the student's desk quietly, read the first question aloud, point to the place in the text where the answer could be found, and leave the student to complete the question on their own: "Johnny. This is the section where you can find the answer. Read it and try to answer the question. Let me know if you need more help." Then I would move on to another student and return later to see if my intervention lasted past the first question. Again, I didn't sit with the student through all of the questions. I tried to encourage independence. Some students could be jump started into completing the assignment on their own; some needed multiple visits, whereby I basically tutored them through the entire assignment. Interspersed with the tutoring, I gave directed praise when I noticed progress: "Good work. Johnny. I'm pleased that you tried the first question. Let's try the second one."

Misbehavior involving failure to sustain effort on the academic task can be attributed to two primary sources: attention deficits and deficits in prior learning. Regarding attention deficits, learning disabilities often manifest as attention problems and involve an element of attention deficit. So, an auditory processing disability might lead a student to lose track of a teacher's oral presentation on a perceptual basis and the attentional aspect might also hamper the student even when they followed what has been presented. Put simply, a learning disability predictably leads to attentional and focus problems like the ones that I'm describing.

Regarding deficits in prior learning, a student's inaction on an academic task, in this case reading, writing, or other text-based activity, might be due to a lack of preparation for the task. Possibly the student is not familiar with enough of the text's vocabulary to properly read the text and gain meaning from it holistically. The text may be dense with unfamiliar words and the student lacks the decoding skills to handle the load. Possibly the student has had no exposure to the context, such as the medieval period, and thus has trouble appreciating the information contained in sentences and paragraphs. Sometimes these deficits in academic knowledge and basic skills can masquerade as merely attention problems. Thus when intervening in a misbehavior, it's important to consider both sources, academic and attentional.

In my first few months of co-teaching, my response to misbehavior, of either academic or attentional origins, was a quick offer of tutoring when the student showed obvious signs of drifting off task. Tutoring was conducted at the student's desk, individually, without interrupting or deviating in any way from the general-ed teacher's lesson. This approach was mostly geared toward counteracting attention deficits and problems of attention, and it was probably deficient in addressing problems of prior learning. When tutoring a student, I might explain a key term that I thought was vexing the student, and I might go to the length of reading a section aloud for the student to help them decode it. I have to admit that in regard to academic deficits, these interventions led to a patchwork engagement of the content at best.

As first semester progressed, I occasionally had the opportunity to address instructional sources of misbehavior by consulting with the general-ed teachers. The teacher's method of delivery can either diminish or exacerbate the impact of attention problems and deficits in prior learning. To combat attention problems, the teacher can deliver information in well-defined and explicit chunks, with a verbal check for understanding at the beginning of each chunk. At the beginning of the reading lesson, for instance, the teacher can ask all students to hold up their book open to the right page. Then the teacher reads the title and first heading clearly, followed by asking students to read aloud the title and first heading in unison. The teacher might stop to check if students know how the title relates to the unit. At the end of the first section, the teacher asks students to read the last sentence in unison. Optimally, the teacher would ask students to find and read aloud in unison a key phrase or word of the section before moving on. Then the next heading should be held up to show the teacher. Whatever strategy the teacher adopts for reading aloud, or any other recurring instructional activity, it should be a routine taught to the students. This is just a quick example. There are myriad strategies for counteracting attention deficits. In my reading intervention course, I applied an incentive-based strategy whereby the student had to know where we were in the text when called on to earn their read-aloud point, thus giving students strong motivation to follow along; this incentive usually elicited greater levels of attention from the underachievers.

Academic deficits can be counteracted by including a quick teacher-led preview of the context before launching into the text. This strategy both connects to and establishes prior knowledge, which will help comprehension. A teacher-led lesson on key vocabulary at the beginning of each unit can establish the context of the reading material to follow. The teacher can administer a graded quiz that asks students to find ten words that they didn't understand in a passage and to copy their definitions from a dictionary. Students could find those words as homework and then read the passage aloud the next day as a group. In general, the more previewing included, the more likely the student is to overcome academic and attention deficits. Strategies for addressing attentional and academic deficits are a major area of scholarly research, and the intended function of the co-teacher was to bring that research into action in joint planning. In first semester, my impact on joint planning was minimal, since there was no common prep with my co-teachers: the principal's realignment of the resource specialists had eliminated it

Finally, organization problems were also predictable, involving recording homework assignments in planners, maintaining school supplies, turning in completed classwork, completing homework on time and turning it in, refraining from drawing on, tearing, or otherwise damaging textbooks and workbooks, and refraining from drawing on, carving, or otherwise damaging desks. At the beginning of first semester, these organizational problems were overwhelming because my students experienced them in unison. They were obviously bogged down in the anxiety of the unfamiliar generaled setting. They were a bit spaced out. Eventually, I learned to anticipate their organization vulnerabilities, and I cruised around the rows and aisles of the classroom checking for school supplies, collecting classwork, flipping books open or interrupting minor vandalism, and prompting for entries into planners. As with my other interventions in first semester, these stop gap measures maintained a minimal patchwork engagement in the curriculum but didn't live up to ideal of the disabled students autonomously responding to instruction in a fashion similar to non-disabled peers.

Violets Among the Rocks

My first semester as co-teacher was mostly spent as an outsider to the general-ed faculty, but a few violets did manage to bloom amid the cold rocky conditions. First, as I have already outlined, I became a fairly effective tutor in the general-ed classrooms. I developed a repertoire of interventions, which I performed autonomously based on identifying my students' needs through observation. I made sure materials were ready, checked students' understanding at key curricular transitions, and helped students recover when they lost the thread of instruction. These interventions at least minimized the impact of the predictable attention deficits arising from learning disabilities.

Second, a couple of my co-teachers began seeking me out as a collaborator. They actually started asking me about ways they might improve the learning experience for their disabled students. These two were the youngest of my four language arts co-teachers and recent additions to the school faculty. Both were recently credentialed teachers in the three years where the principal evaluated their performance in preparation for a permanent contract: in other words, they were seeking tenure.

Karl was a young twenty-something, about 6'3" tall with trim athletic build and handsome Anglo blond appearance: a definite bombshell for a middle school teacher. He might have played tight end in football or forward in basketball. He typically wore blue jeans, t-shirts, button-down cotton casual shirts, cotton pull-overs like rugby jerseys and hoodies, and athletic shoes. He basically followed the fashion statements of skateboarders and surfers, and his wardrobe implied a degree of common cause with the students. He taught an eighth-grade core section. His forte was social studies, so he anchored his language arts instruction in his units on early American history and the Constitution. Betsy was verging on thirty-something, about 5'6" tall with perky Celtic good looks: smooth ruddy cheeks, perky blue eyes, curly cropped blond hair, broad athletic shoulders, long muscular legs, with a few extra pounds around the tummy and hips to soften all that power into a matronly presence. She might have been the captain of the field hockey team. On most days, she wore denim or cotton twill pedal pushers (and less frequently other styles of calf-length culottes), casual oxford blouse or t-shirt, and either flip flops or studier closed-toe leather sandals. She taught a core section of seventh-graders. Her forte was language arts. Instead of merely incorporating language arts into social studies, she implemented literature analysis lessons separate from world cultures topics.

Karl had moved straight from his undergraduate career to teaching. Betsy started her working life after college as a retail store manager for a ground-breaking entrepreneurial company in the emerging body-care market; she was there during their IPO. Karl was deferential and even a bit shy. Betsy was a mature, formidable presence, and she could best be characterized as demanding and even contentious. Karl was single, and I recall that he still lived at home with his folks. Betsy was married with no children (yet) to a thirty-something handsome young man who worked at the premier groundbreaking firm in human resources software.

Both teachers followed reciprocal direct instruction with rows and aisles in a rectangular floor plan facing the board and overhead projector. In fact, their instructional delivery was very similar to mine in reading intervention, with teacher-led lessons that culminated in students working independently after receiving new information; even the furniture was the same, with two-person rectangular tables organized into rows (since the senior teachers had secured all the individual student desks). Karl showed strength in explicitly outlining tasks and then turning the work over to the students. He didn't do much guided instruction or other kinds of leading students. He tended to be a task manager and organizer. Betsy favored delivery of new information and guided instruction. She was a whiz at guided instruction, but she was a bit of an authoritarian and dominator. If a student grew restless or distracted, her first reaction might be to yell at them or remove them to the principal's office. Karl maintained a kind of easy going reciprocity with his students, and some evaluators might call him permissive (whereas I might call him tolerant and accommodating). Karl and his students seemed to like each other. Betsy was in an uneasy truce with her students, and there was an ongoing struggle for power, with the students occasionally defying Betsy to the point where she shouted them down at the top of her voice. On the other hand, Betsy tackled incredibly difficult content in her literature lessons. She was an overachiever who wouldn't take no for an answer. Betsy's students seemed driven to defy and taunt her.

I made similar suggestions to both teachers. The most effective suggestion was frequent progress reports and timely calls to parents when a student was falling behind. Karl's approach was to complete curricular activities at the same time each week. For instance, new vocabulary words were previewed on Monday, worksheets were completed as homework and handed in on Friday, and retention was measured by a test on Friday. Karl graded work quickly and called parents as soon as a student fell behind. He was organized and clear with deadlines of all sorts, and that gave him the ability to inform parents of problems as soon as they arose. Betsy's curriculum was more spontaneous and varied with each unit; she was a bit more project-oriented than routine-oriented. Eventually, though, she learned to call parents early when a student was falling behind in the formative checkpoints of a project. The main impact of this strategy for both teachers was to inform parents in time for the student to complete makeup work and to minimize gaps in achievement.

Frequent progress reports are based on a flexible view of deadlines. Instead of giving the student a failing grade when they missed a deadline, the teacher informed the parent of a makeup opportunity. Under IDEA (i.e. prevailing special-ed law), this flexibility qualifies as a reasonable accommodation made in support of an inclusive placement. Authoritarian teachers might see the flexibility as permissive and suggest that a failing grade would teach the student a lesson in timeliness. But by law and custom, special education should be based on positive discipline, meaning failure is seen as the weakest motive and least-effective lesson. The intervention of flexible deadlines aims to prevent and minimize the impact of school failure for the disabled rather than use it as a lesson, within limits. Wanton disregard for assignments and deadlines can still be characterized as defiance and penalized with failing grades; the student and family must make a good faith effort.

Both teachers were employing a repertoire of daily and weekly routines taught to students explicitly. For instance, Betsy conducted read-aloud lessons in literature the same way every time. In social studies, she led delivery of new information and recording lecture notes in a routine that ran across all units. I only had to encourage the teachers in this direction, since they were already moving forward. I was able to point out where students hadn't understood the routine since I was with them when they lost track of the instruction. I basically gave feedback about what seemed to work.

With these two teachers, I made a least modest progress toward fulfilling my role as collaborative teacher. The reciprocal discussion of strategies and their effectiveness was starting to approach the ideal of collaborative instruction. Yet I still wasn't being consulted about lesson design and other ways to adapt the presentation of academic content to better accommodate my learning-disabled students. That kind of collaboration would be the pinnacle of co-teaching. All three of us were being evaluated that year by the principal. Karl and Betsy had a lot at stake, since they were looking for a permanent contract. I was just an intern. The principal told me that a satisfactory evaluation for me rested on my ability to relate to my co-teachers. Maybe the principal told these two tenure-seeking teachers the same thing, creating the ground for deeper levels of collaboration. Keen observers might wonder if this level of interdependence in a new process was a fair basis for evaluation.

The Old Rocks

My two other language arts co-teachers were senior practitioners near retirement. Both were considered master teachers and they both supervised student teachers for local universities. Ann was a slim Anglo sixty-something of medium height who except for her mildly-wrinkled fair skin and thinning silvery-blond cropped hair could pass for twenty. She favored tailored pants suits supplemented by the occasional business-casual slacks and blouse. Her fabrics were durable and plain wool, cotton, or twill, in solid colors; she wore formal yet functional and fastidious outfits. Her one luxury seemed to be designer shoes, in pumps or flats. Her husband was an assistant principal at one of the district's high schools; they had mature children. She taught core studies (language arts/social studies) to seventh graders.

Ann was the authoritarian in my group of collaborators. She had a reputation among the students and parents for proficiency in putting hyperactive boys in their place through soul-shaking reprimands, critical calls to parents, and trips to the principal's office. Some of my learning-disabled boys were becoming targets of these kinds of interventions, but only outside my presence. When I was present in Ann's classroom, it seemed that the additional authority figure kept the boys calmer, at least to the point where they didn't draw any fire. News of the reprimands came to me through complaints from the student or parent. In case it seems like Ann might have been afraid of me, I will report that she didn't hesitate to reprimand me in front of the class if I didn't carry out my responsibilities with sufficient rigor. My response to these scoldings was to carry out my responsibilities with sufficient rigor.

Those responsibilities consisted of being a top notch aide working to support Ann's every demand. My focus on tutoring skills early in the school year was in large part driven by my need to contribute to her classroom in some fashion. In first semester, Ann never made any kind of overture toward involving me in her planning or instructional delivery, expect to express mild consternation when I wasn't living up to her expectations for a crack aide. Amazingly, I figured out those expectations on my own through trial and error, since she didn't offer word one of advice on that topic. Interestingly, she had been quite generous in mentoring me in regard to my reading intervention course. Ann gave students failing grades on late or incomplete work, with no kind of second chance. She also made no modifications to tests or projects. She was inflexible as a strategy, and she believed failure was a teaching tool. Consequently, almost all of my students were failing at the end of first semester.

Ann was the department chair for language arts. Karl and Betsy had been student teachers under Ann's supervision, and it was amazing to see how her strategies had carried through into Karl's and Ann's classrooms. Ann possessed all the good traits of both teachers, except that she hadn't warmed up to flexible deadlines and occasionally modifying an assignment for an individual student. She followed reciprocal direct instruction, with a rectangular floor plan of rows and aisles facing the front board; she was the only one of my co-teacher to have individual student desks. She had routines for repetitive activities that cut across all units for textbook read alouds, lectures and student note-taking, assigning and collecting homework, weekly vocabulary and spelling assignments, weekly geography fundamentals, and grading and posting progress. She was very creative with project-based learning. Building models of castles and studying fiefdoms and knights with medieval coloring books were highlights for me. I was impressed by the art gallery with an art appreciation exercise for the Renaissance. I also remember a slide show from Ann's trip to Africa. She integrated a writing project with the science teachers on the ideal traits of a prototype robot for exploring space, with students actually drawing or creating a model of their robot in science class.

Projects and other lessons requiring student autonomy were of course a gauntlet of temptation for hyperactive boys, but Ann was an overachiever who didn't take no for an answer. I admired Ann's skills in lesson planning and classroom management, and I had incorporated some of her strategies into my reading intervention course, but I secretly aspired to inspire her somehow to open up to the ways of accommodation and positive discipline. The first step, for first semester, I felt, was to be tolerant of our differences and break the ice. The principal supervised Ann, not me, and I didn't have to be responsible for the way Ann handled misbehavior. I aimed to be an influencer more than an authority figure.

Peggy was the other senior master teacher. She taught core studies to eighth graders. She was in her last year of a long teaching career. She had already announced her plan to retire at the end of second semester. She was a heavy-set Anglo sixty-something of medium height in obviously good health. She had an athletic frame, was not overweight, with a strong chin, broad brow, thick curly brown cropped locks, broad shoulders, booming voice, bouncy stride, vivacious personality, and probably a pretty good right hook in the right situation. She was married with grandchildren. She reminded me of a frontier woman, maybe a matron of a ranch built up from a homestead. She favored well-fitting blue jeans, with running shoes and button-down oxford blouse, sometimes with a jacket or sweater.

Peggy didn't follow reciprocal direct instruction or any

other method consistently. Her floor plan was group seating, consisting of four large rectangles, with each one holding roughly eight students. The seating didn't focus students' attention to the front board or any other point in the room. Students were mostly focused on each other; literally, it was where their gaze would naturally fall. Consequently, students spent most of their time talking to each other on topics of their choosing. It was really hard to tutor my students or get them on task in any way. It was impossible to label misbehavior as defiance, since there was no baseline of compliance to measure against.

On the few occasions when Peggy led a discussion from the overhead projector, the view of the screen was obstructed for most students and the presentation was in small, blurry type that they couldn't read without straining. Moreover, the text on the slides wasn't very well arranged. Delivery of new information and guided practice were not her strengths. Peggy's approach to instruction could best be characterized as passive direct instruction.

On most days, she would post a textbook assignment on the board and assign the students to complete it on their own in class time and as homework. The assignment would consist of reading a chapter and answering some of the comprehension exercises at the end of the chapter. She collected the exercises and returned them with a grade promptly. She would periodically give a test on a unit, which would cover the content from a few chapters. Sometimes she would prepare her own handout for the comprehension exercise.

In periods in which I was present, Peggy spent most of the time at her desk, working at her computer, grading completed assignments, recording the grades, and planning the next assignment. Peggy didn't put much emphasis on routines but the students did basically understand this rhythm of a few graded chapter assignments followed by a graded test.

The lack of active monitoring by the teacher in combination with the group seating made for a mildly rowdy climate among the students. Peggy allowed the students to talk freely among themselves while working on the day's assignment. Basically, it seemed like recess or lunch more than a classroom. Peggy invited students to her desk a few times a quarter for a verbal progress report on their semester grade, but that didn't seem to have much impact on the minimalists and underachievers. My tutoring-based intervention strategy really had no impact, since my students simply would not attend to their assignment with sufficient intensity. I roamed the room, checking for student understanding, and offering help. When I found a student in a receptive mood, I prompted the student to engage a question, but they typically hadn't read any of the chapter and in many cases hadn't even opened their book. Even if they humored me for one question, they would immediately resume socializing as soon as I left their desk.

I found the permissive classroom culture to be unproductive. I was developing an interest in positive discipline because I was inclined toward discipline. If I had to work with either permissive Peggy or authoritarian Ann, I would choose Ann. My tutoring-based interventions worked fairly well in her classroom, where students could only speak with permission (like in my reading course). Students probably should not have been allowed to talk freely, especially with one third of the group being learning-disabled. Peggy tried to maintain a kind of implicit standard of decorum. For major misbehaviors such as profanity, loud language, or interfering with a classmate, Peggy called the offending student aside and counselled them about the need for responsible behavior; she might threaten to call the parents. Minor misbehaviors were blithely ignored. Major misbehaviors were at barely acceptable levels and minor misbehaviors flourished.

Peggy's style relied on students working on their own through long periods of classwork, sometimes called seatwork, for the entire period, day after day. This approach is really difficult on students with attention deficits, especially those who also have reading deficits. Inattention, the leading misbehavior, can blossom into a near total impediment. Since seatwork depends almost entirely on the student's ability to read to learn, reading deficits will be crippling. Students with attention and reading deficits would be better served by the step-by-step format of reciprocal direct instruction, wherein the teacher directly and interactively leads students in acquiring new information and practicing with that information before applying it on their own.

Karl and Peggy had similar instructional styles in that they both had students working on their own most of the time. Karl was a little more thorough in introducing new information. For instance, he routinely led read aloud lessons to preview texts that students would need to understand for the assignment. He might also lead guided practice for the first few steps of the assignment. These preparatory steps launched the overachievers and minimalists into decent levels of attentiveness and sustained effort, and the attentiveness led to a relatively calm classroom culture. The underachievers had at least some grip on what was expected after the read aloud and guided practice, and I could often fix up their understanding with brief tutoring. Karl's floor plan used two-person rectangular tables arranged into rows and aisles (approximating individual student seating) in a layout very similar to my reading course, and that made tutoring easier and more effective.

I must confess that I had no impact whatsoever on Peggy's classroom, except maybe to provide a bit of encouragement and moral support. Overachievers occasionally would ask me for help and that was nice. They seemed to understand the assignments pretty well. I think they got a charge out of the fact that I remained among the students for the entire period whereas Peggy seemed to take refuge at her desk; they probably thought I was a rebel. Peggy was an amiable and caring person, and I felt she was a good role model for the students. Her passive style of instruction made my job difficult, since

I was there to represent the underachievers and minimalists, but I don't think she would intentionally harm anyone. We never got around to discussing strategy, but occasionally Peggy would express her frustration at the poor performance of my students and others in this period. She would say, "I just don't know what to do with these kids. Nothing I do works. No matter what I try, I get the same high level of failure and low level of participation." If she had been younger, I might have recommended a couple of books on reciprocal direct instruction. Instead, I said a few words in agreement, suggested that inclusion was a new strategy, and encouraged her not to take things too hard.

Ann didn't discuss strategy with me either. And, like Peggy, she would occasionally express her frustration to me about the high level of failure in our co-teaching section. Literally, she would use the same words as Peggy. For Ann, though, I had no easy pat response. Her teaching was skillful and even inspired, but she seemed to really struggle with underachievers. They really threw her off. I knew that adhering to failure as a teaching tool would never work for her in inclusion. But I also knew that was a part of her worldview, held at the gut level, like mom's recipe for apple pie.

I was lucky to have Ann as an example to emulate in my reading course. I dared myself to be even more demanding than her but through positive discipline. I shared her utilitarian tendencies whereby I might sacrifice the emotional well-being of my underachievers for the sake of the greater good. I knew that we both had to improve on that front. When Ann complained about poor results, I would just avoid the issue with a curt response: "Okay. Thanks for the info. I'll see you later." I was stalling while I hoped some inspiration would come to me in the form of a subtle outrageous means of insinuating flexibility into her thinking. Fight crazy with crazy!

Karl and Betsy didn't share much about their results with me. As new teachers, they might have been afraid to disclose too much. As a new teacher myself, I was glad to leave it up to them to deal with their results. From my perspective, the two were applying deliberate energy toward improving the performance of their learning-disabled students, so I could claim at least some modest success. I never spoke to the principal about my discussions with co-teachers, and she never spoke to me about them. I felt that I would never develop rapport with my co-teachers if I served as the principal's snitch or conspirator. I kept everything strictly in the family.

Since I've described my co-teachers' wardrobe and other aspects of their appearance, I should probably include the details of my appearance. I retained the same good health that I arrived in, with trim, fit athletic dimensions. I didn't experience any sudden weight gain or loss, skin disorders, or insomnia that might have come from stress; I probably looked a little too healthy. My styled brunette hair retained its somewhat liberal thickness and length, flowing around my ears and approaching collar length, and I continued my clean-shaven ways.

My wardrobe was consistently upper-end business casual. I basically resurrected and updated my fashion statement from my last corporate job. I favored a base of Eddy Bauer pleated cuffed chinos in khaki and blue, their oxford button-down dress shirts in a variety of patterns, and Timberland oxford leather walking shoes. I added in a variety of oxford button-down flannel shirts, sport shirts, and sweaters from Macy's Charter Club. My mom routinely gave me Pendleton wool oxford button-down plaid shirts as gifts and they came in handy in the Delta's humid, cold fall. In short, I was a Diablo Valley preppy aspiring to good deeds in one of working-class Concord's Title I schools. Those who didn't know me personally might have mistaken me for a hunky sales guy looking for directions to the local country club.

Whistle Blower

My first semester as a co-teacher had me mostly on the

sidelines, but there were some accomplishments. For all four of my co-teachers, I developed a style of tutoring-based intervention that counteracted attention deficits and helped my students follow lessons to the point where they at least engaged minimally in daily activities. These interventions flowed with the pace and structure set by the general-ed teachers and didn't require them to change their lessons or other strategies. For the two newer general-ed teachers in this group, I collaborated on a strategy of flexible deadlines and frequent parent notifications to increase my students' completion rate on assignments. But I still hadn't been invited to consult on lesson plans. Except for the suggestion of flexibility, I mostly limited my influence to those activities that could be accomplished by an experienced aide.

This limited role stemmed from a few factors. First, I felt that I should respect each teacher's desire for sovereignty and creativity in their classroom. Teachers typically resist intrusions on their autonomy. I needed to break the ice carefully before they would want to share their planning. Second, I had less experience than most aides. I needed to just let the learning curve unfold. Third, the principal disrupted the intended team teaching scheme when she realigned the resource specialists by subject rather than grade level.

The impact of the realignment was to spread my co-teaching efforts across two grade levels and four teachers with no formal teamwork or common prep for joint planning. Ideally, I would have collaborated with three seventh-grade teachers, followed my seventh-grade inclusion students throughout the day, consulted with my teammates during common prep, and participated with them as a learning community during professional development. Instead, the net effect of realignment on my teaching was that my role was effectively limited to aide.

As the end of first semester approached, I was resigned to my limited role. I was going to make the best of things. Then two visits from district administrators changed everything, mostly because of statements that I alone made to them. In a combination of naiveté and my ancient disestablishmentarian heart, I blew the whistle by opening my big mouth when others wished I would have kept it firmly shut. The visits occurred around Thanksgiving, at the school's central office, in a small conference room adjoining the principal's office. They were held in the spirit of informal interview research on the progress made so far in the grand experiment of inclusion.

The first meeting was held by the district superintendent: a tall, fit, and athletic Black gentleman in a gray wool suit, who was energetic and quite handsome in early middle age. His tone was friendly and warm, yet refined and professional. The seventh-grade collaborative team was gathered for the interview in which I participated. The principal also attended. Ann and Betsy were the language arts teachers, and they were joined by the science teacher and math teacher for seventh grade. I had barely met the science or math teacher, and I had no idea how my students were performing in their courses, but at least I had some actual inclusion experience with Ann and Betsy.

The superintendent conducted his interview in round robin format, asking each teacher a few questions individually. His questions focused on communication with the resource specialist and between team members: Was team teaching having the intended effect? Both the math and science teacher gave noncommittal answers in a gentle and mildly-sheepish tone: "Sure. Yeah. Everything seems fine. I'm getting everything I need." The math teacher didn't mention anything about his co-teaching with the eighth-grade resource specialist. Ann said, in a restrained, mild tone, that I was co-teaching in her core course and I seemed to have pretty good rapport with the students; things seemed okay for now. She left it at that, conveyed an air of contentment, and didn't make any critical comments. Betsy complained about me. She said that I had been regularly co-teaching in her course, but that she felt my efforts had not lived up to the projections of collaboration for team teaching. She wished I would take a greater stake in the success of her lessons, support her more intensely in behavior intervention, and in general be more attentive to struggling students during the class period. In short, she wished I was a better aide. The superintendent received her comments passively and moved on to the next person without making any response or elaboration: "Okay. Thank you for the feedback. And how about you, Robert,...." Betsy's complaints didn't anger me or evoke any other strong emotion, but they magically launched me into detailed critical statements about the failure of the school site to implement the team teaching model.

I informed the superintendent that the team model had not been implemented for seventh or eighth grade and that the teachers in the interview had no common prep or other joint planning. I told him about the realignment of the resource specialists by subject and how it effectively prevented any real collaboration at the grade level and negated collaborative teaching. I talked about how the lack of unity at the grade level led to minimal engagement with my students. Basically, I described how the current situation reduced me down to a tutor when joint planning of lessons and strategies were the cornerstones of collaborative teaching. I predicted that push inclusion would be fraught with low performance and problem behaviors unless the collaborative teaching model was restored to the original plan of grade-level teams with common prep.

The superintendent received my answer passively, with a friendly expression: "Okay. Robert. Thank you for your view of the situation." Then he closed the meeting with a quick farewell: "Well. Thank you for spending some time with me this afternoon. I just wanted to check on the new program. To see how things were proceeding. It sounds like things are going pretty well for this stage in the new model." Then he dismissed us. The teachers quietly filed out of the room. During my remarks, the principal had slid down a bit and leaned against the back of her chair while mildly glowering at me; she narrowed her gaze like a cat ready to pounce. But she just exited with the teachers and made no response. All participants immediately went their separate ways in silence.

About two weeks later, another interview was held by a district administrator. This time the administrator was a consultant authorized by the California Department of Education (CDE) to work with underperforming schools as measured by statewide testing and other factors of school accountability under NCLB. The consultant never presented his credentials, but that was how colleagues described him. He was a White, Anglo, and greying late middle-aged man, with a paunch, perky upright posture, attractive well-tailored light gray suit, crisp white pinpoint oxford shirt, red tie, and polished black leather oxfords. Hiring a CDE-authorized consultant was one of the consequences imposed on underperforming schools by NCLB (as interpreted by California).

The consultant met individually with each teacher involved in push inclusion. He asked me pointed questions about my daily schedule, my seventh-grade students and collaborative team, and common prep. When I gave the consultant the same kind of straight answers that I provided to the superintendent, the consultant seemed genuinely peeved to learn that the school had not followed the original plan for team teaching. My impression was that I had been the only teacher to give the consultant the honest details about the principal altering the plan. My statements alerted him to the fact that the school was obviously out of alignment with the plan, which might have been his plan.

Nobody ever made it clear why the consultant had been called in for the issue of inclusion. But a few weeks after the consultant's meetings with other teachers and me, an announcement was made by the principal that the school would be restructured over winter break. The school's administrators, meaning the principal and assistant principals, would return early from winter break. They would reorganize student schedules for seventh and eighth grade to support team teaching by grade level as originally envisioned at the start of the school year; sixth grade was already organized properly. My reorganized workload for second semester would consist of my reading intervention course, co-teaching my seventh-grade students in two sections of language arts and two sections of pre-Algebra, and one period of common prep for joint planning with the teachers of those sections. Ann and Betsy would be the co-teachers for language arts. I still needed to introduce myself to the math teacher. I would also have to hold almost all of the annual IEP reviews for my twenty-four students in second semester.

The principal never consulted with me about the restructuring for second semester. She didn't speak with me about it in any way, not even casually. In fact, she hadn't said one word to me since the early November evaluation conference in which she had said that her decisions about my performance rested on my ability to engage with my co-teachers. I was starting to have better rapport with my co-teachers, but the site administration was still largely a mystery. On one hand, I had triggered a change that should increase the likelihood of meaningful joint planning. On the other hand, that change didn't occur in a way that would accrue merit to the principal. Even worse, it made her and possibly the superintendent look bad. I knew that probably no one but the Buddha would appreciate me trying to do the right thing and not even he could save me from the principal's wrath at evaluation time at the end of the year. I might be doomed. Yet I had made it to second semester.

My reading intervention course had decent levels of student engagement; I had developed emerging skills as an effective tutor and supportive teacher in my co-teaching duties; and I had introduced the possibility of flexible expectations with some of my co-teachers. My views on flexibility were supported by scholarly research and in accord with CDE guidelines. Tutoring was helpful and promoted attentiveness among struggling students, but my best work had been in at least inspiring a couple of teachers to try flexibility as an accommodation. It wasn't the lovefest the principal seemed to be looking for, which probably would have required me to become the best aide at the site, but I felt good about my contribution. I left for winter break feeling good about myself and hoping common prep with my co-teachers would give me even more opportunities to explore flexibility and other accommodations that would help my students engage with the curriculum at sufficient intensity for growth to occur. I'm inspired to recall how I instituted common prep in my last corporate position to bring peace to the warring factions of the parent company in Oregon and its acquired division in California.

CHAPTER NINE

Peacemaker

Inclusion Reformed

Second semester began with the school realigned to properly support the push inclusion initiative. Students were given new schedules, and teachers had to help them find their way. But the situation did not degrade into chaos. Within just a few days, the students and faculty settled into their routines without any major disruption. Now the seventh-grade collaborative team, meaning the general-ed teachers directly handling my learning-disabled students, worked with me every day, and I served only seventh-grade inclusion students.

My reorganized daily co-teaching schedule consisted of two sections of language arts and two sections of pre-algebra. Ann and Betsy taught the language arts sections, and their courses started the semester on the same trajectory that they were on at the end of first semester. My involvement in my students' math courses brought one new teacher into my co-teaching domain. He taught both sections. Alfredo was a twenty-something recent Italian immigrant who spoke English almost fluently. He started his teaching career in Italy. He was medium-short, slim and fit, handsome with crew cut and clean-shaven. He dressed business casual with dark colored dress slacks, a variety of stylish dress shirts, and black leather dress shoes. He was mild-mannered, restrained, and decorous in all things. He was married and lived with his wife.

His views on child development could be best characterized as ultra conservative and traditional. He sounded a lot like the old rocks when I talked with him about student re-sults: "I try to tell these kids that their future depends on their studies. They just don't seem to care. I really wonder if it's worth it to teach them this material. I can't see them having much of a future." Sometimes he would compare his American students to Italians: "In Italy, the students do their homework. The school day is a very basic affair that takes about half the day. The rest of the day is spent at home doing homework. Students there care about their future. They do their homework."

Alfredo was frustrated by what he perceived as student ap-athy, but he was pretty affable and never really got mad at anybody. Where he saw apathy, I perceived deficits in prior learning, attention deficits, inattention rooted in adjustment problems, slightly boring teaching rooted in rote learning and computation, and state math standards aimed to serve the gifted over the mainstream. Apathy was the students' visceral response to a situation that they were overwhelmed by. They cared about their future. That is why they acted so indiffer-ently to the present.

My initial approach to Alfredo's classes was to implement the same tutoring-based interventions that I developed for language arts. Alfredo followed a highly-structured approach similar to reciprocal direct instruction. The floor plan was individual student desks in rows and aisles facing the front board and overhead projector. Alfredo spent most of the period at the overhead projector, presenting new informa-tion (by demonstrating new problems and solutions), leading interactive guided practice on sample problems, and provid-ing corrective feedback after times of independent practice. He was a real whiz at visual presentation. His slides were well-organized and readable, and he used colored text, colored markers, and other color coding to direct student attention to key information.

Each phase of instruction followed a routine. So, for in-stance, students could anticipate the presentation of new information by the appearance of the routine for it. This routinized and highly-regimented instruction led to impressive levels of engagement and achievement among the overachievers and the upper half of the minimalists, meaning it didn't work at all for my students, some of whom were acquiring a reputation as behavior problems. Alfredo had a significant percentage of each class, meaning roughly half, recording sample problems in their notebooks, interacting with the teacher during guided practice, completing work during independent practice and homework, following self-correction to check their work, and passing tests. He sheltered his high achievers with a seating chart that put them at the center front of the floor plan with the low achievers arrayed along the sides and back of the room. This arrangement created an inner circle of calm attentiveness, which gave Alfredo the feedback he needed to carry on through his day.

Most of my students were on the side of the room, along the wall with the entrance. They filled the three aisles on that end of the room. As a general principle of inclusion, teachers were asked to avoid any form of segregation, even one as discrete as seating learning-disabled students together, but I didn't mind in this instance. At the start of second semester, my students were losing touch with the demanding curriculum. Grouping them at the side of the room gave me ease of access for tutoring and active monitoring. Basically all of my students were off task for at least part of every period.

My tutoring interventions were focused on guided practice and independent practice. My students were relatively compliant when it came to copying sample problems into their notebooks and at least feigning attention to the delivery of new information. To improve their performance on those tasks, I employed active monitoring by standing or sitting at the back of their aisles. As soon I detected misbehavior such as drifting off or interfering with a classmate, I moved forward and prompted the student back on task. My students typically struggled when they had to process the new information on their own and that is when I tried to help with tutoring.

As in language arts, I would monitor my students for signs of misbehavior. The most frequent misbehavior was sitting back and giving up: in other words, inaction. None of my students were asking for help, even though the high achievers were quite active in engaging Alfredo. When I noticed an inactive student during guided practice, I approached their desk, asked to see their work, engaged them in quick reteaching, sometimes modeling a solution to get them ready for the next problem, and prompted them to attempt the next problem. I circulated around the best that I could, which was tricky since the teacher set the pace in guided instruction. For most lessons, guided instruction was followed by independent practice, which consisted of five to ten problems assigned for homework. Students were given class time to start their homework.

A few of my students were able to engage in the homework. My strategic prompting helped them go deeper than they would have without my presence. And those students were able to minimally pass tests or nearly pass. But for most of my students, my constant visual monitoring merely helped reduce the intensity of their misbehavior. My biggest contribution was to suppress discipline problems for the teacher, whose practices only minimally changed in response to my contribution.

Model of Cooperation

My limited effectiveness in the two pre-algebra sections indicated that joint planning and team teaching would not be panaceas. But the two language arts members of my teaching team embraced joint planning by initiating the process of developing a formal model of co-teaching. This idea of formal procedures was hatched at the start of second semester. I recall that it was announced by Ann and Betsy in a departmental language arts meeting in which I was in attendance. Those were the two seventh-grade teachers that I had co-taught with in first semester, and it was their idea. Ann was the department chair for the school. The principal was not involved at that point, but it was proposed that we develop the model and then share it with the principal.

Up to that point, my co-teaching style had been a matter of observing my students in action and applying my research-based training from the credential program. I had ruled by fiat, an approach supported by the faculty's conspicuous indifference toward my students and me. Collaboration on a formal model would give the site's teachers an opportunity to have input on how the gen-ed teacher and resource teacher would work together to accommodate learning-disabled students. The collaboration would culminate in a written set of guidelines on teamwork, which all team members would abide by like a contract.

On the positive side, the teachers were finally acknowledging their responsibilities in inclusion. On the negative side, Ann and Betsy might be looking for a way to mold me into the instructional aide of their dreams. In response to this concern, I saw an opportunity for a switcheroo. This was my chance to introduce co-teaching and inclusion at its best, to apply everything that I had learned in credential courses and on the job. This would be my model of co-teaching, or at least my voice would be properly heard. Fight crazy with crazy! Although I was mildly dubious about the project's prospects, I privately vowed to apply my best peacemaker skills. I wanted this project to lead to an increase in rapport with my co-teachers and improved learning conditions for my students. I made a conspicuous show of enthusiasm when the project was announced.

A timeline of meetings was scheduled for brainstorming and drafting of the co-teaching model. A deadline was set of about a month. I negotiated to start the process by submitting a bulleted outline of suggested strategies for the model. The basic process would be to start with my outline and then have gen-ed teachers provide feedback to be incorporated into a final document. It seemed logical for me to submit the first draft, since I was the only team member with formal training in co-teaching (switcheroo!). I didn't just write my draft off the top of my head; this wasn't a personal manifesto. I consulted textbooks from credential courses and drew on all I had learned directly and indirectly from the credential process. The textbooks covered educational psychology and teaching learning-disabled students in the general education classroom.

My research indicated that I should propose the One Teach, One Support model of co-teaching. It seemed like the best approach for this school, our teaching team, and our particular students. One Teach, One Support relies on strong leadership from the gen-ed teacher in delivering reciprocal direct instruction from the head of the class. The resource specialist strategically supports the lesson delivery with student interventions tailored to each phase of the lesson. Basically, I was already moving toward this approach, but my draft model increased the level of coordinated activity such that the two teachers were explicitly acting in concert throughout the lesson.

One Teach, One Support seemed appropriate to our particular students for a few reasons. First, our learning-disabled students, most of whom were in specialized non-inclusive classrooms the previous year, needed to learn how to respond to gen-ed teachers as authority figures and learning leaders. Like their gen-ed teachers, the learning-disabled students seemed dubious about this transition to inclusion. They needed a structure that emphasized this new reality in an emphatic way. Second, learning-disabled students should eventually lose their dependency on special-ed staff, especially in middle school. High school will require even higher levels of independence for students to remain in inclusion. Finally, this model best accommodated my limitations as a new teacher, since the more-experienced gen-ed teachers would lead in the planning and delivery of content lessons.

In the process of brainstorming, I provided information about the Teach, Teach model of co-teaching, which is considered the gold standard, the ultimate strategy. This model uses flexible grouping of a classroom's students to have two teachers delivering direct instruction in parallel. Student groupings can fluctuate throughout the year based on the skills and content begin taught. Two small groups as opposed to one large group should give teachers a more granular level of differentiation, especially for struggling students. Groupings don't have to be homogenous such as struggling or overachiever. They can be deliberately heterogeneous to give struggling students exposure to positive peer models. The floorplan is designed with boards and seating to accommodate this parallel arrangement.

There was a consensus among the teachers that the Teach, Teach approach would be problematic for our site. Student groupings would probably fall into struggling versus proficient, with the learning-disabled students almost always grouped with the struggling. This mild segregation could lead to stigmatization, and in one of its few directives about inclusion, the district administration had said that it wanted to avoid any kind of stigmatization. There was also a lack of proper spaces for the parallel instruction: that might lead resource specialists to pull out the struggling students to separate rooms, meaning the possibility of stigmatization. Regarding curriculum, Teach, Teach, if executed faithfully, which means in a manner leading to proficiency in grade-level standards, would require a level of joint planning that the faculty wasn't ready for. Most likely, Teach, Teach would descend into the gen-ed teachers coaxing the resource specialist into teaching learning-disabled students modified grade-level content in a separate grouping or even a separate room. This faculty was disciplined enough to resist that temptation, and they chose One Teach, One Support. My co-teachers might wish that I was a better instructional aide, but they were compliant enough to refrain from outright defiance of the inclusion mandate.

My version of One Teach, One Support covered each teacher's role during instructional delivery plus it suggested classroom accommodations and curricular modifications. The basic daily approach of this model was the gen-ed teacher planning and delivering one content lesson for the entire class, and then the two teachers implementing moderate accommodations and modifications to support the learning-disabled students in achieving the lesson's learning goal: in a nutshell, differentiation. Optimally, the two teachers will also share strategies that incorporate differentiation directly into the lesson design before delivery.

The phases of lesson delivery were broken down into new information, guided practice, and independent practice, with each teacher's movements choreographed for each phase. Procedures were included for intervening in disruptive behavior arising during instruction, with procedures mapped to each phase of delivery. The gen-ed teacher led behavior interventions during lecture, with the resource specialist remaining in the background, in a somewhat restrained role. But in guided practice and independent practice, the two teachers act independently, with each one intervening alone in whatever problems they encounter.

Basic classroom accommodations included alternative testing procedures such as a separate room for extra time, reading directions aloud, allowing use of a calculator, and clarification and brief reteaching of directions. Of course, I found a way to include flexibility in the accommodations, which involved the teacher making arrangements for the student to have extra time on major assignments, including calling parents early in a progress problem.

To foster teamwork in the IEP process, my model defined the gen-ed teacher's role in the planning phase of the annual IEP review. Gen-ed teachers were asked to provide work samples, test samples, grades, and a written qualitative evaluation in the weeks prior to the IEP meeting. About two weeks before the IEP due date, a conference was held with the resource specialist and gen-teacher teacher to review the data and preview the teacher's concerns. Guidelines for communicating about IEP matters were established for exchanges between resource specialist and the gen-ed teachers. Gen-ed teachers on a teaching team attended the IEP annual review as a group, with each teacher presenting a quick update on student progress over the past twelve months; they were also available for parent questions. After the annual IEP review was held, and the parents consented to the new IEP, it was distributed to the faculty. The resource specialist and gen-ed teacher worked together to implement the accommodations, modifications, and services defined in the IEP.

My model did not specify any guidelines for the resource specialist and gen-ed teacher to collaborate on lesson design. I felt that the faculty at El Dorado Middle was not ready to share their space with me that deeply. On the other hand, the model did not discourage or prohibit joint lesson planning, so maybe some progress could be made. Despite this mild disappointment, I felt that the model would foster rapport and teamwork, and improve our team's response to student needs.

The written model was completed on deadline and distributed to the faculty. I had been slightly heavy-handed in moving my draft forward and initiating next steps when the project bogged down in overplanning. Feedback and brainstorming meetings had been held, and I had also received written feedback. To conclude the project, I basically gathered all the feedback, wrote the final document, printed it, placed a copy in each teacher's mailbox, and announced the new model in an email: "Dear Inclusion Teachers, Please find in your mailbox the final draft of our new model of collaborative teaching." No one objected, so I took that to mean we had agreement on how to proceed with collaborative teaching. Eventually, Betsy showed the finished model to the principal, who made no acknowledgement of it, at least not to me.

Improved Foreign Relations

The effectiveness of the seventh-grade inclusion team improved with the co-teaching model in place. In addition to the teaching model, the improvement was supported by co-teaching with my caseload in both language arts and math and by a common prep period for the entire team. Moreover, my entanglements with the resource specialist for eighth grade and her teaching team were eliminated, simplifying my life dramatically. I had one straightforward role for the rest of the school year: support and supervise all activities of the seventh-grade inclusion students. We were one month into second semester, it was January 2004, and there were twenty-four students on my caseload.

I began to manage my time in the inclusion classrooms better. It probably helped that my co-teachers now knew that there was a method underlying my movements and decisions. I was clearly perceiving the different phases of instruction and providing the right intervention at each phase. These interventions included simple mechanical maneuvers such as making sure students' notetaking materials were out and ready or that books were open to the right page. When lessons were underway, I visually monitored students to make sure they were taking timely notes during lecture and on pace with the teacher's prompts during guided practice. When I noticed a student who was seriously off the pace, I would gently fix up their understanding. Independent practice gave me an opportunity to visit key students and offer tutoring. At the end of the period, I ensured that my students used their planners to communicate homework assignments to their parents. For my students at-risk for school failure, I paid closer attention to them at key points in instruction. I located their seats in strategic areas of the room to improve access for checking understanding and tutoring. For some students, I would sign off on the planner every day.

A few students were identified as needing structured behavior intervention. These interventions involved a meeting with parents and the drafting of a behavior support plan, which is a basic written plan to be followed by teachers, parents, and students. These behavior plans were occasionally a follow-up to a suspension. My approach to these plans involved increased communication with parents about student progress, typically on a weekly basis. The teacher and I would also look at seating and move the student's seat in ways that minimized distractions. The gen-ed teacher would be asked to visit the student's desk frequently and make frequent checks for understanding. Finally, I would check in with the student more frequently, in non-contingent ways, to help the student feel welcome in this new experience of inclusion (i.e. I tried to cheer them up).

In general, relationships were forming and rapport was deepening for all constituencies in my teaching practice: parents, teachers, students, and even struggling students. With improved communication came an emerging sense of ease in which we basically took care of business without too many problems or conflicts. Maybe we even enjoyed our jobs for brief intervals. Gen-ed teachers started taking care with my students. Harsh language and reprimands were visibly decreasing, and there was less calling students out in class. Modifications based on flexibility were starting to appear: shortened spelling lists for my students, for instance.

By last quarter of the school year, meaning the second half of second semester, my inclusion practice started to click, especially in language arts. My students were engaging in reading lessons. Their materials were ready, they were following the teacher's directions, and they were at least ready to receive a prompt from me when I visited their desk. I could keep them on task without excessive tutoring, even if they were a bit reluctant at times. Disruptive misbehaviors were minimal, at least when I was present. For nearly all students, weekly vocabulary homework and quizzes were being completed, aided by curricular modifications, especially in Ann's class.

My students started to figure out where in the core curriculum (i.e. combined social studies and language arts) they could shine and where they would falter. They experienced success keeping their reading-lecture notebooks, weekly vocabulary packet for homework, and project-oriented tasks such as medieval coloring book, building a castle, making an illustrated timeline, and designing a knight's armor (i.e. Ann at her best). Each project played out over a few days at least, giving my students the psychological space to approach the assignments in a way that fit their learning style. Tests remained problematic, whether quiz or unit level. My students almost never scored above a C on a test, and frequently scored lower. A traditional test is where the student will experience the greatest level of impairment from their learning disability, because it puts strenuous demands on long-term recall without providing any memory aides (i.e. the gotcha approach). Alternative testing formats are a part of inclusion strategy, including the provision of memory aides such as open-note tests, but my skills were limited at that point. I was just pleased to see some strength coming through on the process-oriented assignments. On an individualzed basis, memory aides like open-note tests can be specified in a student's IEP.

It became clear that the real struggle of inclusion at the middle school level would be to help students convert text-based information into long-term memories. Compared to elementary school, middle school asks students to comprehend fairly long passages of informational text on their own and relatively quickly. In addition, middle school asks students to form inferences about textual information: to think on their own. I had a repertoire of classroom maneuvers that I implemented in trying to help my students cope with reading tasks, especially in the case of responding to textual material in writing. I checked in with key students every few minutes. I moved between students quickly, since if I was stuck with one student, others would go without help. I coached students on how to write a truncated response when they were starting to get bogged down in worries about spelling or grammar. I would jump in and write a few words for a student if that helped them continue: I might scratch in a sentence starter on the fly.

In general, my students would fall behind in any writing task. My repertoire provided a kind of patchwork, minimal engagement in the demanding parts of the curriculum that involved a rapid written response to textual information. I was fighting against the logistical limitations of tutoring on the fly, student weaknesses in spelling and writing due to deficits in prior learning, and the neurological effects of learning disabilities.

We were bumping up against the limits of our version of One Teach, One Support. Further improvements in student performance would probably have to come from joint lesson planning: in other words, adjustments to the way information was delivered and to the timing of learning tasks. To their credit, the gen-ed teachers had somewhat shaped their instructional delivery to the needs of students with learning disabilities. There was marked chunking of information, with extra time for written responses in each chunk, with written responses chunked too. The teachers were giving clear, firm expectations for performance at the start of the lesson, and for directions in each step of reading and writing tasks. There was definitely a step-by-step quality to the lessons, and the teachers were adapting to the requirements of the hybrid inclusion setting. We were by no means optimal, but the gen-ed teachers definitely seemed to be on the right trajectory.

That was the situation in language arts. In math, which was a pre-algebra curriculum, Alfredo basically continued teaching the upper-achieving half of the classroom, which was arrayed tightly in the seats closest to the teacher at the head of the room, without much concern for how that impacted the inclusion students, who were located at the outskirts of the room, farthest from the teacher, almost out of sight. The situation described two sections ago basically continued through to the end of the year. Alfredo was a well-organized master of reciprocal direct instruction. His routinized and highly-regimented teaching led to impressive levels of engagement and achievement among the overachievers and the upper half of the minimalists, meaning it didn't work very well for most of my students.

At the last quarter of second semester, most of my students were losing touch with the demanding pre-algebra curriculum. To improve their performance during instruction, I employed active monitoring by standing or sitting at the back of their aisles. As soon I detected misbehavior such as drifting off or interfering with a classmate, I moved forward and prompted the student back on task. A few of my students were able to engage in the homework. My strategic prompting helped them go deeper than they would have without my presence. These students would occasionally ask me for help on their own volition. And they were able to minimally pass tests or nearly pass. For most of my students, though, my constant visual monitoring merely helped reduce the intensity of their misbehavior. Nearly all of my students could capture the new information part of the lesson in their notebooks, and even follow along sporadically with guided practice, but they experienced intense frustration when it was time to develop solutions independently during independent practice: they couldn't apply the new information on their own.

As we moved into the last quarter of the year, Alfredo offered to handle the seventh-grade inclusion classes on his own. He said that he was comfortable handling the situation by himself, and that my time might be better spent on the planning work for my upcoming IEPs. Alfredo confided in me that the eighth grade resource specialist had not made much of an impact on the seventh graders in first semester. The offer of extra prep time was enticing. I took him up on it, missing many periods of math toward the end of the year and using those periods to prep for IEPs. My feeling was that Alfredo was not ready for the kind of joint planning that it would take to improve student performance past what we had done. Maybe it was logistics: we didn't even know each other until second semester, and by then, his courses were well underway. I had worked with Ann and Betsy since the first days of school, and Ann had advised me on how to handle my intervention reading course. Therefore, it seemed, the language arts teachers made deeper inroads into inclusion strategies.

In general, low-achieving schools and low-achieving students perform better in language arts. Statewide testing shows the same trend for all of the state's students: more students are proficient in language arts than math. Possibly joint planning should include those who set the subject-matter standards: possibly one set of math standards for each grade level fails to account for the actually diversity of ability levels found among the student population. Alfredo's offer was very timely, since neither the school administration nor I would have made it through that school year intact without me devoting that extra time to IEP planning. My workload, it seemed to me, was disproportionally weighted toward teaching. Neither Alfredo nor I asked the principal what she thought of the arrangement.

Individual Human Misery

Increased effectiveness of my co-teaching strategies in second semester opened up resources for deepening my relationships with key students. As I approached the second half of the semester, I was able to identify students on my caseload at-risk for school failure and to implement plans that revolved around partnerships with parent, teacher, and student. My credential training taught me to see all parties as collaborators: to improve student performance, the special-ed professional increases communication and cooperation between parents, teachers, and even students. For the co-teaching side, my part of the plans consisted of providing a combination of direct assistance (i.e. tutoring during class time) and consulting with the gen-ed teacher on how to improve their relationship with the student. The consulting had the greatest impact, since the problem behaviors involved either a conflict with the gen-ed teacher or difficulties with the curriculum.

Three brief case studies from this period can provide a glimpse of how a behavior support plan might work. Johnny was mild-mannered, White, of medium height and slight build, well-groomed with long-but-trim hair, dressed fashionably in casual combinations of sport shirts, jeans, and athletic shoes. Johnny was falling behind in language arts and his grade was falling. He would fail soon. He was a student in Ann's class. He was not in my reading intervention course. Johnny's mother was a teacher in a nearby school. When she called Ann to discuss the situation, Ann told her that Johnny just sits quietly in class but does not engage in the work and that he doesn't record homework in his planner or turn it in. Basically, Johnny was not disruptive. He was a nice kid but he just wasn't trying. From a clinical standpoint, Johnny was experiencing the misbehavior of giving up without trying. Frankly, Johnny was so quiet that I didn't even know he was one of my students until his mother called. This is fairly common in inclusion settings. Some students with learning disabilities become masters of disguise and go incognito. Students experiencing disruptive behaviors draw everyone's attention toward them, creating the opportunity of stealth for others.

Johnny's mother was incensed both at Ann's dispassionate objectivity about the failing grade and at my ignorance of her son's presence in the classroom. Ann was obtusely making the point that in her opinion it should have been my responsibility to keep track of Johnny's performance, but I can justly blame her for never bringing the situation to my attention. Ann and I swung into action after the principal called me into her office to tell me that mother had called to complain about Ann. In my conversations with mother, she complained about Ann's strictness and lack of flexibility. The principal, Ann, and I met with the mother to develop a behavior support plan.

The plan centered on increased partnership with the parent. In the plan, Ann and I would both check Johnny's understanding frequently at key points in the lesson, and both teachers would conduct a daily planner check. It was understood that I would try to lead in these accommodations. I checked with Ann every Friday about Johnny's progress and made a weekly progress report to mother: consequences or rewards ensued at home depending on Johnny's performance in language arts. Johnny's performance improved. He maintained a grade of C or better for the rest of the year. I recall that Johnny had maintained a passing grade in math throughout the school year. He had given up in the subject area in which his learning disability had the greatest impact.

Juanito was suspended for fighting in school. He was Hispanic, of medium height and stocky build, dark-skinned with close-cropped black hair, handsome, well-groomed, and dressed fashionably in casual combinations of sport shirts, jeans, and athletic shoes. And I remember that he had a nice parka. The principal summoned me to a conference with her after Juanito's third suspension in a month. None of Juanito's suspensions were related to his behavior in the classrooms where I was a co-teacher, nor was he a student in my reading course. The suspensions involved bullying schoolmates in locations at school outside the classrooms. Even though the suspensions were not directly related to academics, the principal felt that Juanito was at-risk for a change of placement to a restrictive setting. Moreover, his grades were low, and he was at-risk for failing language arts. The principal asked me to develop a behavior support plan to help Juanito avoid further suspensions.

To develop the plan, I applied training in Functional Behavioral Analysis, which I had received from the district and credential training: in a nutshell, misbehavior is a function of the events that precede it and the consequences that follow it. A popular illustration is the way some students disrupt class because a trip to the principal's office provides relief from the stress of dealing with their learning disability on a tough task: even punishment is more tolerable than reading for some students. The function of the misbehavior in this situation is relief from the stress of the classroom: to escape stress, in other words. The best way to deal with this escape behavior is to adjust reading instruction to minimize stress. A behavior plan defines a method for doing that.

I held a conference with Ann to learn about Juanito's performance in language arts. I was a co-teacher in his section. She said that he was basically quiet but didn't engage with the classwork or homework independently. His engagement improved, she told me, when she visited his desk and provided one-on-one instruction. She was concerned about his lack of independence on the grade-level content. Occasionally, Juanito would get drawn into mischief by students with chronic problem behaviors but he never initiated it on his own. Juanito's passive style was the same in math: quiet, not disruptive, but minimal independent engagement with the content.

I didn't conduct a full functional analysis, but I made a hypothesis about the cause of the suspensions. Juanito's experience of minimal engagement was leaving him disaffected and probably a little angry: possibly peers were teasing him about his lack of success. My plan took the approach of improving Juanito's classroom experience. If he felt closer to his teachers, and experienced some success, he would be less likely to engage in aggression toward peers or succumb to their teasing.

I developed a behavior plan, and then met with Juanito's mother and the principal to initiate it. When I spoke with the mother to arrange the meeting, she told me that Juanito was a good kid but he could use some guidance and structure. She felt that he was a little headstrong. She also expressed that she was frustrated that no one had consulted with her until after her son had been suspended for a third time. My conversations with the mother were in English, which she was reasonably fluent in, but it might have been more respectful to have an English interpreter on hand. Interpreters are an integral part of the IEP process.

My behavior plan for Juanito was similar to Johnny's. The gen-ed teachers and I visited Juanito's desk frequently to check his understanding, before he fell too far behind. Optimally, we checked with him at the start of the assignment to prevent problems down the line. Teachers made sure to acknowledge Juanito every day at the start of the period to help him feel welcome: we literally took care to say "Hello Juanito. How has your day been so far?" The plan included provisions for flexible deadlines and extra help on major assignments.

In collaboration with Ann, I held a weekly status call with Juanito's mother. She was definitely ready to do her part when Juanito needed to put extra effort into an assignment. In all my conversations with her, she came across as an evenhanded authority figure who took her responsibility to the school system seriously. She was a good collaborator, and I privately vowed to keep an eye on Juanito, including extra non-contingent contact (i.e. cheering him up), to help him feel at ease. Once the plan was underway for a couple of weeks, Juanito adopted a different tone toward his gen-ed teachers and me, especially in language arts. He had become an active learner. He was following the daily lesson and asking for help. He was resisting mischief incited by others. He opened up to me in non-contingent conversations: he even asked questions about how the inclusion program worked. Basically, he was more positive, active, and engaged.

Juanito was in the section of language arts, Ann's section, where my co-teaching was having the greatest effect. Amazingly, the change in Juanito sparked a change in Ann's approach to him and me. She and his other teachers found a way to be more accommodating. They were flexible with requirements and time on assignments, and they used a supportive tone with Juanito, even when he struggled. Juanito had no more discipline problems that year. The rest of the semester was basically positive, with acceptable levels of achievement.

Matthew was one of the underachievers in my reading intervention course in both semesters. He was White, Anglo, medium height, stocky with an athletic build, fair-skinned with close-cropped blond hair, handsome, well-groomed, and dressed fashionably in casual combinations of sport shirts, jeans, and athletic shoes. He looked like he would make a good guard in little league football. Matthew was always on my radar, front and center. His serious troubles didn't start until second semester was underway. That was when the principal alerted me to an increasing frequency of discipline referrals and removals from class in Ann's core block in the periods when the instructional aide served as surrogate for the co-teacher.

The discipline referrals involved Matthew ignoring the lesson, making oppositional statements when redirected to the task, and hurling insults at the teacher before finally being sent to the principal's office. The principal asked me to develop a behavior support plan to stem the increase in removals from class. Matthew's favorite subject was math. He made a conspicuous show of interest in Alfredo's lectures and guided practice, and attempted tests. Matthew wasn't really learning at grade level but he somehow stayed on Alfredo's good side and received a minimally passing grade.

In my reading intervention course, Matthew would typically give up on the assignment until I visited his desk and tutored him for a bit. To keep him going after tutoring, I would check in with him every five minutes or so. He would sit quietly during new information and guided practice, but he liked to slip in a bit of fun during independent practice. One of his favorite distractions was to fold a piece of notebook paper into a triangular shaped "football" and then engage a nearby peer in a contest of kicking field goals (i.e. striking the paper with index finger through a classmate's fingers formed into uprights). Some days I turned this pastime into a reward: complete a certain amount of the lesson and get a certain number of minutes at the end of class to play football. Matthew's favorite reward was to play football with me, a privilege which I earned intermittently. Matthew was a reluctant learner, and sometimes I was frustrated with the level of prompting needed to keep him on task. But I never experienced oppositional behaviors, and I had not needed to remove him from class. We were kind of pals in my course.

My relationship with Matthew in reading class paid some dividends in the language arts period of Ann's core block, which was when I was co-teacher. Matthew would engage in the assignment with me prompting him. Matthew always needed time to think before writing, and when finally ready, he wrote slowly and carefully. I tried to give Matthew enough tutoring, including written starters, for him to keep up with the pace of instruction. But, inevitably, he could only finish the first half of the assignment. He could approach the lesson but not quite master it. I attributed Matthew's slowness of processing to his auditory processing disorder. He needed extra time to process language-based tasks. He was struggling with the pace of grade-level instruction and it was making him irritable. I should note that in my reading course Matthew was working on modified content at grade level four to five.

When I called Matthew's mother to discuss the discipline referrals, she gave me a pretty good theory of the reasons for Matthew's increasingly chronic misbehavior. Matthew was accustomed to a more supportive level of instruction. He actually preferred the specialized classroom over studying in inclusion with his non-disabled peers. Matthew was considered a good student when he studied language arts in Resource Day Class, which was the term used to describe a homogeneous grouping of learning-disabled students studying modified grade-level content with their resource specialist as the teacher. Basically, Matthew didn't like inclusion, especially not the strictness of Ann, so he was acting out, probably in hope of being expelled from school. Escape was the function of Matthew's misbehavior.

A power struggle was forming between Ann and Matthew. Ann wanted to hold Matthew accountable for his misconduct. She felt that was what he needed. She was suspicious of giving accommodations to a "defiant" student. She felt that Matthew's difficulties were rooted in poor motivation and a lack of discipline at home. Whenever Ann called home to discuss Matthew's falling behind, it seemed to Ann that mother made excuses. When I spoke to mother about Matthew's motivation, she felt that Ann was out of touch and inflexible.

While I was developing the behavior plan and waiting for a meeting with the principal, Ann, and mother, I applied a few strategies to improve Matthew's conduct, especially in language arts. I made more visits to Matthew's desk. I emphasized encouragement and supportive speech. I found time to do more tutoring in language arts and my reading course. Matthew's rapport with me improved, and we had a few good conversations about his negative view of inclusion. But his conduct in language arts continued to decline, with near daily removals in periods outside my presence.

Most concerning, Matthew was suspended from school twice toward the end of the semester for fighting on school grounds, and he was suspended once for aggressive language toward Ann. The suspensions for fighting involved Matthew striking a classmate from out of nowhere. One assault was in my reading course. Matthew entered the classroom on time at the bell, walked directly up to an unsuspecting seated classmate, and punched him hard on the side of the face, unprovoked and without warning. Matthew's resentment toward Ann and inclusion generally was spilling over onto the playground and other classrooms.

The meeting for the behavior plan and subsequent implementation of it helped Ann open up a little. Now my conversations with Ann featured updates on how modified content such as shortened tests were helping and how Ann was checking Matthew's understanding at each step of a writing project, with Matthew making some progress in each period. Removals were down. Matthew was getting some work done in each class period, even if he was a bit short of mastery. Despite the improved progress, Ann still felt Matthew held out on her as a result of mother's alleged permissiveness. Over the course of numerous phone conversations, I formed a productive and supportive relationship with Matthew's mother. This relationship helped me serve as peacemaker between Ann and the mother, the two main parties in the power struggle.

Just when it seemed that Ann was warming up to Matthew, and Matthew was at least minimally complying with Ann's assignments, Matthew was suspended for alcohol possession and consumption at school. He was caught sipping vodka from a clear plastic water bottle. After the suspension, Matthew's mother and the principal formed a plan to have Matthew re-evaluated by the school psychologist for the eligibility category of Emotional Disturbance. The motivation for the evaluation was to have Matthew placed in a Special Day Class (SDC) with special services for children with emotional disturbance. Or possibly Matthew could study in the regular SDC for seventh grade at El Dorado Middle. SDC refers to a small homogeneous group of students who basically spend the entire day in one classroom headed by a special-ed teacher assisted by one or two instructional aides; curriculum is typically modified to below grade level. The principal was going to leave it to the school psychologist to lead the placement decision. When I spoke to the mother after the decision to re-evaluate had been made, she said that she just wanted to get Matthew away from the gen-ed faculty. She felt that they were too defensive and inflexible.

Matthew went on to complete the school year in Ann's class. Even after the decision to re-evaluate, Ann continued her newfound tone of accommodation and modification, and she was actually quite attentive and flexible for Matthew. He basically stopped making trouble for her. Maybe he was relieved to know this would be his last year in inclusion. Matthew had passing (although not stellar) grades in all his classes by the end of the school year, although Ann still insisted that he could do better if his mother wasn't so permissive.

All three students had stable family backgrounds. All three mothers had occupations outside the home. Johnny and Juanito lived at home with their two-parent families. Matthew's family had experienced a divorce in the past: he lived with his mother, and a prospective step-father was on the scene. As far as I could tell, none of the families were experiencing economic hardship.

Ann was at the center of all three of these case studies. Her faith in punishment and inflexible approach to teaching meant that she was going to have a difficult time with inclusion students. One on hand, Ann was holding all her students equally accountable for meeting grade-level standards. On the other hand, she was defying the mandate of special-ed law to provide whatever reasonable accommodation will allow the student to study the regular curriculum with typical peers. Ann, I inferred, was making a statement that only students who can be held accountable for meeting standards without special treatment should be in her gen-ed classroom. But the California Department of Education (CDE) was making the point that students who can meet or even just approximate grade-level standards with accommodations should be in her classroom.

Ann was responding to her gut instinct about the role of maintaining high expectations for all and for the way special treatment might disrupt her classroom. But I was responding to information from the CDE extolling the virtues of the new flexible classroom in including all in a utopia of accommodation and tolerance. Partly, the CDE based its philosophy of inclusion on research that demonstrated special treatment for individuals with special needs will not adversely affect typical classmates. I was exposed to the CDE rhetoric in my research-based credential training. Ann, as the second semester progressed, started to gradually respond to the CDE's philosophy, as represented by me, and she started to experience a reduction in problem behaviors and increase in academic progress.

In contrast to the power struggles rooted in Ann's rigid adherence to high standards, Alfredo had kept the peace in math by adopting a path-of-least-resistance approach. Basically, any student could earn a low passing grade by recording lecture notes in their notebook, scratching some kind of solution in the notebook during guided practice, and not being too disruptive during independent practice. Students could pass on effort: tests would raise your grade but not lead to failure, and when homework was graded, it was more on effort than accuracy. Alfredo could be accused of condoning low expectations and giving a false impression of the student's mastery. But, in reality, the faculty was grateful for his permissiveness, for the time being. To his credit, Alfredo's non-disabled students applied themselves diligently and scored well on tests, and even a few of my students showed solid mastery on tests.

Final unit-level assignments in language arts tended to involve writing at length. To pass any language arts class in Ann's department, learning-disabled students had to face their two greatest challenges: writing fluently and passing tests. It was not possible for them to handle these tasks without significant modifications and accommodations. Betsy realized this fact sooner than Ann, but she eventually responded to this reality as well.

Abigail, the seventh-grade science teacher, taught all my students once a day, dispersed across a few periods. She also taught all the non-disabled students of the grade level. She was considered part of the inclusion team, but she never really participated as a full member. A trim young forty-something mother of medium height, Abigail's fashion statement was similar to Ann's and the rest of the faculty: business casual with cotton dress slacks, cotton oxford blouse, designer leather shoes, and reddish-brown hair cropped in stylish bob. Neither the instructional assistants nor I ever supported her directly. My efforts, and really the team's efforts, were focused on math and language arts, which were the subject areas monitored by NCLB in its school accountability measurements, even though statewide testing measured proficiency in science.

Abigail tended to be calm and supportive in her interactions with the inclusion team. She basically followed a method similar to Alfredo's in basing the course grade more on participation than tests. She was proficient at differentiation: her lessons were well-organized and featured a visual approach with handouts, overheads, and hands-on activities. But the reading level of the materials and complexity of the discussions were not quite up to grade level. She might have been accused of maintaining low expectations. But no one on the inclusion team would have done that. We were grateful for her ingenuity. She was an active contributor to the inclusion team's group approach to IEP meetings. She almost always had something positive to say about the student, and she conveyed the impression that the student enjoyed her class.

There was an elective period every day. About half of my inclusion students were in intervention math or reading in that period, which were taught by the resource specialists (i.e. eighth-grade resource specialist (math), sixth-grade resource specialist (reading), and me (reading)), and we didn't need much support from each other. In general, students with chronic problem behaviors were placed in the intervention sections, which made the situation easier for the elective teachers. The rest of my students were either in Spanish, woodshop, or art for their elective. These courses were not considered vital to the inclusion effort to teach grade-level material. The teachers managed to accommodate, modify, or individualize enough for my students to succeed. I rarely heard from an elective teacher, and when I did, it was typically to praise a student.

Emerging Truce

Spring, meaning the last quarter of second semester, was IEP season for my caseload. Mostly by chance, most of my due dates for annual IEP reviews fell in second semester. This was a fortuitous circumstance. Now that one quarter had passed since the reorganization of the school into the correct team-teaching model, the seventh-grade inclusion team finally enjoyed some cohesion and camaraderie. A daily joint prep period with teammates and dedicating every day to just my seventh graders made the task of holding twenty-four IEP reviews at least somewhat reasonable.

I used the joint prep period to maximum effect for peacemaking. Two weeks before each IEP review date, I sat down with the student's key teachers and interviewed them about the student's performance. I tried to hold these meetings during prep time, although some spilled over into afterschool. I preferred prep time, because afterschool meetings might cross into uncompensated time, and I wanted to tread lightly on that precious resource. I emphasized in-person meetings over asking for a written evaluation form. These meetings gave me an opportunity to soft sell the flexibility approach and its basic principles of accommodation and modification. I think it's fair to characterize these meetings as pleasant occasions for both teachers. By the middle of spring, they were a regular part of our work week.

From the perspective of Trungpa's spiritual warriorship, I applied the skill of nonjudgmental listening. I made sure to listen with an open mind, with empathy for the speaker's reality, and by refraining from defensive speech. In Shambhala Buddhism, this form of communication is seen as a form of relief in itself: problems will often start to solve themselves. In this way, I learned a lot about gen-ed teachers' values, and I saw that they were not totally obstinate, and that they were staring to open up to inclusion.

For most IEP meetings, the entire seventh-grade inclusion team attended as a group, including science and electives. This was not the case in first semester, when the team members would attend one at a time or didn't attend at all. Actually, I can't even remember one IEP meeting from first semester, partially because a few IEPs went overdue and I didn't get to them until second semester. In the meeting, each teacher gave a short presentation of present levels for their subject area. The teachers were careful to be constructive and refrain from anger or casting blame. I somehow remained firmly in the lead as the designated moderator. When the meeting moved to the planning phase, the teachers stayed and offered feedback even though planning was primarily my responsibility. Every IEP meeting that I held, surprisingly, concluded with the parent(s) giving their consent to all aspects of the new IEP.

My success as moderator was probably due to my pre-meeting conferences, where neither the gen-ed teachers nor I were always so agreeable. Gen-ed teachers knew that they could speak frankly to me and that I would try to address their concerns, so they spared the parents the tough talk that they freely directed at me. But the full-team IEP meetings helped heal the distrust that had been undermining the team-teaching initiative, for parents and teachers. Toward the end of the school year, I occasionally dismissed the gen-ed faculty from the meeting after they gave their present levels, and a few times I even dismissed the principal. Concluding those meetings by myself was a way of giving back some of the prep time that the team members had spent with me throughout the year.

My credential training allowed me to maintain a pretty solid grip on the IEP process, but there was one aspect of the process that escaped me that year. Each IEP student should be re-evaluated every three years: this evaluation is called the triennial IEP. The triennial review involves formal assessment of psychological (i.e. cognitive), social-emotional, and academic factors. The assessments generate data that the IEP team uses to determine whether the current placement is providing an educational benefit. In middle school, the triennial is typically a rubber stamp for the current placement, but technically it might lead to a change of placement. My teaching load of co-teaching for four periods, one period of gen-ed reading intervention, and one prep period (divided between reading intervention, school-wide behavior interventions, IEP planning, and IEP meetings) did not give me enough time to conduct the formal academic assessments for triennials.

I received great training at the site. In coordination with a credential course, an assessment specialist for the district served as a mentor for administering the academic assessments. A master teacher in her last months before retirement, the assessment specialist had been available to the school for all triennials. She retired after first semester. She thoroughly trained me in a hands-on fashion. But there just wasn't enough prep time in this model of instruction to conduct the assessments, which take at minimum about three uninterrupted hours for each student.

The district allowed the formal assessments to be replaced by a file review for triennials. A file review consists of generating performance data through work samples, statewide tests, interviews, classroom observations, historical files, and other non-formal sources. I conducted three triennials by means of this shortcut, in cooperation with the school psychologist, who was part-time for our site. I think we did an honest job, but not the best or most respectful one. Parents must consent to the file review, by waiving the formal assessments, and they didn't seem to mind the shortcut. My sales experience came in handy on this issue.

In general, collaborative relationships started to form with my colleagues on the seventh-grade inclusion team as the second semester progressed. As I just described, we really got our act together in our annual IEP reviews. I actually looked forward to those meetings, especially since they afforded parents an opportunity to encounter the team model in a positive way. On the co-teaching side, the team's teachers finally started consulting with me on classroom accommodations and curricular modifications. On their own volition, they updated me on the progress of modifications they had made such as breaking a writing project into smaller chunks for individual students or sending home extra-time packets to get parents involved in projects.

My two roles in co-teaching were joint planning and directly supporting lesson delivery. Of the two roles, I had the greatest impact in joint planning. My consulting with the gen-ed teachers led to changes in lesson design and individualized modifications that actually created a pathway to success for all my students. Feed a man today, and he may starve tomorrow. Teach a man how to fish, and he may feed the entire village for years. Direct support was fraught with logistical limitations that guaranteed limited effectiveness. For push inclusion to work at all, the gen-ed teachers needed to embrace the challenge instead of looking to pass it off to the resource specialist.

The gen-ed teachers on the seventh-grade inclusion team were progressively opening up to the challenge as the year progressed. They were even making gestures of encouragement toward me. But we, meaning the gen-ed teachers and me, still had some reservations. One Teach, One Support, our co-teaching model of choice, had some limitations. It seemed like co-teaching in general had some limitations in terms of the benefits to the students with learning disabilities. Students were starting to engage in the academic content to a significant degree, but it was a minimal, patchwork type of engagement. We all wondered about how to get more consistent results, meaning how to get the students with learning disabilities more involved.

The research that I had seen on the topic of co-teaching

tended to highlight elementary education and partnerships between gen-ed teachers who volunteered as an outgrowth of their longstanding friendship. Successful co-teaching seemed like an anomaly that wasn't ready for widespread implementation. It seemed speculative.

Privately, I harbored doubts. Maybe students with learning disabilities should study academic subjects in small groups in separate classrooms, taught by their resource specialists, with the specialist collaborating with the subject-matter teachers to develop appropriate curriculum: the Teach, Teach model, basically. Maybe intensive collaborating on curriculum could suffice for inclusion. A highly-qualified resource specialist will have a much higher level of skill than gen-ed teachers. If gen-ed teachers won't accept advice from resource specialists, maybe the specialists should stand on their own. In this doubt, I was indulging the gen-ed teachers in their obstinacy. Their problem, some experts might say, was rooted in "organized" and "working conditions": they could learn the necessary skills if only they would embrace them. Gen-ed teachers had lost sight of what is best for children and resorted to what is easiest for teachers.

I was pleased to see the gen-ed teachers put their reservations aside and open up to the challenge of inclusion, at least to a moderate degree. The teachers started to show the sense of responsibility toward their students with disabilities that must have been behind the teachers' successes up to that point with typical children. I felt that I had helped my teammates reconnect to their inner light and remember their sense of basic goodness. My job was not to support their defensiveness but to represent the requirements of special-ed law, the guidelines of the California Department of Education, and the directives of the district administration.

Peace Accord

During the seventh grade's final writing project, the gen-ed teachers' emerging spirit of accommodation and flexibility rose to a crescendo. The grade-wide project involved developing a persuasive essay on a theme of why a company or an individual should relocate to a country of the student's choosing. The thesis argument was supported by evidentiary paragraphs on topics such as commercial activity, natural wonders, cultural attractions, ethnic history, culinary trends, and natural resources: a perfect integration of written composition and world cultures, the two curriculums of the core block. The essay was converted into a four-fold color brochure with imagery to add the multimedia aspect. Ann and Betsy, my co-teachers for core (both from language arts backgrounds), led their students through all phases of research and composition: picking a topic, locating sources in the library (including online), making notes, crafting the thesis statement, drafting the evidentiary paragraphs, adding a conclusion, formatting the final documents, and editing with revision. The project occupied roughly the last month of school in the core periods.

Ann and Betsy seemed to sense that this writing project was a place where all students might experience success. The spacious pace and step-by-step nature of the research and composition process provided opportunities for intervention. Unlike tests, which typically have intense time pressure and put intensive demands on long-term memory, the research and drafting processes were memory aides in themselves. Moreover, the drafting process had ample opportunities for catching up if the student fell behind.

A year of collaborating and training on issues of inclusion had brought the gen-ed teachers the skills they needed to get every student involved. On the lesson level, the teachers implemented visual supports for each student, which vividly divided the writing process into discernable chunks and acknowledged success at each step. Each chunk was taught in a highly-structured lesson. There were frequent checks for understanding and rapid progress reports if a student fell behind. Materials were stored in the classroom, in ingenious folder-based organizers provided by the teachers, such that students could not lose track of their work in the middle of the project. Ann was especially well-organized. Betsy was close, but sometimes her periods broke down into students retrieving their materials and working on their own, which is less effective than a structured lesson that moves the student forward on one chunk. Ann made an effort to circulate around the room and prompt struggling students, typically mine, when they were faltering on the day's chunk, which helped my students maintain the pace.

On the level of individual modifications and accommodations, relaxed performance standards were applied to my students in key aspects of the writing rubric (the performance criteria). Spelling, fluency, and length were all modified for my students in the direction of modestly lower expectations than those applied to non-disabled classmates.

In first semester, seventh-grade students with learning disabilities had done well in the robot essay, which integrated science instruction with language arts. Each student designed a robot in science class for travel to other planets, including the construction of a model. Then in language arts, each student wrote an essay that described the robot's adaptive traits using a descriptive format. Most of my students finished the entire project, which as it turned out, provided a pilot for the accommodations and flexibility applied in the nation essay. In addition, I think my students were excited to be a part of robots, space travel, and model building. They put aside their power struggle with the gen-ed teachers.

I had not been fully connected during the robot essay. I tended to be present during reading lessons on social studies topics. I learned about the robot model and essay from my students when they went out of their way to show me their work. The project proceeded with almost no direct support from me. I was only slightly more involved with the nation essay. Ann kept me informed when a student was struggling,

and kept me abreast of her project's organization, but basically handled all the teaching on her own. I was more involved
with Betsy. I mostly contributed to the periods where students used Betsy's visual organizers to work on their own
during notetaking and drafting (i.e. turning the notes into
paragraphs). Students had already been trained for the task by
Betsy. She also kept me informed about students who were
struggling and her plans for intervention.

So, Ann and Betsy on their own found a way to include
every student in the year's climactic writing project. These
gen-ed teachers had become positive disciplinarians and
differentiation experts. They were succeeding with students
who had learning disabilities, with almost no direct support
from me. I will, however, claim credit for being an effective collaborator and consultant over the course of the school
year. I had led them to a new level of performance, even
though they would probably have been loath to admit it. All
my students earned a passing grade on the nation project. The
success experienced in writing projects provided students
with some relief from the sore feelings that came with low
scores on curricular tests.

CHAPTER TEN

Metamorphosis

Brinkmanship

Recall that the principal had imposed a performance improvement plan (PIP) on me at the end of my first evaluation conference, which occurred in mid-November. The three possible ratings for the principal's evaluation were proficient, needs improvement, and unsatisfactory. She scored me as needs improvement. She was evaluating me as if I was I tenure candidate, even though tenure was not an issue in any way to a first-year intern like me, who was primarily supervised by the credential program that conducted the three-year-long internship. The district sponsored the internship program.

The first conference consisted of a quick debriefing on the principal's observation of my highly-structured reading lesson on identifying the main point and supporting evidence in an informational text. She basically said my lesson design and instructional delivery were "no too bad" and "pretty good." We spent about two minutes on the lesson. I remember that I offered that I had switched from a workshop model to a highly-structured format, which included reciprocal direct instruction. The principal acknowledged the improvement with a look of mild consternation and a knowing nod. We quickly moved on to the next and final topic of the meeting: forming relationships with my co-teachers and participating in the team-teaching process. Those were the two performance criteria of the PIP, meaning that the route to an evaluation score of proficient rested on my ability to somehow please or otherwise relate to my co-teachers in a favorable manner. The principal didn't give me any advice on how to accomplish that heroic feat. She went over the PIP in a perfunctory, matter-of-fact tone. After our brief conversation about the lesson, she curtly said, "Robert. I'm giving you a score of needs improvement. Here is your copy of the performance improvement plan. I need you to look it over and sign it." I looked it over, signed it, and left without further comment. The meeting lasted about five minutes.

The second and final evaluation conference occurred in early March, after hours a few days after the principal observed my reading lesson on the Triangle Shirtwaist Fire. The principal asked me to accommodate her overtime hours, which was okay with me, since I typically went home well after her. It was a dusky and cold early spring evening, and winter humidity was still in the Delta breeze. We met in her office.

As in the first evaluation conference, we started with a debriefing on the lesson observation. She said that most of the students were following me during instruction, but she noticed a couple of students who spoke to each other without permission. She said that the students clearly liked me, but she wondered whether they were following directions with sufficient attention. "Oh. They like you well enough. They definitely like you," she said. I interpreted this statement to mean that students liked me but maybe didn't respect me. The principal was an authoritarian leader: it is better for a teacher to be feared than loved. Likeability was not considered an attractive trait in a teacher.

From her point about students liking me, she moved on to say that maybe El Dorado Middle wasn't the right population for me: "I'm not sure you're what the students in this school need." I interpreted that to mean that I was indulging the working class in ideals better suited to children from an upper class background similar to my own. I sensed a negative evaluation was coming. My thoughts turned to conceiving a Plan B.

I wanted to draw the principal into some sort of negotiation before she made a decision that might deny me access to the second year of the internship. She concluded her remarks on the lesson by sharing an anecdote about a family friend of hers who had worked as an instructional assistant while studying to be a school psychologist. She thought that I might want to try the same approach. Maybe I should re-evaluate my decision to be a teacher. Maybe I would be better suited to school psychologist. At the end of her pitch, she paused, looked me in the eye, and prompted me for a response by her silence.

I remained calm. I responded by saying that I definitely wanted to keep trying with teaching. I asked for time to discuss her remarks with my credential program. I asked her to delay the conclusion of the evaluation until the last minute at the end of March. She granted my request, and we planned a meeting for the end of March. I had created a space for Plan B, even though I had no idea how that might take shape.

I went straight home after the meeting. I immediately sent a slashing missive to the program coordinator and my credential supervisor. I promised a full complement of retaliatory activities if they didn't intervene in what I felt was the principal's malfeasance. My grievance rested on a few key complaints. The internship was supposed to be a three-year investment in training a new teacher; I felt that the principal's evaluation was impetuous and capricious. The principal evaluated me as if I was a trained teacher but I was only a first-year intern. The principal was under no legal obligation to evaluate me for tenure, and she had several years before she would need to make a permanent contract decision. Finally, I claimed that the credential program had taken me for a fall by sponsoring a scenario in which I was engaged as temporary labor in a distressed school embarking on a doomed inclusion initiative: in other words, a burn and churn scheme.

My gut feeling at that point was that the credential program was run by good people. I complained about them because I figured that would motivate them to help me with the principal. My plan worked. A few days later, Wendy, the program coordinator, and Sheila, my credential supervisor, met with the principal to discuss her evaluation. The district's director of human resources, a dapper thirty-something gentleman in a classic two-piece grey wool suit, joined the meeting. Sheila, my credential supervisor, debriefed me after the meeting. In the meeting, she had told the principal that Project Pipeline, meaning the credential program, was disappointed in the principal and the district. Project Pipeline felt that that the principal was not living up to the program. Sheila said that the principal was sticking with her evaluation for now. Sheila said that she felt that I was a good teacher and that she tried to stick up for me. Sheila also said that the problem for me, in her opinion, was that the principal was intimidated by my popularity with students. Before the meeting, I had asked Sheila to uphold my request to delay the evaluation until the end of March. She did. So I still had two weeks to figure out my next move with the principal. I proceeded to fulfill my teaching assignment as if nothing had happened.

In her evaluation, the principal had glossed over, and even ignored, instructional issues rooted in lesson design. She didn't notice whether the delivery matched the lesson design or if the lesson's learning objective was met. She didn't notice the different elements of the lesson: lecture, guided practice, independent practice, and assessment. She didn't check the appropriateness of the materials and visual supports. Most importantly, she didn't notice whether students with learning disabilities had been taken into account. Did the few minor misbehaviors observed disrupt the lesson to any significant degree?

By focusing on minor misbehavior, which didn't even rise to the level of disruptive behavior, the principal focused in on the area in which she knew that I wanted to challenge her and most other educators. She was protecting her authoritarian turf, standing up for fear and intimidation as motivators. She was an old-fashioned authority figure, and I was the next wave, a positive disciplinarian. She wanted to quarantine me in the back office with the school psychologists, before my positivity became even more contagious. What's more, the psychologist's higher pay would be more compatible with my preppy background.

I was really intrigued by positive discipline. Remember that question about manhood that I had been pursuing since high school, when I had read about the fall of the Nixon administration, as if I had been born to ask it. Is there an alternative to aggression, status seeking, and snobbery? Is there another way to be a man? Or just to be an American, be it man or woman? Positive discipline was an interesting answer, so my motives were probably deeper than the materialistic ones that the principal probably imagined them to be. In addition, I would need to become a teacher first before attempting a move to school psychologist. The immediate financial limitations imposed by fatherhood meant that I needed my teacher's income to carry me through a next step such as a graduate degree in school psychology. The principal's pitch was kind but not workable. I was determined to finish the year at El Dorado Middle and somehow continue the internship next year. The principal had said, "I'm not sure you're what the students in this school need." Maybe she would support me applying at other schools.

The principal based her evaluation on a somewhat superficial visual impression of my class during one or two lessons. But my decision to continue with teaching was based on data. In an earlier chapter covering the second semester of my reading course, I described my practice of collecting each daily assignment, giving it a performance score based on accuracy and other factors, and then posting the score in a progress chart for students to follow. The progress chart showed that seventy percent of the students were participating solidly and demonstrating respectable recall in applying new information in independent practice. The remaining thirty percent, mostly students with learning disabilities, were at least participating minimally. My grading data indicated that I was an *effective* teacher. I also had the principal's feedback that students seemed to like me, which was her misinterpretation of their respect for me. The low number of discipline referrals supported her impression.

On the co-teaching side, I had the crescendo of flexibility shown by gen-ed teachers during the choose-your-nation writing project. Co-teachers and I developed and implemented a version of the One Teach One Support model, which was a textbook adaptation of a research-based strategy to our unique needs. Improvements in the level of collaboration and cooperation between team members were obvious in our team approach to IEP meetings. As described three sections ago, the principal, co-teachers, and I collaborated on behavior support plans that were effective. Maybe the principal thought these successes with other teachers were the reasons why I would make a good instructional assistant or school psychologist. But to me they were reasons to continue to explore and learn as a second-year intern.

I was frustrated that the principal had not mentioned co-teaching in her evaluation conference. My performance improvement plan (PIP) from the fall evaluation conference had focused solely on my relationship with co-teachers. But in the present evaluation conference, she only discussed the lesson observation of my reading course. This lapse confirmed my opinion that she was pursuing an agenda more than a genuine evaluation. I took her lack of conviction as good news. Maybe she wasn't that committed to her evaluation. Maybe I could talk her out of it. I had two weeks to figure out what to say.

Plan B

In general, Project Pipeline, the credential program, was supportive in response to my grievances about the principal's potentially-negative evaluation. Strictly speaking, they may have overstepped their boundaries in criticizing the principal. But Sheila, my credential supervisor, had observed my lesson at the same time as the principal, and she knew my value system from teaching me and mentoring me over the course of the year. Sheila sincerely felt that I was making progress toward becoming a good teacher.

Sheila was in semi-retirement, working as a credential supervisor in teacher education while taking a hiatus from a distinguished career as a teacher in elementary schools. She held a master's in educational leadership. In addition to supervising my practicum requirement (i.e. classroom teaching), Sheila was the instructor for some of my credential courses: she taught me the strategy of reciprocal direct instruction. Her approach to training teachers included an emphasis on adopting the right mindset. Sheila called her approach *relationship-based instruction*, which had roots in research from the positive-discipline camp. "Don't forget to love your students," Sheila advised the credential candidates, "to treat them like kin to the greatest degree you can."

Sheila was not just a supervisor to me but a mentor too. A few times that year, she gave me an opportunity to share my experiences and receive feedback from her, a master teacher. I even met with Sheila offline a couple of times for coffee, which I considered a precious opportunity to study one-on-one with a guru. One of my most memorable coffee-house teachings from her came in response to my exasperation at the way the principal seemed to ignore or downplay the merits of my teaching practice. After the March evaluation conference, I had told Sheila that it seemed like the principal was biased against me for some reason, and she only looked for evidence in support of her prejudice. Sheila advised me that it's not just about what you don't do wrong around the principal, you have to go out of your way to be proactive. Principals have a chicken-little instinct, Sheila said, so you have to act in ways that minimize their anxiety. She also suggested that the anxiety factor might be heightened when a strong male teacher and female principal are involved. Maybe I was a bit stoical and single-minded, Sheila hinted. Sheila recommended overt displays of friendliness and cooperation. I am stoical and single-minded, so I took her advice to heart. From that point forward, I adopted a self-effacing and proactive tone in my relations with the principal.

After the credential program met with the principal regarding my complaints about her evaluation, and the principal persisted in her negative tone, the program director, Wendy, arranged a meeting with the president of the district's chapter of the California Teachers Association (CTA), which is the union that most of the state's teachers belong to. All the teachers in a district belong to the same union. Wendy had been president of the chapter for a few years when she was a teacher in the district. At that point in history, California was a closed-shop, meaning all teachers in a CTA district had to pay dues, even if they declined to join the union. Teachers who joined the union enjoyed benefits such as a legal defense fund and affordable disability coverage. Collective bargaining controls the pay and working conditions of all teachers in the district, regardless of membership. In most districts, the union is seen as a division of the human resources department. The district administration and local union chapter are essentially close friends.

Interns, meaning me, were considered regular full-time teachers and were enrolled in the local union chapter per the closed shop, but I also elected to be a union member. I was a card-carrying member of the CTA (i.e. California Teachers Association). The local chapter was called the Mt. Diablo Education Association. Mike, president of the local chapter, was White, middle-aged, tall and handsome at 6'3", with broad European facial features, athletically built with just a hint of girth, styled thick brown hair, and clad in jeans and a flannel shirt. He reminded me of Dick Butkus of the Chicago Bears, at least in appearance. He was mild mannered. Wendy had already told Mike about my situation and he had offered to discuss my options for responding.

As an intern, I had no right of appeal. A new teacher with a credential on a tenure-bound contract has a limited privilege of appeal, but I had none. In giving me two weeks for an informal appeal of sorts, the principal was already being generous. In general, a principal is free to give any new teacher a negative evaluation without facing an appeal, and even without a progressive process of documenting the reasons for the negative score. It's hit or miss for new teachers; this impetuous approach to hiring is encoded in state law. Possibly this is the reason why fifty percent of California's new teachers with a credential quit within their first five years. And possibly it's why this state is facing one of the worst teacher shortages in its history as of this writing.

With no legalistic remedy available, Mike suggested that the principal's continued generosity may be the solution. He advised me that sometimes a principal will let a new teacher resign in good standing to look for a better fit at some other school. I made a plan based on his advice. If, which really meant when, I receive an unsatisfactory evaluation, I will decline to sign the evaluation form. At that point, I will offer to sign in exchange for permission to resign in good standing at the end of the school year. The evaluation documents are sent to human resources and kept on file, and that put pressure on the principal to have a signed form. The time for signing would give me a space to insert my proposal to resign.

Some readers might be wondering if the district's central special-education department had been involved. I had not heard one word (literally) from them all school year, not even from the supervisor assigned to my school site. That lack of oversight is not unusual, since in general, the typical central office leaves the principal and the resource specialists on their own until some kind of litigious crisis with a parent arises. Keen observers may want the average principal's total lack of training or other preparation for this task noted at this point.

With my plan to resign in mind, I waited for the end of March to arrive. I continued teaching. I carried out all of my responsibilities as if I was staying until the end of the school year. Except that I made a point of working harder than ever, especially on activities involving collaboration with the seventh-grade inclusion team. And, in accord with Sheila's advice at the coffee house, I made overt displays of friendliness and cooperation.

Final Negotiations

The final evaluation conference occurred at the end of March as scheduled. The agenda for the meeting was to continue the conversation started at the beginning of the month when the principal had reviewed her final classroom observation with me. The principal's remarks had turned negative, with her hinting that I might want to pursue a graduate degree in school psychology rather than continue on as an intern teacher. I had asked her to give me two weeks to consider her feedback.

We met after the school day, just before dusk, but during business hours. The principal started the final conference by stating that she had not conducted any additional classroom observations. Instead of looking further at lesson delivery, she wanted to consider how things were going for me overall with the faculty. That, she told me, was a normal part of an evaluation, which she had overlooked in the first meeting.

She said that things seemed to be going well for me with the students, but there had been some concerns expressed by my teammates. I asked who it was. She said, "You let a student call Betsy a bitch." By dint of divine intervention, I didn't lose my cool in response to this bit of innuendo about me. I calmly explained the circumstances. Brittney was a White, slim, physically-attractive seventh grader, with long legs, high slender waist, broad shoulders, long straight amber hair, high broad cheeks, expressive prominent eyes, and clear opaque skin: a seventh-grader bombshell. She dressed in the ubiquitous hoodies, t-shirts, jeans, and athletic shoes. She came from a mixed but stable two-parent middle-class household. Despite her glamorous appearance, Brittany struggled with self-confidence at school. I recall that she was both on my caseload and in my reading course, but she was definitely in my reading course. I had met with her parent's at least once about Brittney's minor misbehaviors and academic underachievement. She was a minimalist in reading intervention. She could demonstrate strong accuracy, but only if she really concentrated. She had a tendency to be drawn in by disruptive peers. I never removed Brittany on a referral to the principal's office; I was able to redirect her to the task though normal classroom communication.

On the day in question, when Brittney called Betsy a bitch, it was one of those periods where Betsy had students get their folder-organizers out for a writing project and work on their own. In other words, the structure of the classroom was at its lowest and the probability of misbehavior was at its highest. I was circulating around the room tutoring my students in brief one-on-one sessions amid the din of the increasingly distracted classroom. Betsy was doing the same thing as me. Suddenly, Betsy squares off with Brittney from about fifteen feet across the room and glowers at her. I'm about ten feet away from both individuals, engaging with neither of them, focused on others. Betsy breaks into a manic tirade at the peak volume and pitch of her formidable Celtic voice; the amplitude was pain inducing. She excoriates Brittany, essentially making an example of her among a group of students talking off task.

About a minute into Betsy's soliloquy on the theme of "I'm so tired of you ignoring me, I've already told you a hundred times, when will you finally learn, etc." Brittney broke into tears while staring blankly at Betsy. After a minute of crying, Brittney screamed out, "You're such a bitch. Leave me alone." I had some experience with Brittney and misbehavior, since she was one of the minimalists in my reading course. I calmly walked up to Brittney, in a deliberately relaxed posture, and invited her to take a break outside with me for a bit: "Hey

Brittney. Why don't we take a break outside for a bit?" Brittney immediately walked out the classroom door and I followed her. Outside, out of earshot of the classroom, in a semi-
private spot in the courtyard in front of the room, I sat quietly
while Brittney slowly regained her composure. When she had
calmed down, I asked her if she was okay. She replied with,
"She is such a bitch. She hates me. Why does she hate me?" I
replied gently by saying that Betsy works very hard at her job
and sometimes gets frustrated when students don't do their
best. Betsy was just frustrated, she doesn't hate you or any
other student. Brittney seemed comfortable talking to me
but still kind of agitated. I had her spend the rest of the class
period in a chair in a quiet part of the school office; I didn't
want to risk another breakdown from Betsy or Brittney. Brittney returned to class the next day without further incident. I
refrained from any kind of punitive action.

My training told me that de-escalation is the priority when
a student is severely agitated, especially when the source of
the agitation is a conflict with the faculty. The student should
be allowed to calm down fully before there is any attempt to
teach them a lesson about the situation. Empathetic listening is a research-based, ethical way to debrief a student after
a crisis such as Brittney's outburst of foul language. I took an
empathetic approach, and Brittney calmed down quickly—
my intervention was effective. In addition, I told Brittany the
truth, which I believe will lead her to have faith in me and
other important adults in her life. Thus my intervention in
Betsy's crisis was effective too.

Punishing Brittney would only have exacerbated the power
struggle with Betsy. In response to Brittney's minor side conversation, Betsy should have walked up to Brittney, in a non-
threatening posture, and asked her if she needed help with her
classmates or the task, and then gently reminded Brittney of
the need to work quietly. That was the de-escalation stage of
the misbehavior: try a verbal reminder-warning first. Instead,
Betsy's actual response was a textbook lapse in classroom-

management practices, and it rapidly escalated the minor misbehavior to crisis level. Moreover, screaming at children is always unethical and unprofessional: it's just plain wrong. But it was Betsy's favorite shortcut for handling lapses in her planning and strategies. I had been looking the other way all year, in the cause of being supportive, and now her habitual problem became a reason to give me a negative evaluation. I felt like no good deed goes unpunished.

The principal listened to my description of the Brittney incident, including both escalation and de-escalation. She was attentive and patient. At the end of my testimony, she replied, curtly, "You're just not tough enough." I interpreted her comment to mean that my upright Zen-like approach was too aloof for her middle-class sensibilities. She wanted fire and brimstone. She wanted sinners to be exposed.

She quickly rolled from the not-tough-enough comment to showing me the completed evaluation document with a rating of unsatisfactory on it. She simply said, "I'm giving you a score of unsatisfactory," and then handed me the document to sign. I made my offer: "Rather than sign, I would like to resign effective the last day of school and then look for another position in the district or in another district." The principal's mood conspicuously lightened. She had been sitting up straight while listening to me, but now she sat back in her chair. She remarked that my role in the school was not the right place for an inexperienced teacher. A new relationship began to form on the basis of me being the rookie out of place in advising experienced teachers. I listened attentively and made a few statements affirming this new view. I made it clear that we had a meeting of the minds. At the end of the conversation, the principal threw all the documentation for the evaluation into the trash and then promptly dismissed me for the day. Regarding the district's special-education department, their silence and complete lack of oversight continued.

A couple of days later, when I sent the principal my resignation letter, to become effective June 30th, I asked her for a letter of recommendation to support my job search. She provided it. The letter emphasized that I had probably done the best that I could as an inexperienced intern in the demanding situation of an inclusion program in its first year. She gave me unequivocal praise for my obvious and growing expertise in special-ed law: it had been a great asset to the faculty (i.e. she thought I should be a school psychologist).

My best months at the school came after my resignation in March, which I kept secret until the last week of school in June. It was the last quarter of the year, and, as I already described in earlier chapters, the time when the collaborative spirit finally took hold in the seventh-grade inclusion team. My co-teachers for language arts were stretching to new heights of flexibility and accommodation in the world-cultures writing project. IEP planning was being accomplished as a team, with positive, supportive participation in the annual IEP review meetings. Math and science kept their expectations modest and used participation over mastery as the main criteria for grading. Behavior support plans were leading to a cessation of problem behaviors, and all the inclusion students were heading for at least passing grades. As we approached the end of the year, we had some breathing room. We were going to emerge from this experiment with at least a modicum of self-esteem left. It's fair to say that relations among the team turned in a cordial direction, maybe even friendly.

For my individual teaching practice, I was working on the principal's recommendation for my next job. I made sure to prep good lessons every day for my intervention reading course, and my students settled into a daily routine of highly-structured instruction, with minimal to no serious misbehavior. The principal agreed to be a phone reference in addition to supplying a letter of recommendation. And the district listed me as eligible for rehire.

Sheila and Wendy each wrote me a letter of recommendation toward the end of year. Sheila's letter focused on my compassionate attitude toward the students and their friendly response to me. She also noted the organizational skills that I had demonstrated in developing curriculum for my reading course and in developing a model for co-teaching. Finally, she acknowledged my growing knowledge of IEP law and my emerging mastery of the IEP planning process, including teamwork. Wendy focused on my diligent participation in credential courses, and my earnest participation in all discussions, demonstrations, and assignments involved in the courses. When the end of the school year arrived, I finished filing my IEPs and moved out of my classroom without ceremony. I headed home with recommendations in hand and two months off (no credential courses) to recuperate and look for another teaching job.

It might be of some value to mention the school's scores on the 2004 annual statewide testing for the seventh grade. English Language Arts was 8% Advanced (Overachievers), 28% Proficient (Overachievers/Minimalists), 38% Basic (Minimalists), 16% Below Basic (Underachievers), and 10% Far Below Basic (Underachievers). Math was 4% Advanced (Overachievers), 20% Proficient (Overachievers/Minimalists), 34% Basic (Minimalists), 31% Below Basic (Underachievers), and 12% Far Below Basic (Underachievers). My impression was that the principal's reputation rested with her ability to produce scores of advanced—and to keep special-ed students (i.e. underachievers) out of the way.

Survivor

Today is Wednesday, June 10, 2020, seventeen years after I resigned from my first teaching position. I have been a fully credentialed California special-education teacher for the past fourteen years, receiving the professional-clear (i.e. lifetime) credential on schedule in June 2006 after the three-year internship. I also recently earned a traditional master's degree in education with a specialty in special education from the

Benerd School of Education at University of the Pacific, one of California's leading private universities, in a graduate program designed as a continuation of the Project Pipeline teaching credential.

Despite my contentious first experience in the inclusion scene, I was actually recommended for my credential while serving as a resource specialist in an eighth-grade inclusion program just five miles north of my first school. I basically picked up where I left off at El Dorado Middle, but with knowledge gained from two more years of credential courses. The new school was slightly more ethnically diverse, with student demographics at 40% Hispanic, 35% Black, 10% White, 8% Filipino, 3% Asian, and a few other groups below 3%. It was a Title I school (i.e. NCLB). My caseload was 60% Black, 30% White, and 10% Hispanic. Under my tutelage, my inclusion students were engaged in lessons, well-behaved, and overall made remarkable progress in the grade-level curriculum. I applied all my peacemaking skills, and they really worked. Both the district and Project Pipeline submitted the requisite recommendations to the state licensing agency without reservation.

This positive state of affairs was a dramatic improvement over previous years of the inclusion program. But amazingly, the position fell into controversy the year after I received my credential. In same vein as my first principal, like they were cut from the same cloth, my credential-granting principal said that he was "hearing things" from unnamed people. I retorted powerfully: "Have you noticed the reduction in discipline problems, engagement in lessons, and overall positive tone of my students? Did you see them in the Homecoming Court? Or hear the profuse praise from the faculty?" "I hear that you're not making friends," said the principal. "Are you nuts? The faculty is putting me up for sainthood. My students went from worst to best—in just one year!" Not impressed by my pleadings, the principal bluntly restated his concern. "I hear that you're not fitting in. It doesn't seem that you like it here." "I thought my results spoke for themselves," said me reiterating in an apparently foreign tongue (i.e. results for special-ed students). "There is more to a tenure decision than just results. You're not warming up to people, and that doesn't look good for tenure. I have to think about whether I should keep you here for life." I asked the principal to accept a written appeal and to reconsider his decision. I felt he must have been acting on partial information from an inclusion saboteur on the gen-ed faculty. I wanted to test his resolve. He agreed to reconsider, but in a second meeting he stuck to his decision.

Having completed the internship, I was now on a tenure-track contract with the district. I could have demanded a hearing with the superintendent or school board. On the other hand, there was the nebulous and ill-defined prospect of a negative evaluation, which could either be a minor obstacle or major career killer. To decisively rule out a negative evaluation, I asked to resign with board permission (i.e. in good standing) and for a letter of recommendation. I decided to abstain from going over the principal's head. I wanted to remain the principal's friend, since a reference from him might get me my next job. The principal granted my request and provided the letter a few days later. The principal discarded the evaluation, and I finished that school year before moving on. The site's school psychologist, who was full-time there and the special-ed department chair, also provided a glowing letter of recommendation.

I decided to escape from inclusion politics by teaching a Special Day Class (SDC). An SDC is a specialized classroom that features a small student population, specially-trained teacher, instructional assistant(s), accommodations, and modified curriculum. Ideally, it's a resource for parents to keep their child in school when they have a disability that is too severe for the student to study with non-disabled peers in gen-ed classrooms. The student spends most or all of the school day in the SDC. An SDC is a "restrictive" environment in the era of the "mandate" for "least restrictive environment" (i.e. push inclusion). I focused my job search on SDC programs and found a new job quickly enough to start the school year on time.

My ten SDC years transpired in the city of Hayward, California, in the shadow of my alma mater, Cal State Hayward (now grown into Cal State East Bay). The first two years were in the city school district. My first SDC assignment was teacher for a mental-health collaborative embedded in a general high school. A mental-health organization provided a classroom therapist and two behavioral support staff. They ran a classroom-management plan including a motivation system, and I provided an academic program for thirteen students with mild emotional disturbance, grades nine through twelve. I worked closely with the mental-health team. We enjoyed a rewarding school year. We maintained a disciplined and caring environment with nearly all students making lots of academic progress toward graduation with a diploma.

The next assignment was teacher for an SDC embedded in a general middle school for students with mild cognitive disabilities grades seven through eight; almost all fifteen students were seventh graders. As a result of some unique circumstances, I kept inclusion down to a minimum, so almost all the students studied with only me every day, like a one-room school house. I taught grade-level curriculum (i.e. seventh) for at least a good part of the school year in every subject. I challenged myself to structure the SDC as an intervention aimed at returning the maximum number of students to gen-ed participation (i.e. inclusion). With this ambition in mind, I actually maintained a disciplined, highly-structured, and work-oriented environment with miraculous levels of time on task and academic growth, and minimal misbehavior. I was in my second school year with the district, and the principal decided to evaluate me, even though the district was only offering one-year temporary contracts to special-ed teachers. He observed me in my language arts period, where I was teaching the state-adopted textbook for seventh grade.

His evaluation was based on the California Professional Standards for Teachers, and it reminded me of the classroom evaluations from my internship supervisors. My lessons focused on analyzing short stories that depicted the immigrant experience. He gave me a score of proficient, although it definitely wasn't a lovefest. Unlike past evaluations, this one was completed, signed, and passed to me instead of the trash bin. I still have a copy in my files at home. This was my sixth year as a teacher, which was the year when the principal at El Dorado Middle should have been giving me my first score of proficient in an evaluation. Keen observers may have noticed the difference between principals' reactions when I'm in an inclusion role versus their reaction when I'm in a SDC role.

The proficient year ended in the summer of 2009, the peak of the Great Recession, and the city district was erratic and unpredictable in its hiring practices, especially toward special education. In response, I joined a private school in Hayward that served students with autism and other development disabilities. The school was wholly-funded though contracts with public school districts, who placed students in the specialized facility when their needs exceeded the capabilities of the district's schools. The school site served about eighty students, divided into eight SDC programs. The private school organization, which was certified by the California Department of Education, operated eight other schools in California and several collaborative programs embedded in public schools. From a career perspective, it was considered credentialed service.

At the private school, I was the head teacher for an SDC that served nine (on average) young adults (ages 16 – 22) with moderate autism or other development disability, typically intellectual disability, using a creative combination of functional academics, pre-vocational training, paid employment training, and social-emotional learning. Basically, my students had been placed in this school after experiencing one or more symptoms of serious intellectual disability such as violence toward self or others, irritability, property destruction, debilitating memory and communication deficits, oppositional defiance, and attentional difficulties. They were physically fit, able-bodied, cute and good looking, well-dressed, and socially outgoing. Their condition was described as severe emotional disorder. In a nutshell, they struggled with handling stress of any sort, especially the stressors of school. But I couldn't have loved them more. We got along really well, accomplished a lot, and enjoyed ample good times.

My students occasionally experienced dangerous or destructive behaviors, but the faculty received specialized training, including crisis intervention with physical restraints, and the site's entire staff acted as a crisis team, so the environment was relatively safe. My classroom staff, my students, and I avoided serious injury. I wish that I could give the same good news about property destruction.

I spent eight well-paid, perk-rich years there, whereas the city district was bogged down in layoffs, furloughs, declining enrollment, and nebulous seniority. Interestingly, students from the Hayward city district comprised at least half of all my students at the private school. This position turned out to be the much-mythologized day job that the misinformed public envies. The students had intense emotional difficulties, which I learned to accommodate as a positive disciplinarian, but I only had to manage nine IEPs, whereas a resource specialist position typically involved twenty-five or more IEPs. My free time was spent on my own goals instead of a school district's problems. In these eight years, I became a well-trained Tibetan Buddhist through extensive formal training in the Shambhala community (i.e. Trungpa's spiritual warriorship), then engaged in extensive study with the Soto school of Zen Buddhism, and next completed a traditional master's degree in education at the University of the Pacific. I worked out at the pool or gym at least three days a week most of the time. And I wrote most of the present book.

SDC is the learning environment where a positive disciplinarian is the most in demand and can make the greatest difference. In all three of my SDCs, I emphasized explicit expectations for performance in all things, motivation based on frequent positive feedback about performance, nonjudgmental offers of help on new or difficult tasks, assessment-based instruction, visual communication, and teaching on my feet. I taught whatever rules that I expected students to follow. Being well-organized and highly-structured provided the trunk, but it was accommodation and tolerance that yielded the fruit. I learned to put students under stress but also to support and redirect the minor misbehaviors that arose. I found ways to maintain boundaries with mild teacher-based interventions and remove students to the principal for only the most egregious infractions. All my SDCs were diverse, with students from Asian, Hispanic, White, and Black families in significant proportions, and all the schools were Title I (i.e. NCLB).

The private school was a situation where a highly-trained teacher could make a nice living for years, but a poorly-trained one would fall to pieces in months or maybe even days. I used every skill that I had ever learned regarding motivation, cognitive psychology, time management, literacy instruction, math instruction, social-emotional learning, crisis intervention, and education law. Wrestling and football came in handy too, especially on the defensive side. But my real advantage came from my emerging bodhisattva skills.

Probably my biggest contribution was in taking a mentoring approach to social-emotional learning. I was definitely the boss, but a friendly and empathetic one. I found a way to be a boss and mentor. My students and I spent all day together, 210 days a year, and most students spent three or more years in my program, so we were almost like a family. I did my best to model patience, forbearance, kindness, and gentle speech in all things, especially in situations where I was frustrated or disappointed; I also emphasized empathetic listening. I modeled the emotional intelligence that I hoped they would acquire. Amazingly, my students did eventually demonstrate these helpful traits, inspiring the school's director to frequently praise my program for instilling independence (i.e. maturity) in its students. When pitching the program to parents of prospective students, she would tell parents that my classroom offered them an opportunity for their child, typically a son, to learn from a "good male role model." I also became a mentor to parents, helping them understand their young adult's needs and supporting the transition to adult services.

During my tenure there, the private school organization, which was founded in the mid- seventies, evolved from a nonprofit foundation on a mission of compassion to a commercial educational entrepreneurship. With this evolution came a gradual increase in my class size from nine to fourteen. At eleven students, my staff and I spent an increasing amount of time in crisis intervention but we maintained a relatively positive tone. At thirteen students, it was cruel and unusual punishment for students and staff. That is when I started complaining. And then the school organization forced me out in what basically amounted to a token internal policy dispute over the appropriateness of my single-handed physical intervention during an eighteen-year-old male student's assaultive behavior toward staff and students in a situation where the school's crisis team failed to appear at the scene.

The student was unharmed, classmates and staff were protected from injury, and there were no complaints from the student's guardians. Subsequent discussions revealed that my actions in the assaultive incident had been lawful and appropriate, and that the school's crisis team was the negligent party. But the defensive postures of both sides, especially on my part, precluded a reconciliation. This departure triggered the first time in the fifteen years of my teaching career that I collected unemployment benefits, which helped me move on. My last day at the school was in January 2018. When I described the situation to friends in a Facebook post, I said that my relationship with the private school had ended due to "irreconcilable differences." I took a nice long break on my unemployment benefits and then looked for work in the spring. I found a new job early enough to start the school year on time.

For the past two school years, I returned to working in inclusion for public schools, mostly at the elementary level as a resource specialist. Elementary school draws on all the knowledge and skills that I have accumulated in seventeen years of credential service to the families of the State of California. As the one inclusion specialist for an elementary school of 700 students grades kindergarten through five, I handled initial eligibility evaluations, annual IEP reviews, triennial IEP reviews, and small-group intervention for math and literacy in the learning center. My elementary students were from diverse ethnic backgrounds, including Asian, Hispanic, White, and Black in significant proportions, with a small percentage from economically-disadvantaged homes.

My favorite aspect of this role was helping the IEP team conduct precise, informative evaluations that gave parents a better understanding of their child's learning differences. My second favorite aspect was developing relationships with the students while conducting small-group and individualized academic interventions. Teaching small-groups in the learning center used skills developed in my private school days: I served as lead learner for students and guided them to mature, independent behavior by modeling a positive, caring mindset.

In these two elementary years, most of my students had never been in an SDC; they had always been inclusion students. Based on my knowledge of students who have spent a significant part of their school career in SDCs, the inclusion students appear to be enjoying higher levels of academic mastery and emotional maturity than if they had studied in an SDC. I wish that I could report that the political dynamics of inclusion have improved from sixteen years ago. They have not. It was like stepping into the same conversation, exactly where I left off at the end of my first year. There are still no explicit, clear professional expectations for gen-ed teachers or resource specialists to follow. But my observations of the newest generation of inclusion students tell me that all California teachers need to embrace the challenge of inclusion and continue to help these students experience the educational benefit that they deserve.

Fresh Start

I moved out of my parent's place in Danville at the start of the second year of my internship. On the way out, I used the last of my savings from my corporate days to repay my parents for the expenses that they incurred in my time living with them. I've been on my own ever since. I traveled light and adopted a nomadic lifestyle to accommodate my search for the right teaching assignment. I managed to find modest-yet-decorous studio or one-bedroom apartments within a short commute from wherever I was working. As I described in earlier chapters, my parents continued to sponsor my visits with my daughter Aileen at their three-bedroom house in Danville, and their generosity provided me with an opportunity for thrift in my housing choices.

I encamped in downtown Vallejo first, in an apartment in the historic riverfront area, where the Napa River meets the flowing waters of the Delta as they move through the Carquinez Straight into the north end of San Francisco Bay. I was inspired by the dramatic inland-sea scenery, thrived in the modest rural economy, and enjoyed the company of my offbeat neighbors and neighborhood. My building was a renovated California historic site from the days when Vallejo was the state capital (i.e. 1851 to 1853). Next I moved southward to downtown Oakland to accommodate my teaching position in Hayward.

Oakland has basically been my home since then. I have had

two different apartments in the lower reaches of the Oakland hills. My current apartment is just off the main street of the Laurel Heights neighborhood in the Dimond District. The Dimond District is renowned for its diversity in ethnicity, religion, economic status, culture, and every other kind of cultural difference imaginable. I love its diversity and its geography. My oversized front window affords me a clear vista out over the city to San Francisco Bay and the San Bruno Mountains. The expansive open sky of Northern California illuminates every aspect of my life: the sunsets are amazing.

I can drive a quick mile uphill through my neighborhood to the Sausal Creek Watershed, Palo Seco Creek and Palos Colorado Trail, and Joaquin Miller Park to hike several steep miles uphill and down for a brisk workout among canyons, waterfalls, groves of firs and giant redwoods, ferns, and other lush plant life. The scenery is comparable to the Marin coast or Big Sur. Oakland is in a central location of the Bay Area, just across the bay from San Francisco, giving me easy access to the world-beating range of cultural and outdoor resources in the Bay Area region. The refusenik culture reminds me of my Mission District days, although Oakland is now experiencing similar gentrification. Our refuseniks' comfort zone of cultural diversity can't really be called modest any more, but at least I can still afford my modestly-upscale renovated mission revival-style building, which is an Oakland historical site as an example of classic California 1920s architecture, with a skyline view, hyper-diligent landlord, resident manager, video surveillance, security door, no smoking, and a parking lot. Violent crime among juveniles and adults in Oakland has dramatically decreased in recent years.

My reverie in Oakland was disrupted for three and a half years by a move to Danville, where I moved in with my parents, but this time I helped them with *their* career crisis. Partially due to effects of the Great Recession, and partially due to the dynamics of aging, my father found himself without a job, without a home, and without any assets in his early seventies. Both father and mother had Social Security and Medicare, but that was not enough to stand their ground in Danville, which they seem to feel is their birthright. My parents and I formed a household, with me providing some cash for move-in expenses and paying half the rent while only occupying one bedroom of the relatively-spacious single-family home. The plan was for me to support them in this way while my father pursued his goal of returning to the workforce.

Amazingly, he got back on his feet and returned to work within a few months. We kept the house going for three and a half years, and I returned to Oakland when it was clear that my parents could pay the sizeable rent on their own. I called our house the Bartlett Elders Residence, and we hosted our clan (i.e. growing nuclear family) and extended family members for numerous celebrations of birthdays and holidays. My favorite part of the house was the private garden patio: it was great for reading, studying, and entertaining. Dad was the gardener. I especially enjoyed his roses and finch feeders. I was happy to have had the opportunity to repay all the generosity that my parents had extended to me during my divorce and in supporting my daughter as a divorced dad. We coexisted well in the Bartlett Elders Residence, and what might have been a burden turned out to be a source of joy and delight. I'm both amazed and troubled that my father is still in the workforce full-time in his early eighties! Mom at the same age works part-time. These two super sales people intend to die with their boots on, as in Grey Panthers.

Aileen, my daughter, graduated from high school with high honors and earned a degree in economics from the University of North Carolina at Greensboro. Her youth was free of delinquency of any sort, and she was even free of intoxicants of any sort throughout her education and remains so to this day. She embraces intellectual development free from the fetters of income and status. She is a gentle, sweet soul, with a healthy sense of citizenship. Her struggles with career decisions seem to be about average for a Millennial. She is not too close with my family any more, but she remains close to her matrilineal family. I stayed in regular contact with her through college, but lately she seems to be gradually going her own way. Clan custody appears to have been a success.

Wynda, my ex-wife, left the Bay Area for Seattle when Aileen was eight. She secured a transfer from what became the world's biggest traditional department store chain. She continued to work in finance and security at the corporate level. The affordable conditions in the Seattle area allowed her to become a homeowner as a single mother with a modest house in the suburbs. All her siblings lived nearby, and they too adopted clan custody. My visits with Aileen were reduced to monthly weekends with strategic longer breaks during school vacations: Aileen became a frequent flier on Alaska Airlines.

Eventually, Wynda grew weary of the upheaval in the world-beating retailer and secured a position with a huge garment manufacturer in North Carolina. Her new role would be in sales support. She finally got out of retail. Wynda and Aileen moved to Greensboro just before Aileen's freshman year in high school. Wynda found a nice one-story American colonial to own. My visits with Aileen went down to a few longer visits a year, typically during summer or winter breaks from school. Aileen became a transcontinental flyer on a variety of airways that offered non-stop flights to San Francisco, and I learned to stay in touch with her using Facebook. Wynda and Aileen enjoy the South, and they continue to live peacefully in Greensboro. Wynda was without relatives there until recently, when her bachelorette oldest sister joined her. Wynda never remarried. She published a novel of modest merits on a feminist theme about ten years ago. I have not spoken to Wynda since our separation twenty-five years ago. I learned about her life from Aileen.

My two younger siblings (I'm the oldest), Ryan and Mary, both still live in the San Francisco Bay Area. All the members of clan custody live within forty minutes driving distance of each other. Five granddaughters have been added to the family, with the oldest ones in middle school. They have been raised in stable two-parent households. My mother lives for these children, and she is more pleased with them than she ever was with me as a child. She is not a surrogate parent like she was for my daughter, but she lavishes them with gifts and attention, and she of course is the model of decorum and style when it comes to gatherings.

We gather often as a clan to celebrate birthdays and all manner of holidays, and sometimes just to connect and relax. Occasionally we pull together to help a family member in need. I don't sail with Ryan anymore, but he is one of the few close friends that I have left after my career change to education, and I really appreciate his company on fun outings of all sorts. Whereas we were pretty close friends in my Mission District years, my contact with Mary these days is generally limited to being a guest in gatherings hosted by her as the heir to our mother's devotion to family and child-rearing. Ryan and Mary are both corporate climbers of significant affluence and influence, without the Irish Catholic aspect of my parent's generation. They are, however, humanists with a healthy regard for the Golden Rule.

The fresh start that I indulged myself in at the time of my divorce seems to have taken hold. I have not had any serious money problems since the bankruptcy in my divorce. I had a few bouts with unemployment as a copywriter in marcom, but I have suffered only one brief period of self-imposed unemployment in my seventeen years of teaching. Basically, all of those seventeen years were full-time with a regular contract. My recent two years in inclusion in public general schools have been contentious, and I hope to move this summer to a teaching role or some other application of my education training in a more sanguine setting. Experience and credible sources tell me that working as a resource specialist can become career suicide if one is not ready to move on after a year or so.

By some miracle, I paid steep child support for fourteen

years and funded all the visits, with a high degree of compliance. My credit rating is above average to excellent. Since my late-model Miata in my copywriter years, I have owned three late-model Volkswagen Jettas (Sport Edition), which are now my thrifty compact car of choice. I have accumulated some modest retirement resources. I have enjoyed affordable access to comprehensive healthcare, and I am in excellent health and free of any illness or condition. My life has been free of intoxicants for seventeen years, except for a drink or two on infrequent social occasions (less than once a month); my life is free of cravings, even for caffeine.

I've lived a full life with travel, participation in a spiritual community, professional growth, ample outdoor recreation, fitness, family, and friends. I dated a number of women, with a few brief romances, but I have not found lasting love. It seems that I am too attached to modesty and overachievement for the women of the me generation. They prefer the Epicurean life of pleasure seeking, which I can dabble in but never maintain for long.

On the upside, my seventeen years in special education have provided economic benefits, and they actually look good on paper, at least from a skilled-blue-collar perspective. But from a bodhisattva perspective, the downside of the job has brought the greatest benefits. In Buddhist philosophy, a practitioner at the basic level focuses on their own suffering and the possibility of cessation in their own life. But devoted practitioners who attempt to live by the bodhisattva vow seek to understand the suffering of all beings and to lead the way to cessation for all beings. Job satisfaction for a bodhisattva lies in identifying the true causes of suffering in others and then guiding them in solutions that lead to cessation.

Confusion about how to educate children with mild learning disabilities is systemic, pervasive, and persistent. The lack of clear direction creates fertile ground for unprofessional and sometimes neglectful conduct from teachers and administrators. In my teaching path, especially in inclusion roles, I have been the object of much defensiveness, deception, and irritability while trying to uphold the special-ed laws in the gen-ed environment. My practice as a bodhisattva is to absorb these forms of negativity, learn from them, and apply some kind of compassionate solution to the underlying causes. So, the negativity directed toward me just makes me wiser and more effective, and thus in a way richer. It's almost a kind of perk.

The confusion over inclusion often leaves students with learning disabilities without the educational benefit that they deserve. California needs to address this problem in a factual, structural way, in the clear light of day, without the posturing and polarization that typically arise when the self interests of politics are involved. We need a moment of honesty, however implausible that might seem. Then we need to contemplate that we are good and decent people, and that we should never let deception be a means of solving a systemic problem, especially with innocent children involved. Finally, we need to make an explicit, structured plan to improve, a plan free of deception, shortcuts, and vagueness. As I end this chapter of my story, I am contemplating the question that formed all the way back in high school when I learned about the fall of the Nixon administration. I'm wondering about what kind of contribution I can make to the inclusion discussion as a good male role model. Maybe this book will become the beginning of some good conversations. The.... beginning.

May all beings be free of suffering. May all beings enjoy loving-kindness. May all beings enjoy compassion. May all beings attain equanimity. Om Mani Padme Hum.

ABOUT THE AUTHOR

Robert Bartlett

Robert has lived in the San Francisco Bay Area for the past thirty-six years. He currently resides in the Laurel Heights neighborhood of Oakland. He divides his time between teaching in California's public school system, practicing with the Shambhala (Tibetan) Buddhist community, writing for publication, visiting with family and friends, and enjoying the outdoors. His favorite pastime is hiking in the extensive parklands and wilderness preserves of Northern California, especially in mountainous terrain and on the Pacific coast. Down and Out in Special Education is his first book. Robert holds an M.A. in Education with specialty in Special Education from University of the Pacific, Stockton, California.
Contact: rwb3publisher@earthlink.net

Made in the USA
San Bernardino, CA
13 July 2020